YELLOW & BLACK

A SEASON WITH
RICHMOND

RICHMOND
EST 1885

slattery
MEDIA GROUP

The Slattery Media Group
Level 39/385 Bourke Street, Melbourne
Victoria, Australia, 3000
Visit slatterymedia.com

NATIONAL LIBRARY OF AUSTRALIA

A catalogue record for this book is available from the National Library of Australia

Group Publisher: Geoff Slattery
Editor: Geoff Slattery
Assistant Editor: Russell Jackson
Designer: Kate Slattery

COVER & BACKCOVER: The moment of victory is confirmed when the team celebrates with
the Premiership Cup.
Photos by AFL Photos. Michael Willson (front cover), Cameron Spencer (back cover).

Printed and bound in Australia by Griffin Press

The Slattery Media Group and Konrad Marshall acknowledge the support of the Richmond
Football Club in this publication, in particular, president Peggy O'Neal, CEO Brendon Gale,
Corporate Affairs and Media manager Simon Matthews, Head of Coaching Tim Livingstone,
coach Damien Hardwick and his coaching staff, the football department, and, of course,
the players; and to Tony Greenberg, the club's Editorial and Research Manager,
for his meticulous proof-reading.

slattery
MEDIA GROUP

www.slatterymedia.com

A SEASON WITH

RICHMOND

YELLOW & BLACK

KONRAD MARSHALL

THE AUTHOR

Konrad Marshall has been a faithful follower of the Richmond Football Club his entire life, which was, until lately, a sad and fallow era for the club.

In early 2016, he joined the Tigers with the intention of writing a book about daily life inside a big Victorian football club, exploring and explaining its rhythms and quirks. He could never have dreamed what would unfold over the pair of dramatic seasons that followed.

A journalist for 15 years, Marshall has spent half his career writing for newspapers in the United States, and the latter part at home as a senior writer with Fairfax Media. He has won numerous awards for his sports journalism, his arts writing, and in-depth reporting. He currently writes longform features for *Good Weekend* magazine.

Konrad lives in Melbourne with his wife, Nikki, and their son, Charlie.

↓ **WINNERS ARE GRINNERS [L-R]:** Josh Caddy, Dylan Grimes, Dustin Martin, Nick Vlastuin, Jack Graham, Kamdyn McIntosh, Shaun Grigg, Nathan Broad and Toby Nankervis celebrate on Grand Final day.

For Mum and Dad

YELLOW & BLACK

CONTENTS

↓ **THE FINAL SIREN:** The view from the outer as Richmond booked their place in history!

JOB DONE: Tigers coach Damien Hardwick and captain Trent Cotchin raise the premiership cup to start a night of celebrations

THE MOMENT

Foreword by Damien Hardwick

It was Dan Butler's last quarter goal, about seven minutes left on the clock.

That was the moment.

It was done.

It was over.

The Premiership Cup was going home to Punt Road.

When the moment hit I just felt pure relief. But then you think about family, players, coaches, staff and fans all at once. It means so much to so many and each deserves a hand on the Cup.

Someone once said: "Trophies gather dust, memories last forever" and that never rang more true than in the days following our Grand Final win. Punt Road Oval—and in fact the whole suburb and beyond—was just a sea of smiles and tears. I have never seen anything like it. Pure joy.

We have faced some difficult times as a Club, as a team, and as individuals, and that is what makes this victory so incredibly special. We never fractured, we remained strong, bold and united and that is a very powerful thing.

The care everyone has shown for one another at our Club, the connection we have with one another, it ultimately created a bond that drove a football performance few outside the Club could have imagined.

Football clubs are the sum of so many parts, each playing a role, each connected to our purpose to thrive and win. But there is so much that sits beneath the surface, not seen by those outside our four walls.

This book takes you inside those walls.

—Damien Hardwick, October 2017

PROLOGUE

by Konrad Marshall

As Damien Hardwick noted in his foreword, this book exists to provide a look inside the "four walls" of the Richmond Football Club. We hear these words so often from professional footballers and their coaches. They use the phrase constantly, seemingly as a preface to any remark about perception or performance, to deflect criticism or maintain mystique. But few among us know what they mean—what exactly lies within the hallways and training spaces and meeting rooms of a club—and that gap in our understanding of AFL football is what led to this book. I cannot thank the Richmond Football Club enough for giving me the chance to experience life in the inner sanctum. The idea that a common fan, albeit a journalist, might be let loose in the rooms of an AFL club—to freely wander within those four walls—and then be trusted to interpret what he saw and communicate its substance and subtleties to the world…well, it was an honour and a privilege. For nigh on two years—since the pre-season of 2016—I did this by carving out spare time on early winter mornings, and full summer days, and on the weekends and evenings when I could visit Tigerland. I would go to meetings, attend matches and training, sit in the rooms as the coach instructed and inspired his players. I would interview and profile the athletes and their mentors and trainers. I would sit in on match reviews, or opposition analysis, or selection committee, or board meetings, or in the coach's box on game day. I took a granular approach to the project, too, covering everyone from the club doctor to the welfare officer, from the Football Manager to the recruiting staff, from the star full-forward to the committed volunteers. I should point out also that the book was not written at the end of the 2017 season with all the facts in hand, but in real time, on the run, chapter by chapter, as the year progressed. The book was built much like the season: week by week, win by win, providing a true sense of the team's growing belief and momentum. Through it all, the reasons why things turned out so spectacularly well are not reported through the prism of reflection, but as they occurred, as tweaks were made, and as influences—and influencers—were revealed. For all this time, I felt like one tiny part of the engine that is Tigerland, albeit as an observer, a chronicler of a time that had its highs and lows.

Before I began this project, I remember consulting one of Australia's best sports writers, who said he would not do it—not in cooperation with a club—because the club would promise access that they simply could not, or would not, deliver. "It's like being given a tour of the old Soviet Union," he said. "They're not going to show you the gulags." At times that was true, most often following a loss. In those moments, mourning defeat in the change rooms, try as I might to pretend I was a fly on the wall, I was in fact a conspicuous reporter with a notepad and pen, sitting in a corner, spying on everyone and scrawling down everything that was said and done. If I occasionally felt like an unwelcome interloper, it's because I was one, no doubt. Occasionally, I was asked to leave before an address (or spray) was delivered. I would sit in on some meetings and was excluded from others. I could interview this player, but that one did not want to talk right now. As a journalist, I seek out the unvarnished moments—the dramatic and raw—but a football department, by nature, protects against such exposure.

At first, I chafed against the minor restrictions placed on my work, but, on reflection, they made complete sense. Collingwood midfielder Adam Treloar once made an off-the-cuff remark about the quality of Richmond's list relative to Collingwood's, and that innocuous slight will never be forgotten, to be dredged up and thrown into the ether—or back at Treloar—whenever the two teams meet. If football departments need to be conservative, it is not without just cause. An errant word in football is seldom forgotten.

And so, this is a book written in cooperation with the club, as it had to be. There were many technical details, sensitive terminology and nomenclature around tactics that were removed. More than a hundred choice curse words were deleted from the first third of the book alone. Other than that, Richmond was willing to reveal the raw truth about life at Punt Road, so 99 per cent of the original material remains. There are intimate moments described in these pages that have simply never been relayed to football fans before. And what a club to follow, and what a time to do it. Richmond in 2016 was meant to be a team on the rise. The Tigers had played in three consecutive finals series, albeit for three straight Elimination Final defeats, but they were maturing, or so it seemed. They needed to vault from the bottom half of the eight into the top four—that last, but hardest step up. The internal club slogan that summer was "Next Level". But those hopes and dreams were almost immediately dashed in the season that followed such optimism. The team lost early, and often, and then as the year progressed they lost hard. As the defeats mounted and finals became an impossibility, they turned to youth, which turned those losses into floggings, which turned the eye of the football media on the coaches and the board, the recruiters and the development staff—the entire club. Yet throughout it all, before it was made public, a careful but clinical process of self-examination was taking place. Changes were made in everything from personnel to game plan to culture—changes that produced an immediate enthusiasm, despite the on-field failures. This book—which had been postponed midway through that disastrous 2016 campaign—was revived in early 2017, in what can surely be described as a "strong and bold" decision by the club. This time, despite a 13th place finish, the Board and the football department agreed to allow a book to be written and printed at the end of the 2017 season, no matter what happened on the field. The club clearly had faith that 2016 was, as CEO Brendon Gale noted, "an aberration" and not an abomination. One small sign from the beginning of the season? The players decide when the Jack Dyer Medal night is to be held each year.

→ **PUNT ROAD TRAFFIC:** A sea of Richmond supporters were on hand at the Punt Road Oval to salute their premiership heroes, the day after the Grand Final.

"They chose October second, two days after the Grand Final," says club President Peggy O'Neal. "I think that's a fairly strong statement of intent, or belief." This book reflects all of the above—it is a faithful rendering of both sides of football, from the hell of 2016 to the heaven of 2017, a recovery and emergence that could never have been predicted; a film script could not be so brazen. This story has twin redemption figures in Damien Hardwick and Trent Cotchin, a prodigal son in Neil Balme, a billboard performer in Dustin Martin, along with stories of hard luck, resilience, maturation, friendship and love. And, remarkably, a premiership.

—Konrad Marshall, October, 2017

1

DAY ONE

The first cars begin rolling into the empty inner city park as the darkness yields to the morning. It's 6:38am, and a multi-coloured mob of hot air balloons drift idly across the Melbourne skyline, up into the vanilla and blue complexion of the hour, on the first day of the 2017 pre-season of the Richmond Football Club.

For the players, this dawn can't come soon enough. The team has not spent its long holiday with any burning desire to atone for a quick finals exit—as they did in 2013, 2014 and 2015. No, they had to spend the summer sitting on something worse—a 13th place finish, with a paltry eight wins from 22 games, capped off by a season-ending 113-point capitulation against the Swans in Sydney.

Now their time with that indignity is over. The extended break is done. They won't see another such stretch of time off for a long while. The AFL home and away season lasts only six months but the players' responsibilities run to a full calendar year commitment, each goal and task and expectation insinuating itself into their lives, creeping and spreading into every private space and thought. Even in their time off where no explicit training schedule exists, there are the individual training sessions they are implicitly expected to perform if they want to be among the very best. New recruits quickly learn that "extras" in skills or weights or running or footwork—whatever your perceived weakness—are the rapid way into the good graces and respect of teammates and coaches. It's what the stars do.

These days, doing 'enough' isn't anywhere near enough. The extras are needed to make an impression, and there is no better time to reinforce that impression than right now, Monday January 9, 2017, at the first time trial of a new season—a three-kilometre run around Princes Park in Carlton.

/////////

Country boy Nathan Drummond, one of the most promising athletes at the club but whose two years at Tigerland have so far been stymied by a serious anterior cruciate ligament rupture just before half-time in his 2015 debut, sits in a Subaru XV, waiting to show what he can do when fully fit. Taylor Hunt is also there, behind the wheel of a V6 dual cab Hilux, and is priming himself for a searching run—one he hopes will keep him in the minds of the selection committee. Shaun Grigg, one of the club's pure endurance monsters, is already loosening up on the grass, shaking out his quads and calves.

One by one the premium Jeeps of senior players and coaches fill the car park. Most of the cars arrive quietly but one arrives without decorum, a Dodge Journey peeling into the car park and coming to an abrupt halt, tyres skidding on asphalt. Alex Rance, the back-to-back-to-back reigning All Australian full back, opens the driver's door. The club's best player is the comedian and prankster of the group but also a vocal and intense leader, and he stands proudly now with both arms raised high, announcing his arrival. Clearly in jester mode, he roars: "Happy new year, boys!"

The group gathers now in shorts, singlets and runners, milling together on the nature strip, catching up, chatting about the trips they've made over the break, the things they've seen and done on their short vacations. But they're back at work now. Most of the city is, too. Traffic rolls down Royal Parade from Sydney Road, a leisurely flow of trucks and taxis and single-occupant cars. Cyclists glide past on sleek 20-speed carbon and alloy road machines and spearmint green fixies with wicker baskets and French bells. Women run laps in Lululemon. Old men walk small dogs. Trams, filled to the brink, rumble along one of the few true clear tram routes in the inner city.

The players wander over to physical performance manager Peter Burge and his assistant, sports science coordinator Brendan Fahrner, and pick up their personal heart rate monitors and GPS trackers. Myna birds cheep, rainbow lorikeets sing and magpies warble as the athletes cluster in packs, together forming one giant, idling, itching, scratching scrum. Despite the hour there are no yawns—only a restless, nervous energy. They have been waiting for this.

New Indigenous players Shai Bolton and Tyson Stengle stand together, quiet and shy. Bolton, a silky forward from Mandurah in Western Australia, was brought to the club with its first selection [pick 29] in the national draft (Richmond traded their initial first pick to land Dion Prestia). Stengle, a Rookie Draft selection [pick 6] comes from Portland, South Australia, and has already impressed with his fierce tackling pressure. The new pair can't help wondering how they will compare against mature players—players like time trial kings Brandon Ellis and former rookie Kane Lambert.

Every player here, seemingly, has something specific to prove in this benchmarking exercise. Nick Vlastuin [pick 9, 2012], long mooted as a potential midfielder but obviously needing to build his running engine, is here and hopeful. The results of this session will be important to him. Ben Lennon [pick 12, 2013] is here, too. In the off season Lennon marketed himself to other clubs, penning an online post about his renewed commitment, training regimen and maturity, but no clubs came calling and so he was ultimately retained by Richmond, given a second chance. His contract expires at the end of this season—he has something to prove and a narrow timeline in which to prove it.

Some notable faces are missing, including retired key defender Troy Chaplin, now an assistant coach with Melbourne, the mercurial Chris Yarran, traded to Richmond one season earlier at considerable expense (he never played a game for the club, and retired over a potent mix of personal issues and injuries), and of course veteran midfield star Brett Deledio [243 games], who joined league juggernaut Greater Western Sydney in exchange for a first and third round draft pick.

Others are missing from the track today with minor niggles, including defender Bachar Houli (who sat out much of last year with a hamstring complaint), star forward Jack Riewoldt (who had finger and ankle surgery before Christmas) and boom recruit Dion Prestia (snared from the Gold Coast Suns in the trade period after protracted haggling over the price, ultimately pick 6 in the national draft).

The other big Tiger recruit—utility Josh Caddy—is present and ready. Caddy, 24, was lured from Geelong in exchange for greater opportunity for himself and, in part, because he is a tall, strong follower—the new fashion in AFL. At 187 centimetres he is no Patrick Cripps (190 centimetres) or Marcus Bontempelli (192), but he has height and strength and, notably, counts physical pressure and overhead marking as assets. He plays big, and tall and performed in big moments in his time at Geelong, and before that at the Gold Coast, taken as pick 7 in the 2010 National Draft. Richmond, recognising that captain Trent Cotchin played his best football in that season when alongside the strong-bodied pair of Daniel Jackson and Shane Tuck, is thrilled to have Caddy there to help with the grunt work. Cotchin has just emerged from his own strange off-season. He was awarded the 2012 Brownlow Medal, along with Hawk-cum-Eagle Sam Mitchell, after Bomber Jobe Watson handed in his medal to the AFL—no doubt recognising the writing on the wall—not long before the AFL Commission was to sit in judgment on the fate of the medal amid the eternal Essendon supplements saga. The hope is that Caddy will help fill that same bullocking need—camping in the hit zone underneath a ruckman, ready to farm the ball out, while also drifting forward, allowing Cotchin to play a more damaging role on the outside of packs.

//////////////

There are new members of the football department, too. After an external review of Richmond's disastrous 2016 campaign, a handful of assistant coaches were moved on. Brendon Lade accepted a job at Port Adelaide, while others were let go, including flamboyant development coach Mark 'Choco' Williams, forwards coach Greg Mellor, offensive coordinator Mark 'Wilba' Williams and defensive coordinator Ross 'Jacca' Smith. Their replacements, including former Saint and Lion utility Xavier Clarke, the sacked Brisbane coach Justin Leppitsch returning to where his coaching career began, and the highly regarded Blake Caracella after a successful time at Geelong, are here alongside the likes of Ryan Ferguson, Ben Rutten, Craig McRae and Andrew McQualter. New football boss Neil Balme is also back at Tigerland, having accepted an offer to leave Collingwood and return to the club for which he once played famously and infamously.

He will assume some of the responsibilities of Dan Richardson, who will now fill a truncated role, focusing on talent acquisition. Richardson has embraced the new role and the new structure: "There's certainly a different feel," he says, walking amongst the stretching players. "A handful of voices have gone out, and a handful of new ones have come in. It changes the dynamic." He is matter-of-fact about the coaching merry-go-round that led to close colleagues—friends—now without a job in the football industry: "That's the cut and thrust of the business."

Tim Livingstone, the head of coaching and football performance—in essence the key coordinator and communicator within the coaching department—is here, too. He stands with the last man to arrive, Damien Hardwick, senior coach now for seven years and a man saddled with the great expectations and impatience of the football public.

Hardwick has arrived with second year player Daniel Rioli, who was drafted to the club in 2015 with its first selection overall [pick 15], and who has been living with Hardwick in suburban Bentleigh ever since. Rioli, the cousin of Hawthorn superstar Cyril Rioli and nephew of Richmond legend Maurice Rioli, is a small forward with X-factor, something the Tigers have lacked of late. He is also an exceptional athlete—on average the top testing player at his AFL Draft Combine, with high scores in everything from the beep test to the 30-metre repeat sprints and the clean hands assessment, and he showed as much in his debut season. However, those displays were flashes—performances he needs to consolidate and reproduce in more quarters and more games. His endurance will be crucial.

At 7am they begin warming up on a nearby oval. The three-kilometre time trial is an unpleasant test. The way the trainers explain it, sprinting doesn't hurt because it is over so quickly, leaving lactic acid no chance to build up and begin burning the quadriceps and calves, while true long distance running doesn't hurt as much either, because professional athletes can mostly find a comfortable rhythm to endure. Three kilometres, however, is "one of those in between distances", where the player must hold a significant pace for what feels like an eternity. "Anything longer than 800 metres," says one trainer, "and you just have to settle in with your suffering."

Blair Hartley, the general manager of player personnel and list management, says most of the players would be excited to be here, keen to perform, but many of them—particularly the new recruits—won't have any idea what is about to hit them. The young ones, he says, have been at the club barely a few months, and still don't understand how far behind the senior players they are. "They think, 'I've done the program, I'll be OK'," Hartley says, smiling. "They won't."

They all stand now in front of a little art deco pavilion and split into groups according to what time they're likely to run. The slowest groups will run first and the fastest last. That way the groups will converge towards the finish, allowing the players to encounter fresh faces throughout the 'race'—competitors they can pass or hold off.

And they're off.

And just like that, they're back.

They sprint and stammer to the finish, heaving and buckled over when they cross the line. As times are yelled out from the stop watch, some are annoyed. They scream, expletive after expletive. Rance, walking through the group, is loud: "Through the nose, through the nose!" he bellows. "Talk to a mate. Get him up." Others sit silently, inhale water, stretch, and walk it off. Drummond and Ellis and Lambert are the top runners. Vlastuin and Caddy—both hoping for midfield minutes this season—have posted impressive personal bests. The young ones—like Stengle and Bolton—look spent but remain ready for a full day of training.

They all know that this moment at the end of the run, just after 7am on a Monday morning, is really only the beginning of something. "That's the reality," says one coach. "A few weeks of anxiety for 10 minutes' work."

///////////

Of course, fitness will only go so far.

Hardwick leans against a railing inside the auditorium at Punt Road Oval. He stands expressionless in front of a wall given over entirely to one famous black and white photo of Francis Bourke muddied and bloodied and angry, emerging with the ball, sweat-slicked hair flying behind him. The room is almost at capacity. With the entire playing group here, plus coaches and support staff, more than 60 sets of eyes are upon him.

The group is back from their time trial, having driven from Carlton in a loose convoy through Melbourne, due back at the club and inside the auditorium by 9am. They lock the doors to the room after that. Punctuality is a non-negotiable. The coaches have already had a short training meeting in here, examining the schedule for January and talking about what they think will work and what won't—arguing about which drills to scale back and which need refinement.

The players file in, and most move to a familiar part of the room to find their perch. Tall defender Dylan Grimes and tall forward Ben Griffiths on the right-hand side, near the front; second year players Connor Menadue and Corey Ellis near the front, on the left.

Star on-baller Dustin Martin sits in the exact same seat as every meeting last year, fourth row back, second seat in. Last season he was flanked—always—by Chaplin and Deledio. With them gone, today he has small forward Sam Lloyd and rover Anthony Miles for company.

They all sit patiently through a presentation from new apparel sponsor Puma, explaining the gear they will wear—specifically the new guernseys. The new jumpers, with their breathable mesh underarms and watermarked logos, will no longer be "mustard and charcoal" but instead jet black and vibrant yellow. (The exact yellow is Color 13-0858 in the 'Puma Library'.) They are also locally made, says the spokesman, with a quick turnaround to satisfy the marketplace: "So if you guys get on a run, and the fans come out of the woodwork, we can respond."

Hardwick speaks next. He eschews chit-chat. He wants to know what the team did well before the Christmas break. The answer is defence, but what specifically? He looks at injured defender Steve Morris. "What's our biggest focus this year, Morro? What are we gonna speak about first and foremost?"

"Pressure on the footy?" he answers, quizzically.

"Yeah, pressure on the ball. So we've got some vision to go over, but let's get that front of mind again. Right now. The sessions prior to the break were outstanding, so what we want to show are some rewarding behaviours from that."

Justin Leppitsch stands up. After a tumultuous stint as senior coach of the Brisbane Lions, 'Leppa' has returned to Tigerland, where he once worked under Hardwick as the backline coach and was widely said to have helped mould its champion defender, Rance. He is now the forward line coach, but at the moment he is taking the entire playing list through a series of photos reiterating correct tackling technique, everything from "the pummel position"—getting low in order to hit opponents in their core—to the use of "inside shoulder"—a body-on-body approach that ensures players aren't left desperately clutching at opponents from a distance, relying on hands and fingers to hold onto powerful bodies.

"Decelerating is really important when we're taking ground, and when they're doing what?" Leppitsch asks. "When do we decelerate?"

"When they're facing up?" answers Miles.

"Yep, when they face you," says Leppistch. "When they're looking at you."

The assistant coach reiterates every little thing they've learned so far about tackling, making sure it will apply when they begin training today. The players must remember to slow down when approaching a target—so they can't be wrong-footed by a player looking to dodge, shimmy or baulk. They must remember to bring their legs close to an opponent *before* their arms— because tackling from distance is less effective. They must know to use their shoulder to make initial contact, *because why, Ben Lennon?*

"Because if we bring the leg close, and the body close," Lennon answers, "then all we have to do is hug them."

Hardwick resumes control of the meeting. He asks them to think back to last season—to a game when they applied this kind of pressure. What game would he be thinking of? There weren't many victories to crow about in 2016. An after-the-siren victory against Sydney? A final quarter comeback against the Suns? And not the expected wins over the Lions or the Bombers?

Someone says the Bulldogs game. Richmond lost the Round 16 clash by 10 points, but was ferocious all night.

"Yeah, the Bulldogs game, because it was outstanding," says Hardwick. "We've got to play to that level week in week out. What we've got to do is challenge ourselves to care more and do better. We've spoken about this. I guarantee you, if we play like this we're going to win a lot of games. A defensive mindset is the one thing you can rely on to bring a side closer, and then we can rely on the offensive stuff to win the game. Play like this, and we're going to win."

He shows a clip from training—a mistake—in which Brandon Ellis is caught between two opponents. Ellis seems to tread water, then drifts away from the ball carrier to guard the receiver.

"Brandon, what did you do here?" asks the coach.

"Um, I looked to go back," Ellis says.

"Yeah, go *forward*. What were you worried about initially?"

"The guy behind me."

"So what have you got to sum up really quickly?"

"Whether I can impact?"

"Yeah, and what we're going to say all year is, 'Make the error coming forward'," says Hardwick. "Press up."

Hardwick shows another clip from the same Tigers versus Tigers practice game, this time with five players from one side swamping two from the other. "Look at these numbers—fantastic! How often are you gonna get beaten with those kinds of numbers around the ball? Not often."

He pauses for a moment, then looks around the room.

"Does anyone know what I'm talking about when I talk about a short pitch versus a long pitch? Reece [Conca], you look like you're having a think, or taking a shit."

The room fills with laughter.

"We want to play off a short pitch, by which I mean, we want to turn that ball over as close as we can to the goals. What do you reckon we were playing off last year?" asks Hardwick. "Yeah, a long pitch. Now, if we're trying to force turnovers in the front half—pressing up on the ball carrier—every now and then we're going to get killed over the back, but we don't care, because we *need* to turn the ball over in this part of the ground."

He talks about the strengths of Grimes, Rance, and vastly improved key backman David Astbury. They are all intercept kings—elite at winning the ball back from the opposition. But the club needs players who perform this same role in other parts of the field, instead of so close to the opposition goal, where counter-attacks are difficult to mount.

Hardwick shows clips that illustrate what he's after. Vlastuin flies back with the flight to spoil a contest. Martin charges at a pack and lays three tackles. Lennon stays with the ball and applies four pressure acts in barely 10 seconds of action.

"That's the sort of stuff that's not necessarily gonna get you on the highlights tape, but more importantly, it's gonna get your name up on this board here," Hardwick says, pointing to the Francis Bourke Award, which is voted on by the team and recognises the player that most embodies their trademark values of awareness, belief and discipline, the attributes—among many others—of the sainted Bourke. "We've spoken about this—our desire for workmanlike behaviour," Hardwick says. "We want you wearing your hard hats, because it's great to watch. How did we describe that drill after we did it?"

"Awesome," says one player.

"Exciting," says another.

"It was like we were a different team," says Grigg.

Hardwick seizes on another answer from somewhere in the room. The answer he was hoping someone would offer.

"I heard that," he says. "It was *fun*. It was great. Now let's go do it again. And again. And again. Let's make sure we build on what we've started."

2

IN THE CHAMBER

Inside the war room where the coaches meet, Damien Hardwick always sits at the same end of the big oval-shaped desk marked with goals, arcs and a centre square. When we meet for the first time this pre-season in February, I forget this quirk of his, sit down in his seat, and he lets me have it: "What the hell is this?"

I apologise and slide one space over.

That's also a mistake: "Keep going," he says, waving me across, smiling and laughing and shaking his head. "What do you think this is?"

All coaches, perhaps all leaders, have quirks that define their reign. Hardwick prefers that no one sit immediately next to him. He likes his space—room to think and gesture, an empty desk around him upon which to flick sheets of statistics, a protected zone surrounding his chair so he can stand up and walk to the adjacent whiteboard without bumping someone's knees or elbows. He feels the same way when watching practice matches alone from the edge of the field, and, if space allows, inside the crammed coach's box on game day. Strange really, when you think back on his playing days, when body-on-body was his metier.

This year was the first time he used the summer break to take a large step back from all things football. He took his family on an extended winter holiday to New York and Chicago, a time he would usually spend here, engrossed in thought. "It was like 'Shit, I'm missing training', but it meant the pre-season flew for me, which was great because otherwise you can drive yourself mad, thinking up things you can do more of. It's just been more relaxed. I wish I could have stayed longer."

Now he is back, and so is the weight of planning, and expectation. The pressure to improve is ever-present, not from the expectant and ever-hungry Tiger fans, but from inside Punt Road: "Inside these four walls the pressure is enormous. And we welcome that. The candle is burning."

///////////

I n January, no team really knows how good or how bad it is. The process of finding out is the season. Only one team wins the silverware, however, so the primary AFL emotion is disappointment. It might be the touchstone of the game.

NFL coach Bill Parcells, who had a glorious and storied career, winning Super Bowls and turning franchises around, believed that losing was a far more potent experience than winning. He is said to have stopped coaching, in fact, not because of any extinguished internal fire or desire to win, but because he could no longer handle the losses. The fact that every player and coach embarks on a journey that is likely to end painfully and abruptly is perhaps a single aspect of the sport.

"People think we think about the finish, but we don't really," says Hardwick. "The pressure is always there because it's a performance-based industry, but we put that on ourselves. The feeling before the first game against Carlton this year will be the same as it was last year. We want to win, week in, week out. I want to get the best out of my playing group, get some wins on the board for my staff, and the rest takes care of itself."

And when the results don't fall as intended? "You accept responsibility, accountability, we admit our faults and we move on quickly. The harsh reality of our game is you can do a lot of things right, but if you lose you're seen as a terrible footy club. That mightn't be the case. We do a lot of things better than many footy clubs, but we had a poor year, and our reputation gets tarnished as a result. That's the industry we're in. You don't complain."

But losses have consequences. Accountability is not just a word. I wonder about the hard conversations he must have had with the assistant coaches who left after giving all they had. Hardwick and Lade were premiership teammates. Williams was their coach. Ross Smith was an ally and confidant at two clubs. Terminating those professional relationships must have been trying.

"We always do the dirty work," he says, nodding. "We pride ourselves on being the executioner, as such, and yeah it's hard, because we're emotionally invested in our staff."

They handled it well though, Hardwick says. He hopes he will do the same when his time comes, but he doesn't want to talk about that. "I can understand the interest, but it's not something we talk about. And if we do talk about it, we joke about it, like 'I might finally get to see Greece in summer'," he says, laughing. "The reality? It's gonna happen at some stage. You enter this game knowing there's a bullet out there with your name on it."

///////////

Hardwick knows that after seven years in the hot seat, and a run of losing finals, his future will be the most speculated upon in season 2017, his performance the most scrutinised; perhaps marginally ahead of his close neighbour, Collingwood coach Nathan Buckley, and Port Adelaide's Ken Hinkley; you can throw Gold Coast's Rodney Eade into that 'elite' bunch. The fans—and administrators—of each of these clubs are hungry and impatient.

Last season it was the same. Hardwick is now used to such attention, approaching the job with equanimity. Last season, the two-word slogan within the club was "Next Level". I ask Hardwick what the feeling is now, after that optimism was dashed on the rocks of reality. "The expectation for me is still the same. I remember thinking we could shoot for top four last year, and this year it's gone back to firmly making the finals. I won't back down from that. That's the competitive nature of me, and the team. In saying that, 17 other clubs are saying exactly the same thing. It's an easy thing to say—it's a hard thing to do."

And so he has begun another year of discussions, debates and quarrels with his assistants, all aimed at seeking the "next level" whether the official slogan or not. Such probing is a constant in this environment. Questioning and challenging are encouraged, and it all plays out in the open—whether coaches with coaches or coaches with players or players with players.

Hardwick believes this is part of the default mindset required to play and win finals. Conflict ensures all avenues are explored, all details are shared and understood, and all personnel are on the same page. The game plan that comes from such conflict and debate is expected to lead to winning ways, but the AFL's robust equalisation measures mean, theoretically, that any team can rise.

Of the 18 clubs in the League this season, perhaps only two—Brisbane and Carlton—could be confidently predicted to miss the finals. In such a competitive playing field, with such slender margins and limited standard deviation, unpredictability is all that seems predictable. Sometimes it seems as though a form of competitive entropy exists. What Hardwick, and his team of coaches and leaders, must do is to scrutinise the total game—Richmond's and the other 17 clubs—so thoroughly as to locate and eliminate any inefficiencies in their control, and exploit what they see outside Punt Road.

It is then up to the head coach to take whatever potential for incremental gain exists at Tigerland and turn it into something that can be trained—here we go again—to achieve the "next level". As coach, he is the bonding agent, the emulsion that binds the group together in this purpose.

For all the pressure Hardwick has been under, particularly in the last two seasons, he has shown a clear ability to improve the Richmond list, something that's easily lost in the 24/7, win/loss news cycle.

He assumed the role in 2009, after tasting success as an assistant at Hawthorn under Alastair Clarkson, and he oversaw a Tigers' ascension that was steady and admirable, given the mess he had inherited after the late 2009 season departure of Terry Wallace: 2010 (6 wins), 2011 (8 wins, 1 draw), 2012 (10, 1), 2013 (15), 2014 (12), 2015 (15). But then came last year, which is either the correction Richmond had to have, or an aberration on an otherwise upward curve.

Naturally, he believes it is the latter, noting that the training block before Christmas was good, and the team has started the new year well. But he knows he says this every summer, and so he is fatalistic about such optimism. "All the players will say 'It's been great—the best pre-season ever'. I reckon they would have said that 12 months ago, too, but we'll feed that momentum." That thought he tempers with a little truth. "It doesn't mean it's going to transfer into Round 1."

The coaching group has put a power of effort into the team's defensive philosophy—getting the players to pride themselves primarily on shutting the opposition down, which will make attacking simpler, at least in theory. "It seems an oxymoron, but we'll score more off the back of a better defence," he says. "Offensively, these guys all have talent—they can all play. Defence is probably the easiest thing to fix, because it's an attitude adjustment."

What of the much-discussed, and generally maligned Tiger philosophy of recent years—that the best way to defend is to attack, although mainly by maintaining possession of the football? It was a game plan that aped the successful style of Hawthorn, relying on precision kicking to play 'keepings off' and then cut through defences. It broke down last season, and some would say also in the series of finals losses before. Hardwick is not convinced this is a failed system—he still believes in controlling the ball, but a control based on total trust of each player in the chain. A control that eschews risk-averse hesitancy and instead adopts freedom and belief.

"There was an inability for our players behind the ball to trust our players in front of the ball. And then our players in *front* of the ball didn't have faith that our players *behind* the ball would kick it to them."

The classic circular argument.

"But that reluctance to move the ball forward wasn't by design. It was more that our players lacked confidence, and when you lack confidence in yourself you lack it in one another. No one knows why it happens. People often say, 'You kick backwards a lot', but it wasn't something we aspired to do. It just happens when you go through a slump or lose momentum—you lose that 'look forward' mentality. We have to get that back."

It will not be easy. He also points out that the team has a hardened core of solid players who do not have bucket loads of confidence, who came to the club as late picks in the National Draft, or Pre-Season Draft, or the Rookie Draft. "We've got a lot of guys who are really solid players, playing their arse off for us, but hanging tough," says Hardwick. "They're getting the best out of themselves but sometimes they lack confidence. And the easiest thing to do when you're lacking confidence is to make an easy decision and go backwards. The guys were too cautious last year, but maybe we didn't give them enough licence or weren't clear enough with our messaging."

Hardwick stands over the oval-shaped table now, using the graphic to assist his reflections on the failings of 2016. He points to the area people commonly think of as the wings and corridor—the middle third of the ground. "Our biggest problem has been moving it from the centre back area, to the centre forward area. It's been our achilles heel. But that happens to most sides when you attack from the back half."

The Tigers had roughly 300 fewer entries into their forward 50 than their opponents last year, and that happened because far too often they were trying to attack from the full-back line. Their rate of success in transferring the ball from deep in defence was as good as the rest of the League, but when you are forced to launch so many attacks from back there, producing winning scores is rare. "The Bulldogs, for instance, were *much* worse than us at transitioning from full-back, but they weren't doing it as often. Funnily enough, Brisbane's transition from their back half is pretty good, but they were doing it 200 times more than anyone."

Put simply, winning teams win the ball further up field, closer to attack, and clear of pressure. This is the short pitch the coaching staff wants, instead of the long pitch from deep in defence they were playing. I imagine the long pitch is also the reason it seems to much of the football public that a player like Jack Riewoldt has strayed so far from goal. Pundits were highly critical of Hardwick throughout 2016 for not listening to their advice: "Leave Jack at full-forward". And yet the spearhead *was* often the deepest player in the Richmond forward line—it was just that the forward line had to come away from the goal line to meet the play.

"I could leave Jack in the goal square," says Hardwick, "but the ball ain't getting there. And Jack's an elite one-on-one player, so I'm going to want him up closer (to the play), where he can win a contest. He can stand down there (at full-forward) all day but he won't touch it unless our midfield is on top, turning the ball over in our half of the ground. The year before last, our forward entries were plus-200 and Jack kicked more goals, and the commentators will say 'Jack played closer to goal'. Well no shit, Sherlock—if we're locking it in our front half, Jack's gonna be closer to goal. It's not rocket science." The Riewoldt stats make fascinating reading, and you can make of them what you will, as with all stats. His best season was in 2010, when he won the Coleman Medal with 78 goals, and kicked 32% of the Tigers' goals. Richmond finished 15th with just six wins. Since then it's been 62 (21%), 65 (21%), 58 (18%), 61 (21%), 54 (18%) and 48 (19%). The Riewoldt puzzle will, it seems, be forever front and centre at every pub forum of Tiger fans.

Strategy aside, the coach is clearly excited about his playing list this preseason. He is energised by the arrival of three ready-made players in Caddy, Prestia and young ruckman Toby Nankervis from Sydney. AFL teams change so dramatically each year that part of the off-season challenge is to find a place for every player, being aware that form can be fragile, and no list manager can claim to be Nostradamus. Hardwick thinks of each player on his list like a character in a script. The season is the story into which they fit, and this trio has already shifted the narrative. "The vibe of the side just changes," he says. "The players sense they've got a new group. It's hard to explain but they're rejuvenated."

He loves the way third-year small forward Dan Butler has attacked the pre-season. Butler [pick 67, 2014, yet to make his senior debut] has overcome injury and was also given strong feedback in his 2016 midyear review—"an intervention"—and his response, says Hardwick, has been intense and specific. "Talk about keeping the ball in the forward line, playing off a short pitch, it's guys like him who are going to help us. Just relentlessly chasing and tackling and maybe getting on the end of a couple."

He is enthusiastic, too, about the progress of the middle-tier players, including Reece Conca, struck down by hamstring injuries in three successive seasons, and Vlastuin, who with Caddy, will add bite and muscle to the midfield. He is also eager, along with every Richmond fan, to see what Brandon Ellis and Corey Ellis (not related) can do. The latter pair, both first round draft picks, intrigue for their recent lack of progress.

Brandon Ellis [pick 15, 2011] was one of the most promising players in the game in his first years—an All Australian nominee in 2014—but he has stagnated since. He still runs hard in both directions but ball security is an issue. The wingman has been criticised for playing outside football but Hardwick stresses that has been his role. "For him to progress," he says, "we're challenging him to go to half-back. It's where he played some of his best footy as a kid. He's a good mark for his size. He can win contested ball and he can break lines."

Corey Ellis [pick 12, 2014] is a greater unknown. The left-footer boasts an elite kick but needs to work on his change of pace, on being more explosive, or being manic around the contest—blasting off on the lead or on the chase. He is also quiet. Last season, Choco Williams said Ellis reminded him of the Port Adelaide swingman Justin Westhoff as a withdrawn young man. Williams's unconventional solution was to send Westhoff to work at

McDonald's for a week, behind the counter, forcing him to talk to customers. Maybe they should put Corey on the front desk at Punt Road, he suggested. In the end, they encouraged him to have more say in meetings and on the track, but 2016 was a tough year.

Ellis's talent is unquestioned. In an intra club match only a few weeks ago, he was comfortably best on ground, moving in traffic with the kind of poise and time displayed by silky left footers like Scott Pendlebury and Dyson Heppell. "He just hasn't had a great run at it," says Hardwick. "There's probably a couple of guys who had better pre-seasons, but it's important to give him an opportunity."

Ellis moved out of home recently, too, which the coach sees as a positive step. He's rooming with Nick Vlastuin, a young leader on the up. The mixture of independence and modelling is important, particularly for young Victorian players. Hardwick well remembers his eastern suburbs mates pulling at his coat tails when he began playing for the Bombers. "Living at home in Upwey I was like, 'Do I have to drive all the way to Essendon to go out, or do I go out with my school mates close to home? Simple, I'm going out with my school mates.' It means you're not fully invested in the footy club. Sometimes the best thing is to get those interstate kids who just get fully entrenched in the team."

This assessment of the list is never-ending, from the first gathering of the season to those dreaded exit interviews. The coaches tread a delicate line in their response to poor performance. On the one hand the players are human beings who need to be guided and nurtured, and on the other hand they are an array of individuals with failings that need to be identified and explained. They must then be worked hard, trained and encouraged, augmented and refined, and ultimately transformed and improved.

Hardwick is an admirer of the book *Collison Low Crossers* (Little, Brown & co, 2013), by Nicholas Dawidoff, a writer for *Sports Illustrated* before he embarked on a career as an author. Dawidoff spent a season with the New York Jets, and when discussing coaches, he made a point that rings true with Hardwick—that football coaches have much in common with fine artists:

Cezanne slashed the paintings that dissatisfied him. Giacometti gasped, swore furiously, and descended into melancholy or anguish as he painted James Lord's portrait, often screaming in a rage at the canvas and then scrubbing it and beginning anew.

Inside the club, it is rare to hear a coach upbraid a player. Throughout the week, their voices are always conciliatory, encouraging—at least when the players are within earshot. Coaches talking together in private are naturally more honest—"With him it's always about self-doubt"; "That guy doesn't like the physical contest"; "He's just not a great player"—like teachers in a staffroom. No, the only time the players genuinely cop a roasting is on game day, and then the words can be caustic, particularly when the error is one of submission or passivity. Over the course of 2016, there were more than a few; in truth, Hardwick has hit almost everyone on the list.

He pointed a finger first at Shaun Grigg, after the midfielder called for a handball, instead of running down the clock in a tight loss: "You are possibly the smartest footballer at this club, but that was so dumb!"

He hit Daniel Rioli after a handful of matches, when the young forward produced a few flashes but not enough of them: "Daniel, when are you going to show us why we drafted you?"

He roared at Kane Lambert in a late season match, when the hard runner went missing after being promoted for a crucial game: "I put my balls on the line for you, dropped Milesy, and where are you?"

He spared no one, ripping into Alex Rance, after Rance had elbowed an opponent in the back of the head: "You're a champion, but that was bullshit. I hope they give you four weeks for that crap!"

But Hardwick will also console each one, and shows them genuine affection—in his own time. He speaks articulately with the mature and pragmatic Grigg. He eats breakfast with Rioli at home. When Lambert suffers a broken rib and a punctured lung in a night game, Hardwick drives directly from the MCG to visit him in hospital. He shakes his head at Rance, and Rance shakes his back, and they have an understanding.

Hardwick knows life is not easy for young draftees, in particular. Corey Ellis, for instance, had a constant groin complaint last season, and a young friend died, too. As one coach said: "He played heavy—his head was heavy." Hardwick sympathises. "Sometimes on game day, you forget about the stuff that's going on in their lives and you think they can unpack it all and leave it at the door for two hours," he says. "But sometimes they just can't. It's hard."

He remembers how hard it was on Rioli, only 12 months ago, in his first season. He remembers the teenager powering through 35-degree days of training and sitting silently in the car on the way home to the south-eastern suburbs, then flopping immediately into bed. Hardwick has knocked on the door of Rioli's room to wake him for dinner, watched him eat and then go immediately back to sleep until morning.

The coach has had more than two decades to adjust to the hourly, daily, weekly, monthly and yearly rigours of the football industry—the everyday life of deep concentration and physical exhaustion. But new players do not have that bedrock. "It's tough on those kids," he says. "When they first come in, they're fried."

And yet Hardwick will need the likes of Rioli to perform. Not just him either, but all of them—young and old. Prestia, Caddy and Nankervis. Butler and Riewoldt. Conca and Vlastuin. Ellis and Ellis. The pressure is mounting.

3

THE STORY

The slide consuming a wall of the auditorium is simple. On a black background, there is one sentence in yellow letters: *What is the story of the practice match tomorrow night?*

Hardwick had worked on his presentation a day earlier, in his office across the hall, and slide one was his first thought. "I know what I want to see," he said when putting the finishing touches on his "preso" for the players. "But I'm more interested in what the players want to see, and that's the question I'll ask. What's the Richmond story tomorrow night? What do you want to put on the park? What's that difference you want people to see this year? Personally, I just want to see a physically aggressive side that's prepared to play fast and hard, tackle and chase."

Now he stands in the auditorium, off to one side of his handwork, facing the players in their tiered seating. "What I want you to do," he tells them, "is sit with the bloke beside you and have a 30-second conversation about what story you want to see come out of tomorrow night's game."

He asks Shaun Grigg first. What does he want his family, friends and the Richmond supporters in the crowd to see? "Me and Milesy spoke about excitement," he answers. "When we've got the ball and even when we haven't. The pressure, the intensity, and just free-flowing, exciting footy."

"Great," says Hardwick. "Grimesy, you and Griff?"

"We spoke about wanting to see all the pieces of the puzzle that we've practised over summer coming together. There's going to be lots of mistakes, but we want to see smashing in, and fighting, and celebrating."

"Great points," says Hardwick.

He turns to David Astbury. "Dave?"

"Just not being scared to make mistakes. Just playing with risk and flair and energy. Go for it."

"All great answers. What's the key word on that slide? Lloydy?"

Lloyd takes a moment, ums, ahs, then guesses: "practice".

"That's right. All those points you guys made are great—but understand it's a *practice* match. I want to see a heap of mistakes. What do I mean by a heap of mistakes, Nick?"

"Positive things," says Nick Vlastuin. "Like breaking a tackle, going for your kicks."

"My oath—play the game! All those things we've been working on, let's have a crack. I don't give a stuff about the scoreboard. What do I care about? Process, and effort."

It's time now for specifics. They talk about tactics for slowing down the Crows' ball movement. The slideshow now has a picture of Adelaide forwards Eddie Betts, Charlie Cameron, Tom Lynch and Josh Jenkins. "What can you tell me about these players here, Batch? What do they rely on?"

Batchelor gives the answer the coach is looking for: quick and easy goals over the back, off fast plays. And then he offers the solution: hard-running defensive effort from the midfielders and forwards.

"Yeah," says Hardwick, "running from *everyone* up the ground. The positive is that we've trained this all summer, so if we get this right they will have no impact on the game. Luckily, I've got great backs who can combat these players, but they need help."

They look at a few examples on screen. Footage of Rioli chasing down an opponent, forcing a turnover. Prestia giving up an errant handball to an opponent: "But stiff shit," says Hardwick, "because watch this amazing secondary effort" (Prestia lunges at the opponent, causing the lost ball to spill free again). Dan Butler, zipping across the grass like an out-of-control lawnmower. Vlastuin hitting the heart of a pack and breaking through the faintest of gaps.

Hardwick's next point: the importance of beating the Crows at the coalface. He calls it "the one-metre rule"—not losing a contest when the ball is within one metre of a Tiger player and the enemy. The ball flies into screen in a snippet of footage from the game against Adelaide last year. Hardwick freezes the frame as the ball lands within a metre of both Brandon Ellis and Charlie Cameron.

"*That's* the ball," says Hardwick, pointing at the blurry, frozen yellow Sherrin. "That's the ball that determines whether you win or lose. That's the one metre we're looking for tomorrow night. Put your head in the hole."

With the frame still frozen, he asks who is likely to win the contest. Whose ball is it right now? If anything, it favours Cameron. He lets the footage continue, and Ellis hits the ball first and man second, knocking Cameron down. Hard. The Crow winger doesn't get up.

"BANG!" says the coach. "The one-metre rule. Tomorrow night. Yeah, we're looking for more inside 50s, but it all comes back to this. We've invested in our midfield—that's your bread and butter."

////////////

They go over offensive and defensive strategies. Hardwick points to on-screen labels, sets of coded letters and numerals, and asks someone what they mean—what do they stand for in the broadest sense? One important code this season represents the first and most basic form of defence—the expectation that players will come forward and attack the ball carrier, looking to spoil or tackle or force a little error by their presence. But as for what such monikers mean in the broader sense? No one answers.

"It's a framework. A rough set of guidelines. That's all it is," Hardwick says. "It's not set in stone. What have you guys here all got? You've got *talent*. We have a framework we play by, but understand you get to our footy club because you have talents and strengths." Nank's, for example, is his physicality. "We want to see you compete, open up scoring opportunities, play the game, play on instinct. That's what we want to see. Remember the weapons you all have that we want to exploit. Each complements the other. Some of us are ball-winners. Some of us break lines. Some of us are finishers. But I want to see them all tomorrow night, so back yourself in."

He asks if there are any questions about the next night.

Riewoldt recalls a pre-season game at Etihad a year earlier, against Port Adelaide, in which the Tigers suffered a handful of injuries and Hardwick asked the AFL if the game could be abandoned before the end. They weren't allowed, of course, but even asking that question caused a minor media storm on the eve of the season. The coach had threatened to keep players on the bench anyway, to protect them from further injury. He threatened to see out the rest of the game without a full team if he had to. Riewoldt remembers the moment, and he grins: "Will we be playing 14 on the field at any stage?"

"Maybe, if you make it to the bench," says Hardwick. "Now take your shit jokes outside."

///////////

The schedule for JLT 1—the Tigers' first pre-season game, against the Adelaide Crows at Etihad Stadium on Friday February 24—is regimented. It is timed and planned to the minute. It's all there on a white A3 sheet, stuck to the wall in several places within the Etihad Stadium change rooms.

The game starts at 7:40pm, but it's not just a matter of getting the players into the rooms at 6-ish and then hoping a sequence of activities will happen in the correct order. The dozens of tasks and minor meetings that need to happen are so strictly set that they are not even in five- or 10-minute blocks.

Individual movement preparation—6:54 to 6:57
Inside warm up—6:57 to 7:03
Enter Arena—7:32

In a quiet room filled with snacks and drinks, spare shorts and socks, the club's assistant sports scientist Brendan Fahrner is fitting distance trackers into small pockets on the back of every guernsey. Because the game is being played in a stadium with a roof, they aren't the standard GPS trackers—they're instead using the Catapult Sports Team A Clearsky 2 System. But it works in the same way, monitoring and recording distance and speed.

Neil Balme, the General Manager of football and former Tiger ruckman is there, and someone ventures that they would not have had such technology in his playing days.

"Mmmm," says Balme, whose last game for the Tigers was in 1979. "Thank God for that."

Inside the little room where Hardwick will deliver his pre-match address, the coaches are milling. Hardwick stands at the front, writing on a whiteboard. He does this before every game, setting up his messages. Tonight, they're reminders.

> Defensively: Control the tempo of the game
> Win the 1-metre space
> Win the 5-metre space
> Offensively: Play to your strengths for the benefit of the team

Each team is represented by magnets on a whiteboard, and there are some interesting match-ups. Brandon Ellis, a short, running back flanker this season, will be on tall target Tom Lynch. Tall defender Dylan Grimes will be responsible for the dangerous small forward Eddie Betts. Assistants talk quietly about some of the new tactical terminology being used by the coaches and players this season. One says it doesn't matter. "Things stay the same. Win the ball, kick it through the two tall sticks."

The atmosphere is light. Hardwick is poring over his notes when he spies the forwards coach Justin Leppitsch, coming at him with open arms. "Don't touch me, don't touch me," says Hardwick, snickering as Leppitsch wraps him in a bear hug. "I haven't missed you at all."

Leppitsch talks briefly about his theme for his forwards: bring the music. If it sounds familiar, that's because of what Western Bulldogs coach Luke Beveridge told his players prior to their historic Grand Final win last season. His message was "Bring your instruments". The coach had thought about the vast crowd that would be there watching the game, and how the only way his players would perform and play creative football is if they thought about their strengths and abilities.

It makes sense. There is musicality in football. Training married with improvisation. Genius and discipline. The savants and the studious. There is beauty in both, but neither one is created without slavish devotion to the craft.

Konstantin Stanislavski, the theatre performer responsible for what is known today as "method acting," talked about rehearsal and artistic performance in the same way. He might as well have been describing footy players when he wrote: *What is difficult becomes habitual, what is habitual becomes easy, what is easy is beautiful.*

Finally, Hardwick speaks. He asks the same question as the day before: What's the story? The story is the first pre-season game of the year.

There's nothing better. He looks at Dustin Martin and asks why.

"Footy's back," says Martin.

"Yeah, we're not playing against each other. What goes up a notch?"

"Intensity," says the star midfielder. "Competition."

"And what's the great thing about competition?"

"Makes you better."

"Yeah," says the coach, "and it's how you test yourself."

He runs over a few more key points. Slow the opposition down. Control the tempo of the game. Bring a defensive attitude on the front half and play off a short pitch. Outnumber them. And make mistakes. Make a ton of them. He has a story to share, too.

"When I was kid, believe it or not I was actually an all right basketballer. OK, I was in the seconds," he says, and the players laugh. "But I loved the game. And then I got one opportunity when a couple of guys from the firsts got injured. And I thought, 'You know what, I'm gonna go out there and try my arse off and get into the firsts side'. I wasn't a great player, but I had my chance. And I remember playing that game and getting into the car afterwards, and saying to dad, 'How do you reckon I went?' And the old man went, 'You played it safe'.

"I went, 'Yeah I did'. I didn't go for that gap. You know what I'm talking about? There's a time when you're one-on-one and you've got that opportunity to go, and if you hesitate what happens? You miss out. I thought 'Next time, Damien, I'm going to do it'. And you know what happened? There was no next time. That was it. That was my one big chance. That's what tonight is—a chance for you to go for that gap. I'm *dying* to see *you* play. Hopefully you end up like I did, an elite basketballer. Good luck, have some fun, enjoy each others company. Go get 'em."

///////////

At half-time the players wander inside. They're winning, and enjoying it. At the front of the room sits a table with a large plastic canvas sheet, covered in a series of squares, each with a large player number embossed upon it—like a snakes and ladders board without the snakes or the ladders. Sitting on top of each square is the preferred refreshment of that player, fluids and snacks.

On square 9, for Trent Cotchin, are two red Allen's snakes and a cola-flavoured energy gel pack—the kind marathon runners slip into their shorts and then suck down at the 33-kilometre mark of the race. Waiting on square 31 for Oleg Markov is a muffin and a banana. Dustin Martin, square 4, has eight rice crackers.

Most of the others just dip into a communal plastic tub of mint chewing gum, and take their drinks. Ben Lennon, square 7, has Hydralite and water. Kamdyn McIntosh, 33, has Gatorade.

They have rub downs. They get patched up. They get walking and then into a little circular shuffle-jog. They do leg swings and stretches and bumps, and then they listen. The coaches bemoan a few things. They're dominating possession, which is great, but not using it quite right—a common problem the previous year. The game is close though, and only Adelaide's superior conversion rate is keeping them in touch. The Tigers are winning the inside 50 count (25-18), and they have 14 forward half turnovers and seven inside 50 tackles.

"The pressure has been terrific," says Hardwick. "We've got to continue to do that. Whichever side gets repeat entries is scoring. What do we know about them in the contest? They're really good—they're good around the contest. So, think about that anxiety when you have the ball in tight, and maybe kick it forward. What's that mean for our forwards? They need to be ready and in position.

"Understand I want you to take the game on, but there is also a stage where you can feel it—*They're coming*—and maybe you take that chance to move it our way. But how good is this? We're seeing plenty of moments where the ball is moving forward, and the goal might just have been missed, but that'll come. It will come. So keep playing to your strengths, keep supporting your teammates, keep taking the game on."

///////////

Sitting in the rooms after the win, Dylan Grimes rips the tape off his wrists. Ivan Maric has big bags of ice strapped to his left calf. Batchelor has his right foot wrapped in the stuff. The crowd of 7262 is already filing out of the ground, into the underground car park or across to Southern Cross Station.

Hardwick stands while his players sit. He's happy. Defensively, the team stopped Adelaide from playing the game in their half. They won the contested ball with a high number (141). They got a victory, and played to their strengths.

"Some guys will be happy with their first game," he says, "and some guys will be flat. But we've got time to get better, time to work on things."

Riewoldt takes a moment to praise the work of David Astbury in keeping the dominant spearhead and Adelaide captain Taylor Walker out of the game all night. Applause rings out. Before they leave to stretch, get massaged, eat hot burritos and head back to the club for recovery in the training facility's basement pool, Hardwick asks Alex Rance what he thought, watching the match from the sideline.

"I thought it was an *awesome* game," he says to the group. "Yeah there were some stuff-ups but the pressure you guys put on...and you looked so quick. Yeah, we sprayed a few, but I was just so excited about the opportunities you created. This is the quickest and most exciting I've ever seen this team. I can't wait to play next week."

4

THE MOOD OF THE ROOM

He probably doesn't know it, but Brendon Gale looks comical right now. It's the stool, you see. He's sitting on a miniature red metal stool in the bike shop café opposite Punt Road Oval and, well, he's a very tall man (198 centimetres), and he's wearing a very nice suit (he is the club CEO), and so he looks, well, very odd, sitting at the kids' table next to a row of teeny bikes with training wheels.

But it was the only space left, so he just hunches that big frame over that tiny table regardless, and digs into a plate of pasta primavera and explains how he, like Hardwick, took an extended break this off season; a week relaxing on Victoria's Surf Coast, then home to Tasmania to spend some time with relatives. He went to Hobart, where his wife's family is from. But first he went to see his mum, who's getting on and has an old house and garden, and needed a bit of help around the place.

It was nice, he says. "I grew up in Burnie, and I surfed a lot as a kid. It's a rugged, wild place, but I never really saw it. Most of my childhood I was being driven between Burnie, Devonport, Launceston, Hobart, doing sport. I didn't have much interest in the environment or physical beauty."

Time changed that approach. "Later though I've developed an appreciation.

I took our executive team for a trek on the Overland Track[1] a few years ago—no mobiles, hiking all day, seeing the stars. My home was more of an industrial town. Factories, pulp and paper mills."

When he arrived at Richmond in 1987—drafted at pick 27 from the Burnie Hawks, in the same draft Richard Lounder came as pick one for just four senior games—Gale was a skinny teenager, tipping the scales at just 84 kilos. He would endure a run of injuries in those early years, undergoing two groin operations and an appendectomy in his first two years at Punt Road. He would play nine reserves games in each of those seasons. "Times have changed," he said. "In those days, it was easy to get drafted and tough to get a game. Now it's the opposite, clubs are desperate to see what they've got with their draft picks."

The team was struggling, and in the middle of a run of coaches—Francis Bourke, Mike Patterson, Paul Sproule, Tony Jewell and finally Kevin Bartlett in Gale's first year at Punt Road—but he still thought he was walking into an elite VFL environment. "I didn't know any different," he says. Being in a professional environment—a paid footballer, no less—was thrilling and carefree, until it wasn't. By 1989, the team had fallen even further, 'winning' the wooden spoon, although that was the least of the club's worries, as Gale recalls: "It must have been the second annual general meeting during my time when Neville Crowe announced the club was millions in debt, and the receivers were at the door, and we've got to go and shake cans. The club was impoverished. Certainly, that feeling was palpable, the whole *Save Our Skins* campaign was in swing. We were sent to all corners of the state. The club harnessed past players, too, and organised functions, and the young guys would get buddied up.

"I remember going out to Warrnambool with Ricky McLean and Robbie McGhie. I remember standing on Brunton Avenue rattling tins. We were part of the response. And when I look back now, in those early stages of the draft and investment in recruiting, we just didn't have the capacity."

Bartlett, the 403-game veteran of the club and coach from 1988 to 1991, would come in on the weekend to install speed balls in the gym. Volunteers would be asked to paint the walls. All of it made

---

1   The Overland Track is a 65 kilometre, six-day trek through the heart of Tasmania Cradle Mountain-Lake St Clair National Park.

an impression on the teenager, who would finally make his debut in Round 1 of 1990, and hardly miss a game until his retirement. Gale played 244 games with the club between 1990 and 2001—a largely fallow period—enjoying only two finals victories, but they were big ones with "big thumping crowds" against the biggest of local rivals in Essendon (1995) and Carlton (2001).

He remembers walking back to the club after coming from behind to beat the Bombers in the second semi-final. It was September and so the days were growing longer. He remembers a warm afternoon, children everywhere, kicking the footy, excited. He remembers the after-match celebration upstairs at the club. Having a beer, enjoying the moment. He can still relive that feeling.

"I heard Dimma talk the other day about premierships. He's lucky enough to have won a couple. And he said when they have premiership reunions, you don't get together and talk about 'How great was that premiership?' You talk about what you're doing and how's the family and you hang shit on each other. It's the journey and the relationships you forge, the life lessons. It's a really hard game but it's just a privilege to undertake the journey with these mates you go into battle with. If I'd won four premierships would I say the same thing? I reckon if you asked Luke Hodge he surely would."

Still, Hardwick has said other things about premierships. The coach also spent quiet moments last season pondering a question: What does it mean to have a great AFL career? Playing 200 games is a splendid thing, but if you haven't got that premiership medal around your neck, what is it all worth? Hardwick played in premierships with both Essendon (2000) and Port Adelaide (2004), but during a quiet moment during the break, he thought about those greats of the game—Robert Flower, Nathan Buckley, Robert Harvey—who left the field without a precious premiership medallion. "I wonder how it sits with them?" he thought. "Imagine playing 300 games and not having that? They must go to bed feeling hollow, in a way."

I ask if Gale feels that way. Does it sit badly, not having won a flag? Does he feel as though something is missing? "I'll be honest, I don't. I don't lie awake at night and beat myself up. It would be a wonderful sense of completion, and there's a sense of a little emptiness on Grand Final Day, but I don't define myself by that. But having said that, not having won the cup was a motivator for coming back as an administrator and hopefully having a hand in one from the front office." Gale's mission since he returned to the club as an administrator in 2009— aside from winning premierships—is to shield players from that kind of exposure. The desire to protect and to build powerful scaffolding is strong.

"From day one—as CEO and on the board—I've felt that the most important thing to work on in the organisation was a sense of focus and alignment, and the next to have a business model that makes money. In 2010 and 2011 the gaps between the haves and have nots in AFL were being exacerbated. Badly. The equalisation measures now are thankfully more intense. But our number one priority was that we had to give the footy department everything they need—not want—and then to have no excuses."

Gale didn't naturally expect to return to Tigerland when he retired. People imagine it was part of his grand long term plan as a professional, but it wasn't. When he finished playing he wanted to get on with another part of his life. He worked in the law. He even chose an area of commercial law that would give him the best opportunity to work overseas, eyeing London, Hong Kong and New York. "I was looking forward to that. I'm a pretty curious person. But I also realised I wasn't as in love with the law as I might have been."

He spent time at the city legal firm King & Wood Mallesons and remembers a friend there who was very good at his work, had been a litigator for six years and is now a partner—but he had never spent a day in court. Part of Gale was anxious about leaving such a sharp outfit, dealing with complex matters—banking and project finance—and "going back into footy, dumbing things down." Nevertheless, he joined the AFL Players' Association as its chief executive, during a tumultuous period, and his world opened up.

"I was in the Supreme Court twice in two years on matters related to the League's illicit drugs policy and confidential information. There were injunctions against News Limited, Fairfax and Channel Seven regarding publication of private medical records. So they were high profile matters concerning parts of the law that were evolving around new media. We had a High Court taxation test case, which we won. There was the collective bargaining agreement. Free agency. So it was a really exciting time."

In the end, he was approached by the Tigers through Gary March, president from 2006-13. In Gale's first full season at the club, 2010, the Tigers finished second last, in Hardwick's first year. "The board had drawn a line in the sand—we need to make some changes. The business wasn't performing well. But it was my club, and there was work to be done."

Australian football clubs are not large businesses. Richmond has perhaps 140 staff (including 45 players) and a turnover of perhaps $60 million. "But," said Gale, "the complexity is enormous. The commercial landscape is competitive and cluttered. Sponsors are tricky to keep happy. Membership and attendances are highly volatile, and hard to budget around. Then you have the all-pervasive nature of media scrutiny. Intellectually it's quite challenging."

Nevertheless, Gale quickly set the club a greater challenge, piecing together a five-year plan with the motto "3-0-75"—signifying three finals appearances with at least one top four, zero debt, and 75,000 members. The heading of the proposal was clear and concise: "Transform the club". Results fell only slightly short when by the end of 2014, they had twice played in finals, eliminated debt, and gathered 70,000 members.

"Those numbers were really just the embodiment of our ability to compete. There was a whole series of objectives cascading under each number, based on an empirical approach to what was building capability. We were saying 'We're going to be a legitimate competitor, because right now we're not'."

High membership means the club has consumer strength. No debt means a strong balance sheet and so the club can take commercial risks. Finals means the team is competing where it counts. But in 2016, that team went backwards, dramatically.

Gale was bitterly disappointed.

Unlike some CEOs in the football industry, he is not completely removed from football operations at the club. He goes to every post-game review to hear the coaches, listening but not pushing. "I'll just sit back and get the lay of the land. Why we won. Why we lost. The mood of the room." Occasionally he will come down to the rooms before a game to hear Hardwick rev up his players. For all that went haywire in 2016, he still feels the club has a strong platform from which to continue building.

"Improvement isn't a perfect trajectory. It isn't linear. You're going to have ups and downs. We were very disappointed last year. We expected to be a lot better, and we weren't. And the media gets a hold of it and it's that Richmond thing—*it's been years, your fans are hungry, they're desperate*—and we know they are. We all are.

But we're also really well placed. We understand why we win and why we lose. We can address that. We will."

He says the review that came at the end of the year—supported by consultancy firm Ernst & Young—wasn't based on a single poor year in isolation. Gale thinks of all the facets of performance examined in the review, and all the people saying the same things, and he quotes long-time football guru and advisor to many coaches, David Wheadon: "Patterns are patterns because they're patterns."

The club was getting into finals but losing them, repeatedly kicking off seasons with poor starts, and too often losing all momentum during games that could or should have been controlled. And after the dismal start last year (the Tigers had one win and six losses before beating Sydney after the siren in Round 8) it seemed proper to sit back and have a closer look.

"But remember, over 2013 to 2015 we won the fourth most games in the competition," he says. "But for a kick a two there were a pair of top four spots available. So, we're doing a lot right. People say, 'Only premierships matter', but wins and losses are a pretty important indicator of how you're going."

Richmond attracts this special brand of attention though and Gale knows it, acutely. They're a big club. But unlike Collingwood, for instance, there's a sense of desperation because of how long the club's fans have had to wait for a premiership; every Tiger fan has 1980 inked into the brain. And that's even more pronounced because there was a time when the club used to win *a lot* of premierships—five from 1967 to 1980. "That's part of the reason for those goals—we're an ambitious club and we want to shoot for the sky. It's been 37 years since the time we last saluted. So last year, after looking good, we seriously fell off the bike and people's faith and confidence was all shot', with an *entrenched* hopelessness. Now we're in a very competitive position—but we did have a bad year."

He doesn't feel as though Hardwick is under pressure. Reappointing the coach last year—extending his contract by two years to the end of 2018, making for at least a nine-season tenure—was heavily criticised externally. Was that commitment made to alleviate media scrutiny? Was it reward for the trio of finals appearances? Was it belief? Gale says it was the considered outcome of analysis over the six years Hardwick had spent at the helm when the extension was made.

"Let's be frank, he inherited a plate of shit. The environment, the list, and at the worst possible time—with the inception of the new clubs in Gold Coast and Greater Western Sydney, reducing the player pool in the draft. The first couple of years it was figuring out who can play and how to make it work, all while training on ovals out in Craigieburn, spending time driving instead of teaching. He didn't just walk into a situation he could put his imprint on. We felt he had all the attributes required to grow as a coach, and so we wanted to give him every strength and every confidence to go about his work. Was it about media? Not at all. It was about unity of purpose and belief. Was it giving the coach every confidence and all the strength necessary to go about the work? It was more about that."

On the way back to the office Gale considers the regimented life of the players, the way they are endlessly assessed and guided and trained. Coming from a less constrained period as a player, he wonders aloud whether the club organises and monitors their lives too stringently. "I sometimes wonder whether we shouldn't just let them stumble around and trip over once in a while."

He walks along a path now in Yarra Park, past the floor to ceiling windows separating the players' weights room and the green surrounds of the famous Punt Road Oval, and says he is excited this year by what he believes is a club focus on simple pressure.

Last year, in the pre-season, the team was striving to kick two more goals per game, and thinking about the best way to go from the fifth of 2015 (seventh after the finals loss) to third and possibly a Grand Final. "I think we took our eye off the fundamentals. And the fundamentals are 80 per cent of what we do."

The pleasing thing this year, he says, is the batch of younger players coming through and finding their own space to be assertive and take ownership of the side. It can't fall to Cotchin or Martin or Riewoldt or Rance, he says. "Our best players last year were the same best players of 2013, and that's a worry. So what excites me are the other guys. Vlastuin is tough and hard and quiet, and he's flying. David Astbury, who's been around a while, looks so composed. Conca just needs some love and some luck. Caddy will make us a better team. Prestia will make us a better team. Really impressed with Nankervis. McIntosh is a good player who we lost early. We lost Bachar (Houli), too. There were a lot of guys who were sub-par last year who should get better, too: Brandon Ellis, Shane Edwards. And I think a lot of people just switched off last year. I think when—mathematically—they realised they were done, then they *were* done. They looked ordinary."

Right now, standing here while a dozen staff members sit on benches or on the ground, enjoying lunch breaks that look like impromptu picnics, Gale is pleased. Who knows how long it will last, but he is convinced they are prepared. That they feel ready. Optimistic. Eager. "I'm not sure what the exact word is," he says. "I feel strong. Very strong about the entire club."

This is a far cry from how he felt only six months prior, during the "torturous" final throes of a season without joy. Still, even in those depths— in the rancour and despondence and annoyance of a lost campaign—Gale sensed something else. Call it a feeling of dormant possibility. He quotes the French existential philosopher Albert Camus, in fact, to describe his own wellspring of belief in something better, yet to come.

In the midst of winter, I found there was, within me, an invincible summer. And that makes me happy. For it says that no matter how hard the world pushes against me, within me, there's something stronger—something better, pushing right back.

5

AMAZONIAN DOLPHINS

The training schedule at Tigerland is set weeks in advance. The players can scan the digital document on the club's 'Playernet' web portal and know where they should be and what they will be doing for the next month or more. Each session is mapped, each portion of the day broken down, allotted and digitised. The plan for any given week is left running on flat screen televisions through the training complex, too, inescapable in hallways and gyms and waiting areas.

Yet despite the crushing weight of work and planning demanded of professional footballers, the actual training is something they enjoy—at least at this time of year. In pre-season there is a joy in its action, in the sheer physicality and dynamic abandon of the task—an exuberance in movement. There is lightness, too, in all those usually onerous meetings about "footy fundamentals", with casual humour and familiarity injected even into the names of the drills themselves. Today the group will take part in training exercises variously named "Tucky's Turning", "Shedda's slick hands", and "Pig Dog." The coaches know to bring levity into the room.[2]

On this Thursday morning, back line coach Ben "Truck" Rutten goes over what the players can expect from their pre-season opponent, Port Adelaide on the coming weekend in Mount Gambier.

The dissection that follows is serious, based on research done by Jack Harvey, an opposition analyst for the Tigers who has spent his entire summer looking at all other clubs.

Head of Coaching and Football Performance, Tim Livingstone, introduces Harvey to the playing group, and explains how he has sat in suburban grandstands watching other clubs train, and how he has gone over footage of all their pre-season games and games from last year, isolating useful pieces of vision for each line coach to use. "Jack works without any fuss in the background, but he does a really important job for us," says Livingstone, and the players applaud. "Now here's Truck to take all the credit."

Rutten, who spent 229 games playing for Adelaide as a desperate rival to the Power, takes his cue and points out how solid is Port's defensive unit, but says if you can divide the group—isolating a back flanker or key defender—that each player has flaws that can be exposed and exploited individually.

He goes to the midfield next, and points out Brad Ebert, Ollie Wines and Justin Westhoff, who are all hard runners but, more importantly, are strong in the air.

He explains that their forwards ordinarily like to roam far up the ground, "then fly back at 100 miles an hour", but there is far more method to their ball movement this year. If anything, they are more conservative.

"So, if they try to use the ball by foot, what do we want, Shedda?" Rutten asks of Shane Edwards. "What's important?"

"Slow 'em down," says Edwards. "Force 'em wide."

"Yep, and once we do that, what's important?"

"Outnumber at the contest."

"Yep," says Rutten. "They want to use the ball by foot and be a kicking team—we're going to cut them off. They've spent all summer working on

---

2   Shedda's Slick Hands is a handball game played in a space no bigger than a lounge room, and named for Shane Edwards, who has slick handball skills. Tucky's Turning is a kicking drill, where players need to turn inwards to deliver the ball inside 50, and is named for former player Shane Tuck (who had to be taught which way to turn). And Pig Dog is a game in which a player is shadowed by a physical tag, designed to close down space and force him to perform when fatigued by constant contact.

this, and they're still not perfect at it, so if we get really good gap control we'll force them to do things they don't want to do."

Rutten points out next that, defensively, Port Adelaide has also shown a hunger this season to hunt its opponents, laying high numbers of tackles in the forward half of the ground, and posting strong scores from the turnovers created. They will bring pressure, so Rutten wants the Tigers to think about what they need to do early in the game. He's thinking of an analogy— a concept the team has discussed this pre-season.

They call it "Warner versus Renshaw", and it is based on a comparison of the playing styles of the Australian batsmen Dave Warner and Matt Renshaw, the former a slashing striker of the cricket ball and the latter renowned for composure in protecting his wicket. Later, Harvey clarifies: "The theory is that if there is heat in the contest early, and you have less time and space, you want to protect your wicket, like Renshaw. And then when the space opens up, play like Dave Warner and take that risk versus reward scenario. So basically, play the game on its merits to start, then explore the options when the contest opens up."

All football clubs utilise such mnemonic devices and learning techniques, but the Tigers have a lot of fun with theirs.

Terms that require such explanation fly around the room in all meetings. The umbrella. The junction. The hit-to. The hit-up. D1 and A1. The help side and the skinny side. Tinder. Snapchat. Brady. Trump. Obama. Pluto. Side Pluto. *Double* Pluto. The sweeper. The striker.

Richmond's football analysis manager, Hayden Hill, says the terms are just as likely to change year on year. In 2016, for instance, Richmond spoke most often in terms of green, orange and red—modes of play respectively denoting a fast break, careful movement and a slow play. Hill says a change in the lexicon is a necessary year on year refresher, or else player engagement levels drop.

"Everything changes, but it also stays the same," he says. "New England Patriots coach Bill Belichick made a comment once, 'The biggest challenge is finding different ways to sell the same story'."

"Uranus" has been part of the story at Tigerland for some time. It's a form of defensive cover, where the team creates or maintains an arc of players to own the space or "width" that your opponent might want to use by switching the ball. You would recognise that all-too-familiar modern pattern—

a backwards kick, following by a kick across the ground, and another out to the wing, completing a semi-circular sweep around the defensive part of the oval. Uranus cover protects against that happening. Why is it called Uranus? The term simply apes a former Hawthorn name for the same thing. The Hawks called it "Saturn", based on the celestial body's rings.

"Uranus is also like covering your anus," says Hill. "Saving your arse."

The glossary of terms is daunting, but some are self-explanatory. There are assigned "Brady" players, for instance, a reference to Patriots quarterback Tom Brady. The Brady player is a defensive option sitting just behind stoppages in the back half of the ground, waiting to launch an attack, and this season could be any one of Bachar Houli or Brandon Ellis, Kamdyn McIntosh or Reece Conca. "Nude" players are those who stand alone, like an unmanned defender protecting against a fast break.

But when enough of these terms—simple or otherwise—tumble out in statements and responses during meetings, it is nearly impossible for an outsider to understand. The following is an actual question and answer from the current meeting:

"Just a second. Aren't we moving the striker to the umbrella?"

Yep, so the Trump is the striker in the forward 50 effectively. That make sense?

The best example of such memorisation techniques, however, probably comes from the man hosting this meeting, Rutten. In 2016, he began explaining his idea by screening grainy footage of a strange looking animal—a misshapen porpoise perhaps—swimming through murky water. He looked at the Sudanese-born rookie forward Mabior Chol.

"Marbs, what animal is this?"

"A dolphin?"

"Correct," said Rutten. "What kind of dolphin, Dan (Butler)?"

"Amazonian."

"Yep, an Amazon dolphin, good," he said, and the players started laughing quietly, waiting expectantly for the point to be made. "You know the history of it? No? Right. He lives up in the Amazon River. Known as the river dolphin or pink dolphin. What happens in the Amazon in the wet season? The water levels rise, right? Starts to cover up all the tree roots and the tree trunks, right? Now, Griffo, if you're a fish, and you see a dolphin coming along, where are you gonna go?"

"Into the trees?"

"Bloody oath," he said, and the whole room erupted. Other coaches shook their heads in disbelief. "You're gonna go hide in all the trees roots and stuff. Now typically, dolphins have fused vertebrae in their neck, so they just go straight ahead. So, if you live in the Amazon River and all the fish are hiding in the sides, what do you need to do, Marbs?"

"Look around?"

"Yep, you need to turn your head. So the Amazon dolphin now has evolved, and doesn't have fused vertebrae any more, so it *can* turn its head and see the fish, and be able to survive. So, what's the moral of the story Towna (Jacob Townsend)?"

"Turn your head?"

"Yep. And so we need to evolve. We need to evolve into 360-degree defenders. So when we've got defenders in behind us, we turn our head and see them. Think I'm talking shit, Brando (Brandon Ellis)?"

Then there was silence. This is where all that jovial patter stops, and these silly names are used to make an actual point about football—one that will hopefully stick in the minds of the players, and make them better. In that moment, Rutten screened a clip from an old game, in which an opponent snuck out behind Ellis at a stoppage, and was halfway down the wing before the Tiger noticed. "Brando this is you with fused vertebrae," he said. "We need to turn our head."

Still, all these sentiments could be framed in simpler ways. Take the terms scribbled on the whiteboard inside Hill's office—four words that anyone could decipher.

Fight. Cheat. Scratch. Bite.

They were written there by Justin Leppitsch, the forwards coach, who knows a thing or two about winning and losing after his tumultuous time at the helm of the Brisbane Lions. "It's just a preface to 'Winning is everything'," he says, joking that *Fight, Cheat, Scratch, Bite* could apply to both Essendon's "Whatever It Takes" marketing slogan and the "win at all costs" mantra which pervaded the 2006 West Coast Eagles, who were famous for training incredibly hard but have also been tarnished with allegations of illicit drug taking that still haunts some players in retirement.

"People were talking about West Coast on radio this morning, and how they didn't care about player wellbeing throughout that era, and that's fair enough," says Leppitsch. "But if you're not winning, everyone gets sacked.

That's the reality. You don't hear anyone saying, 'Gee, we had the nicest blokes out there—they didn't win much but they did *so much good* in the community, it was *such an era* to remember, *such a golden time* at the club'. Fight, cheat, scratch, bite? All it means is, we talk all this fluff, but what really matters is winning."

6

JUST THE WAY IT WAS

Trent Cotchin didn't immediately go on holiday after the 2016 home and away season, or even after the conclusion of the finals series. At that time of year he usually finds a warm, quiet place—a secluded island maybe. The year before it was Bali, soaking up the heat, keeping fit by running the dirty humid back streets of Umalas, Seminyak and Uluwatu. This time he stayed home in Melbourne with his wife Brooke and two young daughters Harper, 18 months, and Mackenzie, 6 months, and thought deeply about what had unfolded over the previous six months.

"I had a lot of time to dissect, review, plan and—in a sense—soul search," he says. Then he pauses. "It was probably the worst year of my life."

Good things happened—the birth of his second child, home renovations— "but it was all clouded by my most challenging year, footy-wise. So I just did a heap of work on myself, to try and come back to what I felt was me at my best."

He needed help, but he didn't share that need with many people, and by the end of September, at the funeral of club saviour Neville Crowe, he felt close to breaking down. Something happened that day. Hardwick hugged Cotchin tightly, and told him he loved him. It prompted a seismic shift within the player—tacit permission to strip away his "armour", to take down his "shield", to step out of the dark "cloudiness" that hovered over him.

He quietly sought advice from the people he knows best outside of football. His father. Father-in-law. Close friends. Mentors. "People who don't bullshit—who are honest but supportive. I went outside of my norm. I needed a deeper level of finding myself, and finding the way forward."

Cotchin had been through poor seasons before, when the team failed to fire, when the handful of great players at the club were vastly outnumbered by the not-so-greats. He was on the team in 2010, when bookmakers began paying out on bets that Richmond would finish on the bottom of the ladder— halfway through the season. Last season was tough for another reason.

"I probably felt as though there were times when there was this ..." he pauses again. "'Lack of support' isn't the right way to say it, but that's what it felt like. I thought—selfishly—that I was hung out to dry last year. With not a lot of people coming in and hitting back. This is off the field, I mean."

Cotchin is talking about criticism, and the way it came for him in wave after wave, particularly in the early rounds, when the losses were still a surprise feature of the Richmond season, and not part of its sad anti-climatic denouement.

In 1961, the American president John F Kennedy—answering a question about the failed Bay of Pigs invasion of Cuba—famously referred to an old saying that "victory has 100 fathers and defeat is an orphan." The orphan at Richmond, particularly after a last minute, Round 2 Friday night loss to Collingwood, was Cotchin.

The critics came quickly. On the Saturday they wanted him to cut out the "dinky" little kicks and go-nowhere handballs—or to stop gathering possessions at half-back. On Sunday there were online polls asking whether he should remain skipper. By Monday there was media pundit David King, a former assistant coach at Richmond, calling for him to consider stepping down at the end of the season. Jonathan Brown, who had noted just seven games earlier—following Richmond's aggressive 2015 victory over Hawthorn—that "Trent Cotchin stands alongside Luke Hodge as the two best captains in the AFL", abruptly decided after the Collingwood game that Cotchin had failed miserably to assemble and command his teammates as Collingwood surged.

Tim Livingstone was dismissive of the chatter, but also offered a succinct counter: "Trent gets criticised but he's had 38 possessions, was the highest contested player in the game, the highest clearance player on the ground, gained the most metres on the ground, and still that's not good enough for some people. So that's why I don't bother listening."

There were external defenders. Hodge was one. Both coaches—Hardwick and Nathan Buckley—gave Cotchin votes in the Coaches' award for his performance. Former Essendon champion Tim Watson made a point that few others would—that no one had questioned Shannon Hurn's leadership after an utter collapse by West Coast against an undermanned Hawthorn in their Grand Final rematch a week earlier. Similarly, when Port Adelaide failed to give a yelp against the Crows—destroyed in their home town derby after an irrelevant 2015 season—no one questioned Travis Boak's performance. Melbourne suffered yet another humiliation that round, too, unable to hold off the "top-up" Bombers, but no one door-stopped Nathan Jones on the way into his club.

No club does "under siege" better than Richmond. And so, on his regular spot on Fox's *AFL 360*, star forward Jack Riewoldt said he was "sick and tired" of people questioning Cotchin. Hardwick did the same, only he was "flabbergasted" by the attention paid to his captain. Their defences only fuelled the fire, and as the losses mounted and top four hopes slipped away, then finals became a mathematical impossibility, the attacks continued. They stayed with Cotchin the entire year.

In front of the cameras, AFL players will say that the voices don't matter. They'll say that the noise outside the club is exactly that—noise. They'll say that the only opinions that count are those of their teammates and coaches— 'inside these four walls'. But the venom seeps through. "You can put up the wall for a time, but eventually it cracks," says Cotchin. "I'm one of those people who are typically optimistic, but there were times last year when I began questioning not just others but myself."

It's hard to imagine what it must be like facing the barrage of vicious tweets that come his way after a loss. And not just toward Cotchin. It's common to see Tiger players walking back to the club after a night game, the darkness in Yarra Park illuminated by smartphone screens and the giveaway light blue of the Twitter app. "I wouldn't open it. I know guys do, but I like to stick to the controllables—and that stuff that's being said about you isn't controllable," Cotchin says. "And most people who spout the stuff that could be hurtful haven't ever played a game, or are fat and sitting in their lounge room and think they have all the answers and ideas. But they have no idea."

The advice he gathered to get through it was simple. We all have strengths, we all have weaknesses, so work on the weaknesses and encourage the strengths to come out. Ask for help. Enjoy life. "The greatest lesson for me is that when I sit back and look at myself from outside, I'm trying to be this perfect person, and the reality is that no one is perfect."

Of course, Cotchin was recognised for a kind of perfection not long after his soul-searching episode. With a smile, he says his off-season after that was "interesting", but that vastly undersells his eventful time away from football. Congratulations are in order. In December, Cotchin, along with Sam Mitchell, was awarded the 2012 Brownlow Medal, a by-product of the Essendon supplements saga, after Jobe Watson had handed back the Medal to the AFL[3].

"That was different," he says. "It was strange. Given my values and morals, it's certainly not the way you want to win an award. But I just did what's in my power—to control what I can control—so yeah, no guilt. It's nice to be rewarded but in my eyes 2012 was just another year. We didn't even make the final eight."

And yet it wasn't *just* another year. Having finally completed his first full pre-season, Cotchin played dynamic and damaging football. He won the second of his three club best and fairests (2011, 2012 and 2014) and was the AFL Coaches Association Player of the Year. He was at the peak of his powers, experiencing what is known in positive psychology as a "flow state", where you are fully immersed in your activity—hyper-focused and yet performing almost without thought, each winning move seamlessly shifting into the next. It was, he says, as pure as joy in football can be.

"You go out every game believing that you can't be beaten, whether that be tagged or playing against the best players in the competition. You just have this amazing feeling within that it doesn't matter what happens or what comes to you—you will just perform."

It's hard to say why he hit those heights. The team was playing freer football. He had a big-bodied midfield surrounding him. He didn't yet have the pressure and responsibility of captaincy. "I dunno," he says. "It's just the way it was."

---

3   Watson polled 30 votes in the 2012 season, with Cotchin and Mitchell, then at Hawthorn, polling 26 votes
     to finish equal second. With Essendon players suspended, for the 2016 season by the Court Of Arbitration
     for sport for infringements to the WADA code in 2012 Watson handed back the Brownlow to the AFL in
     November, stating: "The basic principle behind this prestigious award is to honour the fairest and best. If
     there is a question in people's minds as to whether the 2012 award is tainted, the fairest and best thing to do
     is to give it back and honour the history that has gone before me."

An unspoken factor that set the subsequent seasons apart from his zenith is the taggers that immediately began coming his way: Fremantle's Ryan Crowley and his fingernails; Collingwood's Brent Macaffer and those arm locks; North's Ben Jacobs, facing in his direction, instead of chasing the ball. As with the diminutive Carlton captain Marc Murphy, the close attention of a formidable shadow each week seemed to limit Cotchin's output.

Overcoming the challenge of the tag has meant continually working on his endurance, which is not a strength of Cotchin's but is *always* a strength of 'run with' players: "Building a tank has been crucial. You only need half a metre to win the footy and flick off to a teammate."

One Tigers assistant coach (talking to another) said the answer was to send opposing players to him in match simulation and drills. "Tag him hard at training," said the coach. "He's now a two out of 10 for being able to handle a tag—we need to get him to a seven out of 10. Because the carrot is there: 'Do this and you can be one of the best players in Australia'."

And so he has trained in both attack and defence to add new strings to his bow. He is also coming to grips with the responsibility of letting his teammates know when he needs help to break a clamp: "I tend to go insular and feel that if I'm asking someone for help, I'm affecting their performance, whereas they're all telling me, 'You let us know and we'll whack him'," Cotchin says. "It's part of your pride as well. You don't want to admit that you're struggling."

He isn't used to struggling. He is used to performing acts on the field that make people sit up and take notice. He has been doing so all his life, winning the hard football, emerging from the chaos seemingly calm, then punishing the opposition. "If I can do that consistently, I think it'll go a long way toward dragging others with me," he says. "I want to play inspirational football, all the time."

·································

For Cotchin, the football journey has been longer and rockier than many might suspect of a competition poster boy. Drafted at pick two in 2007 (Carlton's Matthew Kreuzer was pick one), he came to a club that he sums up in one word—"inconsistent". Yet it was much worse than even the club's wooden spoon would suggest. "The facilities were shot. Things were falling off walls. Roofs were caving in. It had a rank smell about it," he says. "There were good people. There were bad people. It's been an amazing transformation, put it that way."

He came to the Tigers from the Northern Knights, but arrived recovering from a broken foot. As soon as he started running his achilles "blew up" and he was "off legs"—unable to prove why he had been drafted so highly. He played well through 2008, making his debut in Round 8, and playing every game. Then, while trying to make up for lost ground the following pre-season he blew the achilles in his other leg.

In 2009 he was consistent on the field without starring, hampered by injury and then, at the end of the year, a hip operation (and a third thwarted pre-season). "The greatest thing for me though—as much as you don't want to be so injured coming into your career like that—is that I learnt lessons about managing my body," he says. "It's held me in good stead going forward."

At the time, he was living with former captain Kane 'Sugar' Johnson, (now retired) a veteran of two premierships with the Adelaide Crows (1997, 1998). It gave him a unique insight into the rigours of professional football. Senior coach Terry Wallace was sacked after Round 11 that year, after just two wins, to be replaced by Jade Rawlings, and Cotchin watched the process unfold. "I'm sure there was more going on than I even realised, but seeing the constant stress that Sugar was under—the fractures that started to appear between the coaching group and the playing group—it isn't what you want."

Wallace, he says, was a good coach, who gave Cotchin his first opportunity and who "saw the game well". But when Hardwick was appointed in his place at the end of 2009, Cotchin understood what a unified structure and plan could look like, and how it could be worked towards. "Plough tended to change the game plan every week, and that's probably where the term 'inconsistent' comes in. Some weeks we would beat the team that wins the flag—like Hawthorn in '08—and then other weeks we couldn't compete against the worst team in the competition."

Hardwick brought with him an altogether different manner, displaying the care and kindness required of a coach whose team is young and unschooled, but he also instituted a highly detailed, highly demanding approach to all aspects of the game.

Most sessions that first pre-season took place on spare ovals in the City of Monash, because the facilities at Punt Road were so bad, or because they couldn't train on an oval shared by a cricket club with a rock hard drop-in pitch.

"So, our pre-season consisted of driving out to the suburbs, doing these long sessions just learning (Hardwick's) game plan and structures. Then getting in the car in the heat and driving back," Cotchin says. "Some of it wasn't even physically tiring, but being out there on your feet for three or four hours—*this is what we're doing in a forward 50 stoppage, this is what we're doing defensively, this is the way we want to move the ball across the ground, our wingers want to run this pattern*—it was exhausting. You just felt 'Far out, this is so much'."

That has changed in 2017. Cotchin describes what the new style of play will look like—what the league and supporters will see. "Energy and effort," he says. "Dimma has spoken about a willingness to compete, but I think it's the consistency we'll see." Last season the focus was squarely on scoring just two more goals—12 extra points that would propel their defensively elite team into the top attacking echelon. There is no such specificity this year.

"It's all about playing to your strengths and believing in the gains that will come, and I think that's been a big thing for Dimma, a big shift for him. Given his accounting background, he's big on numbers, structure, and that's important—an AFL team needs a framework to perform at the level, a certain level of planning going into games—but you also need to release the shackles on guys, and I think that's what we're seeing that's noticeably different."

Brett Deledio said something similar last year. Long before he was traded from Richmond to Greater Western Sydney he mentioned (quietly) that it would be nice to play with a touch more freedom, to uncage the animals on field. *Don't tell the coach*, he added at the time. Cotchin laughs: "Maybe he *should* have told the coach."

Watching Deledio leave was tough on Cotchin. The star forward was a mentor, a champion, and the last remaining player who was already at the Tigers when Cotchin first arrived[4]. "Just a great person, and elite talent. My last few years as a junior, I idolised the way Lids played. You never think you're going to lose your star players, but if I'm to be honest I think it's been a good thing for both him and the footy club. I think he was at a point where he was frustrated, and sometimes that can have a negative effect on other guys."

---

4   Deledio was the number one pick in the 2004 National Draft.

Deledio, who is avid about meditation, also taught Cotchin lessons about work/life balance. Cotchin is 26 and was made captain in 2013[5], the season immediately following what is now his Brownlow year, when he was just 22. At the time, he didn't think it would be an issue but, looking back, if the captaincy had come to him a few years later he feels he might have been better prepared. Perhaps though he would have missed out on the opportunity to learn what he has—about himself, leadership, the football club, about other players and their differences and the way an upbringing can impact your behaviour on and off the field. "Everyone's path into the role is different, but on reflection, I wouldn't change mine," he says. "At times you ask yourself if it's the right thing for you, but you wouldn't be doing it if it wasn't."

He has worked on speaking in front of the group and challenging senior players, which was difficult when he was 22 and they were 32. The most recent step has been making sure that his time at Punt Road is 100 per cent committed to football but his time away from there is time to withdraw. "There's just so much more you have to do. There's that phone call on the way home from training about this player, or a conversation with someone before dinner about selection," he says. "So it's been about educating myself but also people within the football club that once I am at home, I need to switch off—otherwise it does consume you."

No one could have blamed him for being consumed. His leadership reign coincided with Richmond's re-entry into finals, in 2013, for the first time in 12 years—but also those ignominious elimination final failures (2013, 2014, 2015). He keeps a nutshell review of each one in his mind.

Against Carlton, 2013, they played a very good first half and an equally poor second half: "First final for a lot of us," he says, shrugging, "and a massive learning curve."

Against Port Adelaide, 2014, the team was fresh from nine consecutive wins to steal a place in the finals, including an amazing victory against the Swans in Sydney in the final home and away round: "That was almost our Grand Final. I'm not into making excuses but a lot of players were cooked. Poorly prepared, we got carried away with ourselves a week earlier, but we

---

5   Cotchin had been acting captain for one game, in Round 4, 2010, in the absence of Chris Newman. He was then the second youngest captain of a team at 20 years, 10 days and had just 29 games' experience.

were also emotionally exhausted. Key players didn't perform. Kane Cornes tagged me out of the game."

Against the Kangaroos in 2015, most of the team played half as well as they would have liked, and they lost by only 17 points: "We were within a couple of kicks with a few minutes to go, and we've played at five out of 10. Tighten up a few little things, and a couple of our players get going a little earlier in the match, and the story is different. We knew we were capable of beating anyone, and that's the hardest thing. But there's no point thinking about who you *could* beat. We *didn't* beat North Melbourne."

The improvement in the list now—the gains he thinks will lead them back into finals contention—will mostly come from within. Caddy and Prestia won't be enough.

He says Shaun Grigg has had an outstanding pre-season, on the back of his best full home and away season. "Daniel Rioli is going to be a superstar. He's clean, he's fast. Not only is he flashy offensively, he works so hard defensively. I think he bench presses more than me—not that that's anything to be proud of—but he came into the club pushing 60-70 kilos and now pushes 30-40 kilos more."

Corey Ellis is a player he believes will sneak up on the League as the season progresses. For the majority of pre-season he was in the rehab group with a groin complaint, but began training two weeks before to the first intraclub game. "He comes in, dominates, and everyone goes 'Gee, we forgot about this kid'. Silky. Doesn't need it more than 15 times to have a significant impact on the game. He's one of the most talented players we have. It's going to be about finding the position where he's going to work best. I think he'll have that career where he gets a few touches early, then a greater impact as the old farts like me fall out of the midfield."

Ben Griffiths is expected to have a big season, no longer competing with the departed Tyrone Vickery for the second tall forward spot. "He's loved by the boys. I think for him to take the next step, he needs to be that demanding player, crashing packs and starting to hurt people. It's probably not natural for him to be like that—he's a lover not a fighter."

Brandon Ellis and Shane Edwards have the most upside, he says. Both could comfortably push into the top tier at the club. "But I think they have been paralysed by the fact that we were so hellbent on playing a certain way, that it didn't allow them to play to their strengths. That's what I'm excited about this year. Shane sees the game so well, so why would you tell him where to run? Just let him do what he does. Give him some parameters—equalise, defend—but do what makes you a great player. Brando is the same. Playing off half-back the instruction must be, 'Yes, deny your man the footy, but also attack, take off'. He's an incredible runner."

Cotchin can't contain his glee at the thought of Vlastuin alongside him in the middle. "Tigger comes in from the backline. He's rock solid. He'll always be there, always show up. He's a tough bastard."

Of course, all those players were at the club in 2016, and none was significantly injured. So what happened? "It's hard to put it down to one thing. Upon reflection, we were kidding ourselves. Because we were focusing on the next thing and next thing and next thing, you forget about the things that matter most. We spoke about this the internal review—there was a lack of connection. In the playing group it felt OK, but you didn't see it on the field."

After a poor loss to Melbourne on Anzac Day Eve, Cotchin implored the group to demonstrate what they meant to each other. He spoke about a lack of care. Now he describes what that looks like in a game.

"Care is a willingness to enjoy the efforts of someone else, to pick them up off the deck when they've absolutely scrapped and fought tooth and nail to even just halve the footy—not necessarily win it. When we were kicking goals, I don't think there was enough energy and celebration. I suppose there were selfish actions, too, which shows a lack of care. That's where I've seen the difference this year, the synergy and cohesion within the whole group. It's easy to say now that 'It's as good as it's ever been', because we probably said the same thing last year, but I think it's genuine."

Beyond the game plan, beyond team unity—individually—Cotchin has come back to pre-season with a few goals in mind. Footwork in the contest has been a priority. Power shooting out of congestion has been a focus. Developing the strength to break a tag, too. "Explosiveness," he says. "I've done the most work I've ever done in the gym this year. It's just reinvigorated me."

The body is leading, he believes, and the mind will follow. "It's all about going back to what you are good at, and removing those demons that have some how come into your head. We all have them. It's just a matter of whether you let them take control."

7

HOW HARD YOU ARE

The whiteboard in the basement office of Richmond's Physical Performance Manager, Peter Burge, is filled with little blue scribbled reminders that make sense perhaps only to him.

Oxidative capacity.
Percentage of VO2.
Level of lactate threshold.

"You've heard of lactic acid, of course," says Burge. "Lactic acid is that painful burning sensation when you exercise. You can put yourself so far into lactate that you can't walk afterwards. So that's just a reminder to me—*to remind the players*—to get on the jog and flush it out."

Olympic swimmers, he says, will get back in the water after they compete, and then swim more laps than most recreational swimmers complete in the most gruelling amateur session, all to clear that lactate from the blood before their next event. Burge teaches the Tigers to do the same after they run. He wants active recovery after every extreme effort, so they can start the whole process again.

When they sense that burning sensation, light exercise creates continuous contractions in the muscles, helping circulate fresh blood to the overworked extremities. Controlled, constant activity flushes out the lactates, allowing the body to return to normal in everything from breathing to heart rate and body temperature, priming the athlete for yet another round of exertion.

"We want them to be able to recover faster so they can produce higher intensity efforts more often. That's the science. That's what I'm trying to build," he says. "When they're not fit, they blow up and hit the red zone and can't recover. But when they're fit, they keep recovering, recovering and recovering and building that capacity."

Unsurprisingly, Burge is one of those at the club who deals most closely with Hardwick. He has his own staff—overseeing strength and conditioning coach Luke Meehan and rehabilitation coach Rob Innes, while working alongside club doctor Greg Hickey, plus a host of physiotherapists and trainers.

He has a substantial purview. His office sits between the gym and pool and strapping area. The players are there now, a Wednesday morning in March, doing circuit training and weights, and the stereo is blasting *Cherry Pie* by Warrant. Dustin Martin and Trent Cotchin are playing table tennis. Burge keeps an eye and ear on it all. In all likelihood, he knows what every player is doing.

He manages medical information and assesses the status of the list—who can train and who can't, and what are they doing to condition themselves. He delegates while giving his staff ownership of their area, whether it be power or endurance, making sure he understands and monitors their decisions. "I need to know *exactly* what they're doing," he says, "and exactly what they're implementing in their programs. And if I don't, I'm not doing my job."

He needs to know how each player is coping, physically and mentally. How long are they training? How many kilometres are they covering? He plans ahead and manages the calendar and all its predictable pre-game and post-game demands, as well the anomalies thrown up by community camps and player appearances. "I basically have 44 balls in the air," he says. "I'm talking to 10 coaches as well. Plus six of my own conditioning team. I get questions thrown at me all the time."

He needs to have the answers, too. He needs to know that, right now, Steven Morris is progressing well in his recovery from a knee reconstruction last season, that Shaun Hampson's back is giving him more trouble than was expected in the new year, and that new draftee Jack Graham will need time to recover from a strained hamstring tendon.

For all other players, the pre-season focus of the fitness department has shifted towards exercises and drills that build strength and speed through the core. The club has new a boxing and grappling coach, Greg "Clanger" Kleynjans—a former mixed martial arts fighter and international referee. Burge says in many ways the aerobic running box is already ticked. "It's rock solid. So, what we're working on now is high intensity training, change of direction, high repeat end speed. And we've certainly spent a lot more time on footwork."

He does this with Meehan, who spent six years working at the Western Bulldogs under Rodney Eade. A footwork exercise might be as simple as a ladder drill, stepping in and stepping out at high speed while knowing where your body is in space. "In a game of football your eyes are up most of the time, looking at the ball or an opponent. You're not looking down, but what you're doing down there with your feet must happen with some precision and intent. We've got to break that down and teach them what it should be like—how quick it needs to feel, how balanced it needs to feel, how strong and stable it needs to feel. You break the drills down, do repeats, and you ask them to do it quicker, with good technique. Then you try to package it into their more functional football drills, and you hope it becomes an unconscious habit."

In the gym, the work focuses on the lower body being powerful, to make sure dynamic movements have a stable base; so they do basic lifts, then the same lifts with speed, then the same lifts perhaps on one leg, and then Burge or Meehan challenge them with load—whether extra weight or a resistance band.

"When players need to make decisions in a game—about where to go or how to move—they have to make an assessment based on what they see, but they've also got to move themselves and move their feet, and be stable and balanced and quick. So we give them the foundation to do that"—Burge clicks his fingers—"without thinking."

///////////

Burge is not well known outside of clubland. Most of those who perform his role are not. Only a select few are, for better and worse. Former AFL CEO Andrew Demetriou, at one point, lamented the growing influence of high performance managers and sports scientists, lumping them together as "phys-eders" and warning the industry about the threat they posed. This was before the Essendon supplements saga erupted, when Dean "The Weapon"

Robinson and Stephen Dank rose to prominence, so the warning seems prescient in hindsight. Yet many in the role are praised for what they do.

David Misson was perhaps the first to be widely recognised for his ability to create a seemingly indestructible group of players at St Kilda during the Ross Lyon years. David Buttifant played two games for Richmond in 1987 but later became one of Mick Malthouse's most trusted lieutenants at Collingwood, and pioneered high altitude training at the Magpies. The most recent and most public "fitness guru", of course, was Darren Burgess, who came to Port Adelaide from Liverpool Football Club and whose arrival coincided with a resurgence from the Power, success based largely on a frenetic running style of play. Under Burgess, the club developed a reputation as "last quarter specialists" who could outrun all others because of their superior endurance program.

Burge, however, believes that there is a good deal of mythmaking around what he and others like him do. "There are some fantastic high performance managers in the AFL. My old boss at Hawthorn—Andrew Russell—is probably the best. He's been involved in six premierships and seven Grand Finals at three clubs, and we don't hear much about him," he says. "There are times when an important player goes down, and you've got to explain why—how it happened—and the buck stops with me. But most of what we do here is within a team environment."

More so than many in his job, Burge began as an elite athlete—one who competed on an international stage. He grew up in Townsville, and was a promising cricketer as a teenager in Queensland, but when he was 16 chose track and field. He started out as a triple jumper and at 18 was ranked fifth in the world for his age. He decided to pursue long jump and began chasing the dream at 19, moving to Sydney and enjoying a productive run of form. He represented Australia at the Commonwealth Games in 1998 at Kuala Lumpur, where he won a gold medal, leaping 8.22 metres, and also at the Olympic Games in Sydney in 2000, finishing sixth (8.15m). He was ranked in the top 10 in the world at his event before he called it quits in 2003. "I had a few good years," he says. "It all clicked into place. Then I retired."

He coached track and field briefly, and was headhunted by Australian Rugby into a strength and conditioning role, working with teenage academy players. Then he joined Hawthorn in 2005 and worked under Russell for seven years, including the 2008 premiership. It was there he came to know

Hardwick, then an assistant to Clarkson. In 2012 he joined St Kilda to lead his own program under new coach Scott Watters, but only lasted 11 months. He didn't enjoy his time there, mainly due to personality clashes in the football department.

"It wasn't working," Burge says. "I wasn't enjoying working there. Just wasn't the right fit."

The opportunity to work at Richmond came up, giving him a chance to reunite with Hardwick, and he couldn't say no. He won the race for the vacant position at Richmond and arrived for the 2013 pre-season, and found an enthusiastic bunch. "They were desperate for success and desperate to be better. It was just about showing them what I want things to look like. Sometimes it can take them time to buy into. The guys were well-conditioned. Were they at the absolute elite level of the AFL? I would argue in some areas they weren't."

Burge had seen what was required in players at Hawthorn and the Saints. What he found at Richmond was a need for players with elite running capabilities. Dan Jackson was one, but he had retired in 2014. Matt White was another, but he joined Port Adelaide in 2013. For that reason and others Burge has been involved with the recruiting team at the Tigers, giving them at least a few thoughts—a potential wish list—and in the past three years the club has targeted certain types of player, namely those who have elite top end speed, repeat speed and endurance, best exemplified by the likes of Connor Menadue and Daniel Rioli, Jason Castagna and Dan Butler. "We were a good team in 2013 and strong in some areas, but other areas we weren't strong enough in—not to be a top two or top four team. We had elements, but not enough. My assessment was harsh but real. The balance of the group now is really, really good. It's changed."

The idea in part is that a rising tide lifts all boats—younger players with frightening speed and stamina force their older, established teammates to keep up. "Some of the older guys will tell you that's what's happened—they're being driven a lot harder," he says. "We still recruit footballers—not just athletes—but it's a running game, and a contested game. You've got to recover to reach the next contest, and be able to perform when you get there."

Burge has the evidence, both data-driven and anecdotal, to suggest improvements have been made.

Take Richmond's most recent pre-season running sessions. The group does repeat sets of one-kilometre runs, in four groups. Group four is the slowest, and they run first. Group one is the quickest, and they run last. "Group two is telling us they're finding it harder to catch group three, and group one is telling us they're finding it harder to catch group two," he says. "Three years ago, group one would run past groups two and three, easily. That's a good sign. That's telling me that the depth of our aerobic ability has grown. The data says it, the players are saying it—new players are setting a higher standard."

Kane Lambert is the most obvious example. He was a good runner when he arrived at Richmond but is now close to the best aerobic runner at the club, throwing down a challenge to Brandon Ellis. "And that's good for Brandon. Actually, it's great for Brandon," says Burge. "He's being challenged and doesn't want to be beaten. And that's what you want—in everything you do. You have to improve your standard and drag each other along."

In the gym, Alex Rance dominates, but weights are largely an individual pursuit. With many players, Burge wants to see increases in strength without gains in muscle mass. If Dustin Martin were to be put on the same program as Rance, he would quickly add four kilograms but lose mobility as a result. Burge and his team need to find the optimal physical condition for every player, according to a complicated matrix. "You see those guys who can bench press ridiculous amounts, but they don't like the contest, won't go hard. That's no use. The functional strength on the ground is the most important thing. Luke Hodge wasn't a big bench presser but he is incredibly powerful in the contest. So, if they rate really well on that contested strength, we tend to worry less about how much they can lift. It's really about what can help them on the field. Do they need to be able to run and have power around the ball? Do they need high end repeat speed? We've constantly got to ask ourselves, why are we doing what we do?"

At some point, evidently, some players were asking the same thing. Burge experienced an overall enthusiasm when he began at Richmond, but there were concerns, too. Call it a lack of buy-in. "Over time I realised a few things weren't adding up and I was seeing things I didn't like. Just people who were a little sloppy with punctuality, and training intensity. I didn't like that at all. I told some people that. There were some things the higher-ups either weren't aware of or didn't want to hear, but I was prepared to say it. It takes time though. It was challenging."

Burge began to grasp how difficult change could be, and how perhaps it needed to be drip fed. The previous fitness boss, Matthew Hornsby (now with St Kilda), had been with the club 12 years—and junking an entire system overnight is anathema to the continuity required within a functioning AFL club.

"I wanted to do things my way, but you need to be careful about the way you make changes. If you do things wrong you can lose people completely, and it's very hard to get them back. I do consciously remember putting the handbrake on at one point and thinking, 'This has got to be a slow process'. One step at a time."

Every club is different. He took various methods with him from Hawthorn to St Kilda, but he also discarded various Hawk philosophies in favour of Saints systems. He has brought a little of both to Tigerland. There has also been personal development required—from both the players and Burge.

///////////

He has a (relatively) healthy list right now. That's the goal of pre-season—good health combined with maximum performance. The point is to improve the players' baseline conditioning so they can handle the skills training and football work and technical game style. The gruelling hot runs need to be balanced with lighter weeks. Some players can handle being pushed to the nth degree without getting soft tissue injuries; with others you know they're going to be on the edge. Burge has a list on his computer of players who are at a high risk of soft tissue injury. This is not sensitive information but based on public history.

Reece Conca, for instance, is on the list. Three serious hamstring tears will do that. Burge watches such players more closely, gathering multiple data sets from his sports scientists like Brendan Fahrner. He looks at what the numbers tell him, and then he looks for flags. If the same flags pop up for Brandon Ellis, who has has a relatively untroubled run with injury, he worries less. "Everyone's got their own threshold. But you still have to push them all, because you're trying to build resilience in their bodies. You just have to avoid pushing them over the edge," he says. "If they can stay on the edge, pulling back here and there, their bodies will get more resilient, and they eventually come good. That's why we call it conditioning.

We're preparing them to handle more stress. And perform."

When Burge arrived he was advised, for instance, to be careful with Trent Cotchin, who had a history of Achilles strains. But Burge has found the captain to be resilient. Dylan Grimes is another who had a significant injury history, namely to hamstrings. But he has been able to play more games in the past three years than anyone would have expected after his early problems. "But I still have a mark over him in my notes, and I know I must be careful with him, because he might have a one- or two-week issue. Grimes is a tall, high speed athlete. How are we going to predict a tear? Are we ready for it? What are we going to do to make sure it doesn't happen, and he can play every game?"

Burge is not ignorant of the perception that Richmond has lacked a bigger-bodied midfielder to support Martin and Cotchin in recent seasons, but he is not trying to create one. Adding weight to a player usually does nothing but, well, add weight. Younger players like Rioli and Menadue need a "critical mass" of sheer bulk to help them lay tackles, break tackles and shift opponents at stoppages. But add five kilograms to the frame of a player such as Cotchin, and he won't be able to move. Not many can carry 94 kilograms, as Sydney captain Josh Kennedy does, and still cover the ground as a midfielder. Pleasingly, Burge has been able to add some strength and weight to Cotchin this season without compromising his running, but he is aware he needs to maintain a balance of size and speed. Besides, Caddy is now here to help with grunt work, and Prestia with clearances, and Vlastuin to split packs. The latter has needed to work hard on his endurance before it could happen, but he is running the best times of his career—an accumulation of work shining through. "Nick's really learning this year about how hard he can push himself. I think he's taken a step. It's one of the areas we try to teach our players. How hard can you push yourself? How far can you push yourself? It's between the ears."

What about a player like young forward Ben Lennon, who has publicly acknowledged his own need to work on speed and power, to gain that crucial metre or so of separation from elite defenders?

"So many things go into being able to get separation," says Burge. "Guys who are slow can get great separation if they're strong and push off well and their timing is good. Ben's not Usain Bolt, but he's not slow. He's actually a dynamic player, but can he be dynamic quarter after quarter, or does he fatigue? And for a lot of young players—particularly if they've had setbacks as he has with injury, glandular fever—fatigue is a significant factor."

Burge's young standouts this season are Menadue and Rioli and Butler, all of whom were rake thin last season but have reaped significant benefits from their gym program. *"And* they're running PB times over three kilometres, and showing great GPS numbers. They've still got more development—they're not there yet—but we've pushed them more in the strength department than we used to do with young players, and they're looking great."

At the other end of the spectrum you have star forward Jack Riewoldt, who has suffered an interruption to his pre-season campaign thanks to finger and ankle surgery. It irks Burge that reporters leapt to assumptions about his fitness based on those procedures. "The perception is, 'Finger surgery, ankle reco, out for a while', when really he's in the gym on a new program going from strength to strength, and being as professional as ever and moving so well. He's doing extra running, self-driven, after training. We don't go telling everyone, but he's in great nick. He's got all these years of training behind him, so it doesn't take long for him to tap back into where he was. I looked at him two weeks ago and thought he was in the best condition of his life."

Shane Edwards, elevated to the leadership group last year, is another who stands out for his application. When Burge first got to the club, everyone told him about the lightning speed of the high half-forward, but the numbers Burge saw revealed plenty of upside. "He's got good agility, he's light, got good side-to-side, but aerobically there was still some improvement. I didn't think he was that quick, and we identified that the way he was moving was a factor. It was his technique, or efficiency. He was trying to power through his running, heavy on the ground, and so we tried to lighten him up. You practise different drills, give him different cues, show him how it should look and then he learns how it feels. We've worked on it for four or five years now, and he has just worked his arse off and believed in the program and he's done everything asked of him.

"I love the way he trains. I never need to worry about how hard he works. He's now what I would consider an elite AFL runner. He still needs to improve, but he knows exactly what he's got to do. And he'll do it when no one's watching. Doing it here is easy, but how you live your life—how you eat, how you sleep—that stuff is harder. You know he is a player who is doing all that stuff right."

He wants to see all the players work this way—no matter how talented they are. When they don't, he gets frustrated because it hurts the team. "It doesn't hurt me—not the 'fitness guru' guy. I'm sick of that shit. It's just bullshit. It really is. But it hurts Richmond."

Burge's little reminders to himself don't end with the whiteboard. He has little notes everywhere, on Post-its stuck to his desk and memorable quotes in the notes section of his mobile phone. He reads them in quiet moments.

Leadership is not a licence to do less, it's a responsibility to do more.

High performance isn't state of the art facilities—it's a state of mind.

"You can drift on tangents easily when you have so many competing needs—sometimes it pays to come back to basics and centre yourself," he says. "When your mind is constantly racing with things, you need to tell yourself why you're doing what you're doing."

Burge knows he is only here for a short time, and so are the players. They are all temporary custodians of the club. The only people who are there forever are the supporters, and he works for them now.

"You get attached to the Tiger Army. Even before I got here I thought 'I'd love to go to that club and have some sort of impact'. When you go into a final and you hear those fans, they're so desperate for something. You just want them to have it. So it comes back to how hard you are. How desperate are you to win it, to be the best you can be?"

8

TEASING DISTANCE

I t's humid in the change rooms at Moe. Richmond is set to play its final pre-season game of the year, against Collingwood, at Ted Summerton Reserve. A pretty ground in the heart of the Latrobe Valley, it is surrounded by tiered concrete seating and suburban streets.

Inside the home rooms of the Moe Lions, the Tiger squad finds space wherever possible. The coaches congregate in a small room at the back of the building. There's a speed ball on the wall and two stationary bikes in a corner. On a low ceiling, long fluorescent lights are caged in steel, shielded from the errant footballs stabbed around the room during warm-ups. Richmond football staff move through the humidity, shuffling about on the blue carpet.

Pasted to the wall are the team's 2017 "rotations guidelines", which will be important in the heat today. Determined by the fitness team, these numbers govern how often each player needs to come from the field for an interchange break. Each player has his own "max rotations"—a high number might be eight, such as for an onballer like Trent Cotchin, while a low number might be three, for key position players like David Astbury. The chart also lists "max time on ground"—a high number, for a key tall like Jack Riewoldt, might be 20 minutes of continuous play, whereas a running player like Dustin Martin shouldn't be allowed on the field any longer than 10 to 12 minutes without a rest.

On a hot sunny day, on a windy exposed oval, rotations could affect what changes they are able to make, and who is likely to play. Project ruckman

Ivan Soldo and rookie small forward Tyson Stengle, for instance, are in the squad to play their first game, but getting them involved in the action is not a priority for the coaches. "With Soldo and Stengle, if we get them on, we get them on," Hardwick says to the other coaches. "If we don't, we don't. Around three-quarter time, maybe we rest a key or a small and give them a run."

⁄⁄⁄⁄⁄⁄⁄⁄⁄

There are 16 people in this room before the players even arrive for their final pre-match address. Midfield coach Blake Caracella is lying on the floor, sliding back and forth on a foam roller. Tim Livingstone sits on a stool at the front of the room, fixing magnetised names to handheld whiteboards—the ones he will carry onto the ground at quarter-time and three-quarter time.

In another room, Josh Caddy is having his back worked on. Clearance specialist Anthony Miles is being rubbed down by two trainers at once. Brandon Ellis is waiting for his turn on the table, stretching his calves. Goal sneak Sam Lloyd is doing the same, and warming up his lower back. Livewire Dan Butler is getting strapped—ankles. Bachar Houli too—left wrist. Dylan Grimes and Reece Conca are laughing while Taylor Hunt is pacing. Dion Prestia eats a muffin.

Alex Rance balances on one bare foot while holding a large blue elastic band in front of his chest. The band is tied to a weights rack, and is stretched and pulled as Rance turns and pivots and balances against the resistant force. He stops only for a line meeting in which the defenders emphasize three things: communication, physicality, and embracing the contest. These are, says defensive coach Ben Rutten, "Richmond men behaviours".

Rance speaks next, and quickly: "We're at the level now where it's not knowledge-based"—he clicks his fingers—"it's just do it"—click—"do it"—click—"do it"—click—"and being consistent with these things. We have to just churn out these contests—seven out of 10, seven out of 10, seven out of 10—which done enough times makes us look like a Rolls-Royce."

In the pre-match address, Hardwick has drawn a line graph on the board. The vertical axis is labelled "RESPECT" and the horizontal axis "TIME". Next to it he's written "Where are we?" and "Where do we want to be?"

Hardwick hasn't marked any point on the graph—the point is that they're low on respect, maybe nowhere on that chart, and they all know it, and as time goes by they want to be higher. Opposition analyst Jack Harvey, sitting at the back of the room, whispers: "Respect. Easy to lose, takes time to get back."

The senior coach though, has a few more words than that. Defensively, he says, set the tone early. Offensively, just play. "Ultimately", he adds, "it'll be our grunt versus their grunt."

He tells a story, too. He went for a jog with Livingstone a day earlier— they do that sometimes through Yarra Park, outside the Punt Road training facility, just to break up a day of training. On this run, Livingstone said that his teenage son had noticed something different in the Tigers this year—a general excitement. What might that be based on, Hardwick asks? What would the kid have seen?

The players murmur the answer together. "Pressure", they say. Immediate pressure. Tight, defensive pressure. Close, urgent, swarming pressure.

"Right," says Hardwick. "Energy and enthusiasm and celebration. I watched our VFL game last night, and the Tigers flogged the reigning premiers, the Western Bulldogs, with Ben Lennon kicking 7 goals, and I'm sitting there—*as a fan*—going 'Holy hell, it's started'. It's all started rolling, boys. All the stuff we've been working on, all the stuff we've trained, it's all boiling to the surface."

He talks about having fun together, enjoying one another's company, continuing the story of 2017 so far. He's excited about the challenge: "Good club Collingwood, aren't they? Let's show them a better club."

They sit on the floor stretching next, and it's getting hotter. Nick Vlastuin contorts his calves. Young ruckman Toby Nankervis, from the Swans, bounces a ball, while Livingstone switches on a gigantic steel fan, six feet tall and industrial. "Look at this," he jokes. "My biggest fan."

A few players, before they go onto the ground, need a quiet space to prepare. Brandon Ellis sits on the floor with his back against a wall, knees up, legs apart, white ear buds in. Dustin Martin sits cross-legged, hands on knees, eyes closed. He looks like a Zen master. Astbury stands—his feet shoulder-width apart, hands on hips, eyes closed—breathing deeply. Lloyd sits on a bench, palms flat on his thighs, still as a statue.

Soon the team is split into two rooms and moving quickly, with fitness boss Peter Burge barking orders. "Left shoulder!" he says as they tackle one another. "Be ready! Intent! *Yes!* You can hear the contact!"

Shaun Grigg is an encouraging voice: "Fierce pressure first quarter! Sausage (Daniel Rioli), Georgie (Jason Castagna), Marbs (Mabior Chol), can't wait to see it!"

The captain, Cotchin, calls them into a huddle. "Today is another opportunity to show gratitude for what we do, to the people who support us. The good thing about us? Nothing changes—whether it's Moe in JLT or Round 1 at the MCG. Embrace those little butterflies."

Riewoldt: "Bring your best piece of the puzzle today."

Rance: "Don't be tense, don't think, just act. We're an action side."

A crowd of 5701 has gathered here. Fox Footy cameras are mounted on cherry-pickers. So, what do the players and coaches say, on the bench, as Collingwood shoots out to a strong first quarter lead?

Grimes comes flying to the interchange first, and he's noticed fumbles: "Too many double grabs on groundballs," he says, gasping for air. "Dropped handballs."

Hardwick has encouraged them this week to pay attention to their anxiety, and when they sense they are surrounded by black and white jumpers to force the ball forward even blindly—by "bludgeon handball" or "blast kick"— knowing they have trained to rely on numbers around the contest. Football is sometimes a fight for fragments of terrain—a land war in which players must be aggressive settlers, forcing the ball in one direction. But they're not playing to that philosophy right now. VFL coach Craig McRae notices they're looking for the wrong chip kick options, and not driving long enough: "Kicks are dropping short," he says. "Our space is out the *back!*"

A Tiger corrals a Collingwood player, and Shane Edwards watches as the Richmond pressure forces the ball to fly out of bounds on the full, from the Magpie's boot. It leads to a Richmond shot on goal: "Nice!" he yells. "That's what pressure does for us!"

Grimes heads back onto the ground, screaming at every player he passes en route to defence: "Spoil, spoil, spoil! Physicality first!"

Cotchin and Edwards run out, too, and Livingstone has a message for them to spread—a shortcoming the entire team needs to know about: "Three tackles so far—*three tackles for the game!* Our D1 isn't there."

Castagna comes off, splashes water on his face, which mixes with the blood from his nose and washes over his chest. Prestia comes off, too, sucking in air. The Tigers are playing tentative football and Caddy notices them refusing to come forward at running opponents, preferring to guard space: "We're passive," he groans. "We're folding back."

When Collingwood is moving the ball forward, Martin says the team is panicking—playing without patience: "We're taking the contest, but not waiting that little bit for our numbers to catch up and get there. We need to pop it up a bit."

By quarter time the team is down 14 to 52. The Magpies are taking marks as they see fit. Their centre-half back, Ben Reid, will have 18 by the end of the game. Jeremy Howe will have 11. Howe was discussed in the team meeting a day earlier as one of the team's key players, an "intercept specialist". "If you're in a position to take this guy out of the contest," Hardwick said, "getting between him and the jump, do it."

Australian football has a long and inglorious history of coaches assigning players to maim opponents. The Tigers don't make those requests in the modern era, but they demand physical pressure be applied to specific individuals. They want them annoyed, disrupted, and worn out.

Today, the most important player to exhaust is young gun Adam Treloar, and not because he chose to be traded to Collingwood instead of Richmond one year earlier, nor because of public remarks he made about the Magpies list being better than that of the Tigers, but because he is a damaging, indefatigable midfielder. In the opposition analysis, Treloar was labelled an "explosive corridor runner".

"He gets one-twos," said Hardwick, "and runs the corridor up and down, up and down, up and down. We've got to make sure we cover him off with physicality. Bloody good player, so let's get on top of him." (Treloar will kick the first goal of the game and have 29 touches by its end.)

The Tigers attack the second quarter with more purpose, and Livingstone sees a comeback: "Five goals to one second quarter and we can get back into this."

The Tigers kick three consecutive behinds—instead of goals, notes McRae—but they're attacking: "That was better. Feels like we're playing our way again," McRae says.

In the forward line, the athletic Chol flies, spills, gathers, kicks, corners, spoils, tackles and is awarded a free kick, and Martin is excited: "Good boy Marbs! Oh, yeah!" The tall forward kicks the ball out of bounds on the full, but no matter, Livingstone can see the signs are there: "Boys, a dozen tackles for this quarter," he says. "Five in total last quarter."

He makes sure next that Stengle is ready to go on, because Lloyd has a minor knee complaint. The rookie stretches, rips his boot stops against the grass, sips some water. Hardwick talked about Stengle during the week, telling the team about his reaction when told he was getting his first game: "'Bout time," he said. "What arrogance," Hardwick laughed, "but we like it."

Lloyd comes off, and Stengle runs on to an encouraging cheer from the bench, McRae leading the way: "*Sprint* on Tyson. Go Tyse—give us something!"

The team trails at half time, 41 to 68, but won that quarter 27 to 16. Inside, Hardwick has written the word FIGHT on the whiteboard. He's happy though—he knows they worked harder and kept the ball in their half. Still, he isn't impressed with what's happening when they go forward—the midfield and defence aren't setting up well enough behind the forwards, to keep it locked in their half, to maintain that all-important short pitch.

"We've *got* to protect against them rolling down the outside with an easy exit, or funnelling through the middle," he pleads. He points out, too, that they're losing the loose ball gets 13 to 27. "That's a work rate issue," he says. "They're working harder than us. I said to you at quarter-time, 'Don't accept what is happening'. You've done that. But keep it up."

Inside the coach's box in the third quarter, the tenor of conversation is opposite to that on the bench. With players absent, the language about their performance is uncensored and unguarded, as it must be if problems are to be acknowledged and overcome. There's a lot of standard football fan anger here as well.

When Riewoldt is reported for a late—but low, and incredibly light—shirtfront, midfield assistant coach Andrew McQualter can't contain himself: "JESUS that's a ridiculous report! What a joke."

Moments later Hardwick is furious with the lack of running and spread, especially from club leaders: "Look at that—I've got Dustin and Trent holding hands in the middle. What are they doing?"

Leppitsch in particular can't get over the loose umpiring: "What was that for?! And a 50?! But Butler gets manhandled in the forward pocket and it's just 'play on'. They're picking and choosing today, boys."

Hardwick picks up the phone and barks down the line to Livingstone on the bench: "Tell Trent he needs to stalk the defence. He's just sitting there floating at the minute—tell him he plays his best footy when he's on the front foot."

Ellis coughs up a ball in a tackle and Hardwick slams a fist on the desk: "Oh Brandon… Stop going to ground!"

Leppitsch is fatalistic: "I'm glad we're doing this now and not in Round 1."

Rutten mirrors him: "We've got our head up our arses, boys."

The team kicks a clean goal from a fast play and Leppitsch picks up the phone with a message: "Just remind the boys—Caddy, Butts, all of them—*that's* the blueprint. Get it forward, kick it to space."

Football analysis manager Hayden Hill, never far from his laptop, has something to offer the room: "Collingwood has had six scoring shots from nine entries this quarter, which is indicative of the game. They're scoring too easily—from 66 per cent of entries all day."

Leppitsch: "We've been a bit off. Our energy, our decision-making, our intent."

Hardwick turns to Caracella and McQualter: "Can you get your mids to stay in the contest? They're fanning back, fanning back, fanning back, and it's killing us."

At three-quarter time, it's 73 to 106, but the performance looks worse than the scoreline suggests. General Manager of football Neil Balme, sitting in opposition to his former team for the first time, says the team simply isn't blocking the Collingwood transition well enough: "Our backs aren't driving back quickly enough, and our mids aren't filling the gaps. We need our mids to play like they want it, and tough backs to play like tough backs."

After a pause, McQualter speaks: "It doesn't matter about this game—we're gonna lose. But is there anything we want to see? Houli onto the wing hasn't worked. Maybe Rioli into the midfield?"

Moments later, after Soldo comes on and slots a goal from the boundary line, Rioli takes a screaming high mark in front of goal. Leppitsch turns to McQualter: "You still reckon he needs to go into the midfield?"

Hardwick is thrilled: "That's the value of these little guys who can mark, like (Hawthorn forward Paul) Puopolo, (and Collingwood forward Jamie) Elliott. They're dual threats. We've got to convince more of these guys to go for their marks."

Rance, in his second game back from a tight hamstring, has been disappointing. What generally makes the champion full-back so good is perhaps not what a casual fan might expect. It isn't elite hands, or a masterful kick, or infallible decision-making. Rance is so good because he is so patient. He prepares so well, and plays with such deep concentration, that he can endure the ball floating into his arc intended for his opponent, and can exist in that state without panic or the need to react early—because of his faith in his own approach to the ball. His timing is a matter of trust, in himself. But Hardwick isn't seeing it today: "Has Alex had any MOPs (marks off opposition)? He just looks off by half a step today."

He looks down at the bench next and doesn't like seeing so much talent cooling its heels, so he picks up the phone: "Hey boys, you see Prestia and Conca and Martin—they're pretty good players. Just get someone off, and get them on."

Leppitsch points out an emerging story in the game—the form of Chol, the rookie: "Marbs has had 12 touches, one goal one, 8 contested, and he's still a work in progress, but he's showing plenty. He's got Buddy Franklin qualities, this kid."

Rutten sees the ball in Collingwood's hands, and watches it flow down the field too easily by foot: "When they're handballing we can apply pressure and shut down the chain. But we're not pressuring the kicker, and nowhere near close enough to the marking player."

In the last few moments of the game, which ends 107 to 113, Grimes gets clotheslined while taking a courageous mark, and Hardwick is quietly incensed that the umpires ignore the incident: "But that one's not a report, is it?"

The players sit shirtless on the blue carpet floor in the rooms, and Hardwick talks about the contest. In attack, they were pretty good. They won the Inside-50 battle. But the final kick forward is the one they need to improve. He's not pleased they conceded the contested ball in the first half, but is happy they won the statistic in the end. Overall, it was pleasing.

"We were *shithouse* early. But we came back, and just fell short. And what did we get?" he asks. "We got a *great* look at Collingwood. Are we going to give them 123 uncontested marks when we see them again in two games time? No way. Good luck getting those against us again. That stuff is easy to fix. Just tweak that teasing distance."

Before they can disperse—before each one can grab one of the hot roast beef rolls wrapped in tin foil on the table, before they can begin gulping Gatorade and Hydralite, before they can check their phones, before Bachar Houli can jump into the bathrooms next door and plunge himself waist deep into a blue wheelie bin filled with ice water—Hardwick has a few notes on the board, with an empty box next to each one.

"Pre-season, tick or cross?" He places a tick in the box. "It's been great. Exciting."

"Game minutes?" he asks, and no one answers. "Well, how many of you cramped out there? *A lot of you.* That's a great result. Tough conditions. Soft ground. Humid. Up and back game. Expended a lot of energy, worked hard." Another tick.

"Form?" he asks, and they nod. "Yeah, that's right, apart from one quarter it's all ticks here. We've had a *great* pre-season boys, so be very happy with where we're at, but understand, it all starts now. Be proud of your form so far. Let's take it into the season."

9

MOB MENTALITY

I t was meant to be a joke.

So, Josh, you mightn't remember the game you played for Geelong against Richmond late last year—but the Tigers were comfortably in front, about to land a late season upset against a top four side, then you nailed the first major of the last quarter, and the Cats stormed home to win by a few points, breaking Richmond hearts. Do you regret kicking that goal?

"I don't regret it," answers Josh Caddy, deadpan. "At the time, I had no idea I would end up at the Tiges. But I knew that Richmond hadn't beaten the Cats in 10 years."

This is correct. Geelong is the club's hoodoo team. The Tigers last defeated the Cats in 2006. At 12 consecutive losses, the losing streak is only slightly less embarrassing than Carlton's run of ignominious losses to Hawthorn (14 in a row, since 2005), Melbourne's routine capitulation to St Kilda (also 14 straight, since 2007) and finally Melbourne's semi-annual inability to compete with North Melbourne (15 losses, since 2007).

"So maybe it was scripted that Richmond lost," says Caddy, now in on the joke and laughing. "And when we play the Cats this year, maybe we'll finally get over the line."

It's an average Friday morning at Tigerland. Mabior Chol is walking the downstairs hallways, barefoot and singing. Ben Griffiths is on the massage table, getting some treatment before training. Players are signing in and weighing in for the morning, and getting changed.

The acquisition of the bullish midfielder Josh Caddy was perceived as one of the big wins of the trade period, unless you're a Geelong fan. After the trade, *The Geelong Advertiser* reported that the club was inundated with a torrent of abuse over the decision to part with the maturing, big-bodied player so cheaply. Caddy, after 24 games with the Gold Coast and 71 games for Geelong, is fast approaching that 100-game mark of his career, when players are said to begin feeling at home on the field and ready to play their best football.

It wasn't a planned move—to leave a club that played in a Preliminary Final for one that finished 13th. "I guess it's just the way footy is now," he says. "Trade week rolled around, and Brett Deledio had an interest in coming to Geelong, and somewhere along the line my name got thrown up as a potential trade because Geelong had no draft picks that would suit Richmond, after other trades."

Caddy heard through his manager that he had come up in discussions between the clubs, although he didn't know which club had first raised his name. He was happy at the Cattery, and had two years to run on his contract there. Nevertheless, now obviously and publicly in play as trade bait, he visited Richmond and met with its leaders, including Neil Balme, whom he knew from Balme's time as football manager at Geelong. He looked at Richmond's plan for him, including more time in the midfield, and recognised that Geelong already had a glut of players playing a similar role.

"You've got to fight for your spot, which I would have done had I stayed, but when other opportunities come up you look at them and go, well, maybe I will have more opportunity at Richmond, fit in better with their list and can give them more of what they need, as opposed to Geelong, with a surplus of that kind of player."

Geelong's champion midfielders Joel Selwood and Patrick Dangerfield are both physical players who push forward. Cameron Guthrie was improving, and Sam Menegola staking a claim, along with the talented Mitch Duncan, and then there's Scott Selwood, returning from injury as a tagger. "There wasn't enough space for everyone, and I was playing a lot as a forward. Maybe I was a victim of circumstance, because I have that ability to play forward. I understand that every player has to be able to play a different position, but at Richmond there's definitely more of an opportunity to play through the midfield and fit in better."

It hasn't been hard fitting in, either. Caddy was already close with midfield coach Blake Caracella at Geelong. He played with Dylan Grimes at the Northern Knights, and also Kane Lambert, and even had a few games with Nick Vlastuin, who was an under-16 there when Caddy was 18. There are others from the same part of Melbourne. Dion Prestia, one of Caddy's best mates as a junior footballer, had already committed to the Tigers and helped nudge Caddy to join him at Punt Road. The pair roomed together in their first years at the Suns, and once they had both signed at Punt Road they found a place to live in Richmond.

"I also know that Richmond had a really disappointing year last year, but I feel as if their year didn't really reflect where they were at. Even in that game against us when I was at Geelong, we came back to win but Richmond didn't have anything to play for, and there were a lot of young guys on the field, and I remember thinking they were a pretty good side. As a player you want success, and I just wouldn't have come if I thought Richmond was going to be winning wooden spoons. Sitting here now at the start of 2017, contrary to what other people might think, I think we're a chance to have some success."

///////////

Dion Prestia felt the same way. Only six months ago, the young midfielder was up on the Gold Coast, where there was little fandom and even less media—no matter whether the Suns were good or awful or indifferent. "They're different worlds," he says, sitting in an office next to the Richmond heat room. "Coming here I thought I knew what to expect, but I didn't. Obviously."

He enjoys being home in Victoria, and back rooming with Caddy, both drafted in the top ten by Gold Coast in the 2010 draft.

It's nice to be near his dad, Osi (short for Osvaldo), and his mum, Delene, and his older sisters Tahlia and Chanel. He grew up with them in Craigieburn, north of Tullamarine airport, but went to school at Assumption College, a Marist Brothers boarding and day school in Kilmore, where on winter mornings the frosted grass of the football ovals crunches underfoot. Shane Crawford played there, as did Billy Brownless and Neale Daniher, Peter Crimmins and Peter "Crackers" Keenan, David King and Francis

Bourke, among many others. Prestia was captain of the First XVIII. "Footy was big there," he says. "Really big."

And now he has come to Tigerland, one of the biggest clubs in Australia—leaving a Gold Coast outfit that to him always felt embryonic, for something fully-formed. "You come into the club here every day and you're headed to the change rooms, and there's the Premiership Walk downstairs, with the Cups on the wall and the photos of famous players, and you just aspire to that. It makes you expect to win every game," he says. "I feel bad saying it, but at the Suns, early on, we were so young that it felt at times like close enough was good enough."

Prestia was injured in his most recent seasons there, too, and he was not alone. He remembers a period during 2016 when he couldn't play but nor could Gary Ablett Jnr, Jaeger O'Meara, David Swallow and Michael Rischitelli, all with long-term injuries. "Our five starting midfielders all missing. And that's just how it was. You don't want to use it as an excuse, but you can't perform with those outs."

Prestia did not treat the switch of clubs lightly. "It was a tough decision. When I got drafted there were 22 of us who were basically 18-year-olds, hardly any from Queensland, and so we grew up together. It was good fun. I'm still close with a lot of them."

Many of that initial group have since scattered—and many of them top-line players. Not just Prestia and Caddy, but O'Meara to Hawthorn (2016), Harley Bennell to Fremantle (2015), Charlie Dixon to Port Adelaide (2015), Tom Hickey to St Kilda (2012) and Zac Smith to Geelong (2015). Prestia still believes if the Suns had stuck together—and not been dealt such a rotten run with injury—they could have been a great team. "But everyone had their own way of getting home by getting traded, and that was hard," he says. "We had so many players who are playing for other clubs now, it's a bit like 'What could we have been?'"

Choosing Richmond was a decision he approached with calculated intent. When he sat down with his manager, Marty Pask, they first had to find a way of seeing through the dismal results the Tigers had recorded in 2016. "We actually didn't put results into the equation," he says. "We know that people have bad games, and teams have bad seasons, and we knew the Tigers were in the finals in the three previous years. We looked at the spine and you've got Rance, Cotchin and Riewoldt, with Dusty on the ball. That looked a pretty good group to come into. I felt they were young, and weren't playing anywhere near their potential, and that they were in the premiership hunt. I wanted to play big games at the MCG, and there's no place better to do that than at Richmond."

He met with CEO Gale and coach Hardwick, too, and was immediately impressed—even by small gestures. "With Dimma, the first thing he said me was 'How's the family? What are they like? What's your girlfriend do?' He had all these questions and it was ages before he even wanted to talk footy. That's one of the big things I took away from him: footy is footy but he was interested in me as a person and not just a player."

He has since found the football program just as accommodating—sensing immediately that he was brought to Richmond to fill a specific need, for his speed of foot (and hand, and mind) around the ball. He feels as though he is one small piece of team that is viewed holistically—as an interconnected unit understood only by reference to its many parts. "No one expects you to do something you're not capable of. They don't expect me to take big marks, or be the contested bull in the midfield, but they hold me to a certain standard based on what I can do and how I can complement the team. And that's a big part of why I wanted to come to Richmond. I knew they had weapons—they just hadn't fired all at once."

It has been challenging, too. Prestia knows he was the "big fish" trade that Richmond and its supporters had wanted and finally landed—giving up pick seven and a 2017 second round selection for his services. "And there are so many supporters," he says. "You definitely end up putting more pressure on yourself."

Settling into life at Punt Road Oval was not what he expected. His impression of big Melbourne clubs—formed, erroneously, from afar—was of an environment where no one socialises outside of the inner sanctum. "I thought it would be this workplace everyone comes to and then goes off and does their own thing. One of the things that surprised me most here was how close everyone is. It's not just little groups of mates, crews and cliques.

"There is no-one here you couldn't call up and have dinner with. There's no awkwardness, which is amazing for how young so many of them are. Dan Butler, Jason Castagna, Daniel Rioli. Jack Graham, Shai Bolton, Tyson Stengle. I look at a bloke like Jayden Short, who is 21, and I feel like he's 26 because he is this confident spark who involves everyone," he says. "I've heard last year was different. That things were low. That there were hard, hard times. But that's all gone. Everyone wants to be here."

//////////

Caddy feels this, too. But he also notes that the way Richmond operates on a day to day basis does not seem that dissimilar than at his other clubs. Many of the differences are slight and unremarkable. He must wear a club T-shirt to meetings at Richmond, whereas at Geelong, players could wear casual clothes. Meetings scheduled for 9:30 at Punt Road begin at 9:30—anyone later than that faces lockout from the auditorium—whereas at Geelong if everyone was there by 9:25, they would start early, and if a few guys strolled in at 9:32 it didn't matter. Perhaps the terminology is tweaked (the "fat side roll around" versus "help side running"), but there is otherwise little difference in the way things are run between a side that won 17 matches and a side that won eight. "A footy club is a footy club," Caddy says. "And these guys are a great bunch of blokes. I suppose if anything, they're a tighter bunch."

His personal game day routine won't change either. "Early in my career I would overthink going into games, trying to do everything perfectly, crossing Ts and dotting Is, and if I didn't it would get to my head. So, I keep it simple and cruisy now. I'm not superstitious. Don't have any weird or wacky rituals."

He gets up early for day games, has breakfast at a café around the corner— smashed avocado and poached eggs, with a long macchiato. In the rooms he warms up dynamically, with squat holds and run-throughs, anything to loosen the tendonitis in his knees. He pumps music in the car on the way to the ground, but then switches it off. He used to listen to tunes in the rooms, but he did so using the online service Spotify, and phones are no longer allowed in the change rooms during games, "so I sacked the music." It wasn't doing anything for him, anyway. Not any more.

"I'm a pretty intense unit when it comes to game day, and I used to pump myself right up, listen to music, have a few *No Doz*, and I probably got a bit over-aroused, so now I just try to keep as calm as I can, because I know I'll be aroused by the time the game starts."

He says he finds it hard to explain what he loves most about football, but then he relates the sensation perfectly.

He loves the feeling you get when your team has the momentum, and is winning every little physical battle. "Everything is going well. Everyone is doing what they need to do. You feel invincible out there."

A defender lays a hard tackle, a rover taps the ball to advantage, a winger spears a perfect pass, a forward takes a contested mark; he handballs to a runner, who is protected by a mean hip and shoulder and ultimately floats a little kick over the top to a man waiting in the goal square, and that man roosts the ball high from the goal line into the packed grandstands.

"For that two hours on the weekend, it's like you're in a big gang, and you're going up against another gang, and winning means having that mental and physical superiority over the other team, this mob mentality that just knocks them over. And that intangible feeling you get when it's happening? That's what I love. You have a bit of arrogance about you, and you puff out your chest a bit, and you look at your teammate and you're just above the other team. You're just on top of them. There's nothing like it."

10

BARBS AND SPINES

I t's 34 degrees outside, but cool in the Graeme Richmond room, the windowless main auditorium at Punt Road Oval. It's a Tuesday in March, a little over a week before the season starts, and a man with a long brown beard, Shane McCurry, stands at the front of the room. Behind him is a slide with the words "Great Richmond Leadership" over a black and white photo of the players doing weights in an outdoor gym on the Sunshine Coast. It's a picture from their pre-season training camp, two months back, in Maroochydore.

"Does that feel like a long time ago?" asks McCurry, the club's new leadership and culture consultant. "Yeah, things move quickly, but it's been a while since you were up there, and we've deliberately stretched the leadership process out this year. It was a conscious decision, because we thought it was important for you guys to see one another perform—not just at camp, but also out on the training track and in the three pre-season games. You've had a chance to see how fair dinkum you are."

Today, the players will vote on who they think should be in their leadership group. McCurry will guide them. He talks about "The Richmond Man"—a new framework at the club, developed in the off-season to represent the best of what they want. *The Richmond Man* plays to his strengths, knows his development areas, and fights on regardless of circumstances. But McCurry wants to know what a great leader really looks like, so he offers his own examples.

The first is a footballer. On the screen in a blue and white jumper is former North Melbourne captain (and current West Coast Eagles coach) Adam Simpson. McCurry began his professional career at North Melbourne in the early 2000s, under Denis Pagan and Dean Laidley, so he knows Simpson well. McCurry joined the Shinboners directly out of high school, spurning a commerce degree to start on the bottom rung of a football club, first in administration but then quickly picking up minor assistant coach duties. "It was a great club to go to, exactly because it was under-resourced," he says. "The upside was that they needed hands on deck, and it meant I got to do a bit of coaching, a bit of recruiting, a bit of forward scouting, a bit with the strength and conditioning guys. I got a real feel for what makes a footy department tick."

Simpson, he remembers, was a great leader not only because he took control on the field—effectively coaching the midfield group for the last five years of his career—but more so because he could read the mood of the group. "If the group was up and about, he'd want to know why, so he could keep it going," McCurry tells the players. "And if the group was a bit flat, he'd get a few of the boys together to figure out what they could do to get the performance back up."

The next face McCurry screens is a man in a suit. Bald, skinny, smiling. It's Todd Greenberg, the CEO of the National Rugby League. McCurry knows Greenberg because of his recent work. After his time at North Melbourne, McCurry worked for the AFL in the Footy Operations department, with a focus on wellbeing and education; former premiership player and coach David Parkin became his mentor. "David was also a trailblazer in player leadership groups—promoting the importance of personal fulfilment for the players," McCurry says. "He doesn't get enough credit for how much of a trend he set, not just in AFL but world sport. Most sports around the world now have a player empowerment model of leadership in place."

McCurry then stepped away from footy, heading leadership, health and wellbeing for the Cotton On retail clothing chain. For the past three years he has worked freelance, consulting with both the Wests Tigers rugby team and the NRL itself, which is where Greenberg came to his attention. McCurry tells the players he admires the Rugby League Chief Executive because he talks about being a "people-focused person" but then, importantly, lives that philosophy. "The Paramatta Eels lost 16 points during the season for salary cap issues, and rather than sending a letter to the club or letting them read about it in the media, he went out and talked to the coaches and players in this kind of format—face to face—sharing the bad news. It was important to him to be respectful of people. And I respect that."

The final leader McCurry praises is a sullen-looking fellow with heavy jowls. It's England's wartime leader, Winston Churchill, and alongside his black and white photo is a quote: *Never give in—never, never, never, never—in nothing great or small, large or petty, never give in.*

McCurry points out that many people don't realise Churchill had two stints as prime minister, and that during his first stint he stepped out onto the road and was hit by a car, fracturing several vertebrae. "He was really crook for a few years, a low point of his life. But then he bounced back to become PM again, and led the Allied Forces to victory over Nazi Germany. Been through significant adversity—and experienced tough times—but stayed positive with a forward focus."

McCurry turns his exercise back on the playing group. Who do they admire as leaders, and why?

Dylan Grimes points to former Tigers captain and current Hawthorn assistant coach Chris Newman as someone who was consistent in every facet of his life, from footy to friends to family. "He was just 100 per cent genuine, but first and foremost his own person."

Jack Riewoldt plucks a leader from outside the code, Dominic Baker, general manager of Wrest Point Casino in Hobart, whom he met recently. Baker, he says, gets to work every morning and walks the floor, talking to the cooks in the kitchens and the cleaners taking care of the rooms. "The first hour and a half of his morning is seeing what they do, learning their names, right down to actually learning how to make up a room when a guest leaves," Riewoldt says. "He learns the intricacies of the business, developing relationships with all the staff, from those who are seen to be the most important, to the people washing dishes."

Josh Caddy points to his former captain, Joel Selwood of Geelong, for his motivation and drive: "He's a pretty intense unit."

Steve Morris, recovering from a knee injury, says he has seen Alex Rance doing everything he can to lead. "Even taking notes in meetings, trying to really get on the same page as 'Truck' in our defensive meetings, so he can be another Truck out on the field."

Shaun Grigg has noticed Daniel Rioli taking under his wing some of the new young draftees—Shai Bolton and Tyson Stengle—whether out for breakfast or doing weights in the gym: "He's just a great footprint for them to follow."

Rance says he has noticed a renewed "positivity" from Hardwick. "That's the greatest shift I've seen, as the ultimate leader of this group—his encouragement for us to celebrate the good we have in us. I've really enjoyed that, the upbeat vibe."

Sam Lloyd offers a tribute to Ivan Maric. The softly-spoken ruckman drew media attention in 2016 when captured on television cameras helping volunteers and staff clean up rubbish in the change rooms after a match. Lloyd says Maric still attends to all those little things. "He's not just driving them—he's doing them as well. He's been doing this for a long time, and he just hasn't gotten lazy."

David Astbury has enjoyed watching Taylor Hunt emerge as an educator in the back line, organising the young defenders.

Jake Batchelor says a big part of leadership is knowing what you do well, then delivering. Jason Castagna and Daniel Butler have done that—bringing energy and speed and desperation to the field. "I love that they know what we need from them, and come in and just do it. I think that's leadership."

McCurry loves the examples: "Sensational," he says. "Give yourself a clap. I mean it. A real clap." And they do.

Two weeks earlier, the group developed their criteria for a Great Richmond Leader, so McCurry gives them a refresher, with a list on the screen.

A Tiger leader plays to his strengths.

A Tiger leader fights and celebrates.

He's calm and composed, regardless of circumstance.

He's consistent.

He's demanding of himself and others.

He takes big actions in big games, turning contests not just through goals and marks but effort and intensity.

He is authentic and genuine.

He is a strong character but a communicator—and a listener.

He has time for everyone.

He is a teacher and a learner.

He is approachable, caring and understanding.

He sets the standard.

He encourages feedback.

The final criteria: "GETS SHIT DONE!"

They also spoke about what a great leadership group looks like, and McCurry lists those qualities. The group should represent the players, and communicate well with them. They should drive development and performance, and own their decisions. "One heart, one mind, one voice," they wrote. "We don't want whinging or cracks to appear."

Team sheets and pens are handed out to everyone in the room—the players, coaches and some peripheral staff—perhaps 60 people. Each has to consider which players they believe are great Richmond leaders, and which group would ensure a balance of personalities.

"Circle anyone who fits that criteria for you," McCurry says. "We're not going to tell you to write a number, or rate players, or only select 3, or 5, or 9 guys. We're giving you a chance to circle whoever you want—no minimum number, no maximum number (of players). You can vote for yourself, and I encourage you to."

The players hunch over in their seats, arms close by their sides, as if completing an exam and guarding their answer sheets. One by one they hand them in. The votes are tallied later, and discussed by coaches, senior players and the executive, behind closed doors.

///////////

McCurry didn't come to Richmond because he sensed a leadership void that he could fill. He didn't come because the list is young and ready to be moulded. He was approached to join the club in 2016 by Brendon Gale, but the Tigers stood out among other teams he might have helped in part because of their most recent, poor season.

"Anything is possible when you get to the depths of those lows," McCurry says. "You get that perspective in the group—we *never* want to get back *there* again—and I think it can be a great foundation."

He met players and coaches and was impressed with their quality, the way they spoke honestly about where they were, and the steps they wanted to take. He talked to a handful of senior figures—Rance, Riewoldt, Cotchin—and saw the faith each had in Gale, Balme and Hardwick. "It was perfect alignment between those pillars of influence, and I'm not just saying that, I was genuinely impressed by those conversations."

The first thing to note, he says, is that as a facilitator he doesn't run the program—the club runs the program. "One of the first things I say to a client if I'm doing work with them is that the biggest indicator of success, for me, is how quickly we can get you up and running the process yourself." At Wests Tigers, within six months he had players delivering their own leadership and culture programs. McCurry works with a group to determine their framework then lets them take the wheel. "Research on behavioural change in team sports says the biggest driver is peer influence. Doesn't matter what the CEO says or the head coach says or the footy manager says, or what I say. If you have a strong playing group with a set of standards that they hold dear, that's the key."

The process of determining the leaders of this playing group, he says, has been the most comprehensive he has seen. "And I think it's been necessary. I know there's been a lot of pressure from the outside to get a result, but we've been comfortable to do it our way. If you are a relatively new group, with new coaches, then having that depth of analysis is the right decision. People might come out and see the leadership group and say, 'I could have told you six months ago to put those guys in charge', and maybe that's the case, but I can tell you that so many conversations will have reinforced those lines of thinking."

The other point to emerge from the search is the number of people qualified to lead. Nine players received 20 votes or more from their peers. A further dozen received at least 10 votes each. "You could throw a net over those guys and put any of them into the leadership group," said McCurry. "Some are strong on field, some off field, some in relationship-building, and some are a combination."

⁓⁓⁓⁓⁓

Three days later, at 12:30pm on Friday, with the first game of the season exactly six days away, Neil Balme stands at the front of the room, whispering to McCurry. "So, what do you want me to do?" he asks. "Tell the boys 'We've got a captain, two VCs, which we think is the right thing to do, etcetera?' Simple enough."

The players file in next, along with the coaches, and media staff, recruiters and list managers, and Gale. Cotchin sits in the back row and wipes the sleep from his eyes. He has an electric razor with him. Evidently, he was caught on the run, so, for a giggle, he switches it on and holds the buzzing device behind the ears of Dustin Martin, who flinches and laughs and shakes it off.

"The decision's been made," says Balme, "on the back of what you guys want. We also talked to the coaches, and the executive, because our leadership represents the club as well as the players. Cotch will be captain again, which was no great…"—Balme is interrupted by whoops and yeahs and *YES!* —"…no great surprise."

McCurry will say later that Cotchin presented as the supremely authentic person at the club, one who will be demanding but yield to his own insecurities and share them with the group. "It's so refreshing," McCurry says. "You don't hear that in footy often, but you should. In leadership courses around the world there's a body of work being done right now on authenticity and vulnerability. They're traits that haven't always been common in male-dominated team sports, but they're getting more time and emphasis, and there's a reason for it. It builds connection. The traditional ways of building connection from the past are still effective, but there's this whole new way of relating to people. It's a generational shift."

Balme continues: "We're also going to appoint two guys as vice-captains, and they'll be Alex and Jack, and they're there to support Cotch. But there are a whole bunch of other blokes in leadership. If you're an AFL player at the Richmond Football Club, you're responsible for your behaviour, and you're responsible for leadership in this place. Different people will be conscripted at different times to run programs, to offer support, so we're all thoroughly involved. But pure leadership, those three boys will lead the way. They have that responsibility and privilege."

Later, in his office overlooking the oval, Balme will explain that the three chosen leaders were comprehensively voted as being among the most influential handful of players. Others could have been included as official leaders for their various strengths, but the feeling between Balme, Hardwick and Livingstone was that 2017 would be a more significant year on the field than ever before.

"OK," Balme says, "so how do we maximise our influence over the players? And one argument is to get a big bunch of blokes into the leadership group, and the other is to say that these three are relatively unique in their own way, and there's a back, a forward and a mid, so there's a bit of synergy and symmetry there, and these guys already have great lines of communication with Dimma. And then we can conscript and use the others as we wish. We think we'll get the best bang for our buck out of these three."

Balme, Hardwick and Livingstone, of course, couldn't be disingenuous and not take notice of the vote from the players, which placed others on a similar level to the selected trio. But nor could the decision be a straight vote count. "We have to say, 'What do we need as a footy management group, to run the team as best we can?' We didn't have a fully preconceived idea of what we wanted, but we thought a tighter group, which we could keep focused, would be best."

Left unsaid is the fact that leaders from last season—Shane Edwards, Ivan Maric and Steven Morris—were left out, in part because each (through injury or form) did not have a great 2016 season. Edwards though, Balme says, is already exerting a strong influence over the younger players. Morris has set impeccable standards from the confines of the rehab group. And Maric did not want to be in the prescribed leadership group, so is not diminished by the decision. "He'll always lead," says Balme. "He doesn't care what he's called."

Later there will be "evolving leaders" or "emerging leaders"—the likes of David Astbury and Nick Vlastuin and even recruit Dion Prestia. But right now the mantle and responsibility falls on the three, because of what they can do with the football in hand. "The game is the game," says Balme. "But it's about how we play together. How organised and disciplined we are. How much they enjoy themselves. They've got to drive positive energy, and that'll drive our outcomes more than anything else."

///////////

McCurry, back in the auditorium, can't let the announcement slip without a final flourish. He wants to share a story that he thinks is relevant to the leadership decision. He has etchings of three animals on the screen.

"They're all extinct, and they all became extinct in the ice age, which was 10,000 years ago. We've got the sabre tooth tiger, the woolly mammoth, and the giant beaver."

Then McCurry asks for Cotchin, Riewoldt and Rance to come up the front of the auditorium. People assume that McCurry is about to assign each of the three players one of the animals, but instead he immediately asks the rest of the playing group to join them at the front. Then he asks the coaches to come up. And then the staff, until everyone is standing together in a tight, milling group, and the stadium seats in the room are completely empty. Then the image on the screen changes, into what looks a bit like an echidna. "We saw those three kinds of animals that went extinct in the ice age," says McCurry. "Does anyone know what that animal there is?"

Someone says a porcupine.

"It's not just any porcupine. It's the Rothschild's porcupine. Scientific name, *Coendou rothschildi*. And that species of porcupine lived in the ice age, and it saw all those animals dying around it, and so it huddled closer with all the other porcupines for warmth. But it found the barbs and spines were spearing one another in the sides, wounding each other. The closer they got together, the more hurt and more uncomfortable they became. So, they moved apart again, and then they started to die again. They had to make an important decision: to stay apart and die, as a species, or come together and accept one another for what they were.

"They wisely decided to stay together. They learned to live with the small wounds of a close relationship, because the most important thing was the warmth given by one another, to help them not only survive, but thrive. And I reckon there's a lot in that for team sports, fellas. Because we're all very different, we come from different backgrounds, we've got different strengths and different areas to work on, and the only way that we can come together and thrive as a group is to accept one another for what we are, and we support one another to get better. We do that, and just like the porcupines, we'll get the best result for our team. Get around your leaders, congratulate them, and look forward to this next phase in the journey."

There is a roar in the room now, and Ben Griffiths, the two-metre tall forward, comes up behind Riewoldt and envelopes him in a long-held hug. Rance finds himself lifted up by three defenders, like a grunge fan stage diving in a mosh pit. Cotchin disappears into the bodies. It's all back pats and tousled hair and rubbed heads and tapped arses. Then they head upstairs for signing day, to sit together and apply black Sharpie signatures to perhaps 500 pieces of memorabilia. The jumpers and footys and photos will be used throughout the year by the club, given to a sick kid in hospital, or a business on a commercial visit, or donated to a community raffle. And so the players sit in a large circle, handing the items from one man to the next, laughing and joking as they go about the business of football.

Rance and Riewoldt are the last to join the group. Before they get there, they speak briefly to Balme in the auditorium, just the three of them together in the darkened space. The football manager is elated that the announcement was met well by the team, and is confident there will be no leaks to media before the formal press release is made in five hours. The full-back and the full-forward, he says, are needed downstairs in a moment, with their captain, for an official photo and club website interviews. But before he can let them go he has a reminder for them: "This is really exciting. It's fantastic," Balme says. "Well done you guys but remember—particularly early—that the message is simple: 'Support Cotch, support Cotch, support Cotch'."

11

PRESSURE POINTS

In the cavernous change rooms of the MCG ahead of Round 1, a quiet man in a dress shirt with yellow and black tie, and big black framed glasses, stands smiling. The unassuming 69-year-old has a flop of silver hair pulled left to right across his scalp. He holds his hands together in front of his waist, and fidgets nervously on his feet. He seems genuinely embarrassed to be there, this old man expected to say something meaningful to 22 young footballers.

Tim Livingstone speaks for him, first noting that aside from the Jack Dyer Medal for Richmond's best and fairest player, there is another other auspicious award at the club named for a past player. It is named for this man. "It's an award voted on by the players for the players," says Livingstone, "and is held in the highest regard because this man is held in the highest regard."

The man is there to present jumpers to four Tiger debutants in Dion Prestia, Josh Caddy, Toby Nankervis and first-gamer Dan Butler. Their families have gathered here for an important tradition—made more special by the guest of honour. "I'm going to go to stats, because his record needs to be mentioned," says Livingstone. "300 games for the Tigers, and importantly 45 for Nathalia—*which he wanted me to mention.* Five premierships with the Tigers. AFL and Richmond team of century. Australian Football and Richmond Hall Of Fame. Jack Dyer medallist, and in his spare time coached the club as well. Please make welcome, Francis Bourke."

The players applaud and the smiles on the faces of Houli, Rance, Prestia, Grigg and Lloyd are almost giddy. It's hard to say much about Bourke without descending into hyperbole but his nickname, Saint Francis, speaks to something. Bourke's name is—perhaps more than any footballer in history—synonymous with bravery. In a 1971 clash with Hawthorn, he broke his leg but continued to play before eventually walking off the ground unassisted.

It is one of many such stories. The legend is best characterised by footage of a battle with North Melbourne at the Kangaroos' Arden Street home ground. Bourke was accidentally poked in the eye, and with blood flowing from the socket and down his face, he calmly moved to the forward line, dived to take a chest mark, and kicked a goal to ensure a close win. A month later Richmond won the 1980 premiership—their last.

"Gentlemen, mums and dads, I am really flattered that the club would ask me to do this job. Your first game for your club, you never forget that," Bourke says. He is envious of them, and would give his right arm to play just one more game, and he tells them as much, remembering his debut in Round 5 of 1967. He was 20 years old. "It's such a fantastic opportunity to find yourself in the team, rubbing shoulders with the tin gods, and the great thing about it is, you just never know where it's going to finish up for you. I came down thinking I'd miss one season of milking the cows at home and I'd be back the following year. That was 50 years ago. Fifty bloody years ago. Make the most of it because time just goes so quickly."

///////////

Inside the coaches' room, ahead of the season opener, Richmond versus Carlton, the coaches talk. The space is decorated this year with new plastic wall decals, with updated branding. Along the back wall are photos of Bourke, Dyer, the legendary coach Tom Hafey, early 20th century goalkicker, Jack Titus, and Australian Football Hall of Fame Legend and Richmond Immortal Kevin Bartlett, who has only this week seen a bronze statue of himself unveiled outside the ground. They are timeless, but the messages on the walls are specific to season 2017.

"STRENGTHS—FIGHT—CELEBRATE" and "Be THE RICHMOND MAN" stand out. Another says "I WILL... Play to my

STRENGTHS ... Show effort, intensity and FIGHT in all circumstances ... See things in the positive and CELEBRATE all that we value as a team."

The coaches jabber away, bemoaning the media coverage this week, which has—in the same flimsy manner as before this clash in 2016—established a simple narrative whereby Carlton is the callow youthful side, and Richmond the more mature and seasoned opponent. In fact, the average age of the Blues is much older. Hardwick warned his players about this during the week: "Don't go falling for that bullshit they're spruiking in the media," he said. "They're not that young. They're not schoolboys."

His pre-game message reiterates the lessons from opposition analysis during the week. The Blues will look for short kicks into the centre—inside 45, lateral, back 45—so the Tigers need to block the corridor, be ready to swoop on forward handballs, and position well to counter the switch. "If we can't turn that ball over, we're chasing arse all day."

At 6:26pm, 54 minutes before the first centre bounce of the AFL season, he speaks to the group. There have been a few players changes but nothing dramatic. He points first to the red square he has drawn around rover Marc Murphy: "Why has this guy got red around him?"

"Simple: he's a bloody good player. A multiple possession player on the outside, and that means he's able to be pressured."

After that the speech is the same as every message this pre-season. Play to strengths in attack—back your hard running, or high marking, or hard ball gets. In defence, immediate blitz pressure is important but covering exits— denying short kicks and forward handballs—is almost more important. "The great thing about those forward handballs is what?" he asks. "It's that they sit up in the air, and you can come in, like Grimsey, and *smash 'em*. That's what we want to see today."

The game will be an arm wrestle, he says—lifting his arm up, then pushing it down, then up and down again—going back and forth in ascendency and intensity—wrestling the air. He's written "RAISE THE FIGHT" on the whiteboard, and that's what he expects. He asks Ben Griffiths to come up to the front and take a laminated picture stuck to the whiteboard and turn it over.

"Not a very good photo at all, is it?" he says. "What is it Georgie (Castagna)?"

"It's a shark," says Castagna.

"From where?"

"Camp."

Specifically, it's a blow-up shark used in a competition on a waterpark obstacle course on pre-season camp in Maroochydore. Back then, in the Queensland heat, in January, the players had fought one another in a stupid wet frenzy for this piece of plastic. Hardwick reminds them how they knocked coaches off docks into the water. How Rance put a handful of players in headlocks. How Riewoldt faked a broken rib to scare the club doctors, and no one questioned him such was the frenetic nature of the game. The coach's eyes are animated. He looks happy.

This time 12 months ago, his address was full of vitriol and anger—he wanted blood, and he wanted his players to want blood as well. This year he wants fun. In the past hour Hardwick has laughed more than sighed, strutted more than twitched. He points to one final message on the board: "BE THE CHILD—BE ALL IN …"

"Think back to when you were a kid," he says. "What don't you have?"

Fear, they answer.

"Yeah, kids are fully invested. You ride a bike, you're riding it to what? To *crash*. You get back on and you go again. I saw that with that stupid shark, you guys being kids, tackling and fighting and going mad. That's the attitude we're bringing tonight. It's fun. It's playing without fear. It's playing like you did with that shark. That was great fun. Tonight's going to be fun."

〰〰〰〰〰

By half time, Nick Vlastuin has registered 10 tackles. The team has scored 7 goals 3 behinds from forward half turnovers—a number unheard of from the Tigers of recent memory. The team has, Hardwick says, "started the game offensively, through being elite defensively."

Entering the rooms at the main break, Rance is almost hoarse: "Just need to put the foot on the throat!"

The coaches nevertheless cover all bases, discussing uncontested mark numbers, pressure point ratings, the size of their defensive bubble, the game time of individual midfielders, the distance they've each run, and who should stay on or go off to begin the second half.

Griffiths is one who will start on the bench. "But give Griff a pump-up," Leppitsch says to Hardwick, "because he's going really well. You know what these guys are like—start them on the bench and they think they've been dropped."

The second half, apart from a lull in the third quarter, is as good as the first. By the final siren, each of the debutants has kicked a goal, including two to Butler and three to Castagna. Dustin Martin plays a dominant game (34 possessions and four goals) that will see his Brownlow odds drop, his contract speculation rise, and have pundits discussing whether he is the equal of the previous two Brownlow medallists, Patrick Dangerfield and Nathan Fyfe.

Martin's kicking on the night is unsurpassed, from low, spearing passes to a 78-metre bomb. His tackling is ruthless, but it is his ability to break tackles that stirs the imagination of fans. His strength in fending off opponents, shrugging them from his back, knocking them over on the run, is perhaps unprecedented. He also shows signs of becoming the consummate team player, giving off three goals he could have kicked himself, and remaining willing to bullock and shepherd so that others might shine.

73,137 people turned up to watch Richmond win by 43 points, having ambushed Carlton with an early three goal to nothing lead that was never surrendered, and eventually built upon. More to the point, there was exuberance to their play—the crash and dash Hardwick has been asking for all pre-season.

///////////

As the song is sung in the rooms afterwards, coaches and staff and volunteers and media stand watching. So too do the VFL players, having walked across to the stadium after their practice match against the Northern Blues at Punt Road Oval.

They're all in club tracksuits. Ivan Maric, who played well in the ruck and feels ready for a recall to the senior team when needed; Kane Lambert, who dominated the midfield and awaits his chance; Jayden Short, who is perhaps next in line for a running back position, should anyone fall out of form or fitness or favour.

Fringe defender Nathan Broad is there, too, as the players sing in a circle and empty 14 bottles of Gatorade on the dancing debutants. Broad leans against the wall and remembers what it was like in his debut, last year, when Richmond beat Brisbane right here, and he was the one being drenched.

"Unreal. Best feeling ever," he says. "Highlight of my career."

Butler, who has just experienced his own dream debut, says the same thing moments later. He won't single out a goal or a tackle as a highlight—only playing his role and the sound of the final siren. "And the banner, fireworks, stadium," he adds, running a hand through long hair sticky with sports drink. "It was a pretty humbling experience. It's not something you do every day—it's something I'll cherish forever."

The media scrum takes hold now, and the players are corralled for radio and print and TV. Rioli is talking to Rohan Connolly for SEN Sports. Former Fitzroy and Brisbane champion Alastair Lynch is doing a piece to camera for Fox Footy, so his former teammate and Richmond VFL coach, Craig McRae, sidles up to say hello.

Hardwick walks the floor, grasping shoulders and clasping hands. One by one he visits the players, offering a whisper or a joke. Houli, who played a quieter than usual game on the wing, but chased hard and harassed. McIntosh, who took a brave saving mark in defence. Brandon Ellis, who risked his body often and began to look at home in the back line. The injury plagued Reece Conca, with a grin from ear to ear, and ice on both calves. Cotchin, who had fewer possessions than usual but set the scene with an early goal. Vlastuin, who ended with 12 tackles. And Riewoldt, who had eight, his most ever.

In private, Hardwick tells the players what he saw. He saw a 1.95 pressure rating. The little-known number is derived by statisticians from an array of identified markers in games, everything from tackles to corrals, physical hits and closed space—1.8 is the average pressure rating, 1.9 is high, 2.0 and above is elite. Richmond has until recently played an uncontested "keepings off" style game, and so has not returned a number as high as 1.95 in many seasons. But Hardwick also wants to know what they saw.

They saw the blitz. They saw the run. They saw celebration.

"But it's not something we've invented overnight," says Hardwick. "We've seen it all through JLT as part of our game. So how do you reckon our measure of respect is going? Yeah, it's trending up. You know how I say about some other sides, 'Gee their pressure's great'? Well, what do you think other sides are going to start saying about us? What are opposition scouts going to look at? They're going to look at 23 forward 50 tackles. Or 34 forward half turnovers, leading to 11 goals 6."

He thinks their Uranus cover was good. They still have work to do—
namely with a few attacking quirks, a reluctance to use that first, instinctive
handball option. But they won. And it's good to have it out of the way.

"The Round 1 game is always the same. You're nervous as hell, aren't ya?
It always feels worth more than it is. But it's just four points. They challenged
us, but there were some significant efforts. I don't like to individualise, so
I won't. You did us proud, your fans proud, and we'll get back on the horse
tomorrow. Enjoy the win. Understand why we won and what it looks like,
and let's look at doing it next week."

12

EMBRACE THE STRUGGLE

The theme for the opposition analysis of Collingwood on Wednesday afternoon is simple: "Start a streak". But a streak, says Hardwick, staring down his squad of 25 players in the auditorium, is just an outcome. The process, he says, is defence.

Defence is everything. On Thursday night, he says, the players need to bring their best blitz pressure—"because we know that wins games"—and monitor their exits—"because we know they like that short inside 45 kick"—and finally fight for the outside—"because our Uranus cover wasn't good enough last time."

The club had a good look at the Magpies during the pre-season, so they understand their opponent and how to beat them: prevent easy exit kicks; pay attention to that all important teasing distance; put body contact on Jeremy Howe and Ben Reid; monitor Adam Treloar and Brodie Grundy through the corridor. "We're not going out of our way to tag blokes," says Hardwick, "but they've got some elite players, so let's make sure we've got an understanding of who they use."

Each line goes into vastly more detail in their analysis. The defensive line, for instance, has a written breakdown of each attacking player at Collingwood, with a photo next to each one. The document is broken into sections such as "medium forwards", and offers a mix of criticism and praise for each player they will try to curtail.

Alex Fasolo, for example, is regarded as extremely dangerous, and clever. Chris Mayne, formerly of Fremantle, works hard and tackles hard. Jesse White is a noted endurance runner with neat skills. Young Magpie hope Darcy Moore, the son of dual Brownlow Medallist, Peter Moore, runs hard and has strong hands. Jarryd Blair is seen as smart and competitive.

The club breaks down all opponents across all lines in this way for every single game. Sometimes weaknesses are highlighted as well. One player can be lazy. Another doesn't like the contest. One goes missing. One is let down by his intensity. Most AFL players—perhaps all AFL players—have one flaw or another. The profile for Collingwood midfielder Steele Sidebottom, by contrast, lists no faults, acknowledging plainly that he is an elite ball user and decision-maker who remains calm and always has an impact: "Just knows how to win possession and use it with class from start to finish."

Offensively, says Hardwick, the Tigers need to play their game but crucially will need to "break the line". By way of explanation, the coach offers footage of Collingwood from one week earlier, against the Bulldogs. In the clip, the ball is in the Magpie forward line and the black and white players are swarming—blocking seemingly every exit—until a Bulldog hits up an elegant short pass to a player in the middle of the chaos. "Why is that kick valuable right there?" Hardwick asks. Then he offers the answer.

Collingwood, he explains, like to maintain an incredibly dense defensive press, meaning almost all their players are in one half of the ground. By taking a mark near the back of that press, the Bulldogs can send another quick, long kick directly out of the maelstrom, to a runner dashing back towards goal.

Next, he shows a clip from the Richmond practice match against the Magpies, illustrating the same point. Dustin Martin has the ball in the back pocket in Moe, and shoots a low pass to Cotchin in the middle of the ground. "Dusty assesses his options, plays to his strengths, finds the skipper through the middle," says Hardwick. "The skipper knows right away that he's broken that first line. He turns, it goes out the back to a runner. Easy goal."

There is applause a few moments later for Jayden Short, Ben Lennon and Kane Lambert, who all come into the side for their first senior game of the year, at the expense of Sam Lloyd, Kamdyn McIntosh and Taylor Hunt. The coach says the three dropped players hadn't necessarily played poorly, but that the elevated threesome had played too well to ignore. "The great thing about you players is there are parts of your game we wanted you to go back and work on, and you've done that, so you get rewarded. You guys are going to help us win the game."

Finally, Hardwick wants to talk about "the story" of the season, and how the team is tracking. He wants to talk about that respect they're trying to earn back. Are people outside the club buying into it? *Probably not yet*, he thinks. He plays another video clip, this one a moment from Fox Footy's *On The Couch*.

Gerard Healy is sitting with David King, Jason Dunstall and Jonathan Brown. The former players and now expert commentators are looking at a graphic that displays the defensive behaviours Richmond exhibited against Carlton. It lists the pressure acts, tackles, turnovers, and scores from turnovers. Dunstall says it's all great, wonderful, well done, but he wants to see it for a full six weeks before he is convinced—and against better teams than the Blues. Brown feels the same way: "You know what the main stat is up there?" he asks. "Versus Carlton."

Hardwick switches off the recording. "Now, we don't normally give a stuff about these blokes," he says. "After all, who controls our defence? *We do*. It is all controlled by us. You speak about the body and how it operates—what's the one thing the body can't do without? *Heart! Heart!* That's the lifeblood of our game, and it's our defence. So, we can come with the right attitude against Collingwood, or we can give these blokes what they want," he says, pointing at Dunstall and Brown and co. "They're waiting to write the story, aren't they? Well, *we* get to dictate that story. And the story is the heart. And it pumps, it pumps, it pumps. It just beats."

///////////

Outside, the oval smells of freshly cut grass. It's dewy and wet and fragrant. The training surface is immaculate and glowing, and it should be, given it is lovingly trimmed five days a week by a meticulous curator. In ice hockey, the rinks are smoothed down between practices and even between periods during games by a giant machine called a Zamboni, leaving a dazzling cross-hatched rink of perfectly smooth ice. The zig-zag pattern of the mown grass here—a warm patchwork quilt of green and darker green—is not unlike that. It is a stage awaiting performers, a far cry from the muddy Punt Road oval of the Jack Dyer era.

The players take their positions to begin light circle work. This is that short training session the day before a match, known as the Captain's Run. The ball zings up and down the oval. From across the field, the distant and familiar slap of boot on ball sounds similar to the patter of ballet shoes, *en pointe*, as they tap and shuffle across the stage. Like dancers, the players too make the unfathomable physicality of their movement look both basic and sublime.

A handful of media stands on a grandstand terrace in the sun, observing and filming. Someone else is watching, too, from behind a fence on Brunton Avenue. It's an opposition scout from Collingwood, having a peek at training. Neil Balme, having crossed from the Magpies in the off-season, recognises him as performance analyst Shane Joules. "We've got a spy," Balme says, grinning. "Better be careful. He might figure us out. Look, someone handballed it to someone else! The yellow team kicked to the other yellow team!"

Australian football is rife with stories of inter-club subterfuge. The Magpie teams of the early 20th century, for instance, used to water down their Victoria Park home ground, turning it into a morass of mud that suited their players, briefly earning the club the nickname 'The Mudlarks'. Spying on training sessions is a far more routine practice in the modern era, because it does have value.

"Training now is so specific that if you come and watch, you *will* get an idea of what we're trying to do," says Balme, now serious. "We were talking the other day about some strategies for our kick outs from full-back, and someone said 'What about trying this?' And someone else said, 'Well, we haven't trained it, so we probably shouldn't do it'. So that's what spies are looking for. If they see something we're training, well, maybe we're going to do it in a game."

Balme is looking forward to the match against Collingwood. Putting his Magpie hat back on, he guesses his old club will have noticed the Tigers' smaller, faster forward line. They'll have observed the increased pressure ratings. They'll be saying their midfield should be able to compete with Richmond's. They'll be saying Richmond is taking the game on more— going long down the line instead of chipping around the edges. "They'll recognise all that we're trying to do, and it'll just be a matter of will."

Balme first came to Richmond almost half a century ago, in 1969. He can picture the old rooms and the bright yellow lockers. "I can remember it like it was yesterday in that sense." Richmond was in the early days of its halcyon VFL era, but the young Balme wasn't overawed meeting the club's star players, mostly because he didn't know who they were. He had come from Western Australia and, at that time, in that place, the most important footy league was the WAFL. "They didn't show much VFL there, so the players weren't household names the way they were in the suburbs of Melbourne."

His coach was Tom Hafey, who came across in his latter years as sweet and genial, and indeed Balme says he was a lovely and decent man. "But he was very, very competitive. Ruthless really. He didn't ask for anything too complicated—just total commitment. He was a real man," Balme says, flexing his arms. "I think the softness was simply him showing empathy for other people. But under Tommy we believed we were going to win all the time, because that's what was expected. There was a certain arrogance about that, which came with performance. Keep trying, bust your gut, crash into them—do anything to make sure you win. He was uncompromising."

The players, too, were vicious in their approach to training and playing. "They were high performance, highly motivated guys," he says. "Royce Hart, Francis Bourke, Kevin Bartlett, Dick Clay, Kevin Sheedy, Michael Green, Barry Richardson, Paul Sproule, Roger Dean. It was a fantastic group. Top of the tree."

Balme says he is happy simply to have shared the stage with them, but he too had a stunning career. It began in 1968, when he played a senior game for Subiaco against West Perth, and lined up against AFL Legend Graham 'Polly' Farmer at Leederville Oval. "Polly was West Perth's captain-coach, and he was 33. I would have been 16, and weighed 12 stone, and even then he was double-teaming grown ruckmen, so you can imagine how many times I got my hand on the ball—not that often."

Five years later, and Balme became a premiership player for the first time, winning the 1973 flag with Richmond against Carlton. But his performance that day is remembered for a pair of wild attacks, including a round arm punch on Geoff Southby, which left the Blues full-back groggy, and a series of hits on Vin Waite in the goal square. Balme says now there was no anger or malice in those events, and certainly no premeditated plan—it was just a primal response to a heated moment. "In those days the intimidation factor was probably a little more marked than it is now. We're a bit better at controlling it now," he says. "When you see vision of it you think, 'That was pretty ugly', but at the time it didn't feel so different from the mood of the game."

Another five years on, after one more flag, and his career was over. He retired at 27 with a degenerative knee, leaving football during the 1979 pre-season, after 159 games with the Tigers. "I was halfway up hill five at Torquay, and the knee just went *stop!* I had a stress fracture inside, and it had just worn out. Back then we had injuries and we just played with them, whereas you have injuries now and you fix them. We created our own problems in a way."

Balme looks out at the field now, as Rioli tucks the ball under his arm for a short sprint, Lambert buzzes around a stoppage, and Nankervis takes set shots on goal. He doesn't have any favourite act on the field that he misses, apart from perhaps spinning out of a pack and kicking a left foot goal. "That was something pretty good to do," he says. "But I think I just liked the smell. You know that smell, of being involved in the contest? It was a great game to play."

And when he could no longer play, he coached, first in South Australia[6], then a stint in the AFL with Melbourne. He moved into football administration next, as football manager at Collingwood, then Geelong, then Collingwood again. Walking back into Tigerland before Christmas felt familiar. "Footy is fairly similar no matter where you are," he says. "We all draft from the same pot, we all play in the same competition. It's really not that dissimilar from club to club."

He sees here a plan in place, a list with the right components, a coach and football department moving in the right direction—particularly a calculated change in the way the players have been empowered, with Hardwick working to make sure the players know he believes in them. "He will help them, but he's coaching them to take responsibility, rather than him taking it all on and having to solve all the problems, because although that's admirable, it's also very hard to do."

The right balance between compassion and demand seems to have been

---

6   Balme later played 13 games for Norwood in 1981-82, during his time as coach of the club (1980-90). The Redlegs, under Balme, won SANFL flags in 1982 and 1984. He then coached Woodville-West Torrens (1991-92).

struck. "It used to be that the players had to adapt to what the coach wanted, but footy is now in a space where the best coaches adapt to what the players need," he says. "We can't ignore the fact that we have to demand extreme performance—but you've got to have this relationship and care as well, so the players know they're allowed to make a mistake and still thrive. Sounds a bit touchy-feely, but this business is all about people."

He isn't sure how the team will go against Collingwood. "I've been in footy for 50 years, and by this time every week—this close to the game—I think we're going to win. And I *know* we're not always going to win, but I always *reckon* we're going to win."

///////////

In the rooms before the game, the coaches eat muffins and ham and cheese rolls, and chat about everything from the security needed to enter an NFL stadium in the United States, to the Danish movie Hardwick watched that afternoon. He can't remember what it was called, but it was subtitled, and it opens him up to ribbing.

"Subtitles?" says Hill. "Did you have some caviar?"

"Nah," says Hardwick. "A latte and a little tabouli."

Player welfare manager Bronwyn Doig brings a tray of coffees into the room, all small. "Do these come in men's sizes?" asks Hardwick.

"Yep," says Doig. "They're for shorter men. Like you."

Leppitsch is standing nearby, assessing the new Puma gear the coaching staff is wearing, including the sheen of the fabric and the placement of pockets. He likes the thumb hook on the zipper quite a bit, and so he furiously pulls the zipper up and down, up and down, up and down, creating a buzzing noise a few feet from the coach. He keeps doing it, mere inches from Hardwick's head. "Is that annoying," he asks him, continuously tugging the zipper. "Am I annoying you?"

Word comes through from the VFL practice match at Punt Road Oval that rookie ruckman Ivan Soldo has kicked four goals. Soldo is a favourite of fitness boss Peter Burge, and so the coaches wonder aloud if Burge will need a cold shower when he hears the news. Soon the players are seated and the pep talk for the evening begins.

The messages are simple. Continue the struggle, continue the story, raise the fight: "It's the primal things," says Hardwick. "It's not being conservative—it's being ultra-aggressive."

Hardwick also has another laminated A3 picture on the whiteboard. As David Astbury approaches to turn it over, the playing group begins a low "whoooaaa" that builds and builds and stretches and increases in volume, like the sound a cricket crowd makes when clapping in a fast bowler on his approach to the wicket. The picture is of a cocoon, and above it is written: EMBRACE THE STRUGGLE.

The important thing to note, Hardwick says, is the hole at the top of the cocoon. The hole is smaller than the butterfly's head, he explains, which means the butterfly must struggle to get out. And there's a good reason for that. The wings of the butterfly are underdeveloped. They're thin. As it squeezes through the opening, the blood rushes to the wings, and only then can it emerge and fly. Cutting a bigger hole—doing things the easy way—won't help. The butterfly must squeeze painfully through the gap in order to flap its wings.

"You've got to understand: the greatest aspect of your sporting life is the struggle. There's a side out there that's going to challenge us," Hardwick says. He leans in among the group now, and gets choked up in the moment. "That hole is going to be there, and so I want you to embrace that struggle. Tonight boys, we look to fly. Love what you do, love the blokes you're playing with. Fly."

After the players leave the room, the coaching group can't help but rib Hardwick.

"Thank you for that," says Tim Livingstone, pausing. "Great speech, *Damien* Attenborough."

"Next week you should do Steve Irwin," says Leppitsch. "*We're crocodiles, boys, and by crikey we snap!*"

///////////

Last season the watchwords at Richmond were "Bold. Manic. Outnumber", and although that never really materialised in season 2016, it has so far in 2017. The pressure wrought by Richmond in the first quarter alone against the Magpies is better than the entire 23 home and away games of the previous year.

Tackling at the coal face. Tackling by chasing. Tackling by cornering. Tackling in pairs. Riding tackles into the ground. Stripping the ball. Hitting the ball. Hitting the body. It all produces what they call "inferred pressure" or "perceived pressure", which means little more than creating a moment of doubt or hesitation in the opposition—that which sees calm players panic, and skilful opponents make skill errors.

The night is summed up perhaps 10 minutes into the second quarter, when Richmond is down by three points but pressing hard, and Collingwood's Will Hoskin-Elliott has the ball. He is starved of options. He can't find a target. So he rushes, and kicks into the corridor. Josh Caddy, already creeping into the teasing space, sprints then marks. In an instant, he is surrounded by four Tigers who all sensed the same interception. Caddy handballs to Martin, who gives to Houli, who gives back to Martin, who surges past opponents in the open field. He finds Prestia, who finds Cotchin, who runs, steadies and goals from 50 metres out.

It is the perfect goal, the result of equalising, then nullifying, the opposition. It is that sought after offensive reward for defensive effort, and it is reminiscent of something written by legendary American basketball coach Jack Ramsay, who led the Portland Trailblazers in the 1970s.

Ramsay believed there was beauty and truth and wonder in sport, but specifically in the gritty contests, and those moments when the opposition is so suppressed—rendered so stunned—that the game is seemingly played by one team. He wrote as much in his book, *The Coach's Art*[7]. The contest is a dog fight and then it becomes ballet—a graceful sweep of patterned movement, counter pointed by daring and brilliance:

> It is a dance which begins with opposition contesting every move. But in the exhilaration of a great performance, the opposition vanishes. The dancer does as he pleases. The game is unified action up and down. It is quickness, it is strength, it is skill, it is stamina. It is winning, it is winning, it is winning!

///////////

---

7   *The Coach's Art* by Jack Ramsay, (Timber Press, 1978).

The rooms afterward are as they always are in victory, a flurry of activity. Some of the club leaders are smiling, like Hardwick ("That was a good one") and Leppitsch ("Never in doubt"), while others are more pragmatic, like midfield coach Andrew McQualter ("Phew!") and the club CEO, Gale ("Five out of ten, for mine").

Behind closed doors, Hardwick is happy that their hard work was rewarded with a 19-point win. The contest was scrappy—they were kept in it by poor conversion from Collingwood—and the result was later described as "winning ugly", but he's proud of them for having faith in their plan. He's also proud they were able to raise the fight when Collingwood had drawn in front—that they won the lead back, pulled away and, importantly, held on. "I look at that game," he says to the group, "and I think '12 months ago, we probably lose'."

"We did," says Riewoldt, laughing. "Could not be more to the day!"

Later, Balme says the team could have played much better. But that is pleasing—when the performance is below expectation but the outcome is victory. To fight back and win from behind, he says, develops resilience and fosters belief.

"It shows that all the stuff we've been talking about—the spirit and intensity and all that intangible shit—that we're getting somewhere with it. If we can get the game right, and this stuff keeps bubbling along, who knows how good we can be?"

13

IT'S A CONTRACT

t's a perfect autumn morning, clear blue sky, a chill in the air. Dew sparkles
on the Yarra Park grassland. And inside the Tigerland gym, all is quiet.
Shane Edwards murmurs softly with medical staff about his injured hip.
Kamdyn McIntosh steps into the sleep room for a short power nap before
training begins. Alex Rance, barefoot, cap backwards, walks into an empty
office carrying a bowl of cereal, and sits with his back to the rising sunlight.

It's 7:45am on Thursday, two days before the Tigers play the Eagles at
the MCG—48 hours before he will (likely) line up on the most dominant
high-marking full-forward in the competition, Josh Kennedy. Adelaide's
Taylor Walker can land drop punt bombs 60 metres from goal, and Sydney's
Lance Franklin can burn defenders with pace and muscle, but perhaps none
take the high, contested mark in the manner of the Eagles forward. "Not
much really changes with my preparation though," says Rance, "whether I'm
playing on Kennedy or a young forward coming through the competition."

Rance is 27 now, so his Mondays and Tuesdays are always about physical
regeneration, shaking out any lingering soreness. Wednesdays might be a day
off, which he uses to focus on things outside of the game. "It's important for
a lot of guys to free up their minds to execute, because it is a really long year.
If you hold onto emotional baggage every week, it turns into a long season."

Thursdays and Fridays he starts to "gear up", and to focus on his strengths.
He won't waste time trying to impress in a handball game at training,

preferring to spend time practising one-on-one contests, marking under pressure, fielding ground balls—anything that will help him intercept the footy in the random space of the defensive arc.

"I've always got to make sure I'm sharpening the axe, to make sure the skills I have are always ready to be put on show," he says. "There's no point in doing training for the sake of it—it must always have a purpose. I'm always asking the strength and conditioning coaches questions—'How is this related to a game?' 'What can I use this for?'—and if they can't give me an answer then I probably won't do the exercise."

He does his research, of course, and there are subtle adjustments. He knows Kennedy is a "hit up" forward—one who gets his possessions by pushing off on strong leads—just as he knows Buddy is an athletic forward who "hightails" out the back of contests towards goal, where he can't be caught.

"You have them in the back of your mind, but as a good defender you can't change your game every week," Rance says. "You've got to ask yourself questions. *'What do they want to do to me?' 'Where do they want to get the ball?'* It's such a large surface out there, what you're playing on. You can't defend everything. You pretty much have to play the percentages—give them a smaller part of the oval than what they're comfortable with."

He knows if his opponent leads to a certain pocket, they will have to beat him on speed. If they move closer to goal, they will have to overpower him. If they think they can take a mark in a small central gap, the kick they receive will need to be perfect.

As an experienced player, Rance relies on this knowledge to come to him in the moment—he doesn't have to think. "I play my best footy when I'm switched on—right in that zone—instead of standing there and going through the motions and watching the ball. But it always comes back to that principle: What do they want to do, and where's the dangerous space?"

Rance wonders about what it was like when footy was less intense. His father, Murray Rance, played in that era, 40 games for Footscray (1986-87) and 57 for West Coast (1988-90), captaining the Eagles in 1989. He hardly missed a game in that period, also playing 140 games for Swan Districts (1981-85, 1990-92). Alex sighs a little, thinking about that "semi-professional lifestyle" and how different it must have felt compared to now, when players must scrutinise their every decision. "You have to think of *everything*," he says. "You have to think of your image when you're walking down the street.

You have to think of what you're eating at all times. In the lead up to games, you must think about whether you've drunk enough water, got enough sleep. You need to think about all these things that contribute to that one day at the end of the week. It's pretty full on."

Football has "gotten big" on Rance in the past. He famously thought about leaving the game at the peak of his powers. As the 2014 season wound down, his team was headed for finals and he was headed for his first of three All Australian guernseys, but he was ready to walk away from the AFL. His mind was made up, in fact. He would leave after 2015, the final year of his contract.

"The reason I was thinking about leaving was my balance in my life. I get very consumed with the guys here. I love getting better, I love the competition, but I felt like I was investing so much time and energy here that I'd get home and have nothing left to give to my family.

"It's funny—the thing that was forcing me away was the same thing keeping me here. I stayed for the guys. There's no other people I'd want to share success with. I think if I were to win a premiership with this side, it would mean so much because of the struggle, because of the hardships you've gone through and those questioning moments."

Last season had its share of such moments. As the team collapsed and the losses gathered a dark momentum, Rance questioned his judgement. As he played throughout those winter months knowing finals would not be part of his year, he second-guessed his decision to stay. He experienced regret.

"It probably was one of the toughest years from an emotional perspective. On field, I put up some of the best stats I've ever put up, but it did cross my mind: 'What have I done? What's the point of this? What am I even doing here? Am I just going to be put through four of five years of pain?' Those thoughts did cross my mind."

When it was over, he was a frustrated onlooker during the finals. He even came back to pre-season training with a "negative mindset" that was hard to shake. "Honestly, it took a couple of weeks for that to melt away. The bitterness was still lingering. I pinged my hamstring early on, too, but it was almost a blessing in disguise, to step back and take stock and take the hands off the wheel for a little bit. For so long I was like, 'This is my performance standard, I've got to keep driving it, if I don't drive others then what's my purpose here?' So it was good to stand back and see that, one, this team can function without me, and two, there are other guys taking control of their own careers. And I probably didn't see that because I always have my head down working."

The poor performance of the team over the past 12 months he puts down to negativity and a lack of confidence. When you're losing, the absence of belief grows stronger, and it snowballs. "You don't believe you're worthy or have anything to offer the team. We had all these talented young guys and a talented list, on paper, but the sense of belief handicapped everyone. It was like we had a V8 engine but we were only running off two or three cylinders."

Instead they worked on showing care, and faith, espousing the notion that every player on the list has talents and is at the club for a reason—chosen for some specific weapon they possess. "We've spouted that before, but this is the first year the younger guys believed it—'I am here, I am talented, I can produce some fantastic football'," he says. "And it's not just about the performance either. It's about the individual and saying, 'We care that you feel valued'. Whether it's a guy who's getting a game in the AFL, or a guy making us laugh in the change rooms, it's that culture that teams always talk about but is hard to produce."

Rance is a vice-captain this year, and was in the wider leadership group last year, but in truth he has always been a leader. It was one of the first traits he modelled as a young man.

He remembers playing under-18 representative football in Western Australia, and an ex-AFL player spoke to his group. He doesn't remember who it was, but he remembers what was said. The former player said he wasn't the most talented footballer, but he got noticed because of his voice, because he was a leader on field and directed others, and that leading made him better in turn.

"I was like, oh wow, I'd never thought of that. Everyone thinks it's all about your running ability, your disposal efficiency. That'll make you a good player, but what'll make you a *great* player is the ability to help others as well. That really stuck with me. And it was one of the things a lot of the recruiters saw in me. It was how I saw the game, read the game, and put others in good positions, too. I've always been outspoken, enthusiastic, mucking around... but driven."

Driving others is something Rance does well. On the training track, he will pantomime movements to the younger players and deliver a lecture: "Listen up!" he'll roar. "Do we understand with all our kicking drills, the focus is look forward, look lateral? Look forward—are there any hit ups? No? Look lateral—if the option isn't there, look for a handball receive. Got it? Let's go again!" He will stare down his teammates before a match, as they walk towards the race, screaming "You put on this jumper it's a contract! It's a damn contract!"

You will also see him pop out of hiding, from inside a wheelie bin, to terrify a passing teammate. And you will see him dancing in his underwear in the Subiaco change rooms after a victory in the rain, wearing only sunglasses and black Y-fronts, singing along to Roy Orbison's *Pretty Woman*, with a boom box on his shoulder. There is a video clip of him online, soaping up the change room floors and then—slicked up and laughing like a maniac—turning the space into a greasy Speedo slip and slide.

He is, according to his captain, "a rare unit".

Rance has embarked on a carpentry apprenticeship. He has earned his pilot's licence. He tries his hand at things he might like, discovers what he enjoys and doesn't, and what he is passionate about and isn't. The thing that kept him around the football club was the improvement he could see in the young players who would come to him asking for help with their footwork, or in reviewing game tape. He got a buzz out of it and thought that professional teaching might be a good fit. So he set up, with others, a school—The Academy, in Essendon—for kids who want to improve their footy but also complete an education with real world skills. On his days off, he's at The Academy, planning its growth, talking to parents and jostling with enrolment numbers. He is across everything.

On the footy field, the thing he most loves is similar: the sense that he is everywhere. "You feel like everywhere you move, you're stopping the play. You're getting the spoil, the intercept possession. It's like you're not even worried about your forward. You know he's there, and you know there are times you have to beat him, but you're reading the play so well. You feel like you're on rails, like the game is being played just for you."

As for specific moments, he craves that long searching kick into his area, when his contest represents the pivot point, where he is the fulcrum against which the play shifts. In repelling an attack, Rance doesn't so much influence the play as completely change its direction—creation and negation at once. "You're standing in front of your player, you see the play coming out in front of you, and you just go and attack and take the intercept mark and switch it out the other way. And it goes forward," he says. "It gives me a chance to say, 'This is my time. This is why I'm here'."

///////////

In the opposition meeting upstairs, discussion centres on the importance of the Eagles stoppage dominance through Sam Mitchell and Andrew Gaff, on their drop off marking players in Jeremy McGovern, Elliott Yeo and Tom Barrass, and of their premier forward, reigning Coleman medallist Kennedy.

A passage of play is shown on screen. It starts with a mark to Yeo, who finds Mitchell in space, who finds Gaff in greater space, who finds Luke Shuey running forward, who hits Kennedy on a lead. The chain of play is clean, unhurried and unbroken—completely unsullied by contest or contact. "This is the way they want to play," says Rutten. "They're a good team when you let them do as they like."

The idea then, is to catch them on the hop, as St Kilda did for much of their game a week earlier. In the first half of that match, the Saints had 13 entries into their forward 50, and scored 12 times. Rutten shows the room what it looks like: a clip of a Saints player spoiling a marking contest, bringing the ball to ground, and launching a quick counter attack through a single handball and quick short pass—two possessions that clear the congestion and force the ball into attack, putting the Eagles defence on the back foot.

The most important point for the Tigers to retain—all over the field—is to "halve" contests in the air. A win in marking contests is not necessary, but a loss is unacceptable. The Tigers simply cannot allow the Eagles to pluck the ball from the sky. The slide says as much: AERIAL POWER!

The team will need to crash packs and spoil hard. Depending on the moment and the conditions, the team will need to consider "bludgeon handballs" that force the ball forward. If they are forced to kick under severe pressure in the wet, "dirty balls" (little scrubbing kicks that force the ball forward along the ground) are acceptable. Whatever happens, the side needs to give its running players a chance, and that does not include bombing long into the arms of McGovern and Yeo.

The team will practise all of this today at training, including a drill called "Houli Kick AKA Don't Kick It To Rance Drill." In this context, "Kick It

To Rance" refers to chipping sideways in the backline, short kicks that were common last year between Rance and Astbury and Grimes, but which are forsaken this year for a more direct game style. It's an offensive drill, where the coaches act as defenders. It trains the players for those situations when they need to kick the ball long down the line, and is designed to test the tall forwards at Richmond, and their ability to mark, but, more importantly, spoil.

///////////

It's 27 degrees and the sky is blue on Saturday at the MCG, but rain clouds are hovering over Geelong and headed for the city, meaning Richmond versus West Coast could turn into a wet weather slog. The Eagles banner is torn to shreds by harsh winds in the pre-game period. The inclement weather could get here fast. In the change rooms, the coaches are talking about tackling—specifically the AFL decision to revise the interpretation of the holding the ball rule on the eve of round three of the season. The new version, they say, allows the umpires to give the player with the ball more leeway, more chance to exercise "prior opportunity"—thus making the interpretation more forgiving. It also tweaks the rule to give lenience to players "attempting" to get rid of the ball. Taken together it's a massive shift, a chop and change approach that the men in the room—Livingstone, Hill, Balme and Hardwick—find bemusing.

The game the previous night, a one-point victory by Collingwood over Sydney, was notable for the high number of tackles and the low number of free kicks which, combined, meant long rolling scrums with no reward. "I don't know what they're doing, honestly," says Hardwick. "One hundred tackles a game turns AFL into a maul. If it wasn't a close match it would have been diabolical to watch."

Soon the players are in the room and Hardwick is ready to reveal his picture of the week. After the rubber shark and the butterfly cocoon, it has become the coach's new pre-game motivational device this year.

"The unveiling," he says. "Alex, you're up."

Rance stands and walks to the whiteboard, but Hardwick smirks and throws up his arm before he can get there, one hand clutching a red piece of paper. "Whoa!" he yells. "Not so fast!"

The room erupts in laughter and applause. Apparently in training on

Thursday, Rance turned wild, buffeting teammates in drills and yelling commands more than a little too loudly. He had to be calmed down, and so Hardwick "sent him off", and they joked at the time that Rance had been given a "red card". Now he is red-faced, but happy.

The picture is turned over. It's a photo of New Zealand Rugby Union player Richard McCaw, captain of the All Blacks and one of the world's best open side flankers.

"The thing he does every week is pride himself on this," Hardwick says, tapping a few words in capital letters on the whiteboard: FIGHT FOR RESPECT.

"He still maintains the greatest thing that ever happened to him was the 2007 World Cup loss. Because it got him stronger up here, in the head, and gave him that mental resilience. He always comes to play, no matter how he's going, because of this," Hardwick says, tapping more words: GROUND ZERO. START AGAIN.

"The game doesn't know what you did last week. It has no idea. It doesn't care. All it knows is what you're going to do going forward."

He taps the next line: GET INVOLVED EARLY—EMBRACE COLLISION ZONE.

"His job was to get in and see where the ball was going and create that scrap. It's the only way our games are similar. I need you doing the same thing."

He taps again: KEEP GETTING UP.

"You're going to win some contests and lose some."

Once more he points to the wall: G.A.B.

"The thing I love about him is he said, 'I want to be a Great All Black'. And every one of you should want to become a great Richmond man. It takes balls though, to play to your strengths. I want to see you go for your marks," he says, pointing to tall forward Todd Elton. "I want to see you run and carry," he says, looking at Bachar Houli. "I want so see you win the ball and get it going our way," he says, waving at Reece Conca. "I want to see it all."

⁄⁄⁄⁄⁄⁄⁄⁄

In the end, Rance doesn't play on Kennedy. Astbury is given the task, and performs well, restricting the gun forward to two goals and little influence.

Rance plays on the roaming tall, Jack Darling, and the Tiger defender has an indifferent first half and a dominant second half. Throughout the contest he shows glimpses of his talent, scooping up impossible half volleys, ghosting in front of targets to take intercept marks, contorting his body at ground level and surging out of defence. He also stumbles, giving away a free kick here, spoiling what he could have marked, at one point facing that difficult decision—to guard your man or leave him—and choosing the wrong option.

He sings the song in the rooms afterwards, in the circle, arm-in-arm with Astbury and McIntosh. Then he slumps into a white plastic chair, sodden from the late afternoon rain, with snippets of wet grass on his white boots. He runs his hand over the back of Dustin Martin's head, and pats Dion Prestia's thigh. He unpeels the strapping tape from his wrists.

Today was not that game "on rails" that he savours, or at least it was but only in patches. Several commentators will place him in the top five players on the field but Rance was simply not at his imperious best. It doesn't matter. Not when you're part of a team that was given no chance of success this season and has just won three straight games to start the year.

"That's up there as one of the most hard-fought and rewarding games," he says, grinning. "You bust your arse in those conditions. I was looking at the scoreboard in the last quarter and it was eight minutes down and I was thinking 'Goodness me, we've spent a lot of energy early'. But for our boys—the young boys especially—to just show up and fight it out, I can't give enough love to them."

Hardwick gives his speech soon after, and the players depart. Rance though, sits alone among the lingering coaches, leafing through sheets of statistics. He isn't looking at his own numbers. He is looking at the other defenders.

Reece Conca, in perhaps his best game for the club, had 25 composed possessions. McIntosh laid six tackles. David Astbury made 10 spoils. "Gee that's a good game," Rance says, about no one specifically, and to no-one in particular. Gingerly he limps down the stepped seating, opens the door and walks out of the room, headed to recovery at Punt Road. He is the last player to leave.

14

WE TALK TO THEM

Seven young footballers sit at a large circular table in a small room just off the main administrative floor of the Richmond Football Club.

The players are mobile forward Callum Moore, tall defender Ryan Garthwaite, small forward Daniel Rioli, rookie ruck/forward Mabior Chol, running defender Oleg Markov, and goal sneaks Tyson Stengle and Shai Bolton.

All are first and second year players, and laid out before them on the table inside Meeting Room 2 are Carman muesli bars, bottles of Gatorade, boxes of Up & Go, Chobani yoghurt pouches, trays of rice crackers, low carb protein bars, bananas, pretzels and a handful of Allen's snakes.

Also present are Kylie Andrew, the club dietician, and Matt Pearce, the head trainer—both ready to offer advice and answer questions on the subject of the day: "recovery nutrition". Bronwyn Doig, the learning and development manager at the club, is also here.

"OK boys," says Andrew, "what we're here for is to help you recover quickly after a training session or a game, because you've always got to play a game next week, or train the next day. So, one thing we need to talk about is *repair*. What do you think you need for repair?"

Markov says protein. And he's right. Garthwaite wonders if carbohydrates will help, too, and they will, says Andrew, but repairing stretched and agitated muscle fibres comes back mostly to protein.

And what do they need to refuel? Carbs.

Clearly, they also need to hydrate, but this group has already been taught about fluid intake in a previous session. Today is about examining the typical foods they might consume immediately after a match. With that in mind, Andrew, the dietician, has also placed dozens of small rectangular pieces of paper on the table, each one with a photo of an item of food or drink, along with the weight, in grams, of carbohydrates and protein in each one. Later in the season, she will take the younger players on group tours of the Coles supermarket on Swan Street, to teach them how to read the nutritional information on the foods they buy, but for today's exercise the flash cards will suffice.

"What I want you guys to do is work out a recovery regime post game," says Andrew. "The amount you need to consider is *always* 20 grams of protein—it doesn't matter who you are or how big you are, you need that. And then you need at least one gram of carbohydrates per kilogram you weigh."

That means a 75-kilo player like Rioli needs to ingest fewer carbs than a 91-kilo figure like Chol, but Andrews says it's easier to just say that every player should have at least 20 grams of protein and 100 grams of carbohydrates. It simplifies matters. "So, what I want you to do," she says, "is take these cards, and put them in front of you until they add up to 20 grams of protein, and 100 grams of carbs."

The players busily add and subtract, and talk about what they like and don't, hence what will work for them as a weekly ritual. They weigh up liquid options and solids, and think out loud.

"I can't do crackers," says Rioli, "they hurt my teeth."

"Good maths man," says Chol, looking at Markov's work.

"But I hate bananas," says Stengle.

Garthwaite assembles his desired post-game menu quickly. A handful of snakes (25 grams of carbohydrates), a banana (20 grams of carbohydrates), a bottle of Gatorade (40 grams of carbohydrates) and a protein shake (25 grams of carbohydrates, and 25 grams of protein).

Bolton has chosen a banana and a bottle of Gatorade. "So, you've got 75 of carbs there," Doig says. "How are we going to get some extra carbs and protein?" Bolton likes the taste of Up & Go (which has 35 grams of carbohydrates and 20 of protein). Done.

"Do we have to eat it straight after a game?" asks Chol. They do. "But what if you're not hungry?"

"Then you've got to drink it instead," Andrews answers. "Choose liquid options like Gatorade—and force it down. If you do this right away, without waiting, you'll recover quicker. You're putting the same petrol in but getting more value for your dollar by putting it in straight away."

What's more, she adds, they'll need to consume that same amount again two hours later. The players groan like high school students assigned a pop quiz, but are told how adhering to a simple and habitual diet will help them overcome the fatigue they're experiencing right now, and also to build the muscle mass they are lacking.

Doig speaks up. "This goes back to something 'Fly' (VFL and development coach Craig McRae) was saying recently, that you guys can give yourselves a competitive advantage over the older boys by doing these things. If there's an older player not doing it, and you are, then you're going to be better prepared. It's all about performance."

It's an interesting comment from Doig, because she is perhaps the one football department employee at the club that people outside the club would least know, and yet she is responsible for the players' performance in a broad and profound way.

Doig, a petite young blonde woman who runs marathons and smiles consistently, helps organise all of the lessons like this, to drive the players' football education. She explains this later in her tiny but incredibly neat office in the geographic centre of the Tigerland complex, which has a window onto a busy hallway but no natural light.

"My job?" she responds. "The stock standard answer is that the coaches teach them how to play footy and be the best athlete they can be. My job is the other side of it, taking a holistic approach to their overall development as a person. The idea is that the on-field and off-field complement each other. If one is going well, the other can, too. If one isn't, the other won't. It's like a dad and mum thing, although I prefer 'older sister'."

For the first through fourth year players, much of what she organises is based on life skills, everything from financial management to sleeping habits. With the older players, she begins to focus on what their future looks like after football, in a few years or a decade. Every season each player must work with her to write an off-field "player development plan", which is part of a robust discussion with their line coach or their "care coach"—the latter being a new development at Richmond, designed to make sure each player has at least one senior mind they can lean on—a mentor with whom they can check in regularly.

Players first meet with Doig, though, on draft night, which for her is primarily about contacting them and their families, welcoming them, and telling them what the next two days look like, "because we get them in here straight away."

Sometimes they live in Melbourne, and so are driven to the club by their mum and dad. Sometimes they come from country Victoria and drive down themselves. Often they have to fly in from interstate—a daunting thing to do at a moment's notice, no matter how much they understand that possibility when heading into the draft day lottery.

Bolton, for instance, is *very* young. Had he been born 20 days later, right now he would still be playing in the under-18s competition in Perth. There was understandably some real concern expressed by his mother about the move. Her son had never left Western Australia.

"So Luke Williams, one of our recruiters, and Daniel Rioli, flew to Perth, picked up Shai and brought him back to Melbourne," says Doig. "It was about making him feel comfortable in that transition, and then having Daniel as a mentor or older brother. They have formed a beautiful bond as a result. And Daniel very much looks out for him."

Once in Melbourne, Doig helps get them settled. The first week or two, the new recruits usually stay with another player, so they can understand what it's like to be a professional footballer. After the most recent draft, that was difficult because some of the senior players were moving or renovating or having children, so young Indigenous players Bolton and Stengle moved in with new development coach Xavier Clarke, staying with him for nearly two months. The two boys stayed together in a serviced apartment joined to one occupied by Clarke, or "X", as he is called at the club.

"X helped make sure they were getting here on time, eating properly, making sure they were going to bed at a reasonable hour, all that stuff, because none of the young boys are used to that kind of structure."

They eventually moved in with their host families, which is a complicated thing to arrange, but made as simple as possible by Doig. Some hosts are based on a form of mates' network. Rioli, for instance, lives with Hardwick and his wife Danielle in Bentleigh. Chol lives with Danielle's best friend Anna, and her husband Roger, and their family in Elsternwick. Rookie ruckman Ivan Soldo lives with another of Danielle's best friends, Amanda and Cam, and their two girls, in Ormond. "He's been there three years and I don't think he'll ever move out," Doig laughs. Both Bolton and Stengle now live with host families in Bentleigh. "So there's this great little geographic pocket of support in the south-east," Doig says. "Dimma says he gets home sometimes and finds Tyson on his couch. 'Righto mate, just let yourself in'."

Accommodation for Jack Graham (from South Australia) and Garthwaite (from country Victoria) was found through the Tigers' member database, which is the usual method, when the 'network' can't deliver. Doig narrows down the potential hosts using several variables: they have to have been a member of the club for 10 years, they have to live within 12 kilometres of the facility, they should ideally be aged 40 or older. "That dials it down to a group of niche people," she says. "It's advertised to them all, which this year was a couple of hundred. If they're interested, they fill in a pre-screening form. I go through each one and see if they're ticking the right boxes. I call them, email them, and short list the group to about six."

Then the club's integrity officer, Steve Wyatt, who also works in player development, goes out to meet the families and perform a site assessment. They need to know what the house is like, and sample the dynamic of the home. "You get a very good feel for people face to face. It's like applying for a job—you look at the CV and it's amazing, but you still need that extra contact."

Even then, the club cannot say if the hosts will be needed, because they don't yet know how many players they will draft from interstate or regional Victoria. The families are left on tenterhooks, then once the players are drafted, Doig and Wyatt sit down with the recruiters to discuss which young man will fit best in which household. "This player might need a family who'll leave them alone, because they're very independent. This one will need a group who'll embrace them and bring them into their family. They're all different—we haven't got it wrong yet."

Garthwaite moved in with a family in Glen Iris. The mother is a physiotherapist and the father a dentist, and they have three boys about the same age as Garthwaite, who looks like he could be their fourth son.

Graham stays with a couple who have been foster parents in the past. But Jack is quite independent—his girlfriend moved with him, and they have their own quarters in the house—bedroom, bathroom and living area.

"Bruce and Maria are like that cool mum and dad, slash aunty and uncle, and take them out for dinner every week and give them some exposure to Melbourne."

Doig also takes each player out to help them buy furniture, using a club connection at Harvey Norman. "They pick their bed and mattress, and it's all very exciting. But it takes them around six months to feel settled in Melbourne, getting used to traffic, or not being with their families, and the rhythms of the club."

Homesickness is a factor. The host families do what they can but Doig tries to be as clear as possible with the players that they should let her know if they are struggling. "Because sometimes there is this fear, 'If I tell the club I'm homesick, and go home, and I'm going to miss a game, is it going to be frowned upon?' So we create an environment where they're supported and they know it. If they're having a bad day, sometimes they need someone to talk to, and generally that's Steve and me. If it persists, we send them home for a long weekend, a couple of days, or get their families over here, just for them to feel refreshed and settled again."

Wyatt, a former policeman and trainer at the Police Academy, also acts as "bad cop", educating the players about risky behaviours, from dangerous driving to navigating nightclubs. The AFL provides its own education, too, around illicit drugs, the role of WADA and ASADA, and gambling in sport. But there is so much for the new brigade to understand. Cultural awareness training. Mental health. First aid. Media. Financial education through the AFLPA induction program. They have a barrister come to the club to walk them through relationships and sexual consent. They do social media training around club expectations—but also online safety.

"If someone is targeting you, here's what you can do. Here's how to make your accounts private, if you want. We talk to them about not worrying what other people say—that what matters is what we think, what they think, what their family thinks. It's continual education about blocking out noise."

The club can't discourage them from wading into the digital ether, because it can be such a positive tool for young and relatively famous men. "Brandon Ellis is a classic example. His business—Uncle Jack watches—started up on Instagram and has gone gangbusters," Doig says. "But they need to understand that in the public domain everyone's an expert, and everyone has an opinion, and some of them are going to put hurtful things up there.

It's difficult. All we can do is make them aware, stay in touch and keep educating."

A large whiteboard rests behind Doig, which shows just how many balls she is trying to juggle at once. Next to the name of every single player on the list is a short overview of their main external pursuit.

Anthony Miles is pursuing a Bachelor of Arts and Teaching. Shane Edwards is training to be a firefighter—something he was inspired to do after Wyatt asked the Metropolitan Fire Brigade to visit the club. Ben Lennon is studying a Bachelor of Criminology, because he wants to join Victoria Police after football. Shaun Grigg is a franchise owner in the Spud Bar restaurant chain, but is also interested in volunteering in a Salvation Army soup kitchen once a month. Next to the name Connor Menadue is the word "Bookie", but Doig laughs. "That is a complete stitch up. I have rubbed that out many times and it keeps reappearing. Connor's actually got an interest in recruiting, and might go out this year and watch talent, report back."

Dylan Grimes owns the Mt Macedon Winery, having purchased the property with his partner Elisha last year. She lives there full-time and he commutes back and forth, then works there on his off days. "They're up to 20-odd weddings for the year, and they do lunches, have a cottage on Air BnB. Gorgeous. Beautiful property."

Markov wants to pursue car restoration, and is doing work experience with a company on his day off. Dustin Martin is starting a business course. So many others are completing building certificates at TAFE, including Taylor Hunt, Jason Castagna, Jacob Townsend and Jayden Short, but also Vlastuin, Lloyd and Riewoldt.

There's another list on the whiteboard, too. Doig and Wyatt asked the playing group to consider things they might want to try in life, but haven't just yet. And so there are reminders for Doig to inquire about how to get a boat licence, or a motorbike licence. One player wants to learn guitar. An older player suggested etiquette lessons for the younger players, and not at all as a joke: "These guys go to a lot of functions, and they have three different knives and forks and don't know which one to start with, so there's table manners, but also networking," Doig says. "Even just learning how to introduce yourself."

Doig has posted sign-up sheets on her door. According to the signed names, a truck licence is appealing to Kamdyn McIntosh, Toby Nankervis,

Miles, Graham and Townsend. "And someone has added Ben Rutten to that list," Doig says. "But I'm pretty sure that's a massive stitch up again, because his nickname is 'Truck'."

A forklift licence seems a good idea to Miles, Short, Townsend and Lambert. There are hunters in the group—including Rioli, Astbury, Grimes and Lloyd—but others would like to try, too, and so Short, Garthwaite, Griffiths, Bolton, Caddy and Lambert each wrote their name under the A4 sign up sheet for obtaining a gun licence.

Doig's phone rings. It's the medical team downstairs. Young Western Australian defender Nathan Broad has been injured. It sounds like a niggle but later turns out to be a serious long-term shoulder injury requiring surgery. Doig plays a part, too, in managing injuries.

If a player gets injured on match day, for instance, she provides support, as someone to lean on both physically and emotionally. She will drive them to get scans, and contact partners and parents to keep them in the loop. Shane Edwards hurt his hip on the weekend, and that information went directly from the medical team to the interchange bench to the coach's box to Doig to Edwards' parents. Chol copped a bad knock to the head that same day in the VFL, and Doig ran from the MCG back to the game at Punt Road, then helped Chol's host mum get into the change rooms so she could hear first-hand from the club doctors how to care for the young man in the days that followed his concussion.

"I've done many ambulance trips on game day, unfortunately," Doig says. "And again, it's about letting the parents know that they're okay, and that someone is with their son."

Last season, when Kane Lambert suffered broken ribs and a punctured lung during a night game, Doig sat beside him in the ambulance as it sped through the dark Friday night to hospital. "Kane, bless him, he's such a gentleman. I remember when we got to the hospital, the poor guy can hardly breathe, and the team there said 'We're really busy tonight, so we'll get you a chair, can you just sit here for a minute?' And Kane was like, 'Bron, would you like the seat?' I said, 'Buddy, thank you so much, but I'm not injured, *you* need to sit down'. But that's the kind of guy he is, so caring and lovely."

Doig never imagined herself in this role, although her tertiary study was a bachelor of psychology and social studies. Her work began at Etihad Stadium in sponsorship, events and marketing. Then she spent time with the AFL in a corporate partnerships role. She's worked at Richmond for five years. "A lot of this job is life experience and the ability to build trusting relationships."

Her phone rings again now, and so she heads downstairs to wait outside the medicos' room for Broad. She will accompany him to scans, where he will learn that his popped AC joint will require a lengthy recovery and place him on the club's long term injury list. It's a sad moment.

She had a happier one near the end of the Eagles game. She was standing beneath the MCG as it rained and poured and the Tigers stormed home. She watched from inside the strapping room, with the volunteer doormen and boot studders and water boys, as Daniel Rioli kicked the winning goal.

Doig could barely contain her smile, and not just for the second-year player, but because she knew his family was in town, that they had flown down from the Tiwi Islands off the coast of the Northern Territory. Doig brought them to training, and took them to the Tigerland Superstore on Brunton Avenue, and got them all jumpers with Rioli's number 17 on the back.

"I dare say they'll be going nuts in the stands," she giggled at the game, as Rioli banged home the sealer on a sodden afternoon. Then she choked up, just for a second. "It's moments like that when you feel like you've won a Grand Final. To see young kids like that have an impact on the game. It's amazing."

15

PERFECT PRACTICE

The purple haze of early evening gives way to the night—a black sky and a star that might be Venus and big yellow lights on tall metal towers and a football field glowing green. Training seems somehow quicker, lighter, more urgent in the evening. The voices seem louder. In full ground drills the players scream and skate across the surface, and the autumn chill in the air begins to bite.

This feels like suburban football. It feels local. It feels like senior league football might have felt only a few decades ago, when footballers were still part-timers who held down jobs by day and trained afterwards.

The scene here and now is quite simply *different* from the specialised and compartmentalised morning and afternoon training sessions of the AFL team, because this is the VFL team, and the VFL players are vanishing into the dark pockets between the light towers, stirring up the dirt on the edge of the field, which muddies and drifts with the falling mist. It even smells like football training.

There is an urgency here that would please Craig McRae, the former Brisbane Lions forward and now Richmond's VFL coach. The three-time premiership player looks on, leaning on the chain link fence around the oval while the players do run throughs and light handball work, fielding ground balls and practising that all-important ability to be clean, and he smiles.

He spoke to these second-string players about putting their best foot forward only half an hour ago, in the Graeme Richmond room. He talked to them about the drills they would do, which are named for some of the regular players in the Tigers team fielded in the next tier state competition. *The Silva Kick. Ballard Hands. Beasley Press.* Before training McRae also put a quote from the American basketball player Kobe Bryant on the auditorium screen, and let it sit there for them to digest: "The key is not the will to win... Everybody has that. It is the will to *prepare* to win that is important."

On the eve of the VFL season, McRae talked about establishing the right kind of culture, the correct high standards, a real connection between one another, and winning habits among them all. He established that his imperative was to see such behaviour on the training track before seeing it anywhere else. He may as well have quoted Ron Barassi, who once told his players at North Melbourne: "'Practice makes perfect' is bullshit. Only *perfect* practice makes perfect."

The guys here tonight come from Leagues throughout Victoria. There are players from "the amateurs" (the Victorian Amateur Football Association), but also the Southern Football League and the Northern Football League, from Leagues in Gippsland and the Goulburn Valley, from the Victorian highlands to the western districts.

Daniel Hull, the Football Operations Manager for the VFL team, brings the players in to Richmond each season. Ordinarily he interviews around 50 players. This year they retained some they liked from last year, and so he spoke to fewer, perhaps 30.

"We go through a process of recruiting strategically to get what we need to complement the AFL list," Hull says, standing near the bench as the players trot around the oval. "If we've got a lot of young AFL forwards, which we do, well, we probably don't need many VFL forwards."

Still, they look at a lot of players. The VFL pre-season began with 40 guys trying out, training with the team, seeing if they had enough tricks to impress in drills and circle work. That group was later whittled down to the lucky 24 on the ground now. But not all of them will play every week.

"It's tough," says McRae. "They all do a full pre-season, and they're all desperate to play. We like to give everyone at least one game to prove themselves. And to give them that chance to play in Richmond colours. It might be the only chance they get."

The number of AFL listed players—including highly rated draftees and speculative rookies—who join the VFL team every week is between 10 and 18, meaning of the 24 VFL players running around the ground right now, four to 12 of them will be needed in any given week. The rest will go back to their regular club, playing for University Blues or Blackburn or Shepparton. "They understand that," McRae says. "A big part of our recruiting is getting really hungry young players."

This VFL club doesn't bring in ex-AFL players or bigger-bodied men to physically support the young and speculative and project players on the Tigers' AFL list. They find players who haven't yet been exposed to "the level", says McRae, and they offer them an elite environment with training programs and facilities. "They're untapped, so you see quick growth. They make it easy on you as a coach. They rock up to training energetic, on their toes, wanting to learn."

Some aspire to playing AFL, and so they can get a close look at a player like Kane Lambert, who is one of the hardest workers at the club but, more importantly, was also once a Northern Blues VFL player. Given a rookie list lifeline by Richmond in 2014, he was upgraded to the senior list in 2015, and has since become a reliable in and under midfielder, and has in recent weeks shut down Collingwood's young tyro Adam Treloar and West Coast's Brownlow medallist Sam Mitchell.

Lambert is the kind of player who sees an off-season not as time to recharge but as time to get ahead, hiring a personal trainer to put on size and work on explosive actions. Even now, on days off from the club, he finds a way to squeeze in some cross training—perhaps swimming, and always some extra weights. "You want to do everything you can, and not put a foot wrong. I just want to get the absolute best out of myself," he says. "I'm smaller, I'm slower, and there are going to be better, more skilful players than me, but I don't want anyone to work harder than me."

Whether the VFL players here reach the same heights or not, McRae is simply glad to give them a chance to be seen, and to improve, and to be *involved*. The VFL coach is—in the words of the club CEO Brendon Gale— "a connector."

McRae encourages even those who miss out on playing for the VFL Tigers to come and watch them from the bench. He asks their families to join them in the rooms afterwards. And during the team's early week game review meeting, McRae tries to screen local footage of the guys playing in their own team, for St Kevin's or Colac for instance, to spotlight just one positive moment. He also gets match reports from the lower level coaches.

"I always like to highlight at least one of the local players, so they still feel we care about them even when they're not playing with us. They might have different game plans but they can still develop the same habits," he says. "It's not easy, because the longer the season goes the less they might feel like part of it, especially if they haven't played. There'll be guys out there who won't play with us at all this season—it's just the reality."

McRae goes out now to conduct full ground drills, leaving me with Shane Harris, 55, a volunteer who hitches a ride from Preston to Punt Road Oval every Tuesday and Thursday night, and then on game day, so he can "help the team". Harris wears the light blue Richmond training top of the coaches, along with club shorts and cap. He has a love of football that is pure. He began coming to Richmond four years ago, to help the VFL property manager.

"I collect all the jumpers and do all the washing," says Harris. "Love it, mate, love it. It's fantastic. My first night coming down to help, I was really hesitant, pretty intimidated by these AFL guys a bit. But they're no different from you or me. From day one they've opened their arms."

He tells me his story. He grew up in a Carlton household, but when he was seven his mother asked him who he wanted to support. Harris chose the team that had just won the 1969 Grand Final, Richmond. "And that was it. My first Grand Final I went to was '73. Dad had tickets to '74, but he wouldn't take me because I didn't do my homework. I was pissed right off. I went to 1980 and '82 as well. Been a bit quiet since then."

Like all Richmond supporters of the last three decades, his highlights are few and far between. He loved the Tigers' last finals victory, in September 2001, against Carlton. But he enjoyed the victory before that, in 1995 against Essendon, more so. He was sitting close to the spot on the wing where full-back Scott Turner flattened Gary O'Donnell. He had a clear view of the Stuart Maxfield hip and shoulder that broke the jaw of David Grenvold. He remembers each of Matthew Knights' three loping, bouncing runs that ended in goals. But he also remembers what happened after both those victories.

After Essendon, he sat at Waverley Park and watched Geelong dismantle Richmond to the tune of 89 points, and with a few thousand others he sang "Oh we're from Tigerland" in the last quarter in the rain—a funereal dirge but also a thank you for a great season. And after the Carlton win, Harris caught a bus to Brisbane only to see his team lose to the eventual premiers, the unstoppable Lions. (Craig McRae was only 18, and had 11 touches and kicked two points in the 68-point Tiger loss.) "It's been a while since we won a final. 16 years," Harris says. "But good times are coming. You can tell. I'd be pissed off if we didn't win a final this year."

Harris has a tattoo of a rose on the inside of his right forearm. When he holds his hands together in front of him, he looks down to his right and sees it, and the three words inked into its branches: "Mum", "Glenn" and "Dad". His mum died 25 years ago, his brother Glenn drank himself to death shortly after, and his dad passed away 11 years ago. Harris found his lifeless father on the floor at home, and his life disintegrated. He had a breakdown. Couldn't find work or a place to live. "I tried to commit suicide," he says, touching the rubber Beyond Blue band on his wrist. "I was in a bad way. I couldn't get a job. Lived in shocking boarding homes all over the place. Shared a four-bedroom home with 20 other people—five single mattresses on a floor. Coburg. Thornbury. Reservoir. I had a massive breakdown, and I was from here to that gate away from walking in front of a train at Reservoir station. A little voice said, 'Don't do it', and I didn't."

The entire time, his only constant has been football. Helping the Richmond VFL squad is only recent—he has been involved with the Preston Football Club for 38 years. He was made a life member five years ago. He works for *The Big Issue*, too, and talks to kids about homelessness. He's seemingly enthusiastic and positive about all things. When Harris says something is "fantastic" he breaks the word into two—"FAN-*tastic*"—and shakes his head afterwards. He means it. Like when he found a decent boarding home. "Clean, safe, spacious," he says. "It was fantastic. FAN-*tastic!*"

He wanders back into the rooms now, beckoning me to join him beyond the sign that reads: "No Public Access Beyond This Point". He strolls down "Premiership Walk", a corridor in the footy department with a photographic timeline of dates and deeds. The flags of 1920 and 1921 are accompanied by a photo of Vic "Flippa" Thorp, the best full-back of his era. The 1932 and 1934 premierships are offset by a staring image of star full forward Jack "Skinny" Titus, who kicked 970 goals for the club, at a stunning average of 3.3 per game. On the wall the 1943 cup—created by the AFL in the 2000s[8]—sits next to a photo of the man whose statue dominates the outside of the club, and who needs little introduction, Jack "Captain Blood" Dyer. For 1967, 1969, 1973, 1974 and 1980 we have the faces of Tom Hafey, Francis Bourke, Royce Hart, Kevin Sheedy and Kevin Bartlett. Harris skips past them all to show me something more important: the room where the boots are cleaned and the jumpers are washed and dried.

People who never played football, or watched it, or wanted to, often have a view of the game—both at a local level but particularly at this professional level—which is tainted by notions of toxic masculinity or unbridled ego, born perhaps of some schoolyard bully who also happened to be a star full-forward, or the drunken antics of a bona fide AFL superstar on the nightly news.

But in truth football clubs are among the most accepting environments in our society—the most welcoming and undiscriminating of community centres. No-one who has been to an under-9s pie night would disagree. Anyone who has worked a canteen or offered to goal umpire or built a banner understands the communal effort. Football clubs rely upon volunteers—and volunteers rely upon clubs.

On weekends Harris gets here three hours before the game starts. He watches the play, runs drinks to the athletes, then stays afterwards packing up, cleaning up. If the AFL team is playing at the MCG, he walks there next. He was in the southern stand last weekend, directly behind an unfathomable Daniel Rioli goal from the boundary line. "SEN-*sational!*" he says. "I thought the place was gonna erupt."

If the team plays interstate, like this weekend, Harris will walk down the terrace-lined streets of this former slum suburb, perhaps to the *London Tavern* or the *Vaucluse* or the *Swan* or the *Rising Sun*, to watch the game at a pub with others from the VFL support squad. On this beautifully crisp Thursday night, it is clear football clubs are not called "clubs" for nothing.

"My best friends in the world are from footy clubs. They're like my family now. Coming here is huge," says Harris. "If I didn't come down and do this—if it wasn't for Richmond—I think I'd be dead now. I come down here

---

8   The first Premiership Cup was presented to Melbourne's John Beckwith in 1959. In the early 2000s the AFL agreed that clubs could create Cups for premierships won pre-1959, at their cost. All clubs have created Cups to represent premierships pre-1959.

and I feel like I belong. There's not much washing to do tonight, but how good is this?"

///////////

The next morning, McRae fronts a meeting for the AFL-listed players who are likely to play in the VFL team on the weekend, Round 1 of their season. It's a short meeting. He has a clip of footage he wants to show, but it isn't a play from the previous week. It also isn't the standard full-ground view, but is instead a close-up. The entire five-minute clip is tight grainy footage of Steven Morris, wearing a microphone, in his return game from an ACL injury.

Morris is otherwise known around the club as "Mozz", because he is a constant buzzing, nagging presence, always acting and demanding. McRae wants them to watch him and discuss. The footage is him on the ground in the pre-match warm-up, in action on the field and directing play from the bench. It is him clapping, sprinting, tackling, waving, panting and screaming. So much screaming.

"Roll around, roll around, roll around! Hit it!"

"Get it forward! Tight! TIGHT! Good! Excellent mate!"

"Scotty, get here. Get HERE! That's exactly what we want! Winning habits."

"Yes, yes, yes, YEAH BOYS, great finish!"

"Yours! Gotta go!"

"Good communication, Sammy!"

"Good body work!"

"Loved your chase to get a turnover here. Awesome. Those little things count."

"Off the back! Off the back about five metres!"

"Great contest! Get around him!"

"Great work Oleg! Greaaat work!"

"Hold it, hold it, hold it! Good work Trent. Sensational brother!"

"Come back two metres. That buys you two metres as well."

"Your help side run out there, *outstanding* mate."

The players watching the clip murmur approval. "Awesome", they say. "Inspiring." They love that it's always positive. That Morris does it over

MOSQUITO FLEET: Once a solitary figure in Richmond's forward line, Jack Riewoldt had the likes of Jason Castagna and Daniel Rioli buzzing around his feet and wreaking havoc among opposition defences in 2017. Castagna's goal late in the third quarter of the Grand Final gave the Tigers a 33-point lead and a firm grip on the Premiership Cup.

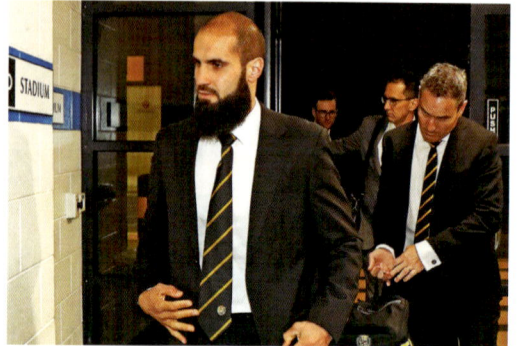

TRIALS AND TRIBULATIONS: Bachar Houli was lauded by Prime Minister Malcolm Turnbull for his work as a multicultural ambassador, but also endured intense public scrutiny over a four-week suspension following the Tigers' Round 14 clash with Carlton. Although he finished second to Dustin Martin in the Norm Smith Medal voting, the coaches gave him the maximum 10 votes in the Gary Ayres Medal, ahead of Martin (8) and Alex Rance (6).

GOAL OF THE YEAR
Daniel Rioli, Round 3 v West Coast

Daniel Rioli scored many great goals in 2017, including four in the Preliminary Final, but his goal in Round 3, against West Coast at the MCG won him the Goal of the Year, presented on Brownlow Medal night. Below, he is surrounded by Kane Lambert, Reece Conca, Dion Prestia and Dustin Martin.

SEE US WITH A GRIN: Jack Riewoldt and Damien Hardwick hug out another Tigers win. The coach embraced his lighter side during the 2017 season, keeping pre-game team meetings fun by revealing a new pictorial metaphor for each round of the season.

DREAMTIME AT THE 'G: Shane Edwards (hugged, left, by Kane Lambert and Shai Bolton) led the way as the club's Indigenous stars celebrated Indigenous Round with a 15-point win over Essendon. Now a 207-game veteran, Edwards was an important midfield contributor on Grand Final day. .

GATORADE SHOWER: Teammates weren't letting the occasion of Shai Bolton's first victory in the yellow and black go unacknowledged, smothering the teenager with affection. The youngster managed six games in his debut season and also provided plenty of spark in Richmond's run to the VFL Grand Final.

BY GEORGE: Dustin Martin and Daniel Rioli swamp Jason "George" Castagna after another of the livewire forward's team-lifting goals. Having broken through for five senior games in 2016, Castagna came on in leaps and bounds during his second season, starring in the Preliminary Final win.

YELLOW AND BLACK: Another victory, another raucous rendition of the Richmond team song. From left: Dan Butler, Kane Lambert, Dustin Martin, Trent Cotchin and Jack Riewoldt. And, the sign says it all: Don't argue became part of football's language through 2017, courtesy of Dustin Martin.

↑ SWITCHING ON: Dustin Martin leads his teammates through another of the cheer squad's magnificent game-day banners; from left: Toby Nankervis, Nick Vlastuin, Alex Rance, David Astbury, Trent Cotchin, Dylan Grimes, Martin and Shane Edwards. Official membership figures of the Tiger Army had grown to 75,777 by the end of season 2017, and no club could have boasted more vocal support.

↓→ BODY LANGUAGE: Jack Riewoldt and Shaun Grigg were two key veterans directing and cajoling their teammates during the 2017 campaign. An emotional player and media whipping boy in years gone by, Riewoldt took on board feedback from teammates and became an important member of the revamped leadership group, with Trent Cotchin and Alex Rance.

TIGER TIME: Richmond players treated every goal like a game-winner in 2017, and that positivity proved infectious. That purposeful focus on celebrating each other's successes was among the hallmarks of a reborn playing group. From left: Brandon Ellis, Daniel Rioli, Shane Edwards, Shaun Grigg, Kane Lambert, Jacob Townsend and Oleg Markov

JACOB'S LADDER: Midway through the season Jacob Townsend thought his AFL career might be finished, but 13 goals with his first 21 kicks when he was brought into the senior changed everything. This revival kick-started a remarkable late-season run for the defensive forward, who'd dominated at VFL level, winning the J.J. Liston Trophy. He celebrates one of his six goals against Fremantle in Round 22, with Trent Cotchin, Jack Riewoldt and Dan Butler.

LEFT: The joker, Alex Rance, has a finger for each of the six goals booted by Townsend.

and over and over again. That there is encouragement but there are also directions. "He's like a coach out there," says Corey Ellis, sitting in the front row. "It's all small stuff, but all of it counts."

McRae pauses a moment in the quiet auditorium. "I'm not standing here saying you've got to be Morro. You've got to be *your version* of Morro. We're not saying, 'Be Steve Morris'. He's Mozz. Buzzing around, that's him. I doubt anyone in the competition does it as well as that. But you've got to find your version of that. If you've got that in your personality, great, but if not you've got to find what it looks like *in you*."

McRae asks them next whether Morris "trains his talk", and of course he does. He is like this whenever he is wearing football boots. "It's not a fluke. He *practises* calling for the ball. He practises *celebrating*. Be loud. I know you can do this Marbs (Chol). *I know it.* I know you're capable of finding a form of this that fits you."

Justin Leppitsch, the forwards coach, is sitting at the back of the room with Balme and Livingstone, and he has a question. He wants to know what was the most important form of communication used by Morris in that clip. What will help the team most? Markov answers.

"Directional talk," says the young defender. "Because at times in a game, we might slip out of concentration, and directional talk brings not only *you* back in but another person back in. If you're switched on, and one step in front of your oppo', and you're talking about it, then everyone else is too."

"Great answer," says Leppitsch. "If you don't have directional talk, we're disorganised. You can say 'Come on boys', 'Lets' go' and 'Get around him' all you want, and all that stuff helps, but the most helpful thing is when someone gets in your ear: 'Oleg, come back a few steps, go right, go right, he's beside you'. I call that 'non-negotiable talk' at AFL level. It's not a choice. You need that. If you don't have it, you become disorganised."

McRae has one more point to make. Volume is important. Your message means nothing if it can't be heard. He has a player in mind that epitomises this: Dustin Martin. "Dusty is the loudest guy on the field at calling for the ball," he says. "You know it. You're almost *forced* to give it to him, like, 'There he is'. As a young player, you can learn something from all these guys whether it's Dusty or Morro or someone else. They do it at training, too. It doesn't just happen. *Screaming* for the ball—it's something you can practise."

The first VFL game of the year is played on Easter Sunday, in perfect conditions at Punt Road Oval. It's warm and sunny with no breeze, and near the end of the second quarter Richmond is dominating North Ballarat, 168 to 9. The fans love it. The supporters look a little rougher perhaps than the average AFL fan, but not by much and at any rate they are among the most dedicated.

Many are here, sitting in the old grandstand or standing behind the goals, solely to see the next wave of Richmond talent—to keep as informed as possible about the depth coming through the lower ranks of the club. Their understanding of the stocks on the Richmond list is better than most professional commentators.

Rookie player Tyson Stengle kicks a goal, and a man sipping a can of *Carlton Draught* nudges his mate with an elbow. "See, that's why they say this guy might be elevated from the rookie list and play senior footy before (suspended first year player Shai) Bolton."

Chol sprints down the wing, takes a bounce, and leans to the right to accommodate his raking left foot kick, and the supporter behind the sticks has another view. "This guy's going to be *good*. Did you see his first half two weeks ago?"

Nathan Drummond, an Indigenous player and superb athlete—playing a tagging role on North Ballarat gun Nick Rippon—chases his opponent down from behind, lays the tackle and wins the free kick. "Fantastic," says the spectator. "That's what Drummo's gotta do if he wants to play at the level."

Down by the bench, McRae is gently coaxing the best out of his players, and calling out encouragement to the field. *Take the contest. Face the game. You're by yourself. Take the one-on-one.* He turns to the players on the bench and sees Stengle with a fat lip. "You all right Wombat?" he asks, pointing to his mouth. "You've got a little bit of blood on one tooth."

He grabs a frustrated Callum Moore as he comes off the ground. "The best thing I can see is that you're playing to your strengths,' McRae says, holding his player by the shoulder. "You're on your toes, and up into them."

He praises the VFL players, too, like Daniel Coffield. "Gee, you're playing well, Coff. So aggressive at the contest. You're looking great, mate."

At half-time the players crowd around inside the Richmond weights room, amongst the dumbbells and barbells and kettle bells. They rest against the lats pull-down machine. They lie down and prop up their legs on the rowing machine. They sit on the bench press.

Injured senior players are here, too, watching, and talking to the players.

Ruckman and club leader Ivan Maric chats to Jacob Townsend while he gets a rub down. Injured forward Shane Edwards has a word to out of favour midfielder Anthony Miles. Draftee Shai Bolton, suspended for striking in a practice match, is here in his tracksuit, and he talks to his mate Stengle. Ben Griffiths, out of the AFL for the second week with a troubling concussion, encourages Chol. Shaun Hampson, who has not played this year due to a lingering back complaint, goes over to Ben Lennon, who is lying completely flat on the floor.

The second half is as dominant as the first. Eventually the score line will read 31 goals, 21 behinds, 219 points to 4.7.31.

The leaves at the top of the plane trees surrounding the oval have turned from green to yellow. It's a golden autumn day. Near the end, a high ball is lobbed into the Richmond defence, which is empty except for a lone Roosters forward. But the ball hangs high in the light as it heads toward him, and a Tigers player hurtles from distance, closing the gap as the ball floats, making up ground while his opponent sits underneath the approaching Sherrin.

The entire time the football is travelling, the Tiger seems simply too far away to make the spoil, but, as it drops slowly and his legs pump furiously he closes the gap and leaps, and turns in air, and shoots a fist skyward. And when that fist reaches its highest point, it strikes the ball, and spoils the mark, and saves a goal, and the player falls to the ground with an ungainly crunch. The player is Steve Morris. McRae walks a few steps to bench and turns to his players. "We're 180 points up, and blokes are playing like that. *Unbelievable*," he says, shaking his head, filled with admiration. "That'll go beyond this week. Habits, boys. It's all about habits."

16

DOING MY BIT

Good Friday. One day before the team flies to Brisbane. Two days before they play the Lions at the Gabba. Reece Conca walks into the gym at Tigerland and music of a different sort than usual reverberates. *Imagine* by John Lennon. *Tears in Heaven* by Eric Clapton. The selection is not Conca's but might as well be—sensitive tunes for a sensitive person.

He's running late for a chat and apologises. He has just returned from a breakfast date with defensive coach Ben 'Truck' Rutten. When Conca explains why he's been out buying his line coach eggs and a latte, he sounds like a teenager caught in a lie, inflecting the final word of each sentence. He grins sheepishly. "I've gotten into a bad habit of trying to kick the ball out of mid-air. I reckon it stems back to when I played soccer as a kid. Anyway, just before Round 1 'Truck' was like, 'If you kick the ball out of mid-air, you owe me lunch. If you don't, I owe you'. I thought 'You beauty, free food'," Conca says, rubbing his hands together. "Then first game, first quarter, there was a ball in mid-air, I went for it, missed it, and bang, there's a lunch for Truck. We made it a regular thing and somehow *all three rounds* so far, I've tried to do it. So, I owe him three lunches."

It's hard to imagine where they bought breakfast on Good Friday, given how many independent cafés are closed around the normally busy precinct near the Punt Road Oval.

It also makes me wonder what it is like to constantly give up such public holidays, not to mention mere weekends. All those weddings and birthdays and christenings. Every family function and impromptu celebration. "Personally, I don't get too annoyed with it," says Conca. "Our schedule is pretty good. We have one rostered day off per week, which a lot of industries don't have. And you get used to that unpredictable schedule.

"You actually begin to lose track of days of the week, and know them instead by the routine. Since we're two days out from a game, for instance, you immediately know you have a main training session, because that's where it fits into a standard preparation. Yeah, we start before 8am, but we'll be finished by 2:30pm, so I think if guys are getting wound up about that then they're stressing about the wrong things."

Conca is originally from Perth—Victoria Park, a suburb 10 minutes south of the Swan River. He has an older brother and a twin sister, and comes from a tight-knit family, originally from Calabria, in Italy's boot. His grandparents, almost 80, still run an Italian restaurant in Perth. The first thing Conca does whenever he goes home to Western Australia is spend time there with them, eating what his Nonna cooks up.

His mother is a home economics teacher, and his father works in construction management. Both are, he says, incredibly hard working, something he grew up appreciating and admiring. They put him through school at Trinity College, where he picked up football late, at 13, because soccer was his first love. But he discovered he was better with a Sherrin. He quickly joined a WAFL Colts team, the Perth Demons, and played senior football at 17. "I wasn't overly gifted athletically," he says. "I've got good agility and speed, and have worked on my fitness at AFL level, but I probably just read the play really well. I think my strengths almost go back to that soccer background—seeing the field."

As a midfielder and roaming defender, he found that he played his best footy when the ball was in front of him. But he also developed a certain calmness in traffic—an ability to use his hands cleanly at ground level, even in the turbulence of midfield action. Richmond selected him in the 2010 National Draft with pick 6—an unexpectedly early selection.

"It was a bit strange. Leading up to the draft, me and my manager expected I might go to Port Adelaide, who had pick 16 (and ultimately selected Ben Jacobs). I was a bit of a bolter, I think because I had quite a good back end of that year, playing a bit of League football, and my National Championships

Carnival wasn't too bad."

"But it really was a bit of a shock. Footy wasn't everything to me. I'd finished school and I was completing a degree in psychology and commerce at uni, because we finish high school a year earlier in WA. It was a whirlwind leading up to it, and then moving to Melbourne was a bit scary, but I was really excited about it. I actually loved every minute, especially those early years getting to know everyone."

In his first three seasons he played 17, 18 and 17 games. He played well, too, developing into an important midfielder, with shrewd awareness and vision in congestion. After 52 games he was ranked comfortably in front of most of his draft class—Dyson Heppell (pick 8) and Dion Prestia (pick 9) notwithstanding.

By 2013, commentator David King predicted Cotchin would soon be the only Richmond midfielder ranked ahead of Conca, whom he described as a blossoming replica of Brownlow medallist Jimmy Bartel: "They don't look flamboyant, but what they do is brilliant."

The burden of being pick 6 came later; not with the emergence of other players his age—like West Coast running machine Andrew Gaff (pick 4) or Gold Coast spearhead Tom Lynch (pick 11)—but with injuries. A broken ankle, multiple stress fractures, hip surgery and groin strains stopped him in his tracks. Conca had a bone called the *Os Trigonum* removed from his heel and, most notably, suffered three serious long-term hamstring tendon tears.

"The last two years, playing so little (two games in 2015, six in 2016), the pressure has really mounted on me, and it's probably only been in the last 12 months I've put some mental things in place to help me deal with that. The injuries have almost been a blessing in disguise in a way, in that they've made me mature and appreciate things," he says. "Post-injury, for instance, I'd always go out and play and train but I was *just so worried* about getting injured. It was almost like 'When is my next injury going to come?'—as opposed to feeling good and focusing on footy. I've worked hard on changing that story in my head."

I saw Conca in the change rooms a year ago, after the most recent of those injuries, in a 2016 pre-season game. He had just completed his first ever full pre-season, was playing well, cementing a new role as a running half-back flank. Then he ripped his hamstring off the bone, one week from the start of the season. Downstairs at Etihad Stadium, he sat in the medical rooms on a bench, crying. Jack Riewoldt cradled him as the tears fell.

"That one probably hit me the hardest, only because I'd got through a fair chunk of the pre-season, which I'd never been able to do, and it's the second half of the last pre-season game when you're *so close* to the season. That was a tough one to swallow. I remember bawling my eyes out for a little bit of time, letting it sink in. It hit me the hardest but it also made me switch on. It rattled the cage enough that I thought, 'I have to do something differently'. I changed my weights program, my rehab, the way I was preparing, the way I was recovering. It was gutting at the time, but I've bounced back."

Now he feels great. Healthy. He's completed six straight games and is performing at the level he knows he can. He loves the backline, too. "We're all between 22 and 27, so it's that perfect mix of age. Everyone just works and we complement one another so well."

He doesn't single out Rance or Grimes or Houli as the standout defender so far, or the young guys in Short and Markov and Ellis, but rather understated tall stalwart David Astbury. "He's athletic. He takes the big jobs in his stride. He's strong. His repeat efforts are incredible. He slips under the radar with his performances but I'll never forget a few years ago before he had a knee injury, he was leading our best and fairest after 10 rounds, which for a key back is incredible. We all know what he can do. His performances over these weeks at the start of the year aren't surprising to any of us."

Conca also feels better outside of football. The injuries in fact forced him to find other outlets for his energy, and so he continued putting time into a diploma in youth work, and volunteering opportunities.

"It's important to me, for balance, because I was just so dedicated and devoted to footy, and I was getting a little caught up in it. And when you're spending so much time *not playing*, rehab just gets so monotonous, so draining."

He works with a group called *Challenge*—a not for profit organisation for children with cancer. It means that one day every week, on a day off from the club, he goes into the Royal Children's Hospital to visit sick children for four or five hours. Many of the kids are terminally ill.

"I'll spend most of my time in the oncology wards, sitting and chatting or playing some games. It's a tough place for kids to be long-term, and any visitors or something different to break it up is massive for them. Most of the kids enjoy their footy, and so we have a chat about who they go for, their favourite players."

He shares a few war stories. And helps the parents, too. "It's so tough on them. They're isolated in these little rooms. Someone has to be with the kids at all times, so maybe I'll just sit with their son or daughter, so mum or dad can go have a shower, or go for a walk and get some sun."

He also volunteers at the hospital every second Monday night, this time in the emergency department from six at night to nine. "I just float around and make sure everyone's comfortable in the waiting room, getting them a coffee or a tea, or a blanket if it's cold. Sometimes I'm just someone to chat to. I'll help look after the siblings, because they can get a bit agitated and worried. If the family has come in a rush I might grab them some games and colouring books. Then I'll float into the emergency wards and make sure everyone is nice and comfortable. It's just my way of helping out."

Some of these commitments help complete work experience hours for his course, but it goes beyond that. After football, he would like to open a centre for troubled kids, helping them get off the streets or to make the most of their time in juvenile detention.

Conca is also known—somewhat facetiously—by Richmond fans for a specific on-field celebration, although not in the brash style of an NFL end zone dance or an EPL player's sprint to the corner pole. His trademark is the 'Conca cuddle', when he leaps onto a teammate after a goal and wraps both arms and both legs around the guy. "It popped up a few years ago. I do love a cuddle. I love celebrating. I love getting around them, and it just caught on pretty rapidly."

Really, Conca just loves helping people and making them feel better. Sharing his own good fortune and happiness is all he's ever wanted to do. "I've come from a lovely family, a great upbringing, and I know that other people have come from terrible situations, with no luck. I just want to be proud of who I've become, and get some satisfaction in knowing that I'm doing my bit."

///////////

An hour later, upstairs, forwards coach Justin Leppitsch makes his opposition analysis debut for the year. The former Lions champion and coach is an ideal fit for a presentation on how to beat Brisbane, and so naturally he plays this up.

"Probably something you need to know before the game, we're playing for the Justin Leppitsch Cup, so..." he clicks a button. The screen displays a silver trophy with a naked man atop the cup, like a miniature Rodin statue, and the room fills with laughter. "I'm probably a bit unhappy with that likeness," he says. "My biceps are much bigger than that."

He continues the casual riff, joking that there was some competition for the "naming rights" to the clash, given that coaching director Tim Livingstone once worked there, VFL coach Craig McRae played and coached there, midfield coach Blake Caracella played there, as did development coach Xavier Clarke. Even the property manager, Giuseppe Mamone, cut his teeth there. One by one Leppitsch screens historic and generally unflattering photos he has found of each man, and the introductions are followed by laughter.

He switches quickly though into business mode. Daniel Rich, he says, is the best player in the Brisbane backline—one who gets a lot of the ball and is damaging with it. Harris Andrews is their intercept marker. Darcy Gardiner is their stopper, he says, then clicks on the player's mugshot so that a red stop sign drops onto the screen. Sam Frost is also a stopper, he says, then clicks on his mugshot to reveal a picture of a shivering frosty snowman.

Their ruckman, Stefan Martin, is their barometer. But onballer and high half forward Dayne Zorko is perhaps their most dangerous player, he says, before clicking a button so that Zorko's mugshot begins bouncing, buzzing and vibrating: "Keep your eyes open for this. He actually runs like that."

Jack Riewoldt, sitting near the back of the tiered room, has a point to add: "Just one thing about Zorko, and maybe everyone can switch on to this. Whenever there's a free kick, he *always* goes and picks the ball up and tries to play on, even when it's not his free kick, so just be alert. Last week I reckon he did it eight times."

Leppitsch continues. Midfielder and captain Dayne Beams is their game breaker and clearance machine. Their wingers—Rohan Bewick and Ryan Lester—are "disciplined and will get back and support where they can. They play hard one-on-one."

Lewis Taylor, winner of the 2015 AFL Rising Star award, needs to be blocked to be rendered ineffective: "If you give him a free run he'll get a lot of the footy."

Former Carlton utility Tom Bell is the team's best runner, and so must be guarded in the forward half because he will stream back towards goal, looking for an open field and unguarded square: "He probably kicks more from the goal line than anyone in the competition—including you Lloydy."

The two young key forwards—Eric Hipwood and Josh Schache—are both talented, he says, but slight. Heavy body contact will help.

In the team sense, what Richmond needs to guard against is the Lions' ability to hit form and hold it. In Round 1 the Lions scored 41 points against Gold Coast before the Suns got into the game. Against Essendon and St Kilda they were on similarly prodigious runs before settling into an arm wrestle, then dropping away, then surging back into the lead.

"They're a momentum team," he says. "The minute you take the throttle off they can actually score pretty quickly. They're a good team if you allow them to be. If you don't, they'll struggle."

He goes over various strategies the Lions have used in the pre-season— U-shaped movement of the ball, going long down the line, pressing defensively, using "handball hustle" through the corridor. "But they're 18th in the League for handball effectiveness," he says. "If we're good defensively in the corridor, we'll turn it over and burn them."

He points to a potentially notable statistic. The Lions are number 17 in the League for switching the ball. But … they switched the ball six times one week ago, and five of those switches ended with the ball in attack.

"So, they're not normally switching, but they switched six times last weekend and five went inside 50—so what would you do if you were coaching them, Nick?"

"Switch it more?" answers Vlastuin.

"Yep, I'd do it a little more," he says, "so let's watch for the switch."

He talks too about a video posted on their club website during the week, of Brisbane's midfield coach Dale Tapping: "He used the word 'composure' about 100 times in his interview, so you can see they're really happy with their effort," Leppitsch says. "We have to make sure they feel *uncomposed* with their game."

Finally, he loads a clip of a Lions play against the Bulldogs, and asks forwards Mabior Chol and Daniel Rioli, sitting in the front row, to watch the footage closely. He wants them to follow the uncontested possession chain of chipping and marking, and to look out specifically for Dayne Beams—then to speak up when they see Beams on screen.

The clip begins, and is sped up to the point that it looks almost like a scene from a Benny Hill episode. Every eye in the theatrette—of perhaps 50 people—follows the seemingly endless chain of kicks and catches.

"Whether they go to this level this week, I don't know," says Leppitsch. "But if they do, this is what I call opportunity. This is where we can cash in, right now."

The clip finishes almost a full minute later.

"Did you see Beams?" he asks, and Chol and Rioli can only shake their head. Leppitsch does the same, crossing his arms and feigning disappointment in the young players.

"No, I didn't see him either. He was on the bench at the time," Leppitsch says, smiling. "I just wanted to make sure you were concentrating."

When the laughter in the space subsides, someone in the back row wonders quietly when the Melbourne Comedy Festival (playing in city venues) came to Punt Road. The mood is similarly buoyant days later, when Richmond comfortably beats the Lions, by 52 points at the Gabba.

True to form in that game, Conca makes at least one failed mid-air soccer kick attempt, adding to his tally of lunches owed to Rutten. He plays well otherwise.

Two weeks on, however, he injures the lisfranc joint in the centre of his foot. It's an obscure injury, but one that ended the career of Collingwood champion Dane Swan.

Initially Conca is supposed to miss a few weeks with the bone displacement, perhaps a month, but scans later inflate that estimate to 12 weeks.

Reece Conca is once more placed on the long-term injury list, and will miss at least half of the season. He can hope only for a late return to the field, perhaps shortly before finals if all goes as planned, which, for him it seems, things rarely do.

17

HARD TO MEASURE

The monthly Richmond Football Club board meeting is held in a large room at a long polished wooden table, slick with lacquer, surrounded by tall black leather chairs with the club logo stitched into the headrest. There are printed agendas and iPads, water jugs and glasses, a cheese selection, grapes, strawberries and crackers.

One wall of the board room is a floor to ceiling window fronting a balcony overlooking the ground, but the blinds are drawn. On the opposite wall, a series of 10 metal silhouettes of Premiership Cups are mounted high. On another surface hangs a massive aerial photo of the MCG, the Punt Road Oval illuminated in the foreground. The final wall is given over to a large oil painting of the Richmond Team of the Century, featuring players from all eras. Titus and Knights. Weightman and Hart. Richardson and Sheedy—all receiving the coach's address from Tom Hafey.

It is 3pm on a Tuesday, and there is a high level of formality to wade through early on, from quorums to matters arising, and quarterly P&Ls to declarations of interest based on previous minutes. Mostly it is questions.

"Does this include depreciation and amortisation?" asks one board member.

"How is evidence to the contrary going to be incorporated?" asks another.

"Do we want to exercise our option?"

"What are the forward projections?"

At the head of a table of heavy hitters sits Peggy O'Neal, a coal miner's daughter from West Virginia turned corporate lawyer, and the first female president of an AFL club. To her immediate right sits club CEO Brendon Gale, followed by former International Cricket Council CEO Malcolm Speed, then 1980 premiership player and former high-ranking police officer Emmett Dunne. To the president's left are former Hay Group managing director Henriette Rothschild, corporate lawyer Kerry Ryan, financial services and investments expert Maurice O'Shannassy, former investment banker John O' Rourke, and club finance chief Michael Stahl. Joining the meeting by conference call are Ernst & Young partner Rob Dalton and former SEEK managing director Joe Powell.

They talk about various projects in their embryonic stages, but discussion moves quickly to gaming, or rather, gambling venues. Specifically, Richmond's investment in the Wantirna Club, where it has 97 poker machine licences that will expire in 2022. At issue is the expiration of the venue lease in 2018, four years earlier than the lease of the machines. It's a conundrum because they don't yet know what the Victorian government will say about those machine licences in 2018—whether they will renew them for a 20-year period, or a 10-year period. "It's the hot topic in gaming circles," says Stahl. "First question everyone asks is, 'Any word on what might be happening with licences?'"

One director wonders aloud whether licences being renewed for a decade might be a problem from a social responsibility standpoint. "I'm not sure that it's prudent to lock ourselves into gaming for years, given that we've had a number of conversations about starting to move out of gaming."

Gale hears these concerns, but tries to temper such worries. "Unlike most other clubs, we are actually doing something about this," he says. "We're not just talking about it."

The CEO goes into some depth here, talking about AFL club funding models and being financially accountable, and ensuring Richmond continues to perform well in the benchmarked and stratified League. The AFL, he says, has asked clubs to come up with strategic initiatives that might generate non-gambling revenue.

"Not just to hold us accountable, but maybe to support us," he says. "They're also coming up with a new set of models for club governance, club constitutions, the way committees operate, etcetera, but I think we're well advanced in that area already."

Not to be deterred, the board asks whether Richmond is continuing to look at funding models for a second gaming venue. "We're always looking at opportunities," says Gale. "But until we're told otherwise, we're open for business. I don't think we're in the position yet where we can say no to gaming—but we are constantly doing things to reduce our reliance."

O'Neal adds her voice to the debate. "We haven't found anything in the last 18 months that has been of interest or suitable or can make money. AFL clubs right now can't afford to be out of gaming."

Later, Malcolm Speed explains this reality in terms of the unfortunately parlous state of finance in almost all AFL clubs: "You have a great season and you might make $1 million. You have a poor season, you might lose $1 million. There's little room for big gains."

It's an idea that becomes clearer throughout the course of the meeting. They talk next, for instance, about club sponsors—a crucial but at times difficult alignment. Beyond branding on signs and websites, sponsors expect player appearances at anything from car dealerships to furniture stores, and they expect regular access to the inner sanctum of the club. Indeed, after this meeting, the Board will head to a private dinner around the corner on Swan Street, with key sponsors invited.

There is a potential new major sponsor in play—insurance company NIB, which previously had a deal with Geelong and now wants to return to the AFL space. They're also well advanced in discussions with Swinburne University about a broader strategic alignment as well as the naming rights for the building at Punt Road Oval, currently called the ME Bank Centre. And finally there is a new deal with Jeep that needs only a signature from the international head of the Fiat Chrysler Automobiles in Italy, Sergio Marchionne. "It has to go across his desk, but it's approved," says Gale. "We're waiting for a good opportunity to announce a new three-year deal. It might also look a bit opportunistic to announce it now because we've won a few games, but the fact is the deal was done in December."

///////////

After a brief break, guests from the AFL arrive, namely Chief Financial Officer and General Manager of Clubs and Broadcasting (and former Gold Coast CEO) Travis Auld, along with Jamie Williams, AFL Club and

Stadium Reporting Manager. They're here to provide an update on where the AFL sees itself and present the findings of the "Club Financial Review", a financial benchmarking document the AFL prepares each year.

Auld puts up a slide with a single line: *Our vision is to be the unassailably number one sporting and entertainment offering in Australia, with our decision-making consistently focusing on six pillars.*

The pillars, he says, are people, strong clubs, new fans, community football, a spectacular game, and industry revenue distribution. He breaks each pillar down into various targets and summarises the 2017 outlook when it comes to such measures as crowds (looking to 32,231 on average), a large TV audience (102 million), and participants (1.47 million nationally).

"These are the things we are judged by publicly," he says. "They're not our KPIs, but you're never going to get away from them."

He also goes through the priorities for this year, including a heightened focus on social inclusion and responsibility, and such developments as the AFL Women's competition, which took the summer by storm in its inaugural season. "We think that went well but we're under no illusions, it's going to be hard," Auld says. "You look at any new competition, or team, and the second year is always much harder."

There's the planned home and away game between Port Adelaide and Gold Coast in Shanghai, working out how to maximise returns from the $200 million purchase of Etihad Stadium, and deciding whether club-nominated AFL memberships should be handed back to clubs. There's also a new Collective Bargaining Agreement with the players, which will take time because of all the League's other investments: "Every extra dollar we invest in a player has to come out of one of those other buckets."

Williams speaks next. He will walk the club's finance committee through the details at its next meeting—but first he offers a summary he calls "the director's cut".

The League, Williams says, categorises the operating revenue of each club by three streams, the first being distribution from the AFL, the second being football income from sponsorship, membership and attendances ("Which I call colloquially the 'meat and potatoes'"), and then non-football incomes (primarily poker machines).

The summary is fascinating. Across the League, 10 clubs reported an operating loss totalling around $17 million. And only three clubs reported an operating profit of over a million dollars, which includes West Coast, Hawthorn, and the Western Bulldogs, as a result of the Grand Final.

Attendances were stable. "You can see that Richmond was third in attendances," says Williams, "which is a great result—considering the on-field performance last year."

He also examines the "show rate" of various members—how many paid up patrons *actually* attend games. Richmond has a strong show rate and sold a total of 72,278 memberships in 2016, on the back of a string of improved seasons.

Football department expenditure is the next topic addressed. They want all clubs to understand exactly why the controversial "soft cap" on spending was necessary to end the "arms race" between clubs—their varying abilities to invest in coaches, trainers and more.

From 2006 to 2011, he says, the compound annual growth rate of football department expenditure at clubs was 11.4 percent. From 2011 to 2014, the growth rate was 10.1 per cent—and showing absolutely no signs of slowing down. "This led to gaps between rich and poor, and operating debt," says Williams. "This is really the backbone of our problem."

Auld points out that when the League created the cap on spending in football departments, the difference between a high- and low-spending club was almost $4 million annually. It is now around $1.5 million. "The chase was okay for a few clubs but it was a problem for half the competition," says Auld. "We've taken a growth rate of 10 per cent down to 2 per cent, which is a really big shift. We plan to hold that for a period, stabilise, and improve some balance sheets. And then we can look at it again."

The presentation goes through good debt and bad debt and various forms of profit, but it ends with Williams looking at the disappointing 2016 season for Richmond and delivering a kind of report card.

Eight wins and no finals means a red cross. "But the debt reduction from 2010 to 2016 has been one of the most admirable things we've seen. It's been a real financial discipline."

Membership of $8.3 million is a great result. Sponsorship of $4.2 million is average, but match returns of $4.3 million is above the average of the larger Victorian clubs ($3.3 million). Corporate hospitality yielding $1.4 million is promising. Merchandising dipped, but that will happen with on-field losses.

"To quote Damien Hardwick, 2016 was a little half step back," he says, referencing a press conference gaffe by the coach from last year. "But on the positive, Richmond is a highly efficient, financially well-managed football club, debt-free since 2013."

Williams says Richmond has consistently proven an ability to "punch above its weight" in terms of memberships (third) and attendances (third)—all without any real on-field success. "The kicker from on-field performance hasn't occurred yet. Accordingly, I see you as 'the sleeping giant'."

Rothschild asks about non-gaming income, and what financial ventures other clubs have pursued or might examine to wean themselves off gambling. Williams notes that Aligned Leisure—a wholly owned subsidiary of the club—is a perfect source of diversification in a League that has few such exemplars.

Rob Dalton, calling in by speaker phone, has a question: "Is there a formula for financial success when teams do go all the way to a Grand Final? The Bulldogs came from nowhere. Are there some lessons we can learn now, to maximise the return when that day does come?"

Auld steps forward to answer, because this point, he notes, has been raised by several clubs. He believes an internal working group might be worth assembling, to talk to a club like Hawthorn and see how the Hawks cashed in on success. GWS has done a lot of work on it, he says, because with their small market they would want to make any finals run count. And the Bulldogs were a little "worn out" in the sprint to the dramatic, romantic end of their 2016 season. "But I guess that's a good problem to have."

///////////

More than two hours into the meeting, it's time for an update from the Korin Gamadji Institute—an Indigenous youth education and leadership program established by and located at the Club. Its director, Aaron Clark, a Djab Whurring man who grew up on a mission in western Victoria, enters the room to present to the Board.

Gale, introducing him, points out that Clark has just won a scholarship, joining the NAB Emerging Indigenous Executive Leaders Program, which was just written up in *The Australian Financial Review*.

Clark is here to give the board an overview and "health check". KGI, he says, has in five years become the community hub they wanted it to be.

More than 10,000 aboriginal people have now had some contact with the centre.

The club also houses the Melbourne Indigenous Transition School (where 22 seventh grade children from regional and remote Australia attend classes) and has ties with the Wirrpunda Foundation (for in-school educational programming). There are netball and football programs, and cultural programs. "It's a 'strength-based' approach," Clark says. "What can kids be great at? How can we use their culture to springboard into something? What pathways can we create?"

He talks next about the annual Dreamtime game against Essendon, and he's brought in a guernsey. On the back is the number 67, which small forward Shane Edwards will wear, to honour the 50th anniversary of the 1967 referendum, in which nine out of 10 Australians turned out to vote to recognise Indigenous Australians as citizens with rights.

The design this year was by Indigenous street artist Josh Muir, and it represents Bunjil, the creator. All the Indigenous players at the Club helped with the design, from rookie Tyson Stengle to emerging forward Daniel Rioli—who, Clark says, is unassuming but strong on matters relating to reconciliation.

"It highlights his maturity. I don't want to underplay the role anyone has played at the club, but Daniel has been really involved with KGI. He's had cousins attend MITS. He's been instrumental in designing the jumper. He makes regular appearances at our programs."

Gale adds, "He's a talented young man, and a potential leader at the club," rapping his knuckles on the table. "Such an impressive young man."

Clark, returning to the reason for all this action, brings to bear some grim statistics. One in four people in Australian prisons are Indigenous. Fifty per cent are incarcerated for low level offences. Once in the correctional system, they have an 80 per cent recidivism rate. And nearly one in two youths in detention are Indigenous. "As a nation, we are currently better at sending Indigenous kids to prison than keeping them at school," he says. "We're not putting these numbers up to blame anyone, but to remind people. Because in doing this, we're denying ourselves—our society—some great people."

He reminds the board that the Dreamtime game averages 1.2 million TV viewers, with an attendance of 81,000. Gale says it's an occasion that "creates a sense of urgency"—where initiatives that might take months or years to receive assistance find help much faster.

Clark moves on to what KGI can do for the club on the field, which includes everything from attracting talent to retaining it. (KGI, for instance, was integral in setting up aboriginal host families for young players.)

Then there is the Laguntas program, which offers football development and heritage education for young Indigenous players in Victoria. Though he is from the Tiwi Islands off the Northern Territory, Rioli was a boarder at St Patrick's College in Ballarat, and was part of the Laguntas squad.

Clark notes that between 1992 and 2012 only 17 Indigenous players were drafted from Victoria. But from 2013 to 2016 eight more players were drafted.

The club's Next Generation Academy in regional Victoria is potentially yielding fruit, too, from a zone that includes the Goulburn Murray, Bendigo, Sunraysia and North Central areas of the state. "It's a real positive," he says. "The ability for us to be courageous in this area is starting to pay dividends."

////////////

Reps from the List Management team enter the room around 5:40pm, with the meeting already deep into its third hour.

Football manager Neil Balme is flanked by Dan Richardson and List Manager Blair Hartley. First, the three men want to look at the 2014 draft, because it was the one in which they made the most list changes and acquisitions in the past eight years.

On screen appear the names of the draftees (Corey Ellis, Connor Menadue, Nathan Drummond and Dan Butler) as well as the rookies (Jayden Short, Jason Castagna, Kane Lambert and Ivan Soldo). Barring Drummond, who just suffered a second ruptured ACL, all have played senior football this year, some as integral members of the side.

"This was an important draft for us," says Hartley. "There was a limited free agent pool and a limited out of contract pool. There was also depth in that pool, because others (drafts) had been so compromised."

Next, they look at overall squad balance, examining a matrix of all players on the list, coded and sorted by age groups and categories including key backs, rebounders, rucks, inside mids, outside mids, key forwards and dangerous forwards. A big purple circle is drawn around a large and worrying gap in the "key forward" area.

Jack Riewoldt is a gun, but he is 28 years old and needs support. Tyrone Vickery is with Hawthorn now. Mabior Chol and Callum Moore are both just rookies, still fairly raw, and will take time. The two most likely to step up are Todd Elton, who has shown positive signs but has been slow to emerge, and Ben Griffiths, now recovering from his second concussion of the year, one of a handful in his career.

But, Hartley explains, after trading out star onballer Brett Deledio, the Tigers now hold two first round picks in the 2017 draft—and there could be as many as five key forwards in the top 20 of the draft this year.

Richardson points out that the team might seem established, but that it ranks 13th in the League for average games played, and is the third youngest on average. They are in fact a young and inexperienced side. "If there's a silver lining to last year," he says, "it is the games we got into these kinds of players: Short, Rioli, Markov, Castagna. Which probably had an impact on team morale and culture, it's fair to say."

They move on to the 2017 strategy around trades, free agency and the draft, although there is in fact little to say so early in the season. The tall forwards available as free agents are limited but include Sydney's Sam Reid, Carlton's Levi Casboult and Port Adelaide's Jackson Trengove.

"It's also been reported that we have interest in (young Brisbane forward) Josh Schache, which is genuine. We've been in discussions with his management," Richardson says. "Josh will be asking for a lot of money, and Brisbane may ask for two first round picks, so we have made no decisions."

Kerry Ryan, from across the table, asks if the club can begin negotiations.

"Yes but no," answers Richardson. "We're allowed to talk about what we would offer, but we can't sign any agreements."

Someone asks for an assessment of Soldo as a marking option—the answer is that he's young, and more of a ruckman. Powell, by phone, asks about Griffiths.

"He's shown real ability at times," says Richardson, "but consistency has been an issue."

"He's a good player but we're really worried about his concussion," Balme clarifies. "It's hard to measure from a risk point of view. But look, he competes well, runs hard, and brings the ball to ground."

"And big blokes are hard to find," adds Hartley. "They don't grow on trees. That's why people like the Hawks will pay Tyrone what they did."

"Concussion is a really big issue for the AFL," says Gale. "This is not like the NFL though—we're really ahead of the game."

As night falls outside, they look at other considerations. Young father-son prospect Patrick Naish is brought up. He keeps looking better, which means Richmond may potentially need to use a hefty amount of draft points to secure him. Hartley says a potential draftee is a like a stock: "A few good games and all of a sudden it goes up."

Richardson adds some detail to the overview Clark provided earlier, about the Next Generation Academy in the northern part of the state, and the Indigenous players beginning to emerge there. Derek Smith from Mildura plays for the Bendigo Pioneers and has good lateral movement and skill. David Smith from Shepparton has played games for the Murray Bushrangers, where he has excited recruiters with his elite speed.

They turn to contracts. Brandon Ellis, now settled into half-back, is one they want to re-sign before he becomes a free agent in 2018. Kamdyn McIntosh has penned a new agreement, but the club would like to wait until others have signed, so that they can break the news in groups. Daniel Rioli is a crucial signature they are working on—hopefully a three-year extension. The big one though, of course, is free agent Dustin Martin.

The commentary around his contract and what the Tigers have offered or should offer or should not offer has been unrelenting across all media. Discussions with his manager, Ralph Carr, have been described in the press as acrimonious or stalled or abandoned, when in fact Richardson says discussions are ongoing and productive. "And frankly I don't see any problem with paying him well, and us winning games."

O'Rourke wonders whether the new CBA has held anything up, but Richardson says that any CBA increase has been written into the offer: "And we're really comfortable with our offer."

Gale chimes in: "His durability is amazing. The only game he's missed was when we suspended him. And we lost!"

O'Shannassy asks, "How will other players feel about it?"

Richardson responds quickly. "They wouldn't have any problem, I think," he says. "The reality of it is timing. He's in form, he's young, he's a free agent, and there's a new bargaining agreement."

Richardson does add, though, that $1.5 million per year—should that offer be made elsewhere—would be difficult for Richmond to match.

"It's a number we probably don't want to afford," he says. "It might have flow-on effects."

He points out that what happened to Sydney, paying Lance Franklin what they did. It is widely accepted that the gargantuan contract for the megastar cost them talismanic ruckman Shane Mumford, but also the ruckman now playing for Richmond, emerging cult figure Toby Nankervis. "Basically, the Swans lost Toby because of what they're paying to keep Buddy."

They talk a little more about the upcoming draft, and how important it will be, how they have had one recruiter for more than a year now spending 90 per cent of his time on this crop alone. It was that early assessment of depth that helped Richmond when Deledio was traded—the Tigers asked for a pick in the 2017 draft, instead of 2016, believing the 2017 crop to be better stocked with young talent. Richmond's pick is tied to the finishing position of Geelong this season.

Gale says, "I just wish the Cats would stop winning games." Then he turns to Hartley and Richardson: "For the record, you have a thankless job, so well done guys."

Balme updates the group on the new players—Caddy, Prestia and Nankervis. "They're culture drivers," he says. "Toby even came back three weeks before he was due from the break. They set the standard."

He talks about the focus of the football department this year—on fundamentals and a consistent game plan. "It's pretty uncomplicated. It's not a new idea to contest hard. We've got a long way to go, but it's all about making us hard to play against. Put it this way, if Tommy Hafey or Tony Jewell were here, they'd be barracking for us."

He talks about how the team is kicking long down the line, and laying forward-50 tackles, and how in both stats Richmond have gone from last in the competition in 2016 to first in 2017—and how it is producing the desired results. "The draw has been relatively kind to us, but you're not four-zip if you're not doing something right. Still, the pressure will come."

He says Cotchin is loving his footy again. Riewoldt has stepped up as a leader and understands the responsibility. Rance has slotted in with unrestrained enthusiasm: "He loves it. We've almost got to hose him down." And as for Hardwick, he seems constantly pleased. "No negativity at all. Prepared to listen to all angles, but still strong enough on his own views."

After one more break, the marathon sitting resumes with a discussion led by Emmett Dunne. It's his initiative: to award life membership to all premiership players, even posthumously, for their service to the club.

He runs through a few numbers. It's been 37 years since Richmond won a flag. In that time they've played in six finals series. 2001 was the last time the club won a final. The point is that finals—flags in particular—are not easy to win.

1149 players have represented the club, he says, 124 of them are premiership players. But 34 of that group are not life members.

"These players we're talking about made a *real* contribution to our club," Dunne implores. "They were paid very little. Had their careers and education compromised. They sustained injuries and didn't get great medical attention, which affected their quality of life. These life memberships are to be celebrated by the players but also their families."

"I support it," says Gale. "When this was put to the Board in 2013, someone suggested it should be a premiership *and* 50 games, but we got some resistance. And I don't know why."

Dunne reiterates just how poorly a lot of these players were treated by the club.

"This was the Graeme Richmond era. *Very* brutal. Premiership players would come to training on Tuesday, be sent to the front office and then told they were off to another club on the Thursday, with no explanation. We'll build some bridges with this."

Previously, the honour of life membership was only available to premiership players if they had also played 100 games at the club. That means players many fans would remember fondly—such as Craig McKellar (96 games), Robert Wiley (95) and Colin Beard (33) would not be eligible. Nor would five players from the club's very first premiership in 1920, says Dunne, including a guy named Bill James.

"Oh my," Gale says to all the board. "Bill James, 1920. Have you heard this story? One game!"

Dunne goes into more detail. Apparently in Grand Final week almost a century ago, Richmond's starting forward was injured and James was the best possible replacement, but had played in a midweek Grand Final of his own in Kyabram. He agreed to play.

"He had to work a double shift on the Friday, came down in a horse and buggy on the Saturday, and played in a premiership," says Dunne. "In the off-season at home, he shot his foot off, and never played again."

It's almost 7:15pm when the meeting finishes, four and a quarter hours after it began, but not before O'Neal can push for an amendment to the constitution, so that the board will have discretion to make any premiership players life members. They quickly run through potential issues.

Are there any problems around cost? *No.*

Is there any sense current life members would feel aggrieved? *No.*

Is there any concern it might dilute the honour, by taking so many new life members at once, or handing them out *en masse*?

O'Neal smiles. "If we have to give out lots of life memberships because we win lots of premierships, I don't think anyone's going to have a problem with that."

18

THEIR BEST PUNCH

The coaches sit in the rooms before the game against Melbourne, and a video clip is played, recorded by Damien Hardwick earlier that day. It's him in casual clothes at home, sitting in front of a game of *Connect Four*, with a furrowed brow, scowling as he scans the yellow and red circular discs in the blue plastic frame. The object of the two-person game is to place four discs of the same colour in a row, while preventing your opponent from doing the same.

The voice holding the camera, that of his 17-year-old daughter, asks a baiting question: "Did I win?"

Hardwick frowns harder, realises the game is over, stands and flails a petulant arm: "Get *stuffed!*"

The coach hates losing. He was considering using the footage as part of a funny but pointed pre-game speech, but in this moment, he decides against that plan. The added novelty isn't necessary.

He brings up the Bureau of Meteorology website instead. It looks like wet weather is approaching. Torrential downpours, in fact. Justin Leppitsch glances up at the time lapse Doppler radar screen and purses his lips: "Well, it's got to be kicked, scrapped, knocked—*whatever*—forward," he says. "You know the rule: 'When it rains, metres gained'."

The players file into the briefing room, and Hardwick asks Dan Butler to unveil the A3 photo of the week. And there it is—a picture of *Connect Four* in its box. "This is the greatest game on the face of the earth," says Hardwick, smiling. "Unfortunately, I can't beat my 17-year-old daughter. It drives me insane. But there's a reason why. What's the object of the game, David? *It gives you a fair hint on the box.*"

"To *Connect Four*?" says Astbury.

"You've got to *Connect Four*, David. So, what do you think I'm trying to do? What am I *playing*?" he asks. "I'm playing too quick. I'm playing all offence. And what do you think my daughter's playing?"

"Defence," answers the room.

"Deny, deny, deny. That's all she does! So, Dad gets frustrated. Dad makes a shit move. Dad loses. She goes in with a defensive mindset and she either wins—or has a draw. With my offensive mind set I either win—or lose."

Hardwick begins getting to his point.

"It takes great discipline to play defence, but that's what we're doing. We're looking for that ability to deny. If you take away their strengths, what are they going to do? They're gonna try to go for it, and eventually, they're going to lose. So, we're going to deny, deny, deny."

He points out that they've trained this system all summer long, and put it in practice in every game. The Tigers are—statistically speaking, after four rounds—the best defensive side in the AFL. "Understand today is all about defensive effort. We win. We don't lose. *Connect Four* boys."

It's such a playful beginning, and so representative of the Hardwick demeanour this season. The man is buoyant, a disposition not based on results but on process. He more than anyone made the decision to change Richmond into a defensive-yet-unshackled team, and now he delights in the plan's application.

Things were so different not so long ago. Exactly one year earlier, in fact, in the corresponding Anzac Eve game against Melbourne, his mood was dark. During that pre-game address, 12 months earlier, his message was desperate. The team was coming off an 11-goal loss to West Coast and he wanted a response. Demanded one. His voice then was twisted with impatience: "You take off the jumper at the end of the game, what do you want it to say?" he asked. "Whoever wore me today gave everything. No short steps!"

But at full-time a few hours later, after the Demons had bullied Richmond in the wet—and in truth embarrassed them—Hardwick was not conciliatory but livid: "We spoke about what that jumper would say. Well, I'm going to give you the answer: We are as weak as piss as a football side."

He turned venomous. Don't let your parents and your girlfriends say you did well, or tried hard, he said. This, he said, was reprehensible. Players jumping out of the way of the man. Dodging the ball itself. "We sit there and pledge allegiance to the thing you wear, and the Melbourne Football Club steamrolls our blokes. Our blokes! No hiding from it... *WEAK!*" he roared, slamming the whiteboard. "FUCKING *WEAK!*"

He said he was sick and tired of it. He told Brandon Ellis he loves him, but he needs to get harder. Bachar Houli the same. Rance was not spared for playing like "an idiot". Nor Martin, for performing like "a schoolboy".

He stood then genuinely perplexed, eyes wide, hands upturned. Was this form the reality, or just the way they were playing "at the moment"? Was this to be their entire season, or their season "just this moment"?

"I sit here and I rant and rave and show bravado, but I can't walk down the street tomorrow. I'm embarrassed to don my colours. I never thought I'd say that. Ever! Hat down, sunglasses on—you should *never* feel that," he said, pausing, scanning their eyes for a flicker of the same fire. "The pride is at the back of the cupboard. We just need to find it. We have to find it."

One year later, back under lights at the MCG, they have their chance.

///////////

Because it is Anzac Day eve, a mounted cavalryman from the Creswick Light Horse Troop rides the boundary slowly, with the eternal flame held high. The MCG itself is lit only by mobile phones, blinking in the darkness.

Leppitsch, who can always be counted on to break the tension, enters the coach's box three storeys above and sees the darkened stadium: "Hmmmm... I dunno how we're going to see the ball."

Below, the players walk across the turf in silence. The teams run through a shared banner with an Anzac shield, surrounded by a patchwork of yellow and black, red and blue, like a knitted blanket on the cold evening. There is the National Anthem, and everyone in the box stands, as does the record crowd of 85,657.

When the Last Post is played, Hardwick hopes the players will remember his message from before the game. To his credit, the coach offered none of the tone-deaf comparisons and parallels between war and football, between trench mates and teammates, between losing your life and losing a game. "Pay your respects, obviously," he said then. "But look at it as an opportunity to reset—to think about what you're going to do and how you're going to play."

And now it's down to business, in the darkness of the coach's box, which is far bigger than you might imagine. The space is tiered, and in the front row are the assistant coaches: Rutten, McQualter, Caracella and Leppitsch. In the middle row sits Hardwick and his right hand, football analysis manager Hayden Hill. In the back row sits the club's AFL compliance officer Jenna Earle, football technology coordinator Simon Reinsch, opposition analyst Jack Harvey, and pro scout Nick Austin. Behind them all, in the back of the room, is Neil Balme.

There are a dozen laptops and a few iPads, not counting the hardware and manpower in the smaller coach's box next door, which adds another six people and as many more computers. The latter team will code videotape as the game unfolds, so that it will be simpler to cut and search later, in the post-game analysis.

The main area is lit mostly by flatscreen televisions. One displays player rotation statistics—the number of changes, time on the ground, percentage of the game played. Another lists team statistics, like defensive contested possessions and forward half turnovers. Another has more individual player stats like kicks and handballs. Another has a live feed of the game, which is about to start.

Hardwick's eyes stalk the field as the players walk to position: "Petracca is starting on ball," he tells the box. "Viney is forward, and Jones is on a wing. Tell our backs to be careful of this."

Rain drifts down quickly as the quarter begins, and soon it starts to sheet across the field. Melbourne's midfield pushes Richmond around and the Tiger response does not please the coach. He speaks into the phone with a message: "Just remind our players, 'When you feel the heat, bludgeon handball and blast kick is our friend'."

That message will go out with the runner—now dressed in pink to avoid any clashes with players or umpires—the club's strength and conditioning coach Luke Meehan. Meehan delivers perhaps 50 messages in a game, running roughly 13 kilometres. Maybe three times near the end of every quarter he tells players the amount of time left. But most of his messages concern rotations. Brendan Fahrner, the club's sports science adviser, sits on the bench beside him, monitoring how long each player has been on the field and who is due for a rest. Nothing is left to chance. Inside the coach's box, they monitor outcomes.

Soon it becomes apparent that the Demons are dominating everything but the scoreboard. Forward 50 turnovers, for instance, have been Richmond's strong suit this season, but Melbourne is winning that count five to one. "It's going to be one of those games," says Hardwick. "We've got shit balance right now. Come on boys: deny, deny, deny."

The ball lands in Riewoldt's hands and he turns and snaps the kick. Hardwick screams the ball towards goal: "Get in, dammit! Get in!" And it does.

He has another message for the bench, to relay through Meehan: "Are you there? Get out to Connor Menadue and tell him his standing position at stoppages is *on his player*, not behind. They're killing us at stoppages."

Rutten notices the players trying to craft perfect plays; beautiful handball chains and neat chips, in the wet, under immense pressure. He picks up the phone: "Can you get a message to our backs? Don't worry about these little handballs—surge it forward."

Hill offers a brief message to the whole box: "Astbury three touches, all handballs. Same for Lambert."

Jason Castagna kicks a behind, and Hardwick is annoyed at the failure of the team to adjust for the kick-out afterwards: "Zone, zone, zone boys!"

A downfield free kick against Conca leads to a Melbourne shot on goal, and Hardwick slams his hand on the table: "Reece! Bloody hell! Referring pressure with a handball in wet conditions is *not* going to work."

Hill offers another update: "The mids haven't touched it. Dion (Prestia), one possession."

Earle takes it upon herself near the end of every quarter to say aloud to the box how much time is left: "Four minutes…"

Harvey notices loose-checking by the Tigers in defence: "That's twice now Harmes has been unattended."

Earle: "30 seconds…"

The siren sounds, with Melbourne holding a narrow advantage, despite the Tigers being badly down in forward half turnovers, five to 13. Richmond is winning defensive clearances six to zero, meaning the backline are doing their job, but the ball appears to be flying right back into their half after every effort to repel the thing. Hardwick sighs as he leaves the box for the on-field huddle. "I'll take three points down after that quarter."

In the huddle, he sends a strong message to the players: to understand the conditions, to deal with the opponent, and to grasp that they will need to play a dour territory game.

At the start of the second quarter, Toby Nankervis charges at a loose ball, sprinting, then strips Melbourne's young co-captain, Jack Viney, and wins a free kick. Balme approves: "Gee he goes, this boy." But Nankervis kicks poorly to a lead in the forward pocket. It creates a turnover, and the ball comes back out of attack. Lambert is there to cut off the play, and he kicks a ball to a different place—the top of the goal square, where the forwards are in a better marking position. Hardwick picks up the phone: "Hello? Just remind our players—*that* kick is perfect. Nank's kick was ridiculous."

Moments later Rance is tackled in the back half, pinned holding the ball after trying to dodge trouble—again the result of players handballing backwards, referring pressure until it became too much even for the best defender in the game to evade. Hardwick smashes his fist on the desk: "Why, why, why are we handballing backwards?"

He fills his own silence, wondering aloud where his midfield has gone: "Has Cotchin touched it?"

Hill answers: "He's had five possessions."

Hardwick calls the bench: "Let's get a message out to the players to raise the fight, please. We're getting beaten in the contest, and they own the outside as well."

It fails to stop the swarming Melbourne midfield. Richmond, cornered again, is caught in another clumsy, panicked handball chain. The wet ball is not helping.

"Kick it! Kick it! Are you there?" Hardwick yells into the phone. "For the fifteenth bloody time, tell them to kick it!"

///////////

When the coach screams into the phone the message is heard by three people on the boundary line. The primary listener is coaching director Tim Livingstone, Hardwick's closest confidant at the club. Livingstone runs the bench. Between players, fitness staff, the runner and the box, there's a lot of noise and action to negotiate.

His backup is Mark Opie, a club volunteer and match day team manager, who listens to the audio feed from the coach's box, and makes a note of every message that comes down, in case one is missed or delayed.

Another coach's assistant and volunteer, Tony Singarella, hears it all, too, listening for positional changes and keeping track of who is on or off the ground. Singarella moves their avatars on an iPad, and each updated move is reflected on the coach's screens upstairs—so they have a constantly updated digital whiteboard.

Livingstone though, is the one who truly cops the earful, as he is now, when the players continue to dodge and handball, instead of crashing and kicking as instructed.

"Sometimes the tension builds when it's a repeated message," Livingstone says later. "It's a bit like umpiring, too: you're only noticed when you get it wrong. But we've got a clear understanding that nothing said is personal. If you're worried about taking offence, you're in the wrong job."

The message against Melbourne, for instance, clearly did not get through to the players immediately. "It might be five minutes at least before everyone gets the message," says Livingstone. "Then it takes time for it to sink in, to take effect. And sometimes you've got to wait for the break to reinforce the idea. There's always a delay."

The runner might carry a few messages at once, but one will always remain a priority, and usually the priority is based on moving a player to a new role or off the ground entirely: *Get this positional change done—send this reminder afterwards.*

"If it's feedback—if it's not a structural or tactical change—you try to do it without the runner, waiting for a rotation or quarter time," he says. "You've got to pick and choose your battles."

⁄⁄⁄⁄⁄⁄⁄⁄⁄⁄

Hardwick knows this but is agitated anyway. He walks away from his seat shortly after. He does this in the box when the annoyance rises. He hovers at the back of the room, paces a little. Sometimes he draws on a whiteboard, marking down stats he plans to relay to his players in a break.

He comes back to his seat now with a plan. He wants Caddy and Martin off the ball, both placed at half-forward instead. Both play with brawn, and can break packs apart, but Hardwick just isn't seeing the speed he needs at the coalface. "Get Prestia, Cotchin and Castagna on the ball."

Inside-50s for the game are now at a perilous 10 against Melbourne's 35. The Richmond defence is under siege.

Houli kicks the ball long into the Richmond forward line, but places it perhaps 40 metres out from goal. It's a dangerous space—the fat side of the ground. If Melbourne wins the ball, it can be gallivanted through the middle, an empty field en route to goal. Leppitsch has seen this exact error too often tonight: "Boys, I don't want to harp on this, but that Bachar kick is *wrong*. We need to stay skinny, because Melbourne want to run it out the fat side. We're creating our own problems."

"Five minutes," says Earle.

Hardwick: "They look quicker than us. They look harder than us. Don't they?"

No one answers. But Caracella's voice steps into the silence. He is calm: "We're looking better this last 10 minutes. We might have absorbed their best punch."

"One minute…"

"Thirty seconds…"

Shaun Grigg takes a free kick on the boundary, goes back and slots a clutch goal from the tightest of angles on the siren. Richmond will go into the half-time break trailing by only seven points. "A goal down," says Leppitsch. "That's a good result, I reckon."

At half-time the message is simple. Caracella helped distil the notion before the players trundled in to the meeting room: "Smart but hard. Crack in but don't blaze in. When it's your turn, go."

Hardwick is direct, and rousing. He wants the goal square attacked. In close quarters, he wants a "surge mentality". No more backwards handballs. "We know their pressure is elite, so let's not refer it to a teammate—let's shoot it forward to another contest. Then we've got it in space and we can use our speed."

He says this is a great test. And Melbourne is a great opposition. "This is a tough game," he says. "But you know what, we're a tough side."

Hardwick believes that such matches tell you something about your football club. He brings them down now off their seats into a close group, standing and facing one another, and he circles them. His voice envelopes them. Will they stand up or lie down? "I know what I think!" he yells. "And I can see in your eyes what you think!"

He talks about friends and family and the jumper. The players are on their toes, and he is on his heels. They have their arms around each other, and he has his arms around them. "We can all lift! We can all surge! We can all hunt! We can win this game!"

/////////////

Early in the third quarter the signs are not good. Again, they are choosing the wrong options, again handballing backwards, again chipping short instead of roosting long, down the line, directly at goal.

Rance plays on, tries to dash out of the back line around one opponent, and then another, and is corralled and tackled and turns the ball over. Hardwick turns to Rutten: "Do you want to speak to him or do you want me to?"

They talk all sorts of contingencies and options. Should Grigg stay in the ruck and tag Jack Watts, who is having an excellent game, using the ball with grace and dare: "That's the difference—their cleanliness," says Hardwick. "Isn't it, boys?"

There are so many questions, most without answers. Should Lambert go into the midfield? Should Houli go to a wing? When should Rioli come off the ground for a rest?

Hardwick picks up the headset and unloads: "Get a message to Dion Prestia that he's had four kicks and EIGHT handballs, and it's pissing down with rain! Tell him to use his bloody strengths and stop playing shit footy!"

The message that gets to Prestia, however, bears little resemblance to the spittle from the mouth of the coach. Livingstone says it would have been filtered by him into something like 'Come on Dion, we need you putting your head over the ball'.

"We both know when he just needs to vent," Livingstone explains. "Like sometimes he'll say, 'Get that guy straight off the ground, now!', but I'll know that the player is five minutes away from his rotation, and Dusty is due, and if we need to hold Dustin on the ground when he's fatigued, that can have consequences. Damien trusts me to hit back at him."

More messages go out to the players now, reinforcing once more the need to kick around the body—even blindly—rather than trying to find a target with their hands. Nick Austin is incredulous: "We're still trying to fix things that we were doing wrong in the first quarter of the game. Unbelievable."

Leppitsch, seeing almost no alternative, suggests they play a "kick and catch" game—spotting up targets, retaining possession, slowing down the play—something closer to the Tigers' game plan last year. Something to take the ball away from Melbourne. Something to kill the heat. If they lower their eyes, it might work. Hardwick shakes his head to say no.

The siren sounds, and Richmond trails 53 to 73. But Hardwick senses the pair of injuries to Melbourne could play a part in the outcome: "They're two rotations down, so that gives us a chance to outrun them."

///////////

After the final break, the coaches get back upstairs. There's no direct elevator, so after they jog from the huddle to the fence, and then up a slight race, and then down into the sub-sphere of the stadium, they need to scale four flights of stairs to reach their perch. They return to the box understandably breathless.

The Tigers kick a quick goal through Riewoldt, and then Rioli has the ball. The coaches lament the fact that their attack is not zoning up—ready for the kick in, should Rioli miss. He kicks the goal. It doesn't matter.

Now Richmond is only seven points down. Hardwick picks up the handset: "Remind them again to raise the fight, please."

When a message like this one needs to be spread to the entire team, it is given first by Livingstone to the four players on the bench, then to the runner, who'll target leaders on the ground, starting with the defence and then moving forward.

Hardwick, who spends almost the whole quarter on his feet, can only hope for the best. Martin kicks for goal across his body, and Hardwick is unusually calm as it fades through the air but twists through the tall posts: "Yes. Got it."

He calls down the line at one point, but cannot hear a voice at the other end: "Hello? Hello?" he asks. "*HELLO?!?!*"

"You're on mute, Dimma," says Earle.

He presses the correct button on the intercom. "I want Menadue to the wing.

Butler forward, please."

A behind is kicked, scores are level, and in the box there is a cool, quiet tension. Free kicks draw the attention of coaches more than before. When a decision goes against them, the assistants are indignant. Like fans. Hardwick though is level-headed. This is not a rare reaction, either, but his default. The coach is generally pragmatic about officiating. "Nah, it was there," he'll say. "Nah, it was too high," he'll tell the others. "Nah, that was clumsy," he'll deflect.

When a free goes against them, he immediately focuses on what it means—on the gap it might give the opposition: *Run* boys," he'll say, hoping they ignore their indignation and sprint immediately into a defensive formation. "Run, run, run, run, run, RUN!"

Riewoldt takes a mark, within range of the goals, and Hardwick wants composure: "Slow it down," he says. "Take your 30 seconds." Jack steers it through—a controlled long range drop punt on a tight angle—and they're up by six points. "Still too long though," says Hardwick. "Five minutes left. Gotta raise the fight again. Send the message."

After the centre bounce, Houli gathers the latest in a handful of clean possessions for the quarter, and finds a target. Hardwick is impressed. "Gee, Bachar's been good."

Richmond scores a behind and has a crucial seven-point break, but McQualter, the midfield stoppages coach, is alarmed by something he spotted at a ball-up in the defensive half of the field: "Jesus, Shorty was behind in that stoppage," he says. "Tell him, 'DO NOT let Garlett get forward of the ball'."

Caddy goals. Richmond is now 13 points up. The coaches don't celebrate in the box. If anything, their urgency increases. There are only so many seconds before play begins again, and so they reshuffle their deck. Hardwick demands an extra man back, beyond the six already in defence.

"I need to get a forward off! *I need to get a forward off!* We need a seventh!" he says. "Rancey onto Hogan. I want Shorty spare."

"One minute fifty seconds…" says Earle.

"One minute…"

The game is won now but Hardwick is still calling plays down the phone: "Get 'em all back please—get 'em all back!"

"Thirty seconds…"

Now they are certain it is won. McQualter turns around, eyes wide, shaking his head: "Let's never talk about this game again," he says. "Right?"

"Twenty seconds…"

The siren sounds, and Hardwick slumps a little as the energy pours out of him: "Phew. Good win boys. That's a great result. Well done, Tigers."

Leppitsch looks up, serious for a second. He is positive and thoughtful. It seems like a light bulb moment: "There's something about this bunch of blokes."

They all close their laptops now, and walk down those staircases back into the grey concrete recesses of the stadium. Halfway down Leppitsch returns to comedy, or realism: "Mate, you'll always take your worst victory over your best loss."

In the rooms, Hardwick leans on a cinderblock wall, grinning and clapping as his players come in off the ground: "It'll be a big song, this one," he says to no-one in particular. They launch into the words, and he stands behind a net, looking on but quietly mouthing the lyrics with them.

The win was far from ideal. Club analyst Jack Harvey says it came down to the "critical moments" in the contest: "The little things and the big things. Saves on the goal line. Smart taps. Individual ground level brilliance. Tackling pressure. Blokes standing up when they had to."

When the players are done with their media interviews, and have their boots off and ice applied to their joints, Hardwick tells them he is proud. He is proud of Houli, and his courage to use the ball with class. He is proud of Cotchin, for warring with his opponents on the boundary line, sparking a melee. He is proud of Riewoldt for taking 500 shots on goal during the week, and seeing his effort rewarded with a match-winning six-goal haul.

A full match review isn't needed this week, he says. There is little to be gleaned from this game. "It was just a shit fight. There was nothing pleasant about it," he says. But he stops then, sensing maybe that he undersold their effort and intent—that which he asked for and which he was given. "It was just spirit. It was a show of heart."

He tells them one more thing. If they don't already, they need to start believing in their season. Five wins and zero losses means something. "You have to ask yourself a question," he says, scanning the room. "Why not us?"

The players depart for recovery. The coach leaves to attend the press conference. The last man left in the briefing room is Livingstone, packing iPads and laptops into his monogrammed "TL" backpack. He muses on the issue of control, and whether it exists in the coach's box—or at least to what degree.

"It's not an illusion, but I do think your game is won during the week. Damien would say that as well," he says. "On game day, coaches can change kicks-ins, stoppage structure, adjust tactics a bit—*usually based on things that aren't working*—but in the end, if you've not prepared and trained, you're in a bit of trouble."

If you want to understand the impact of the game day communication between coaches and players—between football's cause and effect—Livingstone suggests listening to the maxim of Craig McRae, the club's VFL coach.

"'Fly' has a great way of putting it," he says. "On game day you hand the keys of the car over to the players. In the end, they've got to drive."

19

ONE TENTH OF A SECOND

Although it is only late April, it feels like winter. The sky is dark this early on a Friday morning and the clouds above are a blanket of bruised and sullen grey, with patches of faint blue. In the heated gym at Punt Road Oval, a US college football game between southern rivals Alabama and Clemson captures the attention of the physio staff.

Jack Riewoldt watches, too, cycling alone in the heat chamber. Toby Nankervis places his focus elsewhere, on the upper body weights stations, lifting alone, while Ben Lennon, searching for added mobility, twists his legs against rubber resistance bands, working on his core strength and warming up for the day.

They are the only players doing extras so far, until Shaun Grigg walks in wearing a pair of army green dropped crotch pants and a black hoodie. Grigg is—according to Damien Hardwick—the smartest player on the Richmond list. By this he does not mean the best scholar or conversationalist (although he might be) but rather the most astute judge of football dynamics—the fastest interpreter of the way a ball moves through the field, and the way players circle and twist in concentric patterns around it, drawn into or resisting its orbit. Basically, says the coach, Grigg reads the game a fraction faster than most, and a fraction is all it takes.

"I'm just calm out there," Grigg says, sitting down in a quiet alcove on the ground level of the club complex. "I think I've got enough game sense to find the ball and set up other people. I think I can pick the momentum of the contest and the mood of the group. I know when to hold it up if it's been helter-skelter for too long, and when to surge. I always tell the boys, 'My horsepower's up here'," he says, tapping his temple.

The wider football world has only just begun catching up to this notion, the pundits now realising what has been clear to Richmond devotees for some time—that important victorious moments for the Tigers generally tend to involve the unfashionable, ultra-consistent left-foot midfielder in some way. Grigg is what you might call a clutch player—"clutch" being that catch-all American term for an athlete who absorbs the pressure of the moment and crafts a cool response.

Often clutch is used to describe the all-time greats, which makes sense because those players invariably rise to the occasion. Larry Bird, the Boston Celtics power forward, had a knack for saving his most insouciant passing for the NBA Finals. Derek Jeter, the legendary Yankees shortstop, did not own a superior Major League Baseball batting average, but he knew exactly when a base hit was required and so delivered one, time and again, and in doing so delivered New York five World Series. In tennis, there was Jimmy Connors, in soccer Cristiano Ronaldo. The best of them is possibly New England Patriots quarterback Tom Brady, 39, who only two months earlier drove his team to a fifth Super Bowl victory, earning him the moniker of "GOAT" (Greatest Of All Time).

The closest AFL approximation is the much-decorated and universally revered Indigenous champion Shaun "Silk" Burgoyne—a long-time Hawthorn utility who seems to save his surest plays for those fleeting yet somehow elongated moments in final quarters, when epic matches are won or lost.

Grigg—to be clear—is not one of these people. This is perhaps the only time he will be mentioned in such company. But he does share shades of that crucial clutch trait with the greats. Formerly known for his reliability and durability, he is now a cold-blooded performer. Passages of play that win games invariably carry his imprint, with a tap, or a handball, or a seemingly simple pass that opens up the field. He has a knack for taking marks that must be taken, sticking tackles that must be stuck, and kicking goals that must be kicked. Composure has become an indisputable part of his arsenal, and never more so than in the early part of this season.

Against Collingwood, the goal that broke the Magpies' spirit was his.

Grigg earned a controversial free kick by exploiting the new 'third man up' ruck rule, then coolly goaled from 50 metres. Against West Coast in torrential rain, he lined up outside 50, at which point special comments man Dermott Brereton advised viewers to watch out for a short pass ("He hasn't got this journey," he said) but instead the 29-year-old slotted a long bomb to put the Tigers in front. And then against Melbourne, when the game could easily have drifted out of the Tigers' reach following a woeful second quarter, Grigg lined up on the boundary with six seconds left to half-time. The siren sounded only a moment after his snapped kick.

"I couldn't see the ball at all—there was this light obstructing my view," he says. "It was so bright. I literally had no idea where it went. It could have gone anywhere. It could have gone off the side of my boot. It could have gone into the corridor. It could have gone out on the full. But I could hear the crowd starting to roar and I *just* caught sight of it as it curled inside the goal post."

It's a shame he didn't see the ball in flight. Kicking a clutch goal and hearing the roar of the stadium is perhaps his favourite thing in football. He talks to the younger players about such moments—the way they make him shiver. The joy is the leather of his boot hitting the leather of the Sherrin, and that fleeting moment when he alone knows it will be a goal. He knows by combining kinetic memory—*that specific feeling of a flush strike*—and what his eyes tell him—*the early trajectory of the spinning object*.

"No-one watching on TV knows. None of the commentators know. Your teammates don't know. The coaches don't know. But you *know* you've got it sweet," he says. "You wait for the roar, but before that there's maybe one-tenth of a second where you're the only one anywhere who knows. It's pretty spine-tingling."

//////////

But there are lows to go with such highs. One came in Round 22 of last year, after the Tigers lost to the Saints by nine points, in what Hardwick called a "strange old encounter" at the MCG, but which others described as comfortably the worst game of the 2016 AFL season—from any team—a performance without skill or urgency or even pride.

Grigg, playing a new inside midfielder role that year, had been flying throughout the previous rounds but on this day was poor—registering an uncharacteristically low 19 possessions and two tackles. He was also out of contract. "That uncertainty, when you're one of the older guys, is hard," he says. "Especially for the whole season. I felt I was playing well enough to earn a new contract and to keep going, but sometimes that's out of your hands."

And so he walked down into the change rooms afterwards, and listened to the coach's message, which was all about tweaks and little changes and pursuing a new methodology: "Get this thing right," Hardwick said, "and we'll turn it around."

But for all the positivity from the coach, there was anger in the room. The Tigers had only scored six goals all day. They had fumbled, dropped easy marks, and fallen over. Cotchin couldn't contain his disgust: "Guys, I reckon Dimma is just being nice. I reckon we were insipid. *Insipid.* I'm embarrassed."

Rance fed from his captain's distaste, accusing himself and his team of playing like shy children, afraid to assert any kind of dominance: "Just passive. It's ugly footy and I just hate it. We're waiting for Cotch to stand up, me to stand up, Jack to do something brilliant. *Stand up! Stand the hell up!* Take control of your careers."

Then came Football Manager Dan Richardson, quietly imploring the players to realise that their effort—or lack thereof—has very real consequences. "People lose their jobs," he said. "There are people in this room who aren't going to be here next year, because of performances like that."

Hardwick stepped in to cool the moment. "Let's just take a deep breath," the coach said. "No more talk. No more bullshit. Families have barneys all the time. Shit happens. We talk about it. We deal with it. We can all get better, boys. No sooking, let's move on."

For Grigg, despite the routinely pervasive honesty and systematic bald feedback of the professional football club environment, that scene seemed unlike any other.

Yet strangely he understood.

"It was a certainly a shock," he says now. "But it's that tough moment, when everyone is under pressure. It was a shit season. Sometimes you crack."

Ironically, Grigg signed a new one-year deal the following week, setting himself up for another season of football but also another 12 months of uncertainty. He came into another pre-season shortly thereafter, this time without his best friend at the club, Brett Deledio, who had been traded to Greater Western Sydney. Grigg found it tough.

"I never thought that he would go. But that's how the game has gone now. It's fair enough—he wanted to have a crack at a flag at GWS," he says. "It's been different not having him around, particularly outside the club, our wives and kids all spending time together. I've missed him as a mate. But that's the beauty of a footy club—I've got 44 other mates as well."

Grigg is familiar with the way the world is: he was pick 19 for Carlton in 2006 and came to the Tigers after 43 games with the Blues, traded to Richmond in exchange for Andy Collins. He turned 29 in the middle of April and is now the oldest player in the club's best 22. (On the current playing list, only Ivan Maric is older.) Yet very quickly this season he felt energised by the changed attitude of the coaching group and the stated club philosophy of playing to one's strengths. It has made every day fun, and makes his job leading the younger contingent simpler.

"There's this trap when you get drafted, when you're a young player, of thinking you have to make yourself into this AFL superhero, fitting this mould where everyone's supposed to be the same type of person," he says. "But we've just encouraged everyone to be themselves. It's made the environment so much more relaxed, without taking any professionalism away. There are times for hard work, and there are times to have a joke. It's been a massive shift. Massive."

He noticed the tangible effects in the first pre-season game, against Adelaide at Etihad Stadium, when the small forwards ran riot and tackled compulsively. It was something Grigg needed to see. "Everyone says they're going well in pre-season. You hear them: 'We're running well, we're fitter, we're stronger', but it's impossible to confirm because you're not playing against anyone. The first game though, when I saw our young guys play with enthusiasm and pressure, I sort of thought, 'Wow, these guys really have improved'. They've stepped up."

Still, he couldn't have expected a five-and-zero start to the year. "We've played wet scraps and dry blockbusters. We've played games like Collingwood or Melbourne that we might have dropped in the past. But the seniority of the older guys and the enthusiasm of the younger ones is a good mix. Little things are being valued by the playing group, like the pressure the forwards are putting on. You don't get a stat, or a mention by the commentators, but we notice."

And it's fun, too.

"There's this cut-throat seriousness to the business that's always there," he says, "and sometimes you forget that it's a game that you fell in love with as a kid. That falls by the wayside as you think about how you need to improve in this area, or put on muscle, or drop your skinfolds. You need to improve, but a lot of guys forget to work on their strengths, what they're good at, the weapons that got them here."

For Grigg that was always running. He grew up in Linton, west of Ballarat, a small, cold community. He kept himself warm during games by running, always running. He watched his father play for the town, too, his dad's big boots crunching the icy puddles on grounds all about the goldfields region. "The guys who played in that senior team, these country footballers, I idolised them as much as Nathan Buckley, James Hird and Wayne Carey. And I just hung around those club rooms like a bad smell."

He played junior footy in jumpers that didn't fit, or had faded colours, or the wrong pattern of stripes, so long as they were somewhat close to maroon and gold. His dad was the president of the club and his mum washed jumpers and worked in the canteen. The weekends were everything in his life—a world brought low by losses and warmed by wins. The 20 minutes after a victory is something he describes as both the best feeling and the worst.

"Mentally and physically you're gone, you're stuffed. But you're sitting next to your mates. Everyone's dirty and sweaty and some guys have got cuts and bruises, and you're all iced up." In those moments—both as a child and still now as an adult—he revels in chatting about the goal a mate kicked, or the tackle the captain nailed, or that spoil and how the ball bounced and bobbled and how in the *hell* did that end up in his hands? *Did you see that?*

As Grigg got older, he realised that those minutes after a game are everything to him. Everything. The epiphany crystalised one day when he heard a quote from a cricketer, English paceman Stuart Broad, who said something like: *Remember all the teammates who support you, all the coaches who help you, all the fans who cheer for you, but at the end of the day, play for the little boy who fell in love with the game.*

"That just rang true for me, because I remember myself in the backyard, and the change rooms at Linton, and how much I loved it, and then last year how I lost it in the hard times, and how much I missed it," he says. "I don't want to miss it again."

20

LEAVE NOTHING TO CHANCE

Bells ring out in the City of Churches for a Saturday afternoon wedding. St Peter's Cathedral, on the banks of the flowing *Karrawirra Parri* or Torrens River, overflows with revellers. And next door sits the comparatively quiet Adelaide Oval, where the unbeaten Tigers are warming up, one day ahead of playing the unbeaten Crows for top spot on the AFL ladder.

The roof inside the stadium is rather beautiful, shaped like sea shells and sheltering thousands of seats in grandstands named for Bradman and Chappell, Ricciuto and Wanganeen. At one end behind the goals is the grassy hill—a gorgeous gap in the edifice of the venue. It is something of a throwback feature in modern arena architecture, as is the historic manual scoreboard. This is a marvellous venue for sport, many suggest the best in Australia, and, as is the way with all modern stadia, it has a pristine surface.

Adelaide Oval has its imperfections and quirks though, too. The pockets, for instance, are shallow. Walk even 15 metres along the boundary line from the point post, as Justin Leppitsch does now during the captain's run training session, and you are left staring at a wide goalmouth target. The mercurial Eddie Betts has made this pocket famous for the seemingly impossible goals he often kicks here but—*with no disrespect to his legend*—the angle is incredibly favourable. So obtuse, so forgiving. Far more so than on any other AFL ground in the country.

Leppitsch points out as much, standing now 25 metres from goal. "See the way the lines come in?" he says, standing on the chalk dust. "It opens the face of goal and narrows the space inside 50. It leads to a lot of goals, a lot of kicks out of bounds on the full, and a lot of free kicks for deliberate."

He tells a few of the players this because in 24 hours they will enter this serene space and find instead a crucible—a true battle in enemy territory, against a top team, with an infamously rabid home crowd at their backs. The coaches know it will be a factor.

Only a day earlier, in Melbourne, Ben Rutten, a former Crow, began his opposition analysis at the Punt Road Oval not by dissecting Adelaide's offensive brilliance, or the contested ball power of midfielder Matt Crouch, or the run-and-gun handball weaves of their rebounding defenders, but by considering the oval itself.

"It's important we go over there not fearing this ground. The teams that do," he said, pausing, "are beaten before they get there."

Later, he explains that the noise created by this parochial crowd, whether those from Adelaide or their crosstown rivals, the Power—and then contained and amplified within the curved roof design—is deafening. But there is also, he notes, some "history" for certain Tiger players to overcome—a reference to the day Port Adelaide eviscerated Richmond here in a 2014 elimination final. "It's a great place to play footy. It can be a scary place. But it's not something we can afford to fear."

He talked to the players in this meeting, too, about taking an attacking mindset to the game. The Crows have, up to this moment, beaten their 2017 opponents by an average margin of 45 points, and so there is an inherent risk that the Tigers will fall into the trap of playing only to limit that scoring power.

"We're playing to beat—not to stop," he says. "The Crows are the number two team in the competition at winning ground balls, but Richmond is number one."

He shows footage of the Crows losing a final last year against the Swans—three video clips that demonstrate how Richmond can win. In the first, a Crows defender tries to clear the ball with a short kick but it is intercepted. "Covering their exits," says Rutten.

The second clip shows Sydney outnumbering Adelaide in a contest, and a Swan player streeting away with the ball. "Two versus one," he says.

The third clip is of young Sydney onballer Isaac Heeney crashing into a Crow and emerging with the football. "Wanted it more," says Rutten.

"This is what they haven't faced this year," he says, pointing at the screen. "But they're going to get it on Sunday."

//////////

On level one of the hotel where the Richmond team is staying, there is a small room populated with a few chairs and massage beds, the temporary treatment room for the players to receive rub downs and therapeutic massages. Now however, around 5:30pm, it is the venue for the Tigers defensive line meeting.

The players—Conca, Rance, Ellis, Short, Astbury, Grimes and Houli— are dressed casually, having just come from their pool recovery after the final training session. They chat now in the little conference room, debating the size of the flatscreen TV (100 inches?) while sparking a little laugh or two by drawing dicks on the whiteboard.

Rutten, wearing thongs, dims the lights to present a summary of strengths and weaknesses, but the point of the meeting runs deeper. It is ostensibly to voice any final encouraging thoughts or unconsidered insights.

Rance says it's important not to leave it up to the umpires to win their battles for them. "If you're in a marking contest, don't play for the free kick, don't go to ground, don't paddle it out of bounds. We grab that ball. We take it on and we're smart about it, and we keep the game in our hands."

Rutten makes a point about structure, particularly when Nankervis drops back into the path of Adelaide's triple threat of tall forwards in Taylor Walker, Tom Lynch and Josh Jenkins. "When Nank is there, disregard him. He's rucking solo, so he's doing that for a rest, not to provide cover. Don't expect him to be doing any of your work for you."

They talk about having faith in their ability to hold back the tide. Astbury, for instance, returns to the Melbourne game, and the lop-sided inside 50 count. "The backs really, *really* stood up under duress," he says. "I didn't notice we had had that much ball coming our way—we just took it on. I just thought 'This is what we thrive on'."

Rutten clarifies the point. At one time against Melbourne, he says, the Demons had 33 inside 50s to the Tigers' nine. But the two teams had the same number of scoring shots. "That's why we invest in our mental program," he says. "So we can withstand those moments."

The "mental program" is something the backmen have led at Richmond. Two years earlier, Emma Murray, a mindfulness expert, came to the club and began working with individuals. Among the first were Dylan Grimes and Steven Morris. Now Rance, Ellis and Astbury are all faithful adherents. Most take part in one-on-one sessions with Murray, but the defensive line also does regular work as a group.

When playing in Victoria that means gathering them together in person, but for an away game such as this, Murray records a sound file of the session. The words aren't *pro forma*, either. Murray sat in on line meetings during the week, and talked with Rutten about what key messages he wanted reinforced. All he needs to do now is push *play*.

"It's about eight minutes long today," says Rutten, hitting the button. "It's been a short, busy week, but take this time. Connect as a group, you're going to be relying on each other out there."

And so in the darkened room, Houli sits on the floor with his back against a wall, legs straight, hands in his lap. Grimes lies flat on a massage table at the back of the room. Astbury sits bolt upright in a chair, hands placed on his knees. Conca sits cross-legged, chest out, like a boy in the front row of a school photo. Rance lays on the carpet with a hat over his face—Ellis, too, with the glare of the flatscreen on his head. Short is squirreled away in a corner on his back, with his room key tucked into his sock. Now the voice of Murray enters the air.

"I want you to start by closing your eyes and taking a deep breath," she says.

The players' chests rise and fall in response.

"Take your full awareness to that deep breath, noticing your entire body just letting go. Become present in this moment now, and just feel yourself relaxing, everything becoming quiet, and becoming still. And as you take your attention to your breath, I want you to focus on how this visualisation is just one moment in your preparation leading up to tomorrow's game."

Over the next eight minutes, Murray helps them picture how each of them wants to play against the Crows, encouraging them to feel their breath and energy, and the energy between each person in the room—tuning out distractions, and tuning into this space.

She asks them to engage their imagination, bringing images of one another into their minds—mental pictures of them playing, using their strengths. She wants each player to see themselves alongside a teammate now, to see themselves winning together.

"Pay close attention to how you dominate when working with your teammate. Notice how your connection with this teammate will always overpower and beat any Adelaide forward."

She gets them to zoom in on these mental pictures. To focus on how they talk to, cover for, fight with, and sacrifice for each other.

"Focus on the aggression now. Focus on how two players with full aggression can dominate each and every moment of the game."

She asks them to flick quickly through each individual there and what they bring to the contest. To see each face in this room, and feel trust in them. To feel excited by what they see in their minds.

"Make your picture big, and bright. Don't see yourself stopping the opposition—see yourself beating the opposition."

Now she gets them to zoom out, and see the entire backline working as a group—one big machine functioning and firing.

"See the white bright light that connects each of you. See that white bright light like chains, from one player to another player. Every single back makes a link in that chain."

She asks them to imagine any part of the game they want. See it unfold. Watch the ball enter their zone and then be repelled. See it coming toward them. See them beating their opponents. See them corner and control the opposition.

"See the Adelaide forwards getting caught in that chain, caught in that web of chains. I want you to notice that power, aggression and domination when every member of the chain is doing their job and playing to their strengths."

She takes them through celebrating on the siren, in the rooms, and how great it feels within this group.

"Deep breath now, and imagine energy coming into the feet, and legs, and body. Everything is set. Everything is ready to go. Take a deep breath knowing your mental preparation is done. When you're ready, bring your attention to the darkness behind your eyes, and come into the room, ready to go."

They cough and sniff as they open their eyes.

Someone murmurs "Good, good."

Someone else whispers quietly: "Yes."

Someone else again: "Oh yeah…"

Inside the rooms at the ground the next day, everything is set out and waiting for the players. Giuseppe Mamone, the property manager, is the man responsible. He flew to Adelaide a day earlier, getting up at 4am to escort 57 big grey plastic boxes—like gigantic coolers—through freight travel.

The club takes around 1200 kilograms of gear with it to every game, and so each box has to be labelled carefully, with a letter or two, according to the system designed by Mamone. W is for warm-up tops. I is for interchange (meaning blankets and jackets). F for footys (16 of them). MF is for mini footys (23 for the players and coach to sign and disperse to the crowd). BB is bump bags (for floor exercises during warm up). GD is for Gatorade drums. And so on.

M is for miscellaneous, which includes a spare projector (which the coaches sometimes use for presentations), a spare set of scales (because the players weigh themselves before and after every game and training session), a spare mouthguard (because you never know), and a tool box (because the wheels on one of these boxes once broke, and Mamone wants to have the right tools at hand should it happen again).

"We leave nothing to chance. We take everything we might need," he says. "The projector might only get used once a year, or not at all, but at least I know I've got it."

The checklist is daunting. Jumpers, shorts, whiteboards, medical gear, trainers' gear and IT boxes filled with computers, cables and switching terminals. Four boxes of empty water bottles. Foam rollers and chewing gum. Allen's snakes and beetroot juice. Massage cream, Deep Heat, liniment oil, surgical gloves, blister shields, heel lifts, cotton tips and *Wilgrip* (resin). There are ice bags, vomit bags and blood bags. There is narrow tape, wide tape, elastic tape, taut tape, scissors and nail clippers.

Once Mamone arrives interstate, he hires a truck, loads it all up at the airport freight shed, goes to the hotel to pick up a few items like fresh towels and Gatorade that were delivered there, then he goes grocery shopping— for fresh fruit, sandwiches, muesli bars and yoghurt. Once he and his crew arrive at the stadium, they set up massage tables and folding tables for food and drink. They hang signage around the rooms, so it feels like it belongs to the team. When the short training session is done, the gear is left overnight and needs only a refresh two hours before the first bounce.

Mamone started in this kind of logistical role in 1993, when he was

12 years old, at the Coburg Football Club. (Carlton legend Alex Jesaulenko was the coach.) In 2004, he went to the Calder Cannons. He worked with Brisbane in 2008 and 2009. In 2010, he came to Richmond. "I'm 35," he says. "I have not missed one weekend of football since 1993. I've missed weddings, funerals, 21st birthdays. Because I love what I do."

In his lair, back at Tigerland, they do 120 loads of washing a week. Dozens of footys are pumped daily using a device he designed. (Mamone was sick of footballs getting over-inflated or under-inflated, so he worked with Airtech—who design the tire pumps at service stations—to create a pump that inflates balls to exactly 69psi/kpg.)

Mamone is the master of his domain, and detail-oriented to a fault. He has trays of different coloured plastic cable ties, for instance, to seal up those 57 travel boxes for away games. Orange cable ties are for Gold Coast and GWS games. Purple for Fremantle and Port Adelaide. Red for Sydney. Yellow for Brisbane and Adelaide. Why?

"That way, if someone cuts open a box at the airport and replaces it with another cable tie, I'll know, because they're unlikely to have colourful ties. If it's sealed with black or white, I know to check the contents."

Boots are stored in another room, with the boot studder, Ilmar Tiltins, who has been a volunteer at the club for 37 years. And he's not even the longest serving. That honour goes to Ted Soderblom, who helps out during the week, and is 84. He's been here 51 years. Both receive a small stipend for their service.

Mamone though is a full-time employee of the club, and does the job because he loves meeting people, but more so because he enjoys helping the machine function—a perfect cog in something much larger. "I love the players feeling happy with what they've been given—the service we've provided. Whatever they want, just get it. Make everything go smoothly, never a hiccup. That's why I'm here."

///////////

The players get dressed to music. House music. Dance beats. But also Run to Paradise by Choirboys and Jessie's Girl by Rick Springfield. None of the players on the field tonight was born when the latter two songs were written.

The coaches meanwhile go over a few last-minute plans—things brought up earlier in the day during what they call their "contingency meeting", which coaching director Tim Livingstone describes simply as the "what if" meeting. "What if they do that? What if things don't go to plan?" he asks. "It's your plan B for every back-pocket scenario."

If a certain Adelaide player gets out of control, who is the next best Tiger to take responsibility for stopping him? If the Crows are scoring too heavily and we want to play seven defenders, which of them should play spare?

Asking such questions in advance is a necessity. When Richmond played the West Coast Eagles and Sam Mitchell had 12 touches in the first quarter, the decision to send Kane Lambert to Mitchell was not the product of a moment's inspiration—it was planned in one such contingency meeting. "You have to be prepared," says Livingstone. "You don't want to be thinking of a solution during the game. You haven't got time."

And so, they ask, among more than two dozen worst case scenarios, who will follow Crows wingman Rory Atkins if he gets loose? *Possibly the athletic Oleg Markov.*

Nick Vlastuin is playing forward today, but if he is needed in defence, who will go into attack? *Kamdyn McIntosh is the likely replacement.*

If Sloane, the best player in the competition so far this year, begins dominating, who will handle him? *Cotchin at stoppages. Lambert around the ground.*

"But those are just the planned contingencies," says Livingstone. "The game, as usual, throws up things you never expect."

///////////

In the team meeting, Hardwick talks about playing country footy for Upwey, and the road trips through the ranges there. He loves travelling with footy teams. He loved the 90-minute bus ride to Healesville then, and he loves the quick flight to South Australia now.

Back at Upwey, he remembers being 15, and his dad was the coach of the under-17s. His dad would count the boys as they came into the club after a Friday night out, hoping like hell he had enough players for a side. Young Damien would be hoping for the exact opposite, so he could fill in for someone and play.

"I didn't always get a game. But I'll never forget those journeys in the bus. I used to get more enjoyment out of the trip itself than the game. The young blokes getting to hear the old blokes' stories. I think that's where you get that steely resolve, from winning together away. There's nothing better than getting on that plane tonight feeling that winner's ache."

But that is not to be this day.

Richmond beats Adelaide in all areas in the first quarter, but also leaks easy goals out the back. The Tigers dominate yet lead at quarter time by only nine points in what looms as a shootout. Richmond doesn't want a shootout—not against a team with this kind of firepower.

Early in the second quarter, such concerns are realised. The Tigers are pressuring, running, using strengths, stopping high marks, going long down the line when needed, but they quickly fall behind anyway.

Before the game, in the midfielders' line meeting, Blake Caracella foretold a great game of football, a contested game, a game in the style of finals. "You reckon it's going to break open in the first quarter? The second? Third? No. You'll have to fight for this win all game. It might take until the last two minutes," he said. "All game, boys."

But the game is already being torn apart.

The Crows look ominous going forward, their ball movement so slick by hand or foot. In truth it is the result of better tackling and harassment. They are playing harder, tougher and more disciplined football. They kick six goals to one. The Tigers limp in at half-time 27 points down, and in private Caracella sums up the thoughts of the coaching group: "They're big. They move. They shape well. They're clean."

In the first quarter, the Tigers win the contested ball by 13—as well as they have played all year. In the second quarter though, they are beaten by 18. Hardwick tells his players that's the difference. They have been beaten up around the ball. No other numbers count. "I can write E equals MC squared up here, but it makes no difference. What matters is that one statistic: contested ball."

It doesn't get better. In the third quarter, they lose that metric by 17, another thumping. As the goals rain down the sky darkens. Now everything feels hopeless. Bounces pivot sharply away from Tigers. Free kicks go unrecognised. Every Adelaide forward foray ends in a score. They take shot upon shot from outside 50, and shot upon shot soars comfortably through the goals. Not only do they have range—they have radars, too, and a 53-point lead.

The crowd rides it all in a kind of frenzied delirium. As part of the home game entertainment, the speaker system fires a cannon shot every time the Crows kick a goal. It is a deadening thud that echoes around the ground and lets everyone know a blow has been landed. When they are winning like this—seven goals to one this quarter—those blows sound like nails pounding into a coffin. The metaphor is appropriate. Beating an opponent in this fashion seems an act of "killing". The lexicon of football says so. A player with great field kicking skill is "lethal". A forward with a great set shot is a "sharpshooter". A goal kicked from distance is a "bomb". One kicked from a tight angle in a tight game is "deadly". The small forward who lurks in wait is "dangerous". The big forward hovering for a mark is "threatening". Today Adelaide has, and are, all these things.

Yet the crowd does not seem content. They boo at 'missed' free kicks. They boo when the play is halted. They boo over score reviews. They boo even when the score review goes in their favour, indignant that their score was ever held in question—that anyone or anything dare delay their revelry. Sometimes when they don't get the decision they want, they leap to their feet on the terraces and throw fists forward, until *en masse* it almost looks like a military salute.

There is also a complete lack of civil appreciation for any special flourish from the opposition. When Rioli takes an impossible mark—one that might generally bring polite applause—they remain utterly impassive. When Kane Lambert stands under a high ball, absorbs a jarring hit, and struggles to regain his feet, they are unwilling to grudgingly acknowledge the player for bravely taking the hit.

Winning is not enough. Delighting in the loss of the other is their right. I have seen this before, when I once spent a week in the middle of the Richmond cheer squad. Inside a cheer squad, every fan knows that the person sitting beside them shares at least some of the same pride and prejudice, and so they have freedom to scream wildly, at times with caustic abandon. That is what an interstate crowd is like—one giant cheer squad with more than 50,000 members.

And like all fans, they have their favourite targets. If Rance, the pre-eminent key defender in the game, is outmarked, the volume of their disdainful joy lifts. If Jack Riewoldt is spoiled in a marking contest, their glee is unmitigated. But if Dustin Martin should attempt to fend an opponent with his patented "don't argue" manoeuvre and fail—as he does against Charlie Cameron in this match—then the roar is pure ecstasy. This is entirely normal in football, no matter where it is played, and it is to be expected—but at Adelaide or Perth or Geelong such rapture is nevertheless magnified.

And so, 53 points becomes 59 points, then 65 points, and then you get a true sense of how negative momentum feels.

Adelaide marches the ball down the full length of the ground, and the slowly building roar as they fire at goal sounds like a pure and primal release. When it sails through, the snarl is guttural. The sound rolls out from under the curved stadium roof and pours onto the field. It is beyond loud. At times, it is as if the crowd noise has become white noise.

///////////

Then all is silent, except the shuffling of feet as players make their way into the briefing room, not to cop a spray but to hear from Hardwick, who is measured.

"The harsh reality is life throws curve balls at you. Anyone see that coming? I didn't. But we've clearly got some work to do, and we know it. Look at the first and last quarters and we outhunt, we outmuscle, and we get the ball to ground, and we win those quarters. But quarters two and three, from the coach's box, we're trying to flick things around like we're on the Titanic. The magnets are flying—fix this hole, that hole, because the game's gone. It's gone."

He is happy though—in some strange way at least—that the loss is a true "kick in the arse". It should spark resolve. It should inspire reflection. It should demand a reaction, after they lick their wounds and get in the plane home. "The result says we lost by 76 points, but defeat is built on a very fine line—the ball going your way or theirs. Learn from it, but move on. We're five and one. Onwards and upwards. Obstacle versus opportunity."

///////////

The players now have 20 minutes to get changed, eat some hot pasta from a bain-marie cart wheeled into the rooms, then head to the pools under the Adelaide Oval for recovery, while Hardwick heads to his obligatory press conference.

Soon after they're on a bus and off into the night, in silence, wearing beanies and earbuds, headed to the airport, where they hobble across the cool polished floor of the quiet terminal, headed toward the Virgin Australia pre-flight lounge. They settle in there in better spirits, and eat complimentary toasted sandwiches while gulping bottled water. They watch a replay of the match from MCG that day, Collingwood doing what Richmond wanted to do—upset a ladder leader by toppling Geelong.

Riewoldt talks briefly with football pundits David King and Gerard Healy, fresh from their broadcast of the match against the Crows. Club CEO Brendon Gale sips from a glass of white wine with new board member Henriette Rothschild. The stillness of the bus ride is gone, and voices gather in the space. Smiles return.

///////////

On the flight back to Melbourne, somewhere above Dimboola or Horsham or Nhill, Andrew McQualter, the stoppages coach, opens his laptop in seat 9B. The task at hand is coding the game, at first focusing primarily on bounces and throw-ins.

Essentially it means watching footage of the game, and hitting buttons that mark and cut various passages of play, depending on what McQualter wants to highlight—a mixture of good things (green) and bad things (red).

There are dozens of such potential buttons: Body Work, Striker, Brady, A1, D2, Kick-In and more. And McQualter can—with the flick of a key—switch between camera views of the same footage, to close-up or standard feed, or the view from behind either goal, to examine each play in more depth. He knows what he is looking for.

He can click on "Structure" and "Red" for instance, if he wants to mark a poor centre bounce set-up by the midfielders. He can click on "Zone" and "Green", if he sees an example of his players slotting perfectly into their allotted space. "It's mainly the good stuff," he says. "Unless something is significantly breaking down."

The players can later access their own more general and thorough "supercut" of vision through the official stats supplier, Champion Data, including every single moment from the match in which they played a part. McQualter can also go a little deeper, clicking on a grid list of players, to point out an individual's good or bad efforts.

For instance, the screen shows Prestia taking on a tackler and kicking forward, so McQualter clicks "Attack", "Green" and "Prestia", so that the positive piece of vision is stored. Perhaps it will be used during the week to highlight the strong attacking movements of Tiger onballers. Next, in the centre square, Josh Caddy muscles his opponent aside, creating space for Martin to run through, and so McQualter clicks "Body Work", "Green" and "Caddy". In a line meeting in two days he might use such efforts to illustrate what he expects from the bigger mids. In the next sequence, Conca tries to emulate Martin's most famous manoeuvre, the straight arm fend, but Rory Sloane holds on and brings Conca to ground. McQualter clicks "Meeting" and "Funny", knowing he will highlight the error for a joke during a team meeting this coming week.

Next Dustin Martin tries his own fend, but Charlie Cameron catches him and the ball spills free, so McQualter clicks "Attack", "Red" and "Martin".

"But I probably wouldn't show him that," McQualter says. "Ninety-nine times out of a hundred Dusty gets out of that. But we need to code it anyway, because if he has eight of them in one game then maybe there's an issue."

McQualter will spend most of the next day coding. As will Caracella, looking at structure, Rutten, looking at his defenders, Leppitsch, paying attention to the forwards, along with Hardwick and Livingstone and others, examining the tape for whichever moments they consider key indicators— snippets they might show to the entire team, or a line, or an individual.

The result is a matrix of the game represented as colour-coded, time-coded moments. McQualter has been working on his vision for two hours now, but has only barely finished viewing the first quarter.

"If you looked at that matrix now, what would you think?" he asks.

There are very few red moments. It's all green. Richmond dominated.

"Yep. And if you were to watch me code the next three quarters, what do you think's going to happen?"

It's all going to turn red?

"It's all going to turn red."

It's 11:15pm when the plane lands, and the team yawns collectively as bags are picked up. They schlep their belongings now to a bus terminal, and shuttle by shuttle they are ferried to the carpark.

In one bus, Hardwick and Hill sit silently side by side. Rioli and Markov hold an iPhone between them, watching footage of a friend from their draft year, Brandon Parfitt of Geelong, who tore his hamstring badly against Collingwood hours earlier. Rance and Astbury look on. "Oh nooo," says Astbury, watching from the seat behind. "That's shocking."

One by one the players get their keys, and then they are gone, headed home to rest up before a day off, before beginning again. Richmond has only a six-day break before facing the reigning premiers, the Western Bulldogs, at Etihad Stadium, the Dogs' favoured hunting ground. It is midnight in Melbourne at the end of a long, hard weekend.

21

MASTER OF THE MIND

More than a year ago, on a boiling hot day in January 2016, a woman stood alone at the front of the Richmond auditorium. Forty-five young footballers stared down on her, and the picture on the whiteboard at her back—a crude drawing of four squares.

The top right square was labelled "behavioural", referring to kicking and marking and fitness. Beneath it sat "systemic", meaning the game plan and those all-important 'structures' the football public hears mentioned so often but knows so little about. In the bottom-left square sat "cultural", including values and leadership—an area that, through peer feedback and communication, became a recent focus for the club. Above that, at the top left, sat the word "intentional". No explanation was offered.

Emma Murray, in black slacks and loose white sleeveless top, could see the bemused group looking her way, wondering what it meant, wondering who this lady was anyway? Murray runs a business, working with people, using mindfulness, meditation, visualisation and hypnotherapy, among other mental preparation techniques.

The "intentional" quadrant, she told the players, concerns training the mind, and addressing arousal levels. It's about motivation, decision-making, attention, concentration, empathy and resilience. These areas were, to an extent, going unaddressed at the Tigers and other clubs, in part because people too often believe that you either have that competitive steel—the will and focus and hard edge—or you don't. Either you *are* Joel Selwood or Luke Hodge, or you are not. Murray doesn't buy that. "Your mind is just a muscle. It's no different from any other muscle in the body," she told the players. "It's highly trainable."

Murray has worked for two decades with everyone from students to athletes, surgeons to executives, and was herself an elite sportswoman. She was an AIS and VIS scholarship holder as a netball player, and an accredited State League coach in the sport. Her company works with AFL and VFL clubs, VCE students and surgical nurses, elite rowers and ultra-marathon runners. She told the players she was here to give them a taste of what she could offer, and would work one-on-one with any player who wanted private guidance. She had already worked with a handful of the players. She could help, she said.

Athletes are often criticised for being not "mentally tough enough", for making poor decisions or freezing in the moment. Each of these critiques has been made of Richmond in the recent past. They are not the first team to be labelled 'flaky' or 'fragile', yet relatively few clubs have worked as seriously on strengthening emotional control. Hypnosis and meditation have been used in an *ad hoc* manner in Australian rules since the late 1970s (in their last truly great years, between 1980 and 1982, Richmond called upon the West Indian, Dr Rudi Webster[9]) but few clubs have implemented any structured program. The AFL is well behind this curve. Murray cited the US Olympic team, the Michael Jordan-era Chicago Bulls, and even the South Sydney Rabbitohs Rugby League club as early and eager adopters. "You want improvement?" she asks. "Then is it worth looking in an area you haven't looked before?"

Murray glanced at the board, and went through the quadrants again, one by one. People don't lose the ability to kick or mark, she said. And why do players adhere rigidly to structures and set-ups one week, and not the next? If a culture is firmly established, she added, it should absorb the shock of any bumps in the road, shouldn't it? The obvious problem in fluctuating form, she said, was sitting up there on the whiteboard. Top left. The blank quadrant. *Intentional.*

---

9   Webster, nicknamed the "Witch Doctor", left Carlton after the Blues' 1979 flag, to join Richmond under
      coach Tony Jewell, then played a crucial role in the 1980 premiership, the last cup won by Richmond. Webster
      promoted mental discipline, relaxation, hypnotherapy and positive thinking: "The greatest enemy a player has
      is not the opponent on the field," he once said. "It is the one in his head."

"Right now, I want a show of hands," she said. "Whose attention is going in and out of this room? Are you finding that?"

Perhaps three dozen hands rose. Murray called on the players she had helped in the past: did working with her help them maintain concentration?

Steve Morris, seated near the back of the room, said it did. His road to the club was not easy. Although he is the son of dual premiership (1973-74) Tiger Kevin Morris, the nuggety backman was overlooked in successive drafts and moved interstate to play in the South Australian National Football League for West Adelaide, where he endured shoulder reconstructions and knee injuries before an eventual breakout season landed him at Richmond in 2012. Impressing with a fanatical work ethic and unyielding courage, he became a deserved 23-year-old debutant that year, and eventually a member of the leadership group.

Yet his form since has fluctuated. New recruits and draftees constantly threaten his place in the senior side. He is still a leader but is also fighting hard for a permanent place in the best 22. In that context, Morris began seeing Murray privately, to address his concentration problems. He wasn't worried about his focus drifting in and out of a room but in and out of a game. He wanted to work on those "moments between moments" on the field—breaks in the play when the mind would wander. Murray helped train his mind now to snap more quickly back into focus. His process began with posture. Morris would make a conscious effort to lift his chin, puff out his chest, and in doing so he would begin running through the game plan, figuring out where he is in the fray and what he should be doing. In turn, he would communicate better with teammates, instead of sleepwalking through a passage of play.

Murray had also helped goal sneak Sam Lloyd. Like Morris, Lloyd came to Punt Road the long way, first playing three seasons (2009-11) with Deniliquin, where he kicked 110 goals in a season as a 20-year-old (as well as a lazy 65 while playing mostly as a mid-fielder in a premiership team). In 2012 he played club football at Mt Eliza, then with the Bendigo Bombers in the VFL, and in 2013 he joined VFL club Frankston, before Richmond gave him a chance in the 2013 National Draft, at Pick 66. Like Morris, Lloyd faced the difficulty of being on the fringe of selection. In 2015, he played 12 games but was often the dreaded substitute, sitting on the bench for long periods, uncertain about when he would enter the field. Stuck in that green vest on the bench, he had too much time to listen to the arena, becoming distracted by the noise and lights and action.

Wearing a flat-brimmed black baseball cap, Lloyd told the group how he began working with Murray to address mindfulness—searching for a way to stay in the moment longer, without drifting out of the stadium. "It definitely worked. The only thing I was then focused on was what I could do, and what I needed to do," he said to the group. "When I came on, I was ready to go."

Training neural pathways to perform like this doesn't happen in a single session. Murray took out a black marker next and drew a misshapen brain on the whiteboard, complete with squiggly lines for pathways and reactions. Then she drew a little black dot to represent the "fear centre", and a few messy lines leading directly to that negative place. Those messy lines, she said, are pathways, and they have been established and altered since childhood.

Maybe it was something your mum said. Or something a teacher did. Whatever the initial cause, we all create and reinforce these comfortable little goat tracks that lead us to the same reactions, over and over. Some of those reactions are negative and habitual—unless we create new ones, and strong ones. "This is science," Murray said. "You build these pathways without even knowing, but you can choose a different response. And if you choose it often enough, it will become natural."

Craig McRae, at the back of the room, raised his hand. He had something to share from his days at the Brisbane Lions, then on a rampage that was—at the time—unprecedented in the national and professional era of the game. It was also an era, he pointed out, with few mobile phones. When people wanted to reach players during the day they would call the club and be put through to a message bank. Somehow one of the players came up with the idea that if something difficult had to be done—at training or on the field—it was like a call was coming through. The pain was calling. The fatigue was calling.

And so, in a hard-running session the leaders might yell out to group, "Don't take the call! Don't take the call! Send it to messages! Send it to messages!" If a player was being tagged: "Send it to messages!" If a player got hit hard in a game: "Send it to messages!" The Lions developed an enviable brand of resilience off such mental tricks.

Murray loved this input. It seemed a perfect example of setting a new way of thinking—a new pathway that becomes so well-worn that the old pathway is eventually grown over and hidden, swallowed by the landscape of the mind until it exists no more. When the pressure was on, she said, the Lions just didn't have any neural path to quitting. "It just wasn't there," she said. "Those little choices can change what our brain looks like. We can train it, day by day, for that crucial, make-or-break moment."

Tall defender Dylan Grimes, another client of Murray, sat on the right side of the room and raised his voice. He used to get nervous at the sound of the crowd—the way the roar built up and released in big moments, and bubbled with anticipation as the next turning point approached. It was a tough problem to have given the drawing power of the club. Richmond has always been well supported.

The success of the Tigers in that ruthless period from 1966 to 1982, when it won five flags, helped build the "Tiger Army". Many of those duffle-coated foot soldiers were lost in the calamitous late 1980s as well as the mostly inept 1990s and 2000s, when Richmond teams failed to give people a reason to show up. But with successive finals appearances over 2013, 2014 and 2015, the club saw its latent, potent fan base—and membership—rise dramatically. In 2013 the Tigers cracked the 60,000-member mark. In 2014 that rose to 66,000. In 2015, 70,000 signed up. This year, more fans have attended Richmond games than for any other club. If you play for the Tigers, crowd noise is a fact of life.

Yet as the noise built at each game, the pressure inside Grimes did too. The roar too often sent him into a flurry of nerves. His only recourse, with the help of Murray, was to develop positive stories to associate with the aural fury swirling around him. "I just imagined they were saying great things about me," he said. "Then when they roared it was almost like I was being rewarded, complimented before I'd done anything."

Her central task though, she said, was to help players remain connected to how they feel. Be all right with slipping behind in a game, even if your legs are feeling like lead and your heart is pumping. Those feelings are not what bring men undone—the stories they tell are what cause distraction and collapse.

I've never had heavy legs before. How do I run with them? I'm going to play terribly. This is terrible. I might as well give up now.

She wanted to train them to recognise the extraordinary nature of any new feelings and deal with them. "You need to be able to look at a losing scoreboard in a final and be okay with that," she said. "You need to be able to use that piece of information and let it lift you."

Murray pointed out how any story—whether about your accuracy in front of goal, or seeing your family after the game—can take your brain out of the contest, which is why mindfulness is so crucial. Research in her field suggested that 47 per cent of the time human beings are mentally 'off-task', meaning footballers potentially play with only 53 per cent of their attention devoted to the game at hand. If the team is looking for a few extra Inside 50s, or two more goals, or five more tackles, increasing their attention level by 10 per cent might be enough. "You can be off for 20 seconds and miss something vital," she said. "Some tiny physical occurrence, some tiny visual clue the opposition was giving you."

She asked the people in the room then to close their eyes, and think for 45 seconds about one thing.

Go on now.
Be still.
Be silent.
What did you think about?

And who *could* stay on that one thing for the full 45 seconds?

No one. Not one person could hold that singular thought for less than a minute, while sitting in a quiet room. With no crowd. No expectations. No scoreboard. And no peer review. The clear inference: how many of these 45-second units are there in a game of football? (Answer: Roughly 163 consecutive chunks.)

The potential in controlling the mind in those moments is waiting to be tapped. But it takes effort, and Murray couldn't stress that enough. This generation, more than any other, is raised in a distraction-filled society. They listen to music through 'Beats by Dre' headphones before games. In the break room, between training drills, they pick up a *PlayStation* controller. They noodle on the web at the same time as watching a streamed television show at night, while answering emails and ignoring social media alerts. "Your brain is used to pinging from one thing to the other to the other," Murray said. "Then you're asked to step on to the footy field and keep your mind in the moment. That's virtually impossible—without putting in the work."

Hardwick approached the front of the room at the close of the presentation. He enjoyed it. He pointed to the box of quadrants. He looked at "behaviours", and pointed out that the club doesn't recruit boys who can't play. He looked at "systemic" and laughed—these players own their game plan. He glanced at "cultural", and noted that values and feedback have become a key plank in the rebuild of the club. ("We don't recruit dickheads, do we?") Then he turned his head upwards, to the top left, to all that "intentional" headspace they can develop through mental training, mindfulness, visualisation and resilience. He said this is the area in which his team could find the greatest improvement.

"This is the one thing, I reckon, that's holding us back," he said, slapping the whiteboard, then turning to Murray. "I'm not blowing smoke up your arse. You're going to be very important."

///////////

It is eighteen months later now, and Murray has become critical. The team lost to Adelaide, and lost badly, and in such instances, she has a role to play. Following a loss Murray is often called upon in match review meetings to address team mindset issues. Sometimes she guides the entire playing list through a meandering session, 44 sets of eyes closed, 44 pairs of lungs breathing deeply.

She did that after the Crows game, when it was apparent that the players had allowed one lost contest to turn into two lost contests, then a lost quarter, a lost half and an overall obliteration. She was addressing the psychology behind that most mysterious of modern football buzzwords, 'momentum'.

"Out there, when you make a mistake, you feel very alone," she said. "Like it's all on you. But what I'm saying is that you are *all* in *every* moment of the game. You are *never* alone. You don't win or lose off one play, or one player. What *really* hurts a team is when you have a cross instead of a tick, and you carry that cross into the next moment. And the next. And the next. The Seattle Seahawks called it an 'energy whip'. You lose your shit, and spread it to someone else, and we all carry it."

So, if you feel that you've got some crosses happening, she said, put your attention on something you can control. Maybe it's using your feet. Maybe it's using your voice. Maybe it's positioning. Maybe it's celebrating.

"Maybe it's a sheer fight—to put your attention on aggression, because your strength is a little wobbly. Make it a goal of yours that one cross doesn't become two or three or four. But we don't have some magical fairy that spreads belief and gives us courage. This stuff takes work."

Murray does this kind of work not just with the group *en masse*, or with each line, but with groups *within* each line, and with individual players.

///////////

Dylan Grimes was her first acolyte. He came to her at a time when injury plagued his career. "I'd had four or five seasons where I'd played eight or nine games and got injured, done my hamstring. I had this anticipation that I would re-injure myself. I remember coming back and I had a conversation with a coach and he told me that physically I was in the top percentile at the club, but I wasn't performing that way."

Murray, sitting with Grimes in a small room off the gym at Punt Road, interjects: "So what the subconscious mind does—*to keep Dylan safe*—is that when Dylan is on a lead, or extending himself in a chase, or is in a situation where he's done his hamstring in the past, is pull him back. He's not thinking about his hamstrings, but his subconscious mind is saying, 'I'm not letting you do that'. And that's not letting him take his game to that next level."

They worked on that issue, through exercises that focused on his strength, his speed, his fitness—anything that might make him *believe* in his legs. "We did one session, going through some exercises about having faith in my body, and my GPS went through the roof," Grimes says. "Through the roof."

Now he sees Murray once a week, and uses that time to prepare for an opponent, relieve stress in his personal life, or deal with a problem with a teammate or coach.

"Emma's work is sort of the only opportunity you have in the week to do a *brain dump*, or a tune up," Grimes says. "With all your coaches, you don't take stock of your mental state, and confidence is a huge thing in AFL. Huge. And there are such fluctuations in confidence. I could miss a mark out there today at training, and instantly remember a mark I missed in a game two weeks ago, then go into the next game doubting my overhead marking. Now I can come in and go, 'Emma, I don't know why, but two weeks ago I dropped a mark and I just dropped another one out there, and for some reason I'm going into the game doubting my skill set', and we can work on that. These sessions have become just as important as skills training, or weights, or meetings. I can iron out a tiny little thing like that before it grows into something bigger."

Grimes has also worked with Murray on expectations—what he expects will happen on the field, how he expects to beat his opponent, how he expects to make good decisions with the ball. He goes into games now, whether playing on Jeremy Cameron or Eddie Betts, relaxed, expecting to beat anyone, whether an All-Australian full forward or an All-Australian forward pocket.

Murray nods: "A lot of players hope and wish, and go in not knowing what's to come, because they don't reflect enough on the skills they've got, and the evidence of the work they've done. If they go back through their career, and think of their training, they have the evidence—the proof of their ability is right there. Our minds are so easy to manipulate, *if you do the work*, but so many don't do the work, and so they go in hoping and wishing rather than believing and expecting."

////////////

And so in 2017, mindfulness went from a spasmodic part of Richmond's football program, adopted with regularity by only a handful of players, to a full-list requirement. They began by doing regular short sessions in pre-season—three minutes of "attention control" exercises before weights training. Players reported better results, quickly.

Every player on the list was then required to complete two non-negotiable individual sessions with Murray. Three quarters of them came back for more. Some seek her out when they aren't performing well. Others come back when they feel mentally fatigued. Many others return weekly. For some, seeing Murray in the day or two before a game is part of a routine they will not break.

The buy-in didn't stop there. Some mornings she conducts visualisation exercises with groups of players in the darkness before dawn. Sleepy-eyed athletes lie down before first light in a carpeted room, and she walks above them, her soothing voice floating over them, like a lullaby over toddlers at nap time.

Other times, the coaching staff will talk to her about an upcoming opponent, and request a full playing list session in which her words intertwine with team strategy and whatever messages are being reinforced that week.

"At the most basic level, it means these guys can put their full attention to those strengths we always talk about. And that's important—not to let your attention drift off onto outcomes like the score or umpires or injury."

She is elated the club has come on board so enthusiastically. The players, she says, already come to meetings and freely speak up about how they were feeling on the field when they kicked that goal, or the game was lost. Murray is still involved with players from other AFL clubs and says most are shocked to hear how open the playing group at Richmond has become.

"They shudder to think that they could actually go in to their team and say, 'When I missed that goal, I couldn't get these bad stories out of my head.' They're like, 'I could *never* say that.' But we've got this group who are just sharing and growing, and they're so much stronger for it. It's wonderful."

It would be wrong to say that Murray's work was immediately welcomed or beloved by all. Not everyone immediately enjoys meditating, or visualisation, or attention control. It's difficult. "It's like going to the gym," she says. "An overweight, unfit person is going to find their first visit to the gym hard, and exhausting. And they're going to find that they're useless at it. But we all need this. We all need to look after our own shit. Like my 15-year-old son does."

////////////

One more thing about Murray, and that 15-year-old. Beyond her professional training and experience in sport, life has taught her something about resilience. The day before she was scheduled to begin working at Richmond, 18 months ago, her world shifted, or shattered, or both.

Her son Will, then 14, jumped from the pier at Half Moon Bay, up into the summer sunlight and down into the water, then the sand, where he fractured the C5 vertebrae in his neck. He was left fighting for his life, in a coma, from which he emerged with a spinal cord injury that left him quadriplegic. He was still in the intensive care unit a month later when Murray started at Richmond—when she addressed the room and spoke to the players about the "hurricane" you are left inside when something like that happens. It's an analogy she still uses with the footballers, and they with her, when life—and footy—is at its most overwhelming.

They took it on board. The club was the first group to have a fundraiser for Will—an effort led initially by Grimes but seized by all, and turned into a special night in the Maurice Rioli Room on the top floor of the club. "The money was important, but it was also our first night out in the community," Murray says. "We hadn't even seen friends in a group setting. It was just so good for our family, to feel like people had our back. You felt really safe, and loved."

The club kept helping, too. Prominent Tiger booster Russell Telford, of sponsor AG Coombs, became heavily involved in funding and coordinating the renovation of the Murray house, a retrofit that ended up costing several hundred thousand dollars. It meant ramps and automatic doors and lights—a full renovation to create a liveable space for Will. The players now visit Murray there often. "They've really been incredible," she says. "Dusty has a bit of a tradition of playing a game of FIFA with Will the night before each game."

It all counts. Before his accident, Will Murray was a talented basketball player, represented Australia in BMX riding, and was also an elite junior footballer. In under-12s, he was the Victorian state captain. A year later he was best and fairest of his south-eastern junior football League. He was a strong, fast, skilful midfielder and forward, and a leader. "For a time there, our biggest worry in the world was whether Will would be tall enough to be drafted," says Murray. "Now we can barely fit him in his wheelchair. That's why it's so nice for him to still have contact with that world. He loves the connection he has with the boys."

When Will broke his neck, Murray did feel briefly that she had lost him. She wrote about it in the pages of the *Herald Sun*: "My child only knows how to move—he's never *done* stillness. If we can't drive to sport together. If he can't ask me to watch his match—how do we *do* love?"

Instead, Will taught his mum that you can "*do* stillness, too" by just being in the moment—by not lamenting the past or searching for answers to problems in the future. He surprised her, with his focus, and his ability to own each moment in his altered life. "He's great," she says, with a puzzled look. "I don't understand it. It's not what it's supposed to look like. But he's accepting and patient and humorous. He's a master of his own mind. Like I said, these guys could use a dose of my son."

22

THE ACTION FIGURES

Peggy O'Neal strides past the water wall of the National Gallery of Victoria on St Kilda Road, wearing black boots and black wool— naturally with a touch of yellow. The Richmond president and financial services lawyer has just come from a budget briefing for her specialist area of the law, the superannuation industry. Her meeting was understandably dry, and held inside the hulking and charmless Crown Towers, so a walk down the Yarra River to the pleasant bustle of the NGV café seemed a good idea.

The coffee shop is packed because a travelling Van Gogh exhibition is in town, but we sip mineral water in a quiet spot, and O'Neal explains that she is a small contributing patron of the Indigenous collection here. She also supports the building next door, Hamer Hall, and only two weeks ago attended a lunchtime concert by perhaps the world's greatest violinist, Joshua Bell, at the Recital Centre. "We should all make more of an effort to bring beauty into our lives," she says. "Helps give us balance against the negative."

She then chides herself for being too philosophical, but as we meander through her life story, in truth it seems that she, as much as anyone, has garnered perspective on the grand sweep and spectrum of life—from brutality to beauty, poverty to plenty.

O'Neal grew up in a remote mining village in the Appalachian Mountains of West Virginia. Killarney, 560 kilometres south-west of Washington, was a company town, where the miners lived in a couple of dozen homes owned by the local coal concern. Her father was a miner, and so was his father, along with O'Neal's uncles, and great uncles, too. Like the Loretta Lynn song, she was a born a coal miner's daughter, and still has that rural American drawl to prove it. Her education began in a two-room school house on top of a mountain, with perhaps a dozen children spread over seven grades.

"You only know what you know," she says. "I remember that we had wild ponies, and looking back on it, they must have escaped from the mines years ago, when the ponies would pull the carts in and out, and there were little herds of them loose in the mountains. And we'd be out playing in the schoolyard and the teachers would yell, 'The ponies are coming', and we'd all go inside to watch. I haven't thought about that in a long time."

Her home was set on the side of the steep, adjacent mountain, with a railway track running along the creek in the valley below the two slopes. "To go to school, we had to go down the mountain and climb under the coal cars to cross the tracks. I remember the mothers would stand down at the railroad and say, 'OK, go now', and we'd crawl through when the trains had stopped. It felt like a game."

When she was nine, her father quit mining and became a truck driver, and they moved to a slightly bigger town. The school, this time, had an indoor toilet, which she thought was fantastic. "We were so little with the outdoor one that I remember you had to go with a buddy, someone to hold you while you got on the seat. So it was a pretty harsh place, looking at it with an adult eye, but as a child it just was a lot of freedom."

The new town, Grundy, Virginia, (another 180 kilometres further southwest), was just as remote but felt more "aristocratic" anyway—mainly because it wasn't in West Virginia (where the state motto is 'Wild and wonderful', and which O'Neal says remains "a frontier land").

O'Neal went to Grundy High School during the coal boom of the 1970s, when there was a Rolls-Royce dealership in a town with a population of 1200. Young Peggy had great teachers, loved school, and eventually attended college at Virginia Tech. She adored reading and writing—and still does—so she thought of Law School at the University of Virginia, because lawyers get to read and write for a living.

When she graduated, she went to work in Charleston, the capital of West Virginia, at what is still the biggest law firm in the state. She was the 33rd lawyer hired there, but the first woman. "The Law prepares you well for sport in that way—being the only woman in the room," she says. "You have to take on male aggressive environments, to get heard. You learn ways of getting your opinion across—you have to find your way through."

Outside the office, going to court in 1978 would prompt people to ask her, 'Are you carrying the files?' or 'When's your boss going to be here?' Inside the firm, the other lawyers didn't know what to do, and she didn't either. The men would make jokes, and her feelings would be hurt, but she never let it be known. Friday night drinks were tough. O'Neal might go along and stay for half a beer, and then as she left they would say 'Oh, we can have some fun now—she's going'.

"They thought that was kidding," she says. "Anyway, I just persevered. I went back a few years ago and they had a big party for some of us. A couple of the older guys came and apologised. I think it's 40 percent women now. But I got great satisfaction from the Law. I loved solving problems and helping people."

She ended up in Australia as part of what she calls a "typical story". She was visiting Greece on a two-week vacation, and at a bar late one night met an Australian guy doing his six months of backpacking through Europe. Before they parted ways, he said he would look her up, and he did, and they married a year later. Eventually she came to Melbourne, and after flirting with the idea of a career switch, to publishing, instead got her local legal qualifications through the University of Melbourne. Then she needed to settle in to the new country.

The similarities between two western nations, O'Neal says, are perhaps only surface deep. After 28 years she is "getting the hang of the place", but Australia still finds ways to surprise—enough that she still doesn't feel fully integrated, and perhaps never will. She mentions a Leunig cartoon she has on the wall of her home office.

"This guy is lying in bed and he says, 'There's my sock, there are my shoes, there's my toothbrush'. Then he looks out the window and goes, 'But I'm not home'. And I thought, yeah, all my stuff's here, but..." Her voice trails off.

She misses America when she is here, and when she is there she misses Australia. She is caught between two worlds. "That's why I've never given up my US citizenship, even though it means I still pay US taxes. It's where you're from, it's who you are," she says. "I visit regularly. Sometimes you need a big dose of good ole American enthusiasm, to hear that everything's possible, sleeves up, here we go."

O'Neal lives in Richmond. From there to the city and back is her small town. She knows the shops and the people who own them, and her neighbours, and always stops to talk. Now divorced, O'Neal says friends are her family, and she has made many friends through sport. It was always an interest.

"My father was a great sports fan. He played baseball into his late forties in community teams. He was always the pitcher. He loved basketball and played for a long time. Since I was the oldest and he had no sons, I was the one he played catch with and I was the one he taught how to bat, and I liked that a lot."

In her teen years she followed all the high school athletic teams. They were named the Grundy Golden Waves, and played Friday night football under lights in the autumn, basketball in the gym in the winter, track and field in the spring and baseball in the summer. "And I was the number one fan."

It was also that era in which sport became televised, and rapidly bigger, and more richly covered. She convinced her dad to subscribe to *Sports Illustrated*, and she would mail the editors little articles she had written on high school sport. "I wrote them to ask if I could be an intern. They said no."

There were few if any teams for girls, but she did help organise a novelty girls' gridiron match to raise money for school trips. (O'Neal played quarterback.) At university, she played on intra-school teams until schoolwork took over. But she remained a fan, following the Virginia Tech Gobblers and the University of Virginia Cavaliers (known as the Wahoos). "I wrote a column for the University newspaper on girls' sports. I would cover all the competitions, who won and who played well. The love of sport has always been there. I hadn't thought much about it until I became president of Richmond, but it was always there."

When she goes home, or talks to her father on the phone, sport—including Richmond—is always the topic to discuss. "It gives you something to say when you don't really have anything much to say, because your lives are not connected in the same way."

When she moved to Melbourne in 1991, Richmond's 'Save Our Skins' campaign was in full swing, around the corner from her home, and so the Tigers became her team. To educate herself she joined her law firm's tipping competition, and went to her first game with a friend and his wife shortly after the Great Southern Stand opened at the MCG. "It was a beautiful April afternoon, with the sun shining down. We played Melbourne and lost, and I didn't know all the rules, but the guys were running around and I just liked the athleticism, and little by little I started going to more games."

Legal work, at her level, was unrelenting, and in an age when you could not work remotely—*you had to be where the computers were*—it seemed even more so. O'Neal's weekends began revolving around the free-time fun of footy. When working on a Saturday, for instance, she would get to the office at 6am to give herself enough time to reach the ground for the first bounce. Following the team to interstate matches didn't seem like much of a leap.

"It was something different from the law. You start meeting people. Footy is a source of social cohesion and belonging," she says. "I just found it was a great way to take part in what Melbourne talks about most of the year. Footy made the city feel like more of a small town, like I could talk to almost anybody, because it's an opinion business, as we know, and my opinion is as good as anybody else's."

Given she has followed the club since the beginning of the 1990s, I wonder if her favourite player of the past quarter-century is Matthew Richardson or Matthew Knights? Perhaps the gifted half-forward Nick Daffy or the most honest of back pockets, Duncan Kellaway?

O'Neal explains that, as her fandom escalated, she began attending club banquets, and at one such event bid on and won a dinner with the captain and coach—then Wayne Campbell and Danny Frawley. "We all hit it off. I did that for three years in a row, and we became friends, and I still hear from them quite a bit."

She also started sponsoring individual players, who over time became her favourites. The first was then-young ruckman Ray Hall, who finished his career in 2007, stranded on 99 games. "He was really interesting and very smart. He works at DFAT (Federal Department of Foreign Affairs and Trade), and had worked in Treasury as an economist. He's been to Afghanistan and Jordan and is now working for DFAT in Victoria. I had dinner with him last night."

When Hall retired, O'Neal had him pick her next player, and that was Andy Collins, who played 25 games for Richmond before being traded to Carlton in exchange for Shaun Grigg. Before Collins left the club though, he would come to coffee with O'Neal and Hall, and they brought along

Dan Jackson (156 games), so Jackson became her next player. Jackson started bringing Chris Knights, and he started bringing Ty Vickery. This year she is sponsoring Kamdyn McIntosh.

"I don't know many of the players well at all, except my little group. But it's nice to know them as more than action figures. And as soon as you do, you really don't like to hear people yell bad things about your team."

Her connection grew when she was asked by the late Neville Crowe to help set up the Tommy Hafey Club coterie group. They needed someone to help create a legal charter, and so over three years she got an extensive club history lesson while organising luncheons and raising money. Then Greg Miller, who was head of football at the time, wanted to have coffee.

"I thought he would be asking for money, or some free legal work, and he said my name had been mentioned: 'We really want to get a woman on the board and there's been a vacancy—would you be interested?'"

O'Neal had been approached by the board a few years earlier, but as a partner at 'big six' law firm Freehills, found her employers didn't want their senior staff making such demanding external commitments. She asked them again in 2005 though, and this time they relented. "So then I had to decide if I actually wanted to do it, and the club had just lost $2.5 million. But I thought, 'Well, they're not going to ask again'."

She signed on to complete the term of Clinton Casey, who was leaving (Casey was president from 2000-05). Then she took another term, and after eight years was encouraged to stand for president by Gary March, (president from 2006-13) who was stepping down. Ultimately the board said it could work with O'Neal at the helm. "We had a breakfast at a café called Niche on Bridge Road, and that's when it was settled. I sat in the car afterwards and just couldn't believe it."

She got through a day of meetings before realising that she had missed several calls from Richmond communications boss Simon Matthews, who was already lining up interviews with the footy media. She laughs at the memory. "You leap in and make it work. I kept thinking, 'Why not'? You want to think you can do a good job, and that you're not damaging the organisation you're serving. And at some point, somebody had to be the first woman to do this."

She began as president in 2014, when the club had already done much of the hard work rebuilding itself. There was no reform agenda. When people would ask O'Neal's opinion on something, invariably her response was, "What have you been doing? That seems okay."

In describing her role at the club, O'Neal once noted that she is not paid, she is not picking the team, and she is not playing golf with Dimma during the week. "And I don't have Dustin Martin around to my house every week, despite the cartoons. Why do people think Dustin and I are best buddies?" she asks, laughing. "I think a lot of people still have a rather archaic notion about how football clubs operate. But we really try to maintain a line where you have the board governing and management doing, with high paid talent and experts in football."

"It doesn't mean we're not friendly and it doesn't mean I don't enjoy their company, but you've got to be a bit distant from it all. You can't be so attached that your loyalty overcomes what you think needs to be done, and you can't be so detached that you don't know what's going on. It's a fine line to walk."

She recognises though that people in Victoria want these jobs, particularly at Richmond, where a coup attempt—generally ill-fated and destructive—is never far away. AFL club presidents in this state are regarded as establishment figures, mostly business leaders who tend to view the role as a business development opportunity.

"They think, 'This'll give me an entrée into a world that I wouldn't otherwise come into', and it does," she says. "You think you have a network, and you know people, and then you get involved in a football club, and it just gets *bigger*. I've loved that. It's an honour when the Governor-General calls the club and wants to come to a game, and it's fun when you hear from someone in Bendigo who has an exchange student and wants a ticket to see a match. I find joy in both."

In her mind, a football club board needs a balanced range of skills. Gale, as CEO, has skill and experience, not only in law but in football administration. Emmett Dunne is a premiership player with a career in law enforcement. Digital data management and fast moving technology drove other appointments. Each one fits into a different square on the skills matrix. "We need old hands but also younger people who are out in this world, who might know someone who can help with a new problem. The board's job is to test propositions, guide management, but really to bring in news of the outside world."

And not to insist on playing Nick Vlastuin in the midfield?

"We've never once said that," she says, smiling. "But we do talk football outside our meetings."

The Richmond board also commissioned a highly-publicised review of the football department last season, one with a suite of findings that have both been acted upon already and will continue to be acted upon in the longer term. "But I think one of the biggest things we learned was that when we say, 'We're under constant review', we certainly are, but we were doing it *ourselves*. And every so often you need to have external eyes on what you're doing. I think it taught us that we need to be more rigorous in bringing along others, to help. And it should be quite a normal thing, so it's not a review with a capital R."

The club has already acted on recommendations around team building, relationships and leadership—driving a cultural change. Some staff were moved on. "Sometimes it was hard lessons. Sometimes people have done their best, and it's time to get other people to do their best. Sometimes you just need new people, and it doesn't mean the old people didn't do what they were supposed to do. In every organisation you ask, 'Who might be the one to take the next step?', and 'Who out there seems to be the best at this?'"

The football department, she says, was helpful and understanding—and not at all defensive. "They understood that it was not a review *of* football but a review *for* football. It's to help you decide what you need to get to where you want to go."

With that, O'Neal departs, walking out between the two ponds where people throw coins for luck, past a man playing a Chinese violin, headed for Flinders Street station to catch a train to Richmond. Her day began with a flight to Sydney, meetings, a flight back, meetings, this interview, more meetings, and it will be dark when she walks home from Punt Road Oval.

The reset at the club feels complete, and positive. She thinks they have hit upon a formula that will get the side back into the eight, and the four, and more. "Maybe it will. Maybe it won't. We'll see. But people like being at the club, around one another, working together, and that's a good step."

23

SUSTAINABILITY

After a close loss, the coaches tend to sit not in silence, but with quiet questions and rueful laments. Following the Bulldogs game—lost by four points after the Tigers led by five goals, the final moments cruelled by a bizarre free kick against Jayden Short for deliberate out of bounds—the kneejerk response was to lash out at factors beyond Richmond's control, like 27 free kicks to the Dogs and only 13 to the Tigers.

"Thirteen—for the entire night," sighs Hardwick in the Etihad Stadium briefing room. "Happens every time we play the Dogs. Dustin Martin has had 15 contested possessions—how on earth can he not get a free kick?"

But such recriminations are the exception. To a far greater extent, the coaches examine what they themselves got wrong. This time Hardwick recalls a moment when the game needed to be won, and Kamdyn McIntosh chose a short chip kick instead of a riskier long pass. He talks about David Astbury too often looking sideways for a relief option, when the team is better served by him handballing to a running defender. Hardwick would rather lose by two goals making assertive errors than lose by less than a goal being passive.

"So," says Hardwick, moments before the players will be brought in to hear him. "What's the message?"

"Reset, refresh?" offers Leppitsch, looking ahead. "Go again?"

"Maintain the pressure for four quarters," offers Caracella, "and we'll be okay?"

Hardwick writes his message on the board instead: "Could have played better. Harsh lesson. Effort was terrific."

Now imagine another close loss, one week later, against Fremantle. Richmond play poorly all day, and then in the last quarter kick into gear with startling effectiveness, piling on six straight goals—which could have been more—to take a four-point lead with 21 seconds to go. The game is seemingly unlosable from this point on, but what happens next will find its place on the tragic continuum of Richmond anti-folklore. At the final centre bounce, the ball spills free into the hands of Fremantle midfielder Lachie Neale, who measures a low, spearing pass to David Mundy, who marks and—for the second time in three years—kicks a goal after the siren to sink the Tigers.

Two close losses in two weeks highlights how "control" in any game is a fragile concept, and shows just how near Richmond's peak is to its trough.

It does not matter how well prepared they are. The messaging of the coaching group, for instance, remains the same almost every game, with perhaps a tweak of emphasis—hardness this round, ball movement the next. The playing stocks at their disposal are virtually unaltered. Yet taken in isolation, the first quarter against the Dogs and the last quarter against the Dockers were played as well as the game can be played—with a style and commitment that would stand up against any team in the competition. The play in those patches seemed choreographed by yellow and black. But in the remaining six quarters, Richmond somehow could not find any semblance of flow, or even effort. It is inexplicable, and infuriating.

Yet in the rooms immediately after the stunning misstep against Fremantle, Hardwick is not furious. Instead he has a question for his players, written on the whiteboard in green marker: "THE ROOT OR THE FRUIT?"

His concern is not the final moments of the game, *the fruit*, but in fact the first three quarters, *the root*. "The last 21 seconds, if we win that game, it's painting over a lot of cracks," says Hardwick, shaking his head. "We know what works for us—exerting enormous pressure on the opposition. And we didn't bring that. For three quarters, we brought *nothing*."

He points out that for most of the game Richmond was unable to control Fremantle's uncontested marks, or handball receives. The Tigers won the contested possession count but this was an illusion, and even the statistics-driven Hardwick knows this. He does not trust numbers blindly:

"Our ability to compete was as poor as I've seen."

Defensive pressure and aggression are what he demands of the players. Those traits are non-negotiable. "And if you don't come with those two things, you unfortunately cannot play in our team," he says. "That's not to say that we as coaches are not here to help you get that back, but until you do, you can't play, so we go to the well and see what we've got at VFL level to get us back to where we need to go."

Hardwick is composed, and pragmatic, and fair, but the commentary around such losses—particularly such losses in succession, particularly by Richmond—is rarely so balanced. And nor can it be.

Even the most diligent and articulate commentators and experts— champion players and revered coaches—cannot know the internal mechanics of the Richmond process in 2017. They cannot know the precise game plan, or the set plays, or the desired starting position of each player in a particular moment of a game; as against Fremantle with 21 seconds from the finish. Peggy O'Neal has called this "the asymmetry of information". The facts—as known within the club—are by definition trade secrets or intellectual property. This is why, for the most part, the club does not respond to criticism of its methods; to do so would be to reveal that tightly held knowledge. When, in the press conference shortly after the Dockers defeat, a reporter asks Hardwick "What happened?" and he answers, "They marked the ball", it is in part because he is emotional, angry, disappointed, frustrated, but also because he cannot divulge the exact answer. The answer would allude to a plan that could later be exploited. The answer could throw an individual player and his crucial mistake to the howling wolves in the media. The answer from inside, offered to those outside, serves no good purpose. Honesty is not always the best policy.

Accordingly, the commentariat fills the void with conjecture and speculation, dressed up with graphs and footage—and often presented as truth absolute. Some of these views are accurate, or almost, but many are wide of the mark. Feeding off that chatter, into the same vacuum, come the talkback callers, the tweets, and the internet memes. The opinions are binary. Thumbs up, or thumbs down. But not everyone makes such snap judgements.

/////////

It is 10am on a Tuesday, freezing outside, perhaps eight degrees. Any exposed skin quickly turns pink. At a riverfront café in Southbank, near the offices of the league's major statistical provider, Champion Data, sits senior football analyst Glenn Luff—one of the few men in football who can seemingly see inside a club without any preferred access. He sees a changed Richmond this year. "The first thing is the style," he says, sipping a latte. "It's a 'less is more' game style. Last year, Richmond was very much a kick-mark, kick-mark team—hold on to the ball, protect the defence."

But there were problems with this, obviously. The main one was playing most of each game from the Tigers' back half. They could not win the inside 50 count. "I think they only won it three times, which was the least in the competition," Luff says. "It's hard work playing a back-half style of game." (This is exactly the "short pitch" emphasis Hardwick has been driving all season.)

The numbers Luff now sees in Richmond are striking—comfortably the most radical shift by a team this year. The Tigers kick forward more than anyone else, going from 15th in that metric to first. They also kick long, going from 13th to first. They are going inside 50 more, from 17th to sixth. And they are playing a territory game, going from minus-7 minutes in their forward half to plus-4.5 minutes this season.

"More forward half stoppages, more forward half turnovers, and more scoring from forward half chains," he says. "Their scoring increase this year of 12 points, well, it's mostly off the back of their forward-half pressure points going up by 15 per game."

Things have fallen away the last three weeks, with the heavy loss to the Crows and close losses to the Dogs and Dockers, but otherwise the game style has been simple for Luff to analyse. "And it's a sustainable brand," he says. "If you play that way for the whole season, it will bring wins. So for the first time in a while I've been convinced by the Tigers. It's all about whether they can keep that pressure up."

Pressure is a difficult thing to measure. Luff talks about "pressure ratings", which is a measure Champion Data has been working on since 2010. They basically ascribe highly subjective points values to various acts on the field, then count and synthesise the data.

Pressure acts of proximity—chasing and corralling—are observed and recorded and given a value. The highest valued pressure acts are physical—

an effective tackle (one in which the tackled player fails to dispose of the ball) but also an ineffective tackle (when the tackled player manages to dish a handball or squeeze a kick away). Then they record moments when there is no pressure—when teams take possession from "set position"—a mark or a free kick—as well as those moments in general play when there are no opponents nearby.

"Collate all of that, divide by the amount of opportunities, and that's where we come up with this number that represents the average pressure you're putting on per chance," says Luff. "The clubs are getting a feel for a good number and a bad number. And we've heard coaches quote it a lot this year."

Hardwick is one of those coaches. He refers to pressure ratings in press conferences and interviews, but also and most often in private with his players and assistants. Most will not know how the number is created, one of the many quirks in the game's statistical analysis—but all they need to know is that 1.8 is good, 1.9 is elite, and 2.0 or above is off the charts. "It's a challenge for us, trying to explain this shit," says Luff. "But the clubs that want to understand it get value out of it. The Tigers have a mature attitude. They're obviously using it effectively."

Hardwick in fact brought up pressure ratings with his players directly after the Fremantle game, to illustrate the lack of effort in the first three quarters versus their application in the last. "Our pressure for the first three quarters was 1.64, 1.61, 1.46, and then when we decided to actually play, we go 1.94, and we get the game on our terms. No hiding from it. We don't apply pressure, we're not good enough."

The idea has more than a little merit. Adelaide, who looked unstoppable in the first six rounds (so much so that people were already wondering whether the Crows could become the first team to complete an AFL season undefeated) were soundly and surprisingly beaten in recent weeks by the rebuilding Kangaroos in Hobart, and the injury-depleted Demons at home. "North went at 2.03 against Adelaide. Melbourne went at 1.98 against Adelaide," says Luff. "Pressure will kill anyone."

Quantifiable pressure is a facet of sporting endeavour that is being chased all around the world, most notably in the NBA, where an attempt to refine the notion of "hustle" is still being worked upon. In that sporting universe, there is a growing movement to count and revere "the intangibles".

A *Sports Illustrated* feature article by US basketball writer Lee Jenkins pointed out that, starting this season, the NBA had hired 15 statisticians to record every deflection, contest, charge, loose ball and screen assist. Jenkins wrote that "effort is a skill", and the unbeatable Golden State Warriors—despite their obvious talent—were also the hardest workers on the court. Warriors power forward Draymond Green is a believer: "We realise these plays are the difference between the stars that win and the stars that lose. So when you combine the little things we do with the skill and the talent and the dynamic scoring, then all of a sudden you have an animal that's almost impossible to contain."

Of course, this is not a new notion. If you want to look closer to home for a believer in effort over ability, listen to Ron Barassi from the 1977 VFL season, as quoted in the John Powers's 1978 book, *The Coach*[10]: "Nobody's got any right to be proud of natural ability—that came to you through the eye of your father's cock. You didn't do anything to earn it. It's only what you've done with your natural ability—what you've added with that four-letter word 'work'—that's a legitimate cause for pride."

So, pressure, work rate, and the new forward kicking game style, are what Luff sees as giving Richmond a chance to win a final this year—because it all leads to playing the game in their forward half, which is the best indicator of finals success.

Port Adelaide, he says, has returned to being a contender this season for that very reason. "At their peak in 2013 and 2014, everyone used to refer to their speed of ball movement and transition and running power, and we were looking at it going, 'No'. No one was ever talking about how the Power presses up and plays the game in their forward half. *That* was their one wood, not the way they move the footy."

Why does forward-half pressure win?

"It means you have that trick where, if the game isn't going your way, you can still score because you're closer to goal," he says. "You create pressure. You save energy. You protect your defenders. The biggest challenge is conversion."

Conversion, Luff adds, is something of a problem so far for Richmond. Take this statistic: Richmond has created the second most forward half turnovers in the league, but the score yielded from those turnovers is the

---

10 *The Coach*, by John Powers. First published 1978(Sphere), republished 2007, 2017 (Slattery Media).

fifth worst in the League. They are creating chances but not capitalising. Port, for instance, has created only seven more forward half turnovers than Richmond, but has scored 84 more points from their turnovers.

"So the Tigers have created 14 goals fewer than the Power from the same opportunities," Luff says. "I'd need to look closer at that, but perhaps something is off in their finishing. Anyway, that's for the coaches. I can only say what I'm seeing."

///////////

Players and staff roll into the auditorium at Punt Road Oval on Tuesday afternoon for the usual match review, examining the loss to the Dockers. There's a smattering of full kit uniforms but after their cross-training and pool session and flush rubs, the room is more casual than usual. Hoodies. Cargo shorts. Hardwick is wearing jeans. He talks about the game against Fremantle, philosophically.

"We've lost the last three—or we're five and three? Glass half empty, glass half full? We're not quite getting results, but in patches we're showing a better style of footy than we have in a long time. That last quarter—my god—if we string those kinds of quarters together, we've got a hundred-point win. When that win comes, I don't know. Is it this week? I'd love to give you the answer."

They're ready now to go into detail by showing the team snippet upon snippet of action. It will be dissected further in line meetings, and by individuals at computer screens. Players run through vision alone or with a coach. Most of the review examines the first three quarters, and why Richmond was so far out of the contest all day. But this clip begins at the end—in the final moments of the game, when Brandon Ellis vanishes into a pack and finds the barest of openings, lays the ball onto his left boot and sends it floating through for a goal to give the Tigers the lead. The camera lingers on the euphoric celebration, and you suspect Hardwick is going to chastise his players for losing focus—but he doesn't.

"Celebration here, fair enough," he says. "Now watch Jack. What's he doing? He's *organising*. What's he doing with Dustin? What's he saying? What do you want in the middle of the ground? Your best players. So this is outstanding leadership from Jack. Dustin's rooted, but you know what Jack's saying? 'Stiff shit mate, game doesn't know you're tired, we need the best players in the centre bounce'."

He also singles out Bachar Houli for urgently telling players to get back ("Outstanding") and Dylan Grimes waving his arms like a windmill, calling his team to defend ("Look at that").

He lets the vision roll into the centre bounce itself, and asks Cotchin to tell the room what he sees. "We want to keep it inside. Protect the square. Set up in a defensive triangle," says Cotchin. "Looks good."

Now he asks Rance to talk him through the defenders, and what they need to do, roles and responsibilities. "Pretty much all the defenders must have a bloke," says Rance, "and let the mids and forwards do their job getting back."

He calls a forward, Shane Edwards, to come up to the front of the room and draw where the six forwards should be on the oval, in relation to the square. He draws where they should be, including two on the back of the centre square, ready to block an opponent and apply frontal pressure should the opposition seize the clearance and surge forward out of the middle.

Hardwick: "What's the one piece of the puzzle we missed on the weekend, Bachar?"

Houli: "Frontal pressure."

Hardwick: "Yep."

For all the talkback surrounding this win-gone-begging, most see Dustin Martin lining up at the bounce on the speedy Neale as a mistake. They see Daniel Rioli charging in from the wing as a mistake. They see tall defenders standing goal-side of their opponents as a mistake. But none of these structural arrangements are errors.

Rance puts up his hand. He knows that small forwards Kane Lambert and Jason Castagna should be standing on the back of the square, but "Georgie" Castagna is not there on screen—because Rance pulled Castagna back to play as a defender, on his man.

"If I didn't pull George out of there, and I just did my job and took my bloke—instead of trying to be the spare—it would have fixed everything," Rance says. "I should have just done my job, stayed on my bloke, and let them do their job."

Hardwick nods but isn't about to allow one player—a vice-captain—to shoulder all the blame. He understands that the team has failed in their application of the "Bourke" play to protect a lead, "but in saying that, how long to go was there?" he asks. "Did anyone know, on the ground, how long was left?"

Most of the players shake their heads. Someone says they thought 40 seconds. Someone else says they thought a minute. Josh Caddy says he heard 20 seconds. The runner cannot reach every player on the field, and sometimes players simply do not know. Hardwick presses a presentation pointer button, and a slide appears titled, "Last Roll of the Dice".

"If we had our time again, does this moment call for the Bourke set-up?" he asks. "You guys play the game. You've got 20 seconds to go—what could we do?"

Someone says they could bring everybody back, and flood the defence.

"Yeah. So, if we know 20 seconds is left, then this isn't a 'protect the game' scenario, this is the 'kill the game' scenario, and 'flood' is the command," Hardwick says. "One minute and thirty seconds to go, what are we in? *Bourke.* Thirty to go, what are we doing? *Flood.* Always be asking yourself, what are they trying to do now, and what should our response be?"

But he remains encouraging, talking about the myriad moving parts of a football team. "It's easy to sit there having an opinion, knowing what to do on the couch, or behind a computer screen," he says. "You poor guys are those who have to make a quick decision with 20 seconds to go. It's tough, isn't it? But this is also where we take it to the next level."

He wants to see his players making mistakes of the proactive kind—like someone taking a punt to guard the spot vacated by Castagna. "You see something, do something," he says. "Often the first instinct is to protect our position, but that's not the way we play. We play a brave brand of footy that requires decision-making. We'll give you the tools—it's up to you choose when to use them. If you guys think it's time to fight, fight. If it's time to go to Bourke, go there. If you think you need to flood, we flood."

He says they will train it, so they know it, but he is proud of them for giving themselves a chance to win a game they barely even played. "We were out of the game, weren't we? But you fought. Resilience, resistance, all those words come to mind. We just need that composure. Any more questions before we bury this? No? Let's train."

///////////

Hardwick has one final thought before the players leave. He makes an admission, about how insular he becomes after a loss. He says he has method of getting out of his shell. He took it from something said by the club's mindfulness expert, Emma Murray: "To change your emotion, you must have motion."

So, in a funk after a bad defeat, he gets up. He goes out. He walks to a coffee shop to face the world. "You know what I've found? It's not actually that bad," he says, looking surprised. "Were you blokes unlucky? Yeah, you were. The stories that you tell yourself at times like this are often shit, but the reality of life is that we've got a great gig."

He coaches a game, and they play it. "What makes me happy every day is that I get to come in here today and see Oleg's shit moustache," he says, and the room fills with laughter. "That's what makes it great. I get to come to work and see you blokes, and it makes me happy every day."

He says there are too many men to count who would give anything to be in their position, because the job is fun, even when things seem hard, including for those players who are struggling for form, or can't get a game in the senior team—like Anthony Miles.

"He comes in here and he loves you blokes, and as hard as it is for a group of coaches, sometimes we've got to look Milesy in the eye and say, 'Not this week'. It's tough on us, too. Doesn't mean I love him any less. But the one thing that keeps us going is the togetherness of this footy club. I guarantee you our best footy is in front of us. We're going show a video now—this is what it's all about."

The video is a montage of clips from the season so far—of great goals set to music, but it includes the preceding plays that created those goals. Vlastuin marking with courage against Carlton. An intercept possession from Edwards against Collingwood. A spoil. A tackle. A chase. Now there is broadcast commentary over the top, describing Rioli streaming into goal against West Coast and Butler snapping across his body against the Bulldogs, and then against Melbourne, the voice of Channel 7 presenter Basil Zempilas calling the first goal of the game, play by play.

"Terrific battle Castagna! Now over the top. Butler, big man Elton, what can he do? Little handball, Lambert, now Riewoldt! First shot on goal for Jack, and loooook at that! How pretty it is!"

Silence now, and then a Hardwick question: "What were all those goals based off? How did they start?" And then he answers. "Defensive pressure and effort. That's what our game is based around. Understand that you are a good side that is battling to go great."

He cites the Bulldogs, and their 2016 Premiership triumph—after a home and away season that netted only 15 wins and 7 losses—with winning and losing margins throughout the campaign that were both small. He sees similarities in this team, which will fly north on Friday to play GWS on Saturday. Usually that would mean an extensive Thursday "oppo analysis" meeting, but that won't happen this week. The team will go over a few necessary items—kick-ins, structure at stoppages, specific roles and match ups—but the group won't sit and discuss the Giants. Not this week.

"This week it's all about us and what we're going to do to get better," Hardwick says. "I don't give a stuff about the opposition. Understand it's all about us. Get out of here."

24

I'M NOT ASHAMED

The studios of Fox Footy sit in Dorcas Street, Southbank, which—judging only by the address—might sound like some picturesque spot on the Yarra River, but in fact is a windswept side street between busy Kings Way and the Shrine of Remembrance, near a construction company and a Quest apartment block, in an industrial pocket where it is conspicuously easy to find parking spots. It was previously the Melbourne home of the Seven Network, so it has TV heritage.

The pay TV network occupies an expansive two level, open plan office. Upstairs in the far corner is the kitchen, and that's where Jack Riewoldt is surveying the supplied dinner with current Melbourne and former Hawthorn star Jordan Lewis. The two are the regular Tuesday night ("Players Night") guests on the popular evening show AFL360, hosted by ABC commentator Gerard Whateley and *Herald Sun* columnist Mark Robinson.

"What have we got?" asks Riewoldt, peeling back the tin foil from a few aluminium trays. "Please be half-decent."

"Ho-ho," says Lewis, spying lasagne, roast potatoes and a garden salad. "Lazag-nee and greens. Ripper."

The two settle into easy conversation in the space, at a big white bench table in a room designed to look distressed—exposed tin ceiling, rustic wood panels and unwashed brick—paired with slick furnishing. They talk about how they both hit the beach this morning with their respective playing groups, Riewoldt and the Tigers at 6am, Lewis and the Demons at 6:30. (This morning at that hour, it was around seven degrees outside, with a frigid breeze, but even cooler in the water.) Lewis smiles with chagrin, remembering he had to do a "chicken schnitzel" run by the bay. Riewoldt doesn't know what he means.

"You've got to run in, go under water, come out and roll in the sand, go back in, do it again," Lewis explains. "We did it for 10 minutes. Felt like it anyway."

Robinson enters the room next and helps himself to a plate. Whateley is there, too, and wants to know what the review was like at Tigerland after the loss to the Dockers. "It is intensive?" he asks. "I mean, what's the answer?"

"We know what the answer was," Riewoldt replies. "We didn't have anyone off the back of the square. I was watching from the forward line and I could see it but it was too late, and it was like, 'Oh no...' Then it happened."

They're all handed run sheets by a producer, but don't really read them. The format for their appearance is a basic and breezy Q&A, with forewarning about any sensitive topics. Robinson runs through a few pointers for the night.

He wants to talk about the physical attention Melbourne gave to Adelaide star Rory Sloane—which was not just an aggressive tagging performance from Bernie Vince, but also a full team display of intent, in the forms of bumps and hits and verbal abuse from other Demons.

He is also considering bringing up Melbourne running half-back Jayden Hunt, and a rumour he heard about Lewis talking to his new team about "staying together"—not being fractured or tempted by trade offers and contracts elsewhere, but instead building something. "Because you've got to keep them together," says Robinson. "You're not good enough without key players. You can't have a Jayden Hunt-type player deciding he'll start fielding Jason Johannisen-style offers for big bucks."

Lewis plays down the substance of the rumour, but praises his young teammate: "He's an animal. A competitive beast."

"He's in discussion for all the All Australian team," adds Robinson. "As a half-back."

Riewoldt interjects: "Surely there are a few options there," he says. "(Elliott) Yeo. (Sam) Docherty. Rory Laird's in front of him. Jake Lloyd's having a great year."

"Who?" asks Lewis. "Who's he play for? Is it Sydney?"

"Tuohy's having a good year, too," says Riewoldt. "And what about Johanissen?"

"JJ is *not* having a great year," says Robinson. "Not as good as last year."

Robinson also brings up tagging, and a story coming out in his paper the next day, about which midfielders cope best with the tag. The article says there are players who rise for a tag, like Gary Ablett junior, players whose performance doesn't change, like Scott Pendlebury, and players whose output drops. The worst among the latter, claims Robinson, is Riewoldt's uncontracted star teammate Dustin Martin.

"Really?" says Riewoldt. "That doesn't sound right. But I guess if it brings his price down, it helps us."

They talk about other players and issues, and the issue of the day—sledging—in the wake of St Kilda defender Jake Carlisle lobbing a crude verbal grenade at Carlton captain Marc Murphy, regarding his wife. The abuse led to a brawl, and has this week led to a wider discussion in the football media, with many entities including Damien Barrett of *AFL News*, Caroline Wilson of *The Age*, former players and coaches Tim Watson and Terry Wallace suggesting the League needs to act, to form new guidelines or launch an inquiry. Robinson, now in the make-up chair in the room next door, warns Riewoldt and Lewis that the issue is more contentious than they might suspect: "So when we ask you about sledging, just remember to be quite firm about it not being allowed against family. Don't go in there and be lax."

The players are now with the journalist as his foundation is applied, in a room of mirrors, lights and flatscreen TVs, and a rack of shirts and jackets for the various footy shows. There's the navy shirt labelled "Dermott Brereton—League Teams" and the pink floral one for "Kingy—AFL360". A light blue business shirt for "Jake Niall—AFL Tonight" and a crisp white one for "Mike Sheahan—Open Mike."

"Why do you get so much more makeup than me?" Riewoldt asks Robinson. "Why don't I get that much?"

Robinson laughs, and the makeup artist answers for him: "Because you've got a beautiful, youthful face," she says. "Actually, it's because you're not as important as Robbo."

Riewoldt dons the black smock next and slouches in the makeup chair.

Lewis follows. Then they're back in the kitchen, Lewis sipping Diet Coke, Riewoldt water. Footage of Trent Cotchin appears on the screen—today the Match Review Panel gave him a contentious $1000 fine for a "jumper punch" on Lachie Neale. Many think he should have been suspended (and in fact the interpretation of such acts is radically altered in subsequent weeks, after an outcry).

"Ha, I'd get suspended for that," says Lewis, who has an unenviable record of punishment from the League's judiciary. "I'm just going to hold people's jumpers and hit them from now on."

"Bring it up on air if you want," says Riewoldt. "I'll play devil's advocate."

※※※※※※※

It is no small feat for Riewoldt to be here, enjoying such relative ease with the spotlight, cameras and microphones of television. Only three years earlier he was at war with the football media. Criticism seemed to follow him for behaviour on field (mostly over his body language) and off the field (critiquing the club's game plan in public).

But it came to head when Riewoldt was left out of the Tigers' 2014 player leadership group, and grew tired of the questions that flowed from his demotion. Riewoldt, rather than quietly ducking his inquisitors, chose to announce a self-imposed "media ban". He would not continue his regular radio gig on *Gold 104*, nor any appearances on *The Footy Show*, and he would dodge the news media at all turns.

"The thing with the media ban was I was really embarrassed about what happened, when I was left out of the leadership group," he says. "And I just thought people would leave me alone, but it was the opposite. And then I was upset that they weren't talking about the people who were in the leadership group—guys like Troy Chaplin. I hated that. I just thought I had to get out of the media and focus on playing footy, because when you're in media, you instantly become a story. Every week after the show there's something that'll be quoted, and you'll be online or in the paper, and I sort of felt, 'I don't want that'."

Yet he is back now, and loves the format. He thinks this regular TV spot—which he has done for two seasons—also makes him a more well-rounded player.

"If you have to field a lot of questions it forces you to come up with a lot of answers," he says. "It's great to bounce stuff off these guys. Hear a bit of goss'. It's become part of the routine of my week. It's good fun. I feel like it's helped change a lot of perceptions about me, too."

He is also thrilled to be back in the leadership group this season. Riewoldt is one of the smartest football minds at the club, one of those who also avidly consumes football media, and watches all matches. He is a student of the game and a frequent and innovative voice in meetings. This season he also has an incredibly young forward line around him, including Dan Butler (20), Daniel Rioli (20) and Jason Castagna (20), and sometimes Tyson Stengle (18) and Shai Bolton (18). He often stops those guys during training, to show them a trick, or correct a running pattern, or explain a forward stoppage structure.

Riewoldt was no certainty to land a vice-captaincy. He had an inkling he would be welcomed back this season though, and hoped he would, as well: "I felt like I should be, because I think I might be a pretty important part of the puzzle."

He recalls now how, in the privacy of the coaches' room as the selection process unfolded, each of Riewoldt, Rance, Cotchin and Maric were asked to say who they voted for. "And Alex didn't vote for me," says Riewoldt, still looking stung over the full-back's snub. "And we had a pretty big dust-up over that, and it came to a head, and I just said 'You know what, I don't want to be in it if I'm going to continually be judged on past things. I feel like I'm still serving time for a crime I committed years ago, and I'm not even sure it was a crime. I feel like I've got some life sentence instead of ten minutes in jail. I can't do any more—*I truly cannot do anything more*—than I am doing right now to will myself and will the group toward success. You guys have to let go of it'."

They did. But it took time.

////////////

More than a year before, early in the 2016 season, Riewoldt stood outside the auditorium at Tigerland. His peers were inside, being guided through the mechanics of a peer feedback session.

The idea is a tough love, warts-and-all assessment of the individual, and while it is one of the most commonly associated programs with the Leading Teams brand, it is only one of a suite of offerings brought to the club by its former leadership consultant, Gerard Murphy. It is still used at several clubs.

Not everyone loves the concept. Jason Akermanis wrote a scathing column about the process after enduring a session at the Western Bulldogs where his media work and famous handstands following each goal were called into question. Akermanis called peer review "bullying" and in some cases, nothing more than "unrealistic rubbish from a loud minority." He lashed out at a system that would allow rookies to give advice to senior players without "earning the right to give criticism." And he was not alone either. Mick Malthouse, who has coached more games than anyone in AFL/ VFL history, told *SEN radio* in 2010 that what he saw in peer review was "appalling" and could work for some players but easily make others weaker. "I hate it," Malthouse said at the time. "I think it's degrading."

But the idea has also been praised for the improvement seen in those who have been on the receiving end. Gary Ablett Jnr famously received a dressing down at Geelong in 2006, when the senior players savaged his work ethic at training, challenging him to realise his potential and stop wasting his natural talent—a serve that left the gifted young player visibly shaken. In the years following that upbraiding, Ablett went on to win three consecutive AFLPA MVP awards and two Brownlow Medals, becoming, at the time, the undisputed best player in the competition. But Murphy, who is now in a similar role with Port Adelaide, said that the Ablett moment has been mythologised in the same way as has the overall magic dust of Leading Teams. "I was there," he said. "The feedback to Gary was strong but constructive, and Gary was amazing. The way he responded was a credit to the person. The guys were just really frank with him. That's it."

Such sessions happened perhaps once a fortnight at Richmond last season, and were often unpleasant. Sometimes wrenching.

The idea was simple enough. Riewoldt would take a few moments to come up with three words to describe himself. Then a few "stops", "starts" and "keeps"—things he could cease doing, things he might begin trying, and things he should maintain. The group would do the same for him, and confront him, frankly, with their findings.

It took five minutes for a handful of player groups to put together their answers, and with that, Jack was back, sitting on a stool at the front of the room, his feet resting on the bottom rung. He was perched high but the entire team was higher, sitting above him in stadium seating, the lights over them shining down on the front of the room and in the face of the man they were there to critique. "It's pretty full on," Riewoldt said of the moment. "It's confronting."

Rance stood to confront Riewoldt first. The three words his group came up with were "passionate/emotional", "intelligent" and "leader". They wanted him to stop speaking over others, and stop feeling he needed to be the match winner instead of just playing his role. They wanted him to start condensing his comments in meetings. "What you have to say is really important—the first 10 seconds of it—but then it loses impact the more the message goes on." They wanted him to start finding solutions instead of pointing out problems, and to start critiquing his own game. They wanted him to keep asking questions and challenging the group, keep educating forwards and backs by showing them his tricks, and to keep showing interest and care for his teammates. "You're really relatable now, everyone loves spending time with you, and you show a lot of genuine care and a better connection."

Jack nodded, his lips pulling into a flat smile as he took the information on board.

They continued in this vein, using words like "passionate", "temperamental" and "competitive."

They wanted him to be respectful in dealings with all people. To watch his body language on field. To keep driving the social life of the group, to keep delivering home truths, to continue caring, and being generous with his time. The group seemed to want consistency in his character, but Riewoldt wasn't sure what that meant. He questioned them, and Dylan Grimes answered in a plaintive tone. "We feel like one week in our personal relationship with you, we love you and we'll go to war with you, and the next week something will happen and it feels like we're a piece of shit to you," he said.

Jack stared.

"It's a bit of a roller-coaster," said Grimes.

Riewoldt visibly gulped, and nodded quickly while maintaining eye contact.

Others suggested he too often finds ways to be an individual—even wearing older Nike branded training apparel on the track, instead of the newer BLK gear.

Troy Chaplin, who has since retired and moved to Melbourne in a coaching role, summed it up: "We found this really hard because your biggest strength is your biggest weakness, and that's your passion. Sometimes it can be a roller-coaster with you. If you can tidy up everything there's no reason you can't be in the leadership group, because you're among the top two or three influential guys on the list."

Then it was Jack's turn. The three words he estimated the group might use to describe him were "influential", "honest" and "loyal". And the three words he would have liked for the group to describe him—in a perfect world—were "respected", "influential" and "team".

He suggested he would need to stop whingeing, and stop riding the emotional roller-coaster—especially the downs. He would need to start finding answers (instead of problems and questions), and he would need to keep engaging in meetings, and helping others.

He said he was expecting to hear the words "roller-coaster" and "emotional", but was surprised to field criticism that he rips on players for missed kicks and muffed drills. "I don't think I do that," he said.

Grimes immediately mentioned an example from training that week, when the ball wasn't kicked to Riewoldt as he would have liked. "I was like mate, just take a breath," Grimes says. "You were really happy to scream at the guy on the field who didn't kick it to you. I can't remember who it was."

"It was Lloydy (Sam Lloyd)," said Riewoldt, now recalling and not denying the moment.

"That was just one example," said Grimes. "That feedback would have been much better received if you'd waited and told him later."

"I did go up and speak to him and follow it up later," offered Riewoldt.

"I actually thought that was okay," said Lloyd, bobbing up in the front few rows. "Because I acknowledged I should have kicked it to him."

Maric weighed in with a soft voice: "I think we want that direct feedback—bang, it's not good enough—it's just that it carries on a bit too long and loud."

The session began to soften, and warm, soon after. Shane Edwards, who was drafted with Riewoldt in 2006 (Riewoldt was selected with pick 13—Edwards with 26), pointed out just how far the key marking target had come.

"On the field you've always been a star. But off field you've come so far, and we know that's not fully natural for you to be so personal and have small chatty relationships… More than half the time you're the perfect leader…

239

It won't take long or much tinkering for you to be the most influential player here."

Mark 'Choco' Williams, the former Port Adelaide premiership coach, also no longer at Richmond, then weighed in: "On the bench about a year ago you were a pain in the arse, but honestly last year you were outstanding. I would agree with a lot of the stuff people have said before, but you've changed so much. I find you a very influential leader."

Steven Morris offered his own praise: "Playing against you as the opposition in training, it just feels like you're leading this increase in camaraderie in the forward line group really, really well."

Maric chimed in, too: "I love that you care heaps."

The session over, applause filled the room, and the players departed for a session on the track. Later Riewoldt explained that he expected much of what came his way. "With me it's often about that polarising personality stuff. And I understand that," he says. "But it's not performance-based."

He was pragmatic about the process, too, repeating a thought he offered in the session itself. This kind of feedback, he said, is not the way it would be in the real world. In the real world, Riewoldt might sit down once a year with his direct supervisor and a representative from the human resources department, and discuss his performance and goals, and his hopes for a raise. This is much harder, but in airing dirty laundry with his teammates, each of them might learn something about their own behaviour. "It's good for the group," he said. "By peer-reviewing me, everyone's being peer-reviewed."

/////////

There is a sense that Riewoldt has in fact grown in maturity for many years, but that opinions operate on a time delay. It wasn't so long ago, after all, that Riewoldt was in the eyes of the football public a sulking figure, a selfish player, and—to use the description of one curmudgeonly pundit— a prima donna. And yet Riewoldt turned his game and his image gradually, notably roaming further afield and sacrificing goals and glory.

Shane Tuck, a former long-time teammate of Riewoldt's, once told a story to the *Herald Sun*. They were on a pre-season camp in Cairns, and Riewoldt was in the same room as Tuck and six other players. Tuck got a stomach bug, and was up all night vomiting, including all over his bed. Riewoldt was the

ALL AUSTRALIANS

Alex Rance (full-back and captain) & Dustin Martin (Centre)

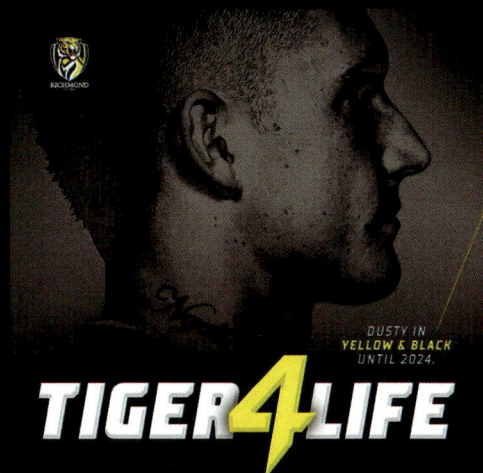

DUSTY IN
YELLOW & BLACK
UNTIL 2024.

TIGER4LIFE

DYNAMIC DUO: Acknowledged as the best defender and midfielder in the competition respectively, Alex Rance and Dustin Martin won All-Australian honours again in 2017. The additional prestige of national captaincy was bestowed upon Rance, and Tigers supporters were soon jumping for joy when Martin ended months of speculation and announced he was re-signing with the club until 2024. Martin's list of awards, including the Brownlow Medal, Norm Smith Medal and Leigh Matthews Trophy, are unparalleled in the game's history.

GEELONG	0.4	2.4	4.9	5.10 (40)
RICHMOND	2.4	3.7	6.10	13.13 (91)

GREAT GOAL: They don't count goals in finals in the goal of the year consideration, but Trent Cotchin's blind turn, spin out of pack, and left-foot wobbler deep in the last quarter of the Qualifying Final would surely have been a contender. Cotchin led the way with an intensity around the ball that saw him with 20 disposals and nine tackles, and win eight votes in the coach's award, behind Dustin Martin (9). Celebrating the skipper's magic moment are the Tiger mosquito fleet: Daniel Rioli, Jason Castagna and Dan Butler.

↑ **FINALS FEVER:** Daniel Rioli celebrates his first taste of September success with the coach. Rioli has lived with the Hardwick family for his first two seasons with the Tigers and on current form, they might not want him to move out.

↑ **BENNY AND THE JET:** Club chief executive Brendon Gale revels in the team success with Alex Rance. A playing member of the team when the club last won a final in 2001, he is now a respected administrator for his role in reviving Tiger fortunes.

YELLOW AND BLACK: One of the more rousing renditions of the club song punctuated Richmond's first finals win in 16 years. For the first time in decades, faithful fans were allowing themselves to believe that a Grand Final appearance was possible.

JJ LISTON TROPHY & AFL PLAYERS' MVP

Jacob Townsend & Dustin Martin

↑ **AWARDS SEASON:** Alex Rance, Dylan Grimes, Sam Lloyd, Ben Griffiths and David Astbury were on hand to celebrate Dustin Martin's AFL Players' MVP Award win. Lloyd would later earn the distinction of being Martin's 'plus one' at the Brownlow Medal dinner, when Martin continued his clean sweep of the League's individual awards.

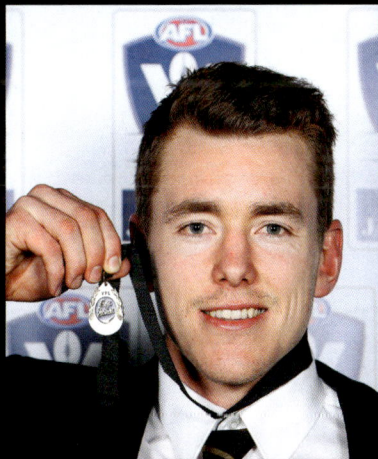

↑ **MEDAL FEVER:** A night before Martin's triumph, Jacob Townsend took out the JJ Liston Trophy as the best and fairest player in the VFL. At one stage of the season the former GWS player thought he'd soon be swapping a football career for carpentry.

↑ **LETHAL:** When Dustin Martin took out the Leigh Matthews Trophy, he became Richmond's first winner of the award since it was inaugurated in 1982. No player in the League better typifies Matthews' relentless approach to every contest.

PRELIMINARY FINAL

RICHMOND *4.3   5.7   11.11   15.13 (103)*
GWS *3.3   5.6   6.10   9.13 (67)*

↑ **BROTHERS IN ARMS:** Richmond players link arms for the singing of the national anthem—an approach they'd adopt again before the Grand Final while staring down Adelaide's much-discussed 'power stance'.

↓ **EYE OF THE TIGER:** Dustin Martin gives Trent Cotchin a knowing glance as he embraces coach Damien Hardwick, but the expression also speaks of a job not quite done. Grand final glory beckoned.

↓ **THE RIOLI DYNASTY:** With four game-breaking goals under Preliminary Final pressure, Daniel Rioli confirmed himself as a vital component of Richmond's remarkable charge towards the AFL Grand Final. No longer will he stand in the shadow of his famous relatives

↑ **BUTLER SERVICE:** He didn't garner the same attention as other Tigers, but small forward Dan Butler's pressure and goals were vital to Richmond's 2017 campaign. He and the so-called 'mosquito fleet' helped turn Richmond from the worst pressure team in the competition to premiers.

GIANT-KILLERS: There was no keeping a lid on Richmond's September campaign once the Tigers overcame Greater Western Sydney to advance to the 2017 Grand Final. Club great Matthew Richardson was among the onlookers barely able to contain their excitement after the Preliminary Final. "Richo" would be named as the official presenter of the Premiership Cup should the Tigers win the Grand Final. Pictured clockwise from top left: coach Damien Hardwick acknowledges the applause, Jack Riewoldt can't contain his emotions: "finally a Grand Final, after 11 seasons"; the song is sung with gusto; and Daniel Rioli celebrates the moment.

2017 BROWNLOW MEDALLIST

Dustin Martin, 36 votes

MIGHTY MARTIN: Dustin Martin polled a record 36 votes to claim the 2017 Brownlow Medal—gaining best-on-ground honours on a remarkable 11 occasions. In 2015 Martin finished seventh to Nat Fyfe and in 2016 was third to Patrick Dangerfield.

COACH OF YEAR: Before the 2017 season, Damien Hardwick had taken the Tigers to 74 wins and two draws from 157 matches, a winning percentage of 47 per cent. He had endured tough times at the beginning, when the Tigers were 0-9, and again in 2016, when the club won just eight matches, and Hardwick was under the gun. He survived, and the rest is history, with the Tigers winning 15 matches in the 2017 home and away season, finishing third, then bursting through the finals series with crushing wins of 51 points, 36 points, and 48 points. He now has a winning percentage above 50, and is the winner of the AFLCA coach of the year award, ahead of his Grand Final opponent, Adelaide's Don Pyke.

2017 AFLCA COACH OF THE YEAR

Damien Hardwick

only player who got up and helped him with his sheets, taking him to the bathroom outside, 50 metres away. "He sat with me during the night and got me something to eat and drink," Tuck said. "I wasn't expecting anyone to help me. How many blokes are willing to clean up your spew?"

The players clearly love their full-forward. They love his creativity and skill, enthusiasm and desire. They love having him on the field, alongside them at training, or being welcomed into his home for a barbecue. Ignoring any little threat to that affection—changing nothing when you've been told to change one important thing—could be fatal. Murphy knew Riewoldt would not let that happen. Reviews seldom go to waste entirely.

"People always change some things about themselves, on the basis that if they don't—if you disregard what your teammates are saying—it's a very dangerous thing to do," he said. "For you and for the team."

And it seems he has changed, or at least the perception of him has changed—catching up with reality.

Rance, who only six months ago could not endorse Riewoldt as a leader, to his face, quickly reversed his position. On radio Rance freely admitted that he "got it wrong"—ultimately praising the goalkicker as one of the biggest drivers of Richmond's 2017 success. He admitted he had clung to judgments from years passed—tarring his teammate with an old brush. "I probably held onto that stuff longer than I should have," Rance said. "I couldn't be more proud of him."

Others this season have spoken of Riewoldt's "even keel" and generosity. He has seemingly gone from petulant to patient—a man with passion to a mentor with compassion. A boy of affectations to a man with genuine affection.

Leppitsch remembers what Riewoldt was like four years ago, before the coach left for Brisbane, when Riewoldt was still a kid. "He used to focus on his hair when he played footy as much as his footy. But he's grown out of that sort of stuff. He's grown into leadership, and care, because he knows he got a young group around him."

Riewoldt has turned into a grinning, jocular presence on the track, like a magnanimous big brother, all headlocks and trick shots. He walks the hallways of the club with a smile, and a greeting for everyone—particularly the quiet ones. He is gregarious but welcoming, yet clever and considered.

Adds Leppitsch: "We're a really young group, the youngest forward line in the competition. Jack's showing guys where to run, putting people in their spots at stoppages. It's a burden—because everyone likes to go out there and play their own game—but he's directing the others. He sees the game and can make sense of it—and he helps it make sense to the younger guys, too. He's a teacher."

//////////

There's a poster in the massage room at Richmond that Riewoldt often looks at while getting a rub down. It says 'The most dangerous saying in footy is *We've always done it this way*'.

"And I look at that and think I'm always challenging—Is this the right thing for me? For us? What's the next thing? What's the best thing?"

If anything has gradually changed in Riewoldt it is that he developed an understanding of how he is perceived, and why, and how to anticipate and respond to any of those preconceptions with composure and maturity. Maturation is, by definition, a process that takes time—it takes people living their life, experiencing highs and lows. Losing his cousin, Maddie, 26, to a rare bone marrow condition in early 2015 was one of those life events. It shook him loose of his emotional moorings, but also centred him. "It rocked my world. It rocked my family. Everything changed for me. But it means I can cry on TV and be comfortable with that and who I am," he says. "I ride the emotion. I show my emotions. I remember after the Carlton game, Round 1, just hugging my old man, and I was in tears, and I'm not ashamed of that."

He has become more resilient, enough to forgo the slights and judgments of the wider world. "People can say stuff about me now, and it just doesn't bother me," he says. "You become a bit soulless about that stuff as an AFL player, especially if you play a long time."

//////////

Showtime. Within minutes Riewoldt is downstairs in a studio with big windows onto the reception area. Five large cameras pan and zoom as the two players and two hosts chat, and the showrunner calls "45 seconds!" They talk again about sledging, remembering a recent incident in which

Heath Shaw was captured on field calling an opponent a "retard". Riewoldt says he thought of a player at his club, Anthony Miles, who has a cousin with a developmental disability. "I thought, if someone said that to Milesy, how would he take it? That really turned me around. Perspective."

The segments begin and they discuss the Tigers' calamitous loss to the Dockers, Melbourne's physical pressure against Adelaide, along with "jumper-punching" and sledging. In 12 minutes it is over, the producer says thank you, and the next guests are ushered in. Riewoldt walks out past desks decorated with team flags and cardboard cutouts. It's dark when he gets into his car and drives away, into the night, ready for sleep and another day of training, scanning the news for potential headlines generated by something new he has said or done.

He is an object of media consumption now, but also feeds that machine. It pays to consider something he said earlier, about the criticism of players, and the way it all too often adopts a personal tone.

They play the game but are judged as if the kicks and marks and tackles somehow reflect their personality, like an actor associated with his most famous roles. Players are tagged as "honest" or "flashy". "Mouthy" or "hard". Players or pretenders. Beloved or reviled. And then the tag sticks.

Yet flamboyant forwards can be boring people. And bellicose taggers can be bookish citizens. Stoic backmen can be petty bastards. And workhorse midfielders can be jaunty raconteurs. Jack Riewoldt flies for marks he will not always take, and snaps goals across his body that should probably be drop punts. But interpreting those acts as character traits says more about the observer than the subject.

"I think that's one of the hardest things for AFL players to deal with," says Riewoldt. "It's one of the things my fiancée and I talk about most. I have no qualms with people critiquing what I do on the field, but they are in no position to comment on me as a person, because they don't know me from a bar of soap."

Unfortunately, for the most part, players are judged on what people read into the tea leaves of a match, whether a sour frown or an over-pumped fist or a triumphant finger pointed at the cheer squad. Such gestures though are hardly revelatory, not when acted out in the turbulence of a game, amid all the psychological upheaval and physical commotion of the modern game.

"On the field, they just don't know what it's like," Riewoldt says, staring and sighing. "They just don't know how *ferocious* it is. They have no idea."

25

MEEP! MEEP!

I t is late on a Thursday, two days before Richmond faces the current premiership favourite, the Greater Western Sydney Giants, on their home ground in Blacktown, New South Wales. The autumn sky is clear and bright but the players are in the gym. Flat screens broadcast LeBron James and his Cleveland Cavaliers destroying the Boston Celtics in the NBA finals, but the sound system is pumping hip hop and the players are lifting heavy weights. Dustin Martin sits on the floor with his back against a bench, a barbell with 100 kilograms resting across his lap. He raises his hips, over and over, easily shifting the weight. Dylan Grimes stands on one foot and throws a medicine ball sideways against a wall, then switches feet and tries to catch the leather weight as it bounces back at him, again and again: "Ha!-*Iss!* Ha!-*Iss!*" David Astbury crouches at the *Torsenator*, a machine with a heavy, hinged pole, with metal discs at the top. With one arm, the tall defender pumps the weight above his head at an angle, and growls.

The players work their legs (for strength in the contest), they do jumps and squats (for explosive movement) and they punish their glutes (because the *gluteus maximus* constitutes a crucial pivot point for running). They get "flush rubs" from trainers afterward, working the lactic acid from their strained muscles, and later in the day will see chiropractors, and do pilates and yoga, wolfing down a club-supplied chicken and pasta lunch some time in between.

Upstairs there are other exercises that must be completed. The players need to work one more muscle: the mind. Emma Murray is there to help, today in the forwards room—a small windowless space filled with beanbags and a little couch. Sitting down right now, sharing a yellow bean bag, are Justin Leppitsch and Craig McRae. Next to them on a black beanbag sprawls Daniel Rioli. On a small couch sit Dan Butler and Shai Bolton. On the floor, on the remaining beanbags, are Jason Castagna and Tyson Stengle, who has a footy in his hand.

These are the small forwards at Richmond, the footballers referred to this season as "the mosquito fleet".

Their buzzing presence is designed to tackle and harass in the front half of the ground. They are the shortest and quickest players on the list but, perhaps—this year at least—the most important to the group. In 2017, the Tigers have put a premium on forward half turnovers and on making opposition defenders panic. Instead of relying on tall timber to mark the ball, they are counting on these players to scramble and scoot, create chaos and scrap goals.

Daniel Rioli was the first to make an impact. Rioli is a famous name at Richmond. His great-uncle Maurice played 118 games for the Tigers, and won the 1982 Norm Smith medal in that losing Grand Final. His cousin Cyril has a Norm Smith of his own, to go with four premiership medallions won with Hawthorn. While at the Ballarat football factory otherwise known as St Patrick's College, this Rioli intrigued recruiters with patches of movement, moments of touch, hints of awareness, and the ability to kick a freak goal. He never dominated matches, but impressed all by staying at the cold country Victorian school from year nine onwards. Then he went to the Draft Combine and stunned onlookers with his unique mixture of high end speed and endurance.

He came to Richmond with a potent combination of flair and intent, and had to be reined in during his first pre season, after practising trick shots after training once too often.

Leppitsch loves that he is driven and composed throughout an up-and-down season—one in which his pressure is a constant but possessions and goals have fluctuated. "He's not a complainer," says the forwards coach. "He listens in and tries to do his best. He doesn't give you all these reasons and excuses why something didn't happen or can't happen."

Dan Butler is an interesting one. He was the first of the fleet to make an impression on the season—his breakaway pace and tackling fury in many ways embodies the 2017 Tiger revival. Not sublimely skilled, and prone to fumble (perhaps because his background was primarily in soccer), Butler's game is built on effort and presence. Importantly, he doesn't get seduced by the ball, and knows his role. At times Leppitsch even wishes he was a little more selfish, and hungry—more demanding as a target. But that's not Butler.

"He doesn't speak a lot," says Leppitsch. "Quiet kid. Respectful. Hard-working. Almost a coach's pet. If anything, you'd like him to give more feedback—what he's thinking and how he's feeling. But he's a no fuss guy."

Castagna plays differently. He seeks out space with his speed. At times it looks as though his legs are moving far too fast for his feet, or his mind, such are his energetic stumbles and recoveries. As a junior at Marcellin College and the Northern Knights he played with maniacal intensity, too, so his job inside Richmond's forward 50 this year is nothing new. He lives with Butler, too, and the pair compete in everything they do. After a long-running table tennis battle, in fact, Castagna found himself on the losing end of a costly bet, forced to have the initials "DB" tattooed onto his backside. At the start of the year both doubted they could fit into the forward line together, but in truth they sit snugly in opposite pockets.

"He's a terrific kid," says Leppitsch. "Really hard worker, and complements the other small forwards because he *does* get targeted. He's a good receiving player. He's a bit more upbeat, vibrant. Not loud, but he's a got a cheeky, fun side."

Shai Bolton has his own footy pedigree. He is part of the Noongar Indigenous nation of Western Australia—a language group that has produced such champions as Graham 'Polly' Farmer and Lance 'Buddy" Franklin. His father Darren played two games for Fremantle in 1999, after a long WAFL career with Peel Thunder and South Fremantle. Bolton came to Richmond from the little coastal city of Mandurah, 75 kilometres south of Perth, and initially struggled to adjust to Melbourne life. But the second youngest player in the AFL feels more relaxed with every week in this city, and has self-evident natural gifts—from explosive pace to lightning lateral movement, and the ability to jump and land with uncanny grace. One Western Australian talent scout observing his junior career noted simply: "He does things on the football field that I've never seen another player do."

Tyson Stengle has his own story. His father died in a car accident when he was young, and his mother struggled with alcoholism and incarceration. When Tyson was four years old he was removed from his home in South Australia, and taken in by his grandmother. She too, passed away and the teenager found himself with his nan and pop, Emily and Cecil Betts, who are related to Adelaide star Eddie Betts. Despite the obstacles encountered in his early years, he remained focused. As one recruiter noted: "A lot of kids in that sort of situation go off the rails. Tyson just kept choosing the right path." He poured his energy into football, and became a supremely balanced ground ball player, with strength through his hips—hard to tackle, harder to predict. He sees the game well and uses the ball even better.

"Tyson hardly speaks, but when he does it's actually pretty funny," says Leppitsch. "He's got real spunk. He's just a highly talented kid making his way, and he's got some unbelievable AFL traits."

They have great nicknames, too. Stengle plays well when connected to the ground, moving fast and low through crowded spaces, and so he is known to teammates as "Wombat". Bolton has electrifying pace, and so tried to create his own nickname—"Usain Bolton"—but it would not stick. Rioli is called "Sausage", because sausage roll becomes "Sausage Rioli". Castagna is called "George"—because his surname is similar to that of the Seinfeld character George Costanza. Butler has the closest to that standard Antipodean name shortening convention, and is simply called Butts. There are worse things to be called[11].

The five of them have brought new flare to the attacking half of the ground, but they are still young. Rioli is 20, as are Castagna and Butler. Bolton and Stengle are 18. They need guidance. Each of them works with a line coach, and a care coach, and development staff. Sitting in front of them now is another helper, the smiling Murray.

She wanted to get this group together to talk about the "stories" in their head—the things they tell themselves during the games, the way they react to and interpret moments, and the labels they give their successes and failures.

---

11   Nicknames at the club—perhaps all clubs—are like that. Take Alex Rance. He is known as "Tross". Why? Alex Rance. Alex. Al. Albatross. Tross. Connor Menadue is known as "Gong". Why? Because Menadue becomes Menadugong, which becomes Dugong which becomes Gong. When Jack Riewoldt first got to the club, champion forward Matthew Richardson was the "top dog" among forwards, and so Jack became known as "Pup".

"As a group, many of you are new to the game," she says. "And as small forwards, you can make mistakes, get caught with the ball—*struggle even to get much of the ball*—so we want to make sure you go into each match with some key things to place your focus on."

Leppitsch speaks: "I just think it's important to talk about the challenges you face. The more honest you can be with that stuff, the more we can grow and improve. We're going to have challenges, so don't be embarrassed when you come across one. The bloke right next to me (McRae) played your position for a long time, so others are here who've done it before."

Murray wants to address their best and worst, which has been on display every single game for the past month. Against both Fremantle and Melbourne, Richmond was inept for three quarters, then piled on goals to storm home in the final stanza. Against the Dogs and the Crows, the Tigers played scintillating and high-scoring first quarters, but drifted thereafter. "We're talking about blow-your-mind incredible quarters, and quarters where you've gone completely missing," says Murray. "So, we want to get a picture of what it's like when it's awesome, and what it's like when it's not awesome, so we can work out what the difference is. Does anyone want to throw up what looked different in the first three quarters last week against Fremantle, compared to the last quarter?"

A brief silence is filled eventually by Castagna: "It's an obvious one, but the ball from the centre was coming in a lot more, and we were getting more entries."

"Talk personally," urges Murray. "What did it *feel* like for you in that last quarter, compared to the first three quarters."

"I think I just felt more *in it*," he answers, "because we were kicking goals and creating chances."

"And if you think of the first three quarters, and the thoughts running through your head, what was different?"

"I remember thinking that I couldn't get near the ball," Castagna says, shaking his head. "They were intercepting it, and taking my game away from me, because I want the ball on the ground."

"Were you trying to work out what to do in that scenario, or just stating that fact: 'Shit, my game is taken away from me'? Were you looking for a solution or just in panic mode?"

"I remember thinking like, 'Is it me? Is it my fault? Should I be somewhere else? Or is it the delivery?' I didn't really have an answer."

Dan Butler pipes up: "It just felt like every time it came into our 50 they had so many numbers back, and we were helpless."

Leppitsch interjects: "What do you think you guys can do about that going forward, to help me, to help the coaches, to help yourselves? What would Jack (Riewoldt) do, Daniel, if there were spare numbers back and he was coming off the ground?"

"Tell someone," answers Rioli. "Get on the phone."

Murray asks Butler if he shared being outnumbered with anyone else while he was on the bench.

"Probably not until quarter-time or half-time or something like that," he says.

Leppitsch points out a detail pertinent to the Tigers' scoring power in the last quarter: "We had even numbers," he says. "So potentially that information could have changed the game earlier. It's not your fault—but don't underestimate what you're seeing and feeling. There's a lot going on but tell us what you see, and maybe we can set up differently. We'll take notice. Identify it, crystallise it, share it."

Murray points out that communication with coaches is an issue with other player groups at Richmond, too, especially when the game is pressing against them. Under duress many players go into survival mode or what she calls "chimp mode".

"Our emotions will *always* make things bigger, and worse, than they really are. So you need to continually check in for the evidence, and the people who are going to *give* you evidence are the coaches. They'll tell you if there aren't enough numbers forward. But you must keep checking in—the evidence will put the emotions back where they're meant to sit. And you'll never get in trouble for giving too much information".

Rioli tries to explain what it was like to watch the ball drift into the Richmond forward line early against Fremantle, only to see it plucked from the air, intercept after intercept. "It was hard to get involved," he says. "You keep going back and setting up, but it keeps happening, like you're doing it all for no reward. But in the last quarter, we score, and we score again, and then you feel like you're amongst it. It's hard to explain. You feel like you know the game more. I felt like I was playing my best footy. Like I was in the game."

Murray nods. She wants to move into solutions and strategies now.

"Daniel, you just did a great job explaining what happens when we feel it's not going right for us. We go, 'Oh my god, it's not coming to ground, my game is being taken away'. And for small forwards, this is more crucial for you than anyone on the field," she says. "Now consider that every thought you have has a corresponding physical picture."

Murray can see the players rolling the idea around in their heads. She doesn't see the exact glimmer of recognition she wants, and so she restates her premise.

"If I'm talking about something really sad and really awful, I'm going to drop my shoulders, look down, and I'm going to be really heavy, and I'm going to talk slowly. And as small forwards everything you do relies on your energy, your speed, your excitement—so when you go to a bad thought, your shoulders will round, your hips will shift, your feet will go flat, your eyes will go down, and you'll go quiet. And when that edge is taken off you—as a small forward—your advantage is gone," she says, clicking her fingers. "Just like that," she says, clicking again. "You rely on that *really sharp* X-factor to beat the opposition, and if you go to that negative thought, your X-factor is *gone*. And so regardless of whether the ball comes to ground or not this time, when it does come to ground, you guys are not quite ready. Does that make sense?"

The players nod attentively, and Murray moves on. She has discussed with Hardwick a plan to stop those negative thoughts happening, and it will begin with each player finding a thought—an idea or a word or an image—to remind them of what it feels like to be energised and alert and ready to win. To do this, she wants to go back one week, and to remember the game they played—both the good and the bad. She will guide them.

"Get into a position where you're nice and comfortable. When you're ready I want you to close your eyes, and I want you to really start to focus on that breath. Take your full attention to that breath. There's lots of noise and distraction going on outside of the room..." [The players' lounge is on one side, the video editing suite on the other, and so athletes and technicians and coming and going and chattering and laughing.] "...but just bring your full attention to your breath, and let that noise drift away. Become aware of the breath *on the in*, and the breath *on the out*. I want you to take your mind and attention and bring up your picture of your *best* football last week, and maybe it's one play you want to repeat over and over, or maybe it's a whole quarter, but I want you to get a really clear picture of what that looks like.

What are your feet doing? What is your body is doing? What are your shoulders doing? How are you standing? How are you moving? What does your *best* running look like, your *best* contest work look like, and while you are looking at that, I want you to tap into what it *feels* like. Where does the energy come from? Is it coming from your feet, your legs—where in your body? What does it sound like when you play that football? How often do you use your voice? When are you using it, and what are you saying?"

Murray pauses now, leaving the players with their own imaginary rolling replay of effortless gathers and elastic snaps and floating leaps and cat-like landings. She lets them linger on those blind turns and predatory tackles and unlikely goals and a single wagging finger. And then she returns to the exercise.

"Now I want you to put that feeling aside, *close that screen*, and I want you to bring up a picture of parts of the game where it was *not* working well, where you were *not* playing your best football, and just watch it like you watch a movie. I want to ask what is missing in this picture from when you play your best football? What is different? What is the key thing that's missing? And when you've got that answer I want you to open your eyes, come into the room, and you're going to share it with the group. This is coming from your subconscious mind. What did you see? What was missing? Who's going to share first?"

Bolton offers his answer first: "Getting to the next contest," he says. "Working hard across to the ball. That was gone."

Murray nods, and asks Rioli for his own missing link. "My worst would be like Shai's, but it's fighting for the outside," he says, referring to the need for a forward to keep his opposing defender between him and the goals—to give him a chance to seize the loose ball in space, whether through a lead or an ugly bouncing ball rumbling forward into the attacking zone. Fighting for the outside means seeing the ball first, and being ready to cut off any counter attacks, but it requires discipline. "I remember going through my vision and just being too slow to react to fight for the outside. If I would have done that, I would have been in a good position. I feel like when my feet are on, my game is on, and I'm more composed."

Murray turns to Butler, who breathes in deeply before speaking.

"My problem was reacting to the ball," he says. "When I'm playing better I'm reacting quicker, because I have better body positioning. So my stance. In my worst footy my stance is off and the oppo' is reacting quicker."

Murray stops now to make a point. She notes that the players initially explained their missing mojo—their worst football—in terms of how bad things felt, how the game seemed out of their control, beyond reach. It was as if they, as individuals, were a factor outside the equation. But what each player has told Murray suggests there is much within their purview to address and remedy.

"Daniel," she says, "when you're playing, no matter who you're playing against—*no matter what team, what opponent, what ground*—can you control your feet and fight for the outside?"

"Definitely."

"And can you maintain that every minute of the game?"

"Definitely."

"And Butts, what about you? Can you control your stance—no matter who you're playing, how good they are, or where the ground is?"

"Yep," says Butler. "I can control my stance, and my readiness."

"Tyson, was there a difference between your good football and your bad football? What looked different?"

Stengle says his feet are the key. McRae, who has coached him all year in the VFL, says Stengle looks markedly different on screen depending on how the game is going. If Richmond is winning he faces the ball always, eager to scoop it up and dash away. When the Tigers are losing his body seems distracted—he is unsure where to turn. "Every time you're around the ball and you present to it, you do something great," says McRae. "If you're facing away from it? Hit and miss."

Murray asks Stengle if he can face the contest the entire game. More importantly, can *anyone* stop him from doing so?

"No," he says. "I can do that."

Murray wonders aloud what Bolton can do to keep himself in the match.

"Move my feet, so they're never still?" he says, unsure if his answer is enough. "If I'm still, I feel like I'm not in the game as much."

"That's a really good one," says McRae. "Behind the goals, I can see the difference in you with even just a little jog towards the ball, versus standing still, hands on hips."

McRae asks Murray to go over a point she made in a meeting earlier in the week, something he remembers about "motion versus emotion". He thinks it might be applicable here.

"Motion changes emotion," Murray says, scanning their eyes. "Think of it this way, a bad emotion has the ability to make us feel slow, heavy, and small. But motion itself—making a move with your body—makes us feel quick, energised and fast. As small forwards all you need to remember is: 'Still equals bad football' and, 'Movement equals good football.' *When you're moving you feel good. When you're moving you feel good. When you're moving you feel good.* Yeah? When all else fails, get on your toes, get moving. Whenever your mind goes to a bad thought, go to your feet."

Castanga leaves for a massage, but Murray wants to finish with one last little exercise. She wants them to go back to their breathing, eyes closed, and to see their best football again in their mind, to focus on that perfect football and make it bigger and better than ever before. "Now I want you to ask yourself: what word sums up my best football?" she says. "Get the first word that comes to mind, and as soon as it comes to mind, open your eyes and tell me what you got."

Bolton says "quick". Butler says "speed". Rioli says "composed". Stengle, too. Murray writes each word on the whiteboard, next to each player's name.

"See that word?" she says. "That's the *only* word you're allowed to have the entire game. That word came from your subconscious mind, and it linked to that picture of your best footy. When you say that word, your body's going to give you that picture. Your body knows what that word means. Your mind knows what speed looks like and sounds like and feels like. It knows what quick means to you. It knows how composed looks in you. Every time it doesn't go right for you, go back to your word and back to your motion. Just trust it, stick to it, write the word down, and keep reinforcing it."

McRae nods: "We'll remind you. And some guys like writing these things on their hand, on a bit of tape, whatever."

Leppitsch tells a story from his playing days. As a tall, tough defender he knew he had to physically *own* his opponent, and so he would constantly say to himself: *"Make it hard, make it hard, make it hard"*. His point is that the opposition will figure out each of their strengths and address them in the contest. He looks at Bolton: "They'll try to slow you down." He looks at Rioli: "They'll try to knock the composure out of you." He looks at Butler: "They'll try to block your run." He looks at Stengle: "They'll try to keep you still."

"These words are entry points to the rest of your game," Leppitsch says.

"It works—it really does."

Nearing the end, Murray now lightens the mood. She says this group—this mosquito fleet—would do well to watch a few *Road Runner* cartoons before a game. She's joking, but these players are fast and small and joyful, like the *Loony Tunes* cartoon character.

Playing as many as five of them at a time—a swarming, young forward line around a solitary tall forward in Jack Riewoldt—has been one of the most novel but successful strategic ploys in the League this season. It has gone from necessary novelty to competitive advantage. Where the opposition once saw a weakness they now see a conundrum. The forward setup prompts unexpected questions for opponents: How tall can our defence be against these guys? What happens when the ball goes to ground? How do we deal with all that speed?

"You guys have a real strength together, if you stick together and stick to your best football, and remember what that looks like," Murray says. "Meep! Meep!"

McRae: "The other thing about doing this exercise as a group is that you can help each other out. You can remind Shai if he's looking slow to remember '*quick, quick*'. If Butts is looking sluggish, tell him '*speed* mate, *speed*'. Tell Daniel, if he's looking flat, '*composed* mate, *composed*'. When you do, it becomes really powerful."

Murray agrees. With this group, if any of them sees the others standing still, the first thing to do is tell them to get moving. "Speaking of moving, we've probably gone overtime," she says, standing. They go to leave and she smiles. "Get moving. Go, you little road runners."

26

NUMBERS DON'T LIE

The football department at Tigerland is quiet by 3pm on a Friday. The coaches and players have departed, to rest up at home, ahead of the next day's game against Essendon. But there is one man still inside his boxy little office, still hunched over his laptop screen. The figure with spiky black hair wearing shorts and a hoodie is mostly unknown outside the club, but Hayden Hill is a man in whom Hardwick places great faith. Hill is the football analysis manager, a mixture of statistician and tactician. And right now, he is enjoying his only free time of the week—the quiet half day he sets aside for tech innovation.

He doesn't have time to noodle with pet projects after a game. After games, he usually goes straight home and begins his report—an analysis of the match, with data as the foundation.

Statistically, how did individual players perform? And the different lines? And the team as a whole? He looks at nothing in isolation because, as he is fond of saying, "the game interconnects".

"My job is to analyse why we won or lost—because of X or Y or Z," Hill says. "And more often than not, it's because of X plus Y and a little Z—and maybe a W, too. You can't look at stats in isolation."

"It's also my job to recognise that while X might have been bad today, over the past eight weeks X has been a strength, so let's not overreact," he says. "Vice versa, if we've been scored against from stoppages in the past three weeks, it's my job to inform everyone that this is now *an official trend*, and needs to be investigated."

Hill also needs to understand and uncover those games when the result masks the truth—when the Tigers win but should have lost, and when they lose but should have won. He looks at dozens of indicators—from Inside 50s to scoring shots, clearances to turnovers—which, when combined, will tell the true story. "Often you can say that—mathematically and historically—if we play this game 100 times, we probably lose 99 times. Last week against GWS was the flipside. We would win that game 99 times out of 100, with those metrics."

He is referring, of course, to the latest close loss in the Tigers' season. After dropping tight games to the Bulldogs (five points) and Fremantle (two points), the Tigers led the Giants for all but one minute of play, until Jeremy Cameron kicked a goal after an end-to-end transition filled with missed spoils, bad bounces, fumbles and ill-fortune—another low Richmond moment for the footy media to discuss, forensically and voraciously.

Hill doesn't dwell on that single shambolic passage of play ("the outlier"), but instead the bulk of all measurable information, and what it can tell him. Against the Giants, every key statistic except for clearances went in the Tigers' favour. They won the Inside 50 count by 16 when, statistically speaking, teams tend to win games if they can prevail in that count by just eight.

Ultimately the Tigers lost by kicking four goals nine behinds from set shots—their worst conversion all season. "We really should have won that game," he says, shaking his head. "People say, 'Why don't you spend more time on goal-kicking?' but there are only so many hours in the day." If Richmond does extra goal-kicking practice, something else in the training program must make way. Perhaps they won't have time for ground balls. Or the drill that trains them to move the ball Inside 50 cleanly. "And there's no point in training goal-kicking if the ball isn't going to get inside 50 cleanly."

None of this is to say the Tigers are doing everything right, and losing only because of bad luck in big moments. The losses in the past four rounds have been played in a markedly different way to the run of wins in the first five rounds. Hill says it comes down to two things. First, the amount of times they score from going inside 50 has dropped from 50 per cent (League average) to 37 per cent (the worst in the League). Second, their accuracy has faltered. Essentially, they are creating fewer scoring opportunities, and squandering what little opportunities they have. More worrying still is an overall slump in their ability to win contested ball inside 50.

"We'll have to break down why that's happening, because contests won and contests lost is still why most clubs win or lose games," Hill says. "People have this weird theory that if you move the football well and you're a good kicking side you can avoid that, but the reality is that it's almost impossible to move the ball from one end of the ground to the other without there being some form of contest.

"People say Hawthorn is a really good kicking team and not a great contested ball team—but the Hawks have always been a great *pressure* team, and pressure is a form of contest. There are still three phases in football: offence, defence, and contest. You've got the ball, they've got the ball, and the ball is in dispute. It's a really old theory, but still true."

That's the start of Hill's week. After that he works on holistic analysis, including what might be happening right now to correct the scoring woes. He looks a little deeper, for instance, at the scoring pattern within each recent game.

"I've looked at the numbers, and over the past five games half our score comes from one quarter. In every game, we have one big scoring quarter, and three poor ones," he says. "My thought is that we're really inexperienced in the forward line, and inexperience gives you spasmodic performances. Outliers exist, but history proves that young guys do get tired, even this quickly in the season. Still, we only needed one more goal in each of the last three weeks and we would be eight and one. So it's not all bad."

Hill's five-page match report takes a day to complete. He feels more creative and analytical in darkness, so the night owl often finishes at 3:30 in the morning, then sends the material to the coaches, recruiters, football managers, the CEO and a few others. He fields any responses and follow up questions, then creates custom reports on demand.

Our midfield against their midfield.

Our midfield against midfields across the league.

"It gives you a good balanced perspective about how the boys are travelling," he says. "Sometimes inside these four walls you get a little caught up in how your guys are going, but until you compare yours against theirs, you don't have a clear view."

Hill also works on player ratings, using spreadsheets, stats and feedback from coaches to quantify each individual performance. "If you just go purely off stats, Dustin and Trent are your best players every week, so our coaches look a little differently," he says. "We see weaknesses much more. We see defensive efforts much more. And they're harder to quantify."

He counts corrals, chases, tackles and spoils but the biggest one to consider is positioning. Positioning can't be tallied like kicks and handballs, but coaches can examine the way a player adhered to structure—or not—and then give their game a subjective rating.

Did that midfielder stand near enough to the winger at stoppage?

Did that forward maintain a good enough teasing distance to prevent the switch?

Did the spare defender occupy the right space throughout the game?

"Poor defence isn't really about missed tackles, or bad spoils," Hill says. "It's about being in the wrong spot, or not working hard enough to be where you should be."

Every player, with the help of coaches, is given a rating from good to bad—dark green (five), through light green (four), orange (three), brown (two) and red (one)—on a range of performance indicators. Defensive impact. Offensive impact. Possessions. Metres gained. Positioning. Blitzing, stalking, and protecting. Structural compliance. Bodywork. Winning or halving contests. The ratings are combined to produce an overall grade for each player. Against GWS, Alex Rance was the only player to achieve the desired dark green.

They do the same thing at VFL level, too, so that when, for example, young forward Ben Lennon's name is raised as a possible elevation to the senior team, the entire coaching panel can look back at the ratings chart and say with confidence that Lennon has been dark green for the past four weeks, instead of relying on someone's general view of how he has played in that period.

"People in football have incredibly short memories. Coaches, supporters, me, everyone," he says. "So, a big part of my job is to resolve that issue: 'Look guys, he had a poor game on Saturday, but he had four green games in a row before that'."

Hill does a large amount of "oppo" work as well, examining the team Richmond will play not just this week, meaning Essendon, but also the week after, meaning North Melbourne. He just finished his statistical analysis of the Kangaroos, in fact, so that opposition analyst Jack Harvey will have the report in hand when he goes and watches them play against Carlton on Sunday.

"The report tells Jack: 'This is what they're strong at, this is what they're poor at, this is how they attack, this is how they defend'. Jack can challenge the numbers as well, and then we'll sit together and look at the tape next week to reach a conclusion."

On game day Hill sits directly next to Hardwick. His job is to watch the numbers, and feed relevant figures to the coaches in the box. He has developed a sense for when to pepper him with data and when to stay silent. He also knows when to rebut or disprove what people are feeling or thinking about the contest.

"Sometimes an opponent will get three disposals in a row, and a coach might go, 'This guy's *really* hurting us', and I can say, 'He's not—he hasn't had any ball at all until now'."

Some stats are more telling than others. Hill pays close attention to clearances, scores from Inside 50s, and opposition intercept marks. He also tries to keep track of the flow of the contest—of what has been happening in the last five minutes, the last ten minutes, the last quarter, and all game.

During breaks, the information he passes to players is generally "feel good" data. The team might like to know, for instance, if they have racked up 25 tackles in any given quarter. "That number might mean nothing if the game is being played a certain way, but if the players see it and think it means they're going in hard, then it serves a purpose," Hill says. "Players' heads can be all over the shop at the best of times, so the last thing you want is to overwhelm them."

\/\/\/\/\/\/\/

Hill's office is basically bare, as befits a man who keeps an incomprehensible amount of data on his computer. In the corner sits a tall stack of old AFL Prospectus books, along with a stack of the annual AFL Record Season Guides. The only ornamental touch in the room is a framed signed jumper from 2011, congratulating him on 10 years of service to the club. He started at Punt Road in 2001, and not in the football department either.

Hill grew up in Bendigo, completed a Bachelor of Computing (with a minor in Applied Statistics) and first worked at an IBM manufacturing plant in Wangaratta. He found work at Richmond by responding to a classified advertisement for an Information Technology Officer, but he only applied on a whim. He wasn't sure he even wanted the job. He had it in mind to work for a big company, Hewlett Packard perhaps, and travel the world doing IT consulting jobs.

"I also had no idea that people worked at the footy club full-time. I just assumed the players trained on Tuesday and Thursday night and played on weekends. Now I hate it when people assume that."

Hill quite literally started at Richmond as the office IT guy, fixing desktop computers and maintaining networks. He was the man you called if your mouse was broken, or the printer wouldn't print. He was 23 then, and is now 40. He inched his way into the Football Department gradually.

Terry Wallace was the first to ask for his help, primarily on match day, supplying basic statistics. The role grew in complexity each year, in large part due to Hill's appetite for empirical data. Anyone who has watched *Fox Footy's* coverage in recent years would be familiar with the statistical niche carved out by former Kangaroo David King. King was an assistant coach at Richmond from 2005-09 and worked often with Hill; together they learned how to read the game by spreadsheet. "I remember seeing all these numbers and instantly asking myself how we could use them. I'd go home and study them and do correlation testing."

He began building a database, too, and feeding information into it, from draft transactions and trades, to the heights and weights of players, and their ages, by club. This database is what he is working on right now, in this much-cherished Friday afternoon spare time. It was initially just a passion project of Hill's, but former football boss Greg Miller saw it and bought into the idea.

It has grown radically more complex, however, and now dozens upon dozens of users within the club access it daily. The players use it first, doing their daily "wellness testing". (The first thing they do when they arrive in the morning is answer questions on an iPad about how they're feeling, how they slept, what their mood and motivation and energy levels are like.) Naturally the coaches and physical performance staff add their own information, but also recruiters and scouts. Media staff use it to log player appearances. If a player raises an issue with medical staff, the conversation will be logged. If one of them brings up a personal problem with welfare staff—*maybe they're homesick, or perhaps they've broken up with a girlfriend*—it will be recorded in the database so the coaches know. Every morning, in fact, the coaches receive an email with all the previous day's database "transactions". Nothing escapes the number cruncher.

"It's their permanent record," says Hill. "And we're continually looking at ways to grow it, so we can predict which players will make it or won't make it. Predicting is our big thing now. That's what I'm playing around with today."

How?

"I've got one function, for instance, where you can choose a year number, like year three in the League (meaning third-year players like Corey Ellis and Connor Menadue) and we can compare their metrics to all other players of the last 15 years, after three years in the system. It helps us understand whether—by the numbers—a player is tracking with the elite at the same stage in their career, or not," he says. "It just helps take out a little bias, because the recruiters have all got their favourites, as do the line coaches. I want to be able to say, 'History shows us that guys who are playing like *this*, at *this* stage in their career, go on to become *this*.' We would never base anything solely on numbers, but it gives us some evidence to consider alongside what we see."

Hill has had more freedom and responsibility to explore these areas under Hardwick than any of his senior coaches so far. And not because of Hardwick's background in accounting, says Hill, but because the coach takes an evidence-based approach to everything he does at Richmond. "Whether it's stats, or vision, Dimma just wants proof," Hill says. "Whether it's Warren Buffet or Mark Cuban[12], you find that successful people always want information."

Hardwick has said as much, too. He spent time during a recent off-season salivating over the IT processing power of NBA clubs, including time spent visiting the Houston Rockets. He was captivated especially by their attempts to measure space on court—essentially trying to quantify a void. Hardwick sees vast gains yet to be made in AFL analysis, and so places great stock in what Hill brings to the club.

He says: "Some people will look at a game and justify what happens by gut

---

12 Buffett, a multi-billionaire from Omaha, Nebraska. is renowned as the world's leading investor; Cuban, another billionaire, and entrepreneur, is the owner of the NBA's Dallas Mavericks.

feel. I'll always want to look at the analytics: *I know what you're saying, but I'm seeing this, and it doesn't match up.* Some might argue that we over-analyse, but I'd rather that than be caught out. That's just part of my preparation, and how I like to be. I love a good matrix. Numbers don't lie, mate."

The biggest growth area in football, according to them both, is assessing the on-field equity of players. They sound like followers of Billy Beane, the hero of *Moneyball*, Michael Lewis's best-selling book (and movie) based on the 2002 season of the Oakland Athletics baseball team. The Athletics, through general manager Beane, implemented the first sophisticated—and successful—player valuation system, and used that system to recruit and trade, largely based on numbers. The team that season exceeded all expectations.

Hill acknowledges that the US leads the way in the field, always looking for the next means of reducing the probability of mistakes. Australian football, by contrast, does not lend itself to easy quantification. "I don't think we can ever reach their level. There are too many variables in the AFL," says Hill. "The NFL is all about discrete, set plays. And baseball is a completely controlled game. Our game is so random by comparison."

Hill also can't imagine a day when his computer might tell Richmond whom to draft, or how much they should pay a recruit.

"You pick the wrong player, it costs you a spot on your list and a lot of money, and I think those kinds of mistakes will reduce as we understand better the measurable abilities required to play AFL. But we trust our eyes and ears much, *much* more than the numbers," he says. "The most important attributes of elite athletes aren't quantifiable anyway. You can't quantify someone's drive. You can try with psychometric testing, but you'll never know for sure."

Does he know anything for sure about tomorrow night, when Richmond plays Essendon in the annual Dreamtime at the 'G blockbuster?

"Certain things are clear. Essendon is a corridor-centric team, and you have to be really ready for that, because if you're not then they will move it through the middle very quickly," he says. "They also take a lot of uncontested marks. They took almost 150 against the Eagles on the weekend. Every defensive principle is important. But we need to make sure that we win the contest initially—*that's always the most important thing*—and then don't let them control the ball by foot."

"Individually, Fantasia and Daniher are the keys when they win, so those two need to be stopped. Hurley down back is a key. He's their leading 'possession gained' player, which comes back to his intercept marks. With the most disposals in the Defensive 50, he's their leading rebounder, too."

This game will be primarily about what Richmond does and not what Essendon brings. If the Tigers play strong, contested football, and keep the ball in their forward half, and force turnovers, they will win. In that sense, Essendon should be irrelevant. All opponents are, in a way.

"You usually have a good idea of how a team wants to play. You rarely walk away scratching your head wondering what they did," says Hill. "You could give me Essendon's game plan, put it on the table right now, and it probably wouldn't help us."

Geelong, he says, was the best team in the competition for years, and everyone knew exactly how the Cats played. But how they played was also something they practised every day, every week, for years.

"And then there's you, who for one week is practising to stop it," Hill says. "Geelong was predictable, but predictability doesn't always hurt you, because you're always going to be more predictable to your teammates than the opposition."

Leigh Matthews once said the same thing of his dynastic reign at the Brisbane Lions: "They know the way we play. But we know it better."

Hill knows that the Tigers need to bring pressure if they are to win the game. Essendon will know that pressure is coming, too.

And so, he will bring his computer to the ground as always, and he will measure and monitor as the match unfolds, and he will feed the coaches what information he can, and the players will act on it, or they won't. And as they succeed or fail in each moment of each quarter, Hill will revise and re-compute, and the coaches will reconfigure their plans, and one team will win and one team will lose, and the truth is that it will probably be hard to pinpoint exactly what compelled the players to play as they did during each momentum shift. They will be able to say what happened, but the question of "Why?" will always be more difficult to answer.

Hill can only hope his rolling analysis finds its mark, that it gives the Tigers a clear view at the gaps in the Essendon matrix they can exploit—that statistical sweet spot to target with the Tiger weapons. His work is a science, but an inexact one.

"No one gets this stuff right 100 percent of the time," he says. "The key is getting it right more than wrong."

27

OUT OF THE ORDINARY

welve men—boys, really—stand on the crest of a hill between Punt Road Oval and the MCG. There are 1212 trees in this place, including 58 thriving species, but the boys stand nearest to a dead one. It is designated by the Melbourne Cricket Club as tree Number 143, and today it is little more than the stalk of old red river gum (*eucalyptus camaldulensis*), silvered and dry.

Known as "the scarred tree", it is more than a few hundred years old, and has a cavity the size of a tall man on one side—a gaping dark maw in its trunk, created when Wurundjeri men of the Kulin nation harvested its bark for canoes. They did so at gatherings here, where they would meet strangers and share stories and dance together.

The boys gathered here now are from different mobs, too—from the Gunditjmara and the Wathaurung among many others—and they dance. They wear no paint or animal hide, but instead cargo shorts and torn acid wash jeans, Santa Cruz t-shirts and baseball caps. And they prowl together lowly over the grass, stamping their feet and chanting, creeping and rearing up to strike.

"Good boys, good," says Jamie Thomas, the cultural adviser guiding them through their war cry. "We'll do it one more time and then you can go inside and chill out."

The boys are guests of the Korin Gamadji Institute. Korin Gamadji is Wurundjeri language for "grow and emerge", and that's what Thomas sees when he watches the young men practise their war cry, which they will perform tomorrow night in front of 85,656 people, when Richmond plays Essendon under lights.

"The initial part of the dance is about honouring your ancestors, and all the people who are around us—opponents, the crowd, and people in TV-land. And it's also about honouring the earth," Thomas says. "As the tempo of the dance builds, it's the analogy of the tiger, the thylacine, which is known to the Bonnarang woiworrang people of Tasmania as the Lagunta. It's stalking its prey. The beat speeds up and there's that *creep, creep, creep* before we pounce and attack, to devour our opposition. It's about ability, agility, and lifting yourself up for a big stage."

Thomas has tattoos on both hands. On his left are the words "ngaju dardi gunni", and on his right is "mgathook peemeejt maara". Both mean "I'm a strong Aboriginal man"—the first in the language of his grandmother's country in western Victoria, and the other in the tongue of his paternal lands in East Gippsland.

He holds a pair of heavy sticks, too, each one with a single long tapered edge. They're hunting boomerangs. Thrown sideways, like the rotor on a helicopter blade, they are perfect for bringing down wallaby or emu. Thomas has seen a man at the World Indigenous Games throw one more than 100 metres from a standing start.

"But they're also used in music, like a tap stick," he says, banging them together. "It's bearing arms, yeah? Sort of saying 'I'm going to sing at you before I throw at you'. I'll introduce them to you—before you get introduced to them."

Thomas has done these dances all over the world. In China. In England. And he has done them on the MCG, too. The cry he helped compose this year, when translated, means "We are strong, we are intelligent, I am the Tiger".

But he says the dance is not about race or religion. He likens it to the famous New Zealand haka, which is performed by Maoris and white men alike. If you are selected in an All Blacks team, he says, you do the dance. It is a gift. An offering.

"The war cry is about us saying 'Here is something we can give wider Australia. This is us. *This is all of us.*' For these young guys to have that opportunity—to feel that you're representing your ancestors and your culture and your people—it can be life changing."

One day later, in the early evening before the annual *Dreamtime at the 'G* game, Neil Balme enters the Richmond rooms. "Shit time of day for a game, I reckon," he says, smiling. "You've got all day to worry about it."

The coaches are sprawled about the briefing room, watching a match between Gold Coast and Melbourne, being played in Alice Springs. And so they talk footy, naturally, but not in a serious way.

They see a player celebrating a goal by sprinting to the forward pocket with his arms out by his sides, mimicking an airplane: "That shit should be banned," says one coach. "We should have a no wankers policy."

Hardwick notices how well the Gold Coast defence is handling the Melbourne forward line: "Bloody hell, Steven May is a good player," he says of the Suns co-captain and full back. "Reckon you could fit him and Rancey in the same side?"

Mainly though, the men in charge of the Richmond playing group chatter about life. They talk about teaching their teenage children how to drive, and the pros and cons of doing so in the labyrinthine car park of the Chadstone shopping centre.

They talk about an episode of the football comedy show The Bounce, which dredged up an ancient clothing commercial featuring Hawthorn champion Jason Dunstall wearing a wool jacket and red felt shirt: "He looked like a lumberjack pimp!"

They talk about the blueberry muffins brought in by the support staff, and how these ones aren't as good as the banana variety of last week, and nowhere near as good as the raspberry ones the week before that.

They talk about a game of golf in Queensland, long ago, when it was so hot and humid that if Hardwick struck a good tee shot, he would sit in his motorised cart and refuse to play out the hole, instead declaring: "I'll take a par."

But talk turns soon enough to the game. Hardwick notes that there is a two-minute gap between the Dreamtime ceremony and the first siren, which won't leave long enough time for a ground ball drill, so they will need to do that in the eight minutes beforehand.

They filter into line meetings next. The midfielders seem ready. Connor Menadue talks about using his running ability, and pushing forward. Sam Lloyd talks about using the footy well, using his footy smarts. Dion Prestia wants to bring belief.

Caracella says they will beat the Bombers through the midfield, spreading quickly from stoppages, and stopping uncontested marks. They need to be mindful of the fact that Essendon will try to run the ball quickly through the vacant middle of the field. "That's when *they've* got the ball. But what can we do before that?" he asks, pausing. "Win the bloody ball *ourselves*. Just like last week. Be good inside, and control the outside."

Grigg speaks: "Go out there with confidence, boys. Don't think about what's been or what if—just play in the moment."

McQualter says the pressure will come. The Bombers can score heavily. They move the ball quickly. They will threaten: "The challenge then is to know it, to recognise it, and get back into your game—as quickly as possible."

Cotchin has something to add. He wants them to think about the emotions that stir in the gut when they're on top. He wants them to take a moment to dwell more on the mindset they intend to bring than the actions they expect to perform. He wants them to remember something specific, something individual, something that is theirs alone about those early season victories.

"Look for that feeling from when you were at your best. That's what we need to go back to—how it felt in here," he says, tapping his heart, "and not in here" he says, tapping his head. "Find it. Hold onto it."

Moments later in the briefing room, with all the players and assistant coaches on tiered seating in front of the coach, Hardwick discusses his A3 picture for the day. Today it's not a picture but a printed message: *To accomplish the grand, you have to focus on the small.*

His speech riffs on all the threads one might expect from this starting point.

Big games are won in small moments: "The fundamentals. That's all you need to focus on. Big crowd—but the game doesn't change."

The struggle is what makes the game great to play: "That anxiety. We've been challenged this season. And most of the time we've responded."

The need to deal in process—not outcome: "The ability to tackle. The ability to chase. It's all about whether we're prepared to work our arses off. Or not."

He talks about the many moments within a lifetime: "There are 20,000 moments in a day—16,000 are now gone, and you've got 4000 left. What are you going to do with them?"

He talks about playing the Richmond way: "We love what we do. We love who we are. We play with spirit. We play with passion. We dare to be great."

Then Hardwick does something he almost never does—he singles out one player. The coach has plenty of chances to do this in any given season. He could have asked the team to lift for a player in his 200th game, for instance, or a boy on debut. He could demand that they rise to salute a player coming back from injury serious. He could tell them to protect a guy facing up against his old club for the first time. He could highlight a fringe contributor who has forced his way back into the top 22. He never does.

But tonight, he highlights Shane Edwards, also known as Shedda, and before that as Titch. Hardwick honours him because of this game, in this round, and because Edwards is wearing the number 67 tonight in honour of the 50th anniversary of the 1967 referendum that acknowledged Aboriginal people as citizens of this country.

He tells the group he appreciates what Edwards brings to the football club—what he has brought for 11 years now. He points out that including this Dreamtime game, Edwards will have played 192 games for the Richmond Football Club—the most ever by an Indigenous footballer[13]. He says Edwards is a special man, and then his eyes grow misty, but he blinks through that as he looks out at the silent group in his thrall.

"I love Shane Edwards," he says, pausing and pointing to the small midfielder. "And I want to see the love for Shane Edwards tonight, because he's part of our family. Like Bachar is. Like Lloydy is. Like Jack is. We do things for our family. We fight for them. We stand up for them. Stand up with Shane Edwards tonight."

//////////

The Indigenous heritage of Shane Edwards was once something that people overlooked. Perhaps his skin seemed too pale. Perhaps he didn't speak about country and clan. Perhaps no one asked. Perhaps we just assumed.

Caroline Wilson of *The Age* wrote a feature story about Edwards in 2012, in which she apologised to the player for overlooking him when mentioning

---

13   Indigenous players who had played more than 100 games for Richmond are Phil Egan (125), Maurice Rioli (118) Richard Tambling (108) and Andrew Krakouer (102).

the Aboriginal talent that had come through the doors of the club. But many others had missed it, too. Edwards was left off various AFL Indigenous mailing lists, and even missed invitations to train at Indigenous camps. Although as Wilson wrote: "It was not so much his Indigenous profile he was avoiding, but any level of profile at all."

His father, Greg Edwards, once told *The Adelaide Advertiser* that his son might be the "most invisible" player in the competition to reach 150 games: "And Shane always says he hopes that never changes, because that's the way he likes it."

Edwards was shy in his early career, and that persisted as the seasons came and went. Only recently has he become a voice. *Dreamtime at the 'G* has helped. A position in the 2016 player leadership group at the club did wonders. He is also 28 now—maybe he just needed to grow up a little.

Edwards came to the club from Golden Grove High School in Adelaide, and weighed no more than 65 kilograms. He was talented, like his father, who played for Central Districts and was the youngest player in SANFL history to kick 100 goals in a season.

Edwards's grandmother, Monica, was from the Arrente tribe, west of Alice Springs and one of the largest groups in central Australia. She was a member of the stolen generation, and ultimately married a German man. Their daughter, Tara, Shane's mother, was also a talented basketball player.

Edwards, sitting earlier in the massage room at Punt Road Oval, remembers what this place was like as an 18-year-old. "None of this was here," he says. "The club actually had worse facilities than what I had playing at North Adelaide before I was drafted. It was a bit of a shock to come to such an historic, big club, but with such poor physical surroundings. It was smaller. The weights were old and rusty. It was almost what you imagine a poor suburban club would look like. The young guys now wouldn't understand how much better it is."

Nevertheless, he was in awe, star struck even—dazed, as if in a dream. At first, he lived with the captain, Kane Johnson. "It was really good to just know what the most professional player at the club did. And because I was always around 'Sugar', I think maybe the older blokes were nicer to me than they were to some of the other younger blokes. The mentality then was 'Earn your stripes before we'll talk to ya'."

Initiation by intimidation no longer exists.

"That went out the door when Dimma came," Edwards says. "Now we're all about embracing the young guys and making them feel comfortable—nurturing them instead of letting them figure it out for themselves, or making them prove themselves before you help them."

Edwards has taken a special interest recently in Nathan Drummond, Daniel Rioli and Jayden Short. Upon their arrival, he bragged to each one that whichever debutant he guides always gets the first senior game: "The Shane Edwards Mentoring Program works pretty well."

He mentors Bolton and Stengle, too—not because he was told to, and not because they are Aboriginal either. "You see a lot of yourself in them, I suppose, and not because they're Indigenous but because they're undersized and light for their position, and they're playing out of their weight division a lot. They need a bit of support."

He thought they might need it during that run of defeats this year, but they didn't. He says they understand—as all professional footballers do—the wafer thin, incremental nature of the gains required by the group to turn losses into wins. "Everyone was about five percent off where they needed to be," he says of that four-game losing streak back in May. "Collectively, that's a big problem. But it's also not like it requires a big fix."

Edwards simply needs to focus on closing down space, providing run and carry, helping others find a way into the game, or an avenue to goal. Edwards is among the top handful of players in the AFL this season for goal assists. That's his role. The younger guys need reminders about their role, too, and that's where he can best help. Generally, a few losses won't dent the confidence of debutants and second-year starters.

"They're still high on the buzz of getting a game. For them, it's all about letting them know how close we are, and what little things they can do to take us there. And it's also about letting them know they need to step up," he says. "They have to understand that getting a game isn't enough. It isn't nearly enough."

⁂

The game starts badly for the Tigers as they concede three quick goals. Orazio Fantasia crumbs and delivers. Joe Daniher lines up a set shot and converts. Brendon Goddard fires a running kick from range, and finds his mark. The new spunk. The young gun. The old head.

The Tigers get those back, however, with three long bombs from set shots by Sam Lloyd, Josh Caddy, and Edwards.

By half-time, the Bombers are four points up in an arm wrestle, and Hayden Hill is feeding Hardwick good news, confidence-building data: "At the end of the day, our transition numbers are really good. It's just conversion."

The game continues, and the second half is a contest of comical misses, strange free kicks, sheer dominance from the Tigers with no real reward. Richmond's profligacy threatens to let the game lurch out of their control, but individual efforts from Ellis, Cotchin, Martin, Rance and Lambert deliver victory.

As the siren sounds, Jack Riewoldt sprints to Edwards and hugs him. He looks him in the eye, then whispers personal congratulations in his ear. Riewoldt has kicked more goals than any player in Dreamtime games. He loves this stage. He loves his teammate.

"He always does that," Edwards says later. "I reckon it's a special game for Jack, because he made his debut in Dreamtime (Round 9, 2007). But he really gets around me that week. He always does. We just have a special bond like that. He's good for a hug."

///////////

Greg and Tara Edwards were watching in the stands. They had flown to Melbourne to see their son play in what has become his favourite game of the year. Later, in private, Shane told his dad what Hardwick had said in the rooms beforehand, about love, and family.

"My old man was like, 'Do you know how lucky you are, having the coach say that about you in front of everyone?'," he says. "Honestly, I didn't even know I'd played the most games by an Indigenous player for Richmond. *I had no idea.* But it's something I'll never forget. It took me by surprise. I just felt really special."

Hardwick has always helped Edwards, too, and not just as a warm presence. Importantly, the coach has given him permission to do the things he does on field, from a look away handball here to a blind turn there—sliding past one opponent, baulking another, spinning away from the next and driving a low flat pass through a thin gap onto a moving chest.

"When I got drafted, I had a lot of bad habits," Edwards says. "My kicking and marking, how I try to dodge players and look for options, it was all a little bit…out of the ordinary. I was told to change it—to copy the good players at the club. But Dimma adjusted around my skill set and said, 'You know what, you play shit when you're trying to play like someone else, so play like yourself'."

The coach never corrected his kicking technique, in which Edwards throws his right leg across his body, scything his foot low over the grass, like a soccer player taking a corner kick. In 2010 Hardwick told Edwards he would play him in every single game that season—no matter what—and play him on the wing, too. It was one show of faith in many that kept being made, and keep allowing Edwards to do what he loves most.

His coaches will hate to hear this, but what he loves most is doing those things that no one else can—or would even try.

"You know once you've done it," Edwards says, smiling. "You hear the crowd go 'Whoa', and your teammates look at you and sort of shake their head. That's the best feeling. It might be a perfectly timed crumb, or just getting out trouble, an unorthodox handball, a long goal, or just winning a contest against a really good opponent. In centre bounces when you're next to a gun and you run away with the ball, that's extra good. You always—*always*—feel like you'll win the next one."

28

GOOD AS NEW

In the rooms beneath Etihad Stadium stands a man with short cropped grey hair and glasses, and a branded *Epworth Hospital* bumbag.

He wears hot pink, and carries with him a case labelled 'RFC Suture Kit' and another—about the size of a lunchbox and covered in red fabric—with the word defibrillator in the title. It is unlikely that Dr Greg Hickey will need either of the latter two items tonight, but he has his standard set of tools ready for the Round 11 match between Richmond and North Melbourne; or rather, he has half a dozen such bags and boxes and kits, and brings them to all games.

He must. "I'm the club doctor—the primary care physician for 45 players and 10 coaches," Hickey says. "I'm the first port of call for any medical, and sometimes psychological, issues. It can be someone injured in a game, or at training, or having social issues off the field. Every day someone will come to me with something. Gastro maybe. A cold. Jack (Riewoldt) had a cold last week."

Here comes one such player now. It's Sam Lloyd, the small forward who has played more VFL than AFL games this year—a victim of the new look Richmond forward line that places a premium on speed rather than factors like Lloyd's natural gifts, which include an ability to weave through constricted spaces, to time his leaps and nudges and blocks, and to bend the ball to his will. Tonight, he has a new haircut. "Samuel," says Hickey, nodding. "Looking sharp today."

Lloyd though, is feeling flat. He's getting over a nasty cold. He would like a *No Doz*. It's not uncommon for players to want one of these caffeine pills before the game. The practice is not rife. Nor is it against the rules that surround the use of supplements. So Hickey hands them over and reassures Lloyd. He will feel better when the game begins: "Get a bit of adrenaline flowing. You should be right."

Hard-running midfielder Kane Lambert sidles in next. He, too, has a minor cold, particularly some persistent sinus congestion. The physician hands him a nasal spray.

It might seem paternalistic for a professional to help grown men navigate everyday lethargy and a sniffle, but the alternative is allowing them to solve such problems themselves. That can have disastrous consequences.

St Kilda player Ahmed Saad, looking for a little pep before a 2013 game, consumed an energy drink called *Before Battle*, only to learn that it contained the banned substance *methylsynephrine*. Saad was banned from football for 18 months.

If Lambert didn't consult Hickey, didn't get the nasal spray, and instead went to his local chemist and purchased an over-the-counter box of cold and flu tablets, he could, in fact, end up ingesting pseudoephedrine. "It's a stimulant, so that could be four years," says Hickey. "Seems harsh, but they all know that. Them's the rules."

Dion Prestia is the next to enter Hickey's medical suite—a little anteroom off the main stretching and preparation space viewers might recognise from television. The small midfielder and star recruit has come for an *Imodium* tablet. Prestia sometimes gets an upset stomach before games, and so takes the pill to feel a little better. He has also been plagued for more than a year with knee trouble. Specifically, Prestia has ITB friction syndrome, which, Hickey says, is not a serious injury but can "hang around" and be an annoyance.

"If your knee gets really sore, don't wait long before letting us know," Hickey says, knowing a local anaesthetic takes time to take hold. "If it's half-time and you're feeling it, speak up."

The players warm up now, and Hickey wanders among the group, and they approach him in dribs and drabs. Houli and Riewoldt, each with nagging joint pains, receive a couple of paracetamol and codeine. Speed machines like Rioli and Menadue take *Quinate*, to prevent cramping. Brandon Ellis drinks pickle juice, which serves the same purpose. Because Hickey knows each of their physical foibles, they relax around him. Kamdyn McIntosh walks over and stares directly at the doctor. "Reg, I just want you to know," he says, face stiff with seriousness, "I'm on tonight." (He is called "Reg" as a nod to the champion Cats player and coach, Reg Hickey, who played in Geelong's 1931 and 1937 flags—the latter as captain-coach—and then coached the club to back-to-back flags in 1951 and 1952. The nickname was bestowed when Hickey arrived at Tigerland.)

Within minutes, the players are inside the briefing room, and Hardwick is ready to share his message. There are reminders about match-ups and mindsets and the fundamentals he espouses, and by halfway through the season they have changed so little, each pointer could be recited from memory.

What changes every week though is the coach's sermon. It always starts with a joke, and tonight is no exception: "Last night at home the footy was getting boring," Hardwick says. "So I went on *YouTube*, but the buffering was too slow. I don't know what Daniel (Rioli) was looking at in his room!"

Once the laughter has faded and the players are silent but still smiling, Hardwick begins. He says that in the darkness of the night, in his quiet home, he stumbled across a short documentary about the Cherokee nation— one of the largest Native American tribes. The picture stuck to the briefing room whiteboard tonight speaks to an ancient Cherokee story. It is a photo of two wolves, attacking one another. One looks poised and ready with fire in its eyes—the other is a snarling ball of fang and frenzy. The two wolves, Hardwick explains, were part of a conversation between a Cherokee grandfather and his grandson. He says there was a terrible fight between them. One wolf was filled with anger, envy, sorrow and spite. The other was filled with joy, peace, friendship and love.

"So," says the coach, "the grandson asked the grandfather, 'Which wolf is going to win?' And the grandfather said, 'The one you feed'.

"It's about being positive. Being at peace. I'm looking forward to seeing how quick we can be, how much spread we've got in us, how much pressure we put on them, and how much joy and friendship we play with. I love watching you blokes play. Feed the good wolf."

///////////

Greg Hickey grew up in the south-eastern suburb of Murrumbeena. One of four brothers, he was a good student, but becoming a doctor was not a considered decision. "I'd like to say there was some massive driving ambition in my younger life, but I went through school and got the marks required to get into medicine. It just seemed a good idea at the time."

He went to the University of Melbourne for six years, followed by three years of clinical training at the Royal Melbourne Hospital. He pursued no specific area of medicine. "Sports medicine interested me, but that didn't exist as a specialty—it was boutique stuff."

He ended up in general practice instead, working in Bendigo, also playing football there. After a year in the UK, he returned to Bendigo, set up his own practice, and began working with the South Bendigo Football Club as their club doctor. It coincided with the development of a College of Sports Physicians training program at the Australian Institute of Sport, which led Hickey to spend two years in Canberra, learning sports medicine while working with the Canberra Raiders NRL club. "I didn't know anything about Rugby League—typical Victorian," he says. "But I enjoyed helping out with their players."

On his return to Melbourne, he worked for a season with the Geelong reserves, and it was off to Richmond next, working for the reserves in their premiership-winning season, 1997. He smiles: "I was the doctor for the last premiership Richmond won".

That same year, the Melbourne Storm NRL club was formed and Hickey was approached. He worked there for six years, and loved it, and it shows sometimes in conversation. A colleague recently brought up the subject of the Geelong midfielder Joel Selwood, who was knocked in the head more than once in a game this season, and left the field with blood streaming from his scalp.

You might expect Hickey to take a protectionist stance on the topic of head high contact, because he is a doctor. But he is also a football fan. He dislikes those moments when a player leans in to initiate contact, dips down looking for a clip, drops the knee when chased, or uses an arm to lift a tackle into the head. "I get really angry with these free kicks," he says, sounding bemused. "Much more than I should."

His view is not incongruous with his profession. He simply doesn't like high contact, and believes there is a duty of care on all players to prevent it—and not just the tackler. Furthermore, incidental contact or light contact, he says, shouldn't be paid as a free kick. He likes the way Rugby League adjudicates such matters. There the referees pass judgment based on the force of the hit or the tackle. High contact is only an issue when it becomes heavy contact—or dangerous.

When Hickey finished at the Storm he returned to Richmond. It was the start of 2004. He has been there ever since, in a little office off a ground floor hallway at the Punt Road Oval, between the players' change rooms and the gym. The day before the Kangaroos game, he sat amongst his shelves of syringes and *Betadine*, gauze swabs and scissors. Crutches of various heights leaned in one corner, next to a bright yellow hazardous waste disposal bin. In another sat a towering stack of big blue cardboard envelopes, holding the MRIs of various footballers' knees and ankles and shoulders. In yet another, there is a file cabinet with a combination lock, holding the valuable and private medical history of each athlete.

The past week at the club has been quiet on the medical front. Young forward Callum Moore injured his ankle in the VFL. It was initially thought to be a routine sprain but on closer examination by Hickey seemed more likely to be a more serious *syndesmosis* disruption, meaning appointments with orthopaedic surgeons and an arthroscopy. Hickey put together a recovery plan, beginning with two weeks in a moon boot, after he had checked the wound. He then informed the fitness and coaching staff. Then it is his job to monitor and update progress.

The club has a few chronic injuries to deal with this season. Ruckman Shaun Hampson has been frustrated by a disc injury that gives him constant lower back pain. Hampson has seen numerous specialists and had various interventions. He sees a chiropractor once a week—Michael Sexton, the former Carlton centre half-back, who played 200 games including the club's 1995 premiership—but nothing has helped in a significant way. "I think it'll just take time," says Hickey, "but we've been saying that for a few months now."

During a game, Hickey fixes little cuts and gouges. Sometimes, but not often, they require stitches, but usually these wounds can be taped during the game and sewn up later. Once every few weeks he has to manage concussion—a time-consuming process but a necessary one.

This season concussion, and its possible long-term implications for players, has dominated discussion around the game like no season before, and tall forward Ben Griffiths's year has been severely affected. The 200cm target flies high for marks, glides into packs, and has suffered as many as seven heavy heads knocks in his career, a handful of which caused him to miss matches with concussion, including twice this season. He missed eight of the first 11 rounds recovering from the side effects.

"Ben is probably the most dramatic concussion patient I've had," says Hickey. "Griffo is a sad one, because he's almost at that point where if he has one more he'll have to consider retiring. He's not quite at that point yet, but if he got concussed again it wouldn't surprise me if he said enough was enough."

Hickey has seen more than a few promising careers cut down by bad luck. Mark Coughlan comes to mind. The bullish midfielder won the Jack Dyer Medal in 2003 when he was just 21. "He was the B&F, the poster boy," says Hickey. "Then he did his knee the following year and he was never the same." Coughlan dealt with osteitis pubis, ankle problems, and then ruptured his ACL a second time. When he returned, he battled recurrent hamstring strains, and finally a meniscus tear in his knee. "Cogs lost some pace—and he wasn't our quickest player to begin with. By the time he got back the speed of the game had changed, and moved on without him."

His last game was the final round of 2009, which was also the farewell for the skilful and popular Nathan Brown, cut down with the most gruesome broken leg in 2005. "That was really sad in the sense that we saw how exciting Nathan was—he was at the peak of his powers—and we never saw the best of him again."

The flipside, of course, are those players who suffer such an unjust run and yet persevere and succeed. Nathan Foley came to Richmond in the rookie draft (Pick 4, 2004) and was immediately dealt an achilles injury, followed by a knee injury and operations on his lateral meniscus. The latter complaint became degenerative, meaning he not only grew accustomed to the pain but also to the exacting preparation and extra training required to retain any of his ground level speed or agility or burst. Foley's stoicism saw him selected in the 2007 All Australian squad of 40.

"He just kept going and going," says Hickey. "There couldn't have been anyone that worked harder than Axel (Foley). For him to turn out the player he became—that was a great story. Little guy, never gave up, and worked hard to get everything he ever got. Eventually though his achilles ruptured again, and that made it really hard for him. He still came back though—that was Axel."

///////////

Thankfully there are no such dramatic moments in the contest tonight. Between the benches and down the race, under the stadium seating next to the auditorium for press conferences, is a sterile space with a sign on the door that reads 'Suture Room'. It feels like a small hospital ward inside, with privacy screens, plastic chairs, a surgical lamp and a yellow biohazard bin ("Danger: Destroy by Incineration"). But Hickey walks past this room tonight, and never needs to go inside.

At quarter-time he sees blood on the jumper of Dylan Grimes, but the cut needs nothing more than a quick antiseptic wipe.

At half-time Dustin Martin wanders in with a nasty graze on his knee: "Reggie boy," he asks. "Have a look?" Hickey bends down and smears a liberal dollop of creamy gel on the wound, his own special mixture of *Vaseline* and *Rectinol*, to stem the bleeding and numb the pain.

Prestia's next. The knee is giving him trouble. Hickey knows it is time for a local anaesthetic. Pain-killing injections coincidentally became a topic of discussion in public only that week. Hawthorn champion Dermott Brereton, recounting the latter part of his career, explained how a persistent knee problem meant he would have had more than 250 "jabs" throughout his career. On the same day, former Sydney full-back Ted Richards revealed that without a dozen pain-killing injections he would not have been able to play in the Swans' 2012 premiership.

This approach is not without controversy. In America's brutal NFL, the use of the pain-killing drug *Toradol* is so widespread that in some cases half a team will line up each game, each player waiting for his shot of "Vitamin T". And there are physicians who believe that treating athletes with *Lidocaine* or *Diclofinac* or *Bipuvacaine* or any other such drug constitutes a violation of their Hippocratic oath. Others believe that painkillers are basically a doping substance.

Five years ago, for instance, Dr Hans Geyer (then deputy director of the World Anti Doping Authority Laboratory in Cologne) asked why it should be legal to use drugs that switch off pain, when it is illegal to use drugs that switch off fatigue. He pointed to German walker Andreas Erm, who won a bronze medal at the World Athletic Championships in 2003 after receiving pain-killing injections several times during the race, and asked the question: "Can you tell me this is not performance-enhancing?"

Hickey bluntly busts the popular myth that scores of players on every team are taking the field only with the numbed comfort of the needle, at least in the AFL, or at least at Richmond. "We're half-way through the season and so far we haven't had to use a local anaesthetic once," he said. "To be fair, that's unusual. By this point in the year, usually someone has a little finger fracture, or bruised rib, or AC joint that might need a local for a couple of weeks."

As for his obligation to players, Hickey says he would never do anything that might make a player more susceptible to injury, not only because it is morally repugnant but because his job is to keep players healthy—not to exacerbate or aggravate their physical woes. Keeping footballers fit is his position description.

And so he quickly prepares a syringe, wearing surgical gloves as he unwraps each part from its sterile plastic packaging. He draws the anaesthetic into the chamber, while Prestia lies on his left side, his troublesome right knee bent slightly as the needle goes in, and out, and in again, touching up the area where the *iliotibial* band meets the outer joint. Hickey massages the knee a little, to spread the substance around. And then the onballer is up.

"There we go," says Prestia, winking. "Good as new."

He won't be able to play for the first few minutes of the quarter, as the medicine takes hold, but the process was surprisingly quick and easy, without so much as a grimace from the player. "I think they get into a 'no pain' mentality during a game," says Hickey. "If you tried that tomorrow, it'd hurt like hell."

/////////

In the second half, there are a few more minor blows for Hickey to address: blood noses to Menadue and Butler; muscle cramping in Houli, Riewoldt and McIntosh. All these are result of high performance. Menadue played with grit and maturity. Butler's game was good enough to earn him a Rising Star nomination. Riewoldt comfortably beat the gifted Kangaroos stopper Robbie Tarrant. Houli had 38 touches. McIntosh, as he promised before the game, was 'on' tonight—repelling North Melbourne attacks all evening, at one point running almost half the field, bouncing the ball four times.

The whole team looked strong. Brandon Ellis, zipping through traffic. Martin, again seeming without peer. Toby Nankervis shrugging aside Todd Goldstein, one of the best ruckmen in the game. The Tigers won by 35 points, putting the game to bed in the third quarter, but in truth, had they kicked more accurately the result would have been established far earlier.

///////////

Afterwards, there are few things left for Hickey to do. Reece Conca, recovering from an operation two weeks ago to repair a *Lisfranc* ligament injury, comes into the rooms and takes off his moon boot. Hickey unrolls the little bandage over the stitches in the top of his foot, and notes that it looks a lot better than it did, and his ankle movement is good. Conca is eager to begin rehab. He wants to know if he can start swimming.

"Yep. You should be fine," says Hickey. "But no weight at all. The time off means it'll heal solidly and give you the best chance to push hard when you recover."

Ben Lennon, coming off a four-goal performance in the VFL, pokes his head in the door to ask how Conca is doing. "He's good," answers Hickey. "But if you see him weight-bearing on that foot, smack him," he says, grinning. "Give him a bloody good thrashing."

In the down time after the victory, the doctor writes a referral for scans for Todd Elton, who injured his shoulder in the VFL game that day. He will miss a month of football.

He also writes one for Ivan Soldo, who appeared to jar his hip during the same match and is now standing and hopping and doing heel raises as commanded. Hickey applies pressure to the ruckman here, contorts his limbs there, but all seems well. He hums as he looks over the tall young man.

"Hopefully you've just jammed the joint a little. I can't see anything dramatic."

"But probably don't go out tonight, right?" Soldo asks.

"Why not?" says Hickey.

"You serious?"

"Well, don't have a million beers or anything, but you seem fine," Hickey says. "Life's for enjoying. You're not going to do any extra damage standing still."

Riewoldt enters the room next—Hickey's last patient for the night. The star forward has persistent effusion in the right knee, which basically means fluid in the knee, a sign of bleeding or inflammation. The injury is known to the doctor, and it is not acute. He had planned to see Riewoldt post-game to give him a shot of cortisone, an anti-inflammatory. It's given now because the players are about to enter their bye week, and the cortisone will allow the joint to settle down faster during the time off from training. Riewoldt is flying with Daniel Rioli to his home in the Tiwi Islands the next day, with Dylan Grimes, Jayden Short and Shane Edwards, as well as Craig McRae and Justin Leppitsch.

The big goalkicker lays flat on his back, leg bent, knee raised. He stares at the ceiling, and the needle goes more than an inch deep into the joint. Riewoldt doesn't even blink. Then he stands and rubs his hands together.

"Thank you," he says, smiling. "Now to get some magic Tiwi water on it."

The players all depart now, headed to recovery at Punt Road Oval, before driving home, going to sleep, waking up and then scattering. Ellis is going to New Zealand to get away—mobile off, eyes and ears open. Martin is also going to New Zealand, but to visit his father. Nathan Broad, Jason Castagna and Dan Butler are jumping into a van and driving up the Sapphire Coast to Sydney. Sam Lloyd is going home to Deniliquin, and on a short camping trip with Alex Rance, David Astbury and Ivan Maric.

Hickey is staying in Melbourne and having a rest, his season only half over.

"A good night," he says, zipping up the last of his kit bags. "No injuries, a great win, a week off. I think our work here is done."

29

INSIDE OUR HEADS

One coach throws a footy at his feet. Another pushes a tackling bag into his path. Brandon Ellis hits the bag, charges at the Sherrin, scoops it lightly, and handballs it back. Again he charges, and again the swinging heavy sack hits him, and the back flanker makes a sound like gas escaping a pressurised tank—*ish!*—with every contact. *Ish! Ish!*

"Nice Brando!" yells Hardwick. "Spend time over the ball. Good, good, good. Yes!"

Ellis has spoken of this before—his need to be first in line for this drill. For the 23-year-old running player, it has become an almost superstitious routine designed to improve the contested side of his game—to do better at fielding all those ground balls that bobble about the backline like leather chaos. He never leaves a session at Punt Road Oval without making sure he has done the drill ten times because, he says, defence is like "life and death". This drill offers the perfect preparation, and also a "free mind and free spirit".

In truth, something else is responsible for his newly found calmness and lightness of mood. It happened six months ago, on the Richmond pre-season training camp in Mooloolaba. The club was trialling a new team building exercise. It was called the 'Triple H sessions' and it meant that a single player would stand in front of the group and share three personal tales: a tale of a hero, hardship and highlight from his life. Ellis immediately knew what his would be.

"I wrote it all down, I couldn't wait to share. But I was so nervous because no-one knew my story," says Ellis, sitting now inside Tigerland, remembering that moment in summer. "I sent Cotch a draft of what I was going to say, and he was like 'Mate, you're going first—I don't care what you say'."

And so, he found himself in front of the group, in the air-conditioned conference room of a Sunshine Coast resort, on the Sunday night before a brutal five-day training camp. He wore thongs, tan shorts and a black T-shirt, and clutched his iPhone. He was too scared to improvise—"shit-scared, actually"—and so he read from the bright little screen in his hand.

He told a story first about his dad (Dale), mum (Nancy), sister (Kate) and brother (Sean), and the moment that rocked them. It was about his hero—his father.

"He was diagnosed with cancer. I came home from school one day with my brother and sister to find him and mum crying on the floor. I asked what was wrong and he told me, and I ran to my room. My world crashed down on me. He had these lumps in his throat."

Ellis was in year 10 at the time. His father had overcome kidney cancer in the past, but now it was in the throat and the diagnosis was that it was more insidious and more powerful.

"They said 'You don't have long to live. It's way too far gone. We can't cure it'. They said 'Start saying your goodbyes and cherish what time you have with your kids and wife'.

He came into my room and we just cuddled in my bed for hours. I didn't want him to leave. Didn't want to believe it was real.

He was my right-hand man, who took me to training, never missed a session or a game, took me to gym, kicked the footy with me in the pouring rain for however long I wanted, and so much more.

My best mate came over that night and I overheard him in the lounge room with my dad, who said, 'When I'm gone, can you please look after Brandon, to make sure he goes down the right path'. Hearing that killed me.

So, I gave up footy. Stopped going to school. I just wanted to be with him all the time.

The doctors said, 'You can have the treatment but it's pointless'. He goes 'Stuff that, I'm a fighter, I'm not giving up on my kids. Give me the treatment, I'll do anything'.

Coming home from school, seeing him get his chemo and his radiotherapy was not a good sight. He lost all his hair. He was so skinny. He looked like he was just dead, there in his chair. He said to me, 'Whatever you do Brandon, go back and play footy. Do it for me.'

Six months later, the lump was gone and he's still here today. They said it was a miracle. Now he's healthy. He hadn't had a drink in 20 years, but now he loves a Jim Beam and Coke every Friday with mum. Life's too short.

He's taught me to never give up, always work my arse off. He was the one who would drive me to the pool for recovery. Nudge me to do an extra gym session. I wanted to do it for him, and nothing has ever motivated me more. I play AFL for my dad."

Ellis sniffed, and sniffled, and wiped away a few tears. Most of the room—45 players and 10 coaches—did the same. And then he began his tale of hardship, in North Carlton, in a first-floor Housing Commission flat, where he grew up sharing a bunk bed with his brother in a tiny room.

"I got bullied through primary school and high school. I got reminded every day that I was poor and had nothing. I used to walk a different route home so that people wouldn't know where I lived, because I felt so uncomfortable, embarrassed and ashamed."

He takes a deep breath now, and crosses his arms, and one leg bounces as he explains how it was hard to bring home friends, or girlfriends. He didn't bring anyone there until high school, in fact, because so many of the kids he grew up with had called him scum. His father, before the illness, worked packing orders in a chocolate factory, and his mother took care of her three kids.

"My parents had no money. They've still got no money. But when I got drafted, I promised them as soon as got some money I would start looking after them. I got my family out of the flats a few years ago. I got them a rental property in Moonee Ponds near me, and pay half their rent. It's the first time my mum and dad and brother and sister have had a backyard in their life. They can't get the smile off their faces."

They each have their own bedroom now. Ellis's mum has a veggie patch, and a lawn. His footy career gave them a new life—so different from the one he remembers from the flats.

"I've seen a lot of things happen. I've lost people close to me. I've seen a lot of crime. My mates have been stabbed right in front of me. When I was little we badly wanted a trampoline, so my mum and dad saved up 200 bucks to buy us one. You couldn't get us off it, until one morning we woke up and someone had burned holes

in it with cigarettes. It shattered us.

Mum used to do our washing and put it on a shared clothesline with everyone else from the flats. So many of our clothes got stolen, so I used to go to Melbourne Central with my mates on the tram, and steal clothes, rip the tags off. Just so I could have some nice new tops.

Over time, I've had to develop some tough skin, and could have easily gone down the wrong path. I know I'm reserved, pretty quiet, and don't speak up a lot. I know I hang out with my mates outside footy a lot, more than I should, and should probably spend more time with you boys, but they've all been through it with me, and we're so close because all we had was each other. Now you know my story, I can finally open up and feel comfortable, talking to your boys about it."

His highlight came next, and it was the day he was drafted. Ellis began playing AFL Auskick at four, at AG Gillon Oval in Brunswick. When he was seven, his uncle, Shane Francis, coached the under-10s at West Coburg, and fudged the paperwork to allow him in the team. Playing two years out of his grade, little Brandon won the best and fairest anyway.

He grew up a Collingwood supporter, but in his teens his cousin's Nanna, Judy Francis—who was the cook for the North Melbourne Football Club—told him he could go into the club with her if he switched to the Kangaroos. Soon he was lurking in corners at Arden Street, mouth agape as Wayne Carey, Glenn Archer and Anthony Stevens trained. Brent 'Boomer' Harvey is still his idol. He saw what they all did, how hard they worked and how much fun they had, and it was all he ever wanted to do.

On draft night, he couldn't have friends over to the family flat—it was too small. So his Calder Cannons coach offered to host. Ellis could bring as many mates as he wanted. He wanted to go to a Victorian club, but it looked unlikely. GWS had 11 of the first 14 picks that year. Brisbane had two. Port Adelaide had the other one. And Fremantle wanted him at Pick 16. Richmond, with pick 15, was the first local club in the draft.

And so they read out pick 14, Devon Smith, to the Greater Western Sydney Giants. Ellis sat on a couch, crossing every finger and toe. Richmond began reading out a number, and then the name 'Brandon'. He never heard the name Ellis...

"Everyone just erupted, and there was a big stacks-on. It was the best feeling in the world."

Chris Newman called. Brett Deledio called. Cotchin called. Hardwick called, and Ellis accidentally hung up on him. Within two days he was at the club, going through an induction, and then he was at the airport ready to head to Arizona for a high-altitude camp. He grabbed a chocolate bar, and remembers Deledio appearing in front of him with a message: "Would Gary Ablett be eating a chocolate bar?"

"I threw it in the bin. Shit, potted by the vice-captain on day one. But I learned a good lesson straight away."

He moved in with a host family, eventually bought his own place and lived there with Steven Morris before fixing it up and selling up. He bought another place, and he lives there with Nathan Broad and another friend, a school teacher. He has just completed an eight-month renovation. It is his castle.

"So yeah, feel free to ask me anything you want. Anyway, that's my story."

The group applauded and cheered and immediately stood. Players approached, and held him close. For Ellis, it was the beginning not just of a training camp or a new season, but of another phase of his career. Perhaps his life.

"By the end, people were crying," he says now, back at Tigerland after a midweek training session. "I felt like I became a new person. And I just felt so much closer to the group, so accepted. It was massive for me. *Massive.* It's like I can finally be who I want to be."

Like Cotchin, Ellis no longer thinks he must be perfect. It was easy to think otherwise when his career began. His annual match tally since he arrived at the club reads 21, 20, 22, 22, 22 (and now every game in 2017). Put another way, he has missed just three games in six years, and is beloved by the fans. Social media provided ample validation.

"My first three years it was all love. All praise. If I had a bad game, no problem, people would just pump me up," he says. "But last the last three years, you just get people attacking you. *You're shit. I can't wait to run into you in the street. Brandon Ellis is crap. Why is Brandon Ellis getting a game?"*

"I try to laugh at it, but your family sees it and it hurts them," he says. "So, I just don't give the keyboard warriors anything to use. I've never written back to anyone. Just brush it aside, let them have an opinion—they'll have one anyway. Tom Mitchell had 50 touches the other day (against Collingwood in Round 9) and people *still* put him down."

This season, he has shifted to the backline and loves the new role. And the backline loves having him. Against North Melbourne, and Essendon before that, Ellis had 30 possessions and a goal. He attributes that form—indeed the form of the entire team—to the Triple H sessions that have happened almost every other week at the club since Ellis spoke. It has kept them closer, on and off the field.

"There's so much love for each other," he says. "We stay positive, we stick tight, we don't let anything in the cracks, or anyone inside our heads. And we know our best footy together is good enough to beat anyone."

//////////

When Hardwick hears of such endorsements, all he can do is smile. He didn't really know the sessions would produce such an outpouring, or be so popular, but he had an inkling they could prove important.

"You always bring different things to the group at different times, but this idea of 'connection' was something I delved into late last year," he says. "It seemed more relevant this season."

The coach didn't learn the exercise on a leadership course, nor did he hear about it from another coach, nor see it in action at another organisation. He read about it in a book, by Jon Gordon, a self-styled American leadership and teamwork guru who has worked with everyone from Fortune 500 companies to school districts. The book was called "You win in the locker room first: The seven C's to build a winning team in business, sports and life", and it featured many of the methods used by American football coach Mike Smith, who led the Atlanta Falcons through one of the most striking turnarounds in NFL history. The 'Triple H' idea came under the "C for Connect" chapter (along with exercises titled "The Defining Moment" and "If you really knew me, you would know this about me").

Gordon is that kind of author. His books have titles like "The Energy Bus" and his chapters have names like "Don't let your reptile eat your positive dog". But the Triple H exercise is a method that has worked with everyone from the Clemson University football team to the UCLA women's basketball program. It worked at Richmond, according to Shane McCurry—the man who leads these sessions at the club—because of the trust within the group. McCurry saw it in that very first session with Ellis.

"There was just not a single head in the room that wasn't solely focused on the person up the front, and it wasn't in a way that made them feel isolated," he says. "It was that focus and that presence—that idea that 'We're right here with you, we know you're doing it tough up there, talking about these things, but we're behind you'."

The idea is simple, too. We lack any depth of knowledge about most people we meet, says McCurry, whether the person sitting at the next desk, or the guy one locker down. "You know about them, where they've grown up, where they live, maybe the name of their partner. But you don't often get to that next layer down, and I think any team can benefit from getting to know one another at that deeper level."

At times the program can sound exactly like the kind of pop psychology too eagerly lapped up by sporting organisations and commercial sales teams. Gordon himself is fond of canned inspirational quotes: "Humility doesn't mean thinking less of yourself, it means thinking of yourself less" and "True leaders don't create followers, they create more leaders". But there is nothing hokey or semantic or plastic about the Triple H method—certainly not as practised at Richmond.

"It's pretty confronting, but it's also like a load off their mind," says Tim Livingstone, the coaching director. "It creates conversations and understanding. We're talking about stories of sickness and broken homes. Put it this way, if you've got to put your arse on the line for your mate, and take a hit on the field, you're more likely to do it if you have some care for what he's trying to do, and what he's been through."

The season so far since the sessions were introduced has been an emotional learning curve for the group. Every player willing to share his story has spoken with awe about watching a teammate cry, or shake—about how it felt to lay themselves bare.

Shaun Grigg spoke about his hardship. He was a teenager playing senior cricket for VRI Delacombe, south-west of Ballarat, when a friend collapsed and died while batting. Mal Hughes was 41 years old, and had a heart attack at the crease, while batting. Grigg was presented with his bat that week, at the funeral. "Next week I made 112 not out, using his bat. I was 16," Grigg says. "It was a hardship, but it was probably the best thing I've ever done."

Ben Griffiths found his hero at home, and many of the players do. It is easy to be awed by the people who raise you. In the case of the tall forward, it is his father. "He's the kind of man I want to be," he says. "His sister has a terminal disease. She also has the maturity of a 12-year-old. The way he looks after her and loves her, it's really admirable. He just shows this care. All the time, he just cares."

Bachar Houli found his highlight transformative. It was the birth of his first daughter, Sarah. He admits until he saw his wife, Rouba, giving birth at the Werribee Mercy Hospital, he didn't fully value or appreciate his own mother, Yamama, or father, Malek. He told the other players as much. "I made a promise that day—an oath—that every time I see mum and dad I'm going to kiss them. Hand or forehead or cheek," he says. "Because what more does a mum or dad want? They want to see you come and show your affection for them. I see them smile every time."

Ellis isn't sure the results on field would be the same this year without Triple H. Despite every team bonding exercise, every trip away, every Mad Monday, every interstate game, every induction and every community camp, he says it has taken these sessions for the players to truly show one another who they are, and why they are the way they are.

"We don't want to be fake," Ellis says. "We want you to know, 'This is who the fuck I am'. We've taken a massive step forward this year in how much we care. We're connected now. I feel like we're forming a brotherhood."

30

TWO PLUS TWO IS FOUR

After the bye, the home and away season settles into the heart of winter. Training meetings begin in near darkness, day games end in a sodden rainy twilight, and the dramatic ups and downs of football matches all seem distant as soon as they have passed, almost as though they never happened, or happen long ago.

In Round 13, at home, the Tigers pounce on Sydney—the form team of the competition—with an early six-goal lead. It is an ambush—slick and unseen. But they squander that chance, running out 9-point losers.

They respond a week later, doing what they should, comfortably controlling all four quarters against lowly Carlton. They are never threatened.

In Round 15, playing away against Port Adelaide, Richmond capitalise on the inaccuracy of the Power and run over the top of the home side for a rousing 13-point win.

But against St Kilda at Etihad Stadium comes a reality check, perhaps, or an aberration—an horrendous stumble at least—as the Tigers are obliterated by the Saints, simultaneously humbled and flattered by the 11-goal margin.

A week later at the same venue, they recover to account for Brisbane, but they know they are winning ugly. In the rooms after that last victory, while the players sing and Ivan Soldo is doused in *Gatorade*, Hardwick does not even watch the song. He stands with his assistants in a briefing room, and he writes the word "CLINICAL" on the whiteboard. "We haven't got this yet," he says to the others, tapping the blue letters. "The polish isn't there."

What to make then of more than a month of football played in such a snakes and ladders way? If you were to ask Tim Livingstone, Richmond's Head of Coaching, he is likely to point to the cartoon on the wall of his office, behind his desk, which he does early the next week.

The comic is a pair of stick figure drawings. He uses the diptych occasionally in presentations. The first scene is labelled "Your plan", and in it sits a man on a bicycle, riding up a steady, smooth and mild incline towards a finish line. The second scene is labelled "Reality", and in it sits the same man on his bike, staring ahead at a much longer path—one beset with pits and peaks, storm clouds, rocks and only the faintest barest outline of a flag in the distance.

The latter picture could quite easily represent the last month or more of football by the Tigers. It could also represent the recent history at the club. Livingstone points to a deep watery trough in the second image.

"There's 2010," he says, recalling his second season at the club, when Richmond lost the first nine games by an average margin of 52 points, when the club was likened to the dying days of Fitzroy, when a Facebook page called 'I hate it when I'm kicking the footy around and Richmond try to recruit me' quickly gained more than 50,000 followers.

Next Livingstone points next to a steep rise with a rocky outcrop and a nasty drop. "There's 2013, maybe 2014 and 2015," he adds, remembering successive years in which the Tigers reached the finals only to be ejected immediately. Last year was another steep drop.

His challenge then—and the challenge of the entire club—is to reconcile those two narratives and smooth the level of output, so the win-loss ratio of the team is never skewed so dramatically. Livingstone's job is instruction and coordination. He is a facilitator and friendly presence.

Coaches, players and administrators pass through his second-floor office as though it is a kind of high school form room. They steal Mentos from a large glass jar he refills every week. They interrupt and convene impromptu gatherings, and Livingstone—a funny man—is genial about all such intrusions.

He studies his craft, too. His bookshelf is thick with tomes both instructional and inspirational, with everything from "They call me coach" and "The Art of Kick Building" to "The 7 habits of highly effective people."

He also has a wonderful guide to the game pinned to his noticeboard: *Football – A few hints, by J.F. McHale, Collingwood coach.*

"That's amazing, isn't it? That's his football game plan and protocol," Livingstone says. "Some of it is ahead of its time, for nineteen-twenty-whatever."

There are 15 pointers for game play, and most are excellent. McHale, the legendary Magpies coach, advises that you should always play in front and never take defeat badly or crow over a victory. *Don't kick into your man on the mark*, it reads. *This is an unpardonable mistake and often leads to disastrous results.*

His 12 points for training are less relevant. In fact, most are dated and somewhat strange.

Don't eat foods that are too rich, such as suet pudding. Avoid sprinting for trams and trains immediately after breakfast. Take a cold bath every morning unless you are feeling unwell. *Drink a glass of cold water before going to bed*, it says. *In this way, the intestines receive a good cleansing.*

But Livingstone knows McHale didn't coach a record eight VFL premierships without a certain hardness of character. He points to the final note: *Remember what you are undertaking to do. Nothing is worth undertaking unless it is worth doing properly.*

One wonders what McHale might make of what Livingstone is working on now. In downtime, he is looking over the latest Player Wellness Reports. The players complete these each day, entering information into an iPad about how they're feeling and what they're thinking. They tap screens to rate their level of 'General Fatigue' from 'Excellent' to 'Very Fatigued'. They do the same for how they are 'Coping' and their level of 'Motivation'. They rate their 'Muscle Soreness' for each of the Lower Back, Glutes, Quads, Hamstrings (from 'No Awareness' to 'Very Sore'). How they slept is gauged on a sliding scale from 'Excellent' to 'Terrible'.

The data and anecdotal information is then assessed by an analytics team, examined for spikes and patterns. Some players always report being tired while others never will, so abrupt changes to their patterns are more important. That's when club welfare officers get involved. Why aren't they sleeping? Are they stressed? Do they need a new air-conditioner or heater? Should someone from the club check to make sure their mattress is the right one?

On another wall in his office sits an A4 colour-coded chart, the result of a profiling exercise that measures and sorts all players and coaches into various styles of thinking. Psychometric testing has long been a part of corporate organisational psychology. The MBTI (Myer-Briggs Type Indicator) and the HBDI (Herrmann Brain Dominance Index) are the most popular. The more detailed assessment tools are the OPQ (Occupational Personality Questionnaire) and the Saville Consulting Wave, but the core idea behind all such tools is the assessment and categorisation of capabilities and behaviour. Livingstone says the survey used by Richmond is called "Insights Discovery". Its results are based on a questionnaire that takes around 20 minutes to complete, before ultimately providing each person with a set of four ranked "Insights Colour Energies" including Fiery Red, Sunshine Yellow, Cool Blue and Earth Green. (Dustin Martin for instance, is a placid and calm individual in person, and so tested as Earth Green.)

The idea of such profiling is to increase self-awareness within the group, and to recognise the different traits individuals bring to the team. Livingstone says the players and coaches use the colours as a basis for framing interactions—a kind of shorthand for dealing with others. (I have heard players reference the system in meetings: "Sorry, that's probably borne of my Red personality.")

If talking with midfielder Shaun Grigg, for example, knowing he is a Blue will tell you to be prepared and perhaps not to be flippant. (On a good day, Blues are cautious, questioning and formal. On a bad day, Blues are indecisive, suspicious and cold.)

Greens, including the quiet ruckman Ivan Maric, need patience and time to answer, and should not be forced to make quick decisions or deal with surprises. (When things are going well, Greens are encouraging, patient and relaxed. When things are not going so well, they're docile, plodding and obsequious.)

When dealing with a Red, such as Jack Riewoldt, be direct, brief, and focus on results—don't hesitate, waffle or focus solely on feelings. (Reds are assertive and competitive, but their dark side is aggression, intolerance and control.)

Finally, Yellows, including Alex Rance, want flexibility and entertainment, not so many details or too much solitary work. (Yellows are enthusiastic and persuasive figures, but just as easily indiscreet and hasty.)

Hardwick is high Blue and high Red—a personal style that has permeated much of the Tigerland footy department. Dr Pippa Grange, a former AFLPA psychological services manager, once assessed the culture at Richmond and found it to be high detail, high control and high loyalty. She encouraged Richmond to be more creative, more lateral thinking, more relationship-focused, because they were a highly task-oriented bunch. This season it seems the penny has dropped.

At any rate, Livingstone has always been a nurturing sunny Yellow. His personality plays well against that of Hardwick. The two are rarely apart. They jog together with Hayden Hill through Yarra Park most Tuesdays and Thursdays, sometimes stretching their route to the Tan Track around the Royal Botanic Gardens. Even when they leave the office they remain connected, Hardwick most days calls Livingstone on the drive home.

"Sometimes we'll just chew the fat. Sometimes he'll want to vent. Then he'll think things through and come back 12 hours later. His feedback is constant in that way," Livingstone says. "We're both always thinking, always talking. He knows he's a bit of a sledgehammer about things and I'm more of a diplomat."

New staff and players routinely report as being amazed—even confronted— by the way players and coaches are so intricately evaluated (and then supported) at Tigerland. Craig McRae, who played in three premierships during the Brisbane Lions' halcyon days, then coached at Richmond before spending five years as development manager at Collingwood, returned to Richmond in 2016 to find measurement and tracking had reached a new level in his absence. Defensive coach Ben Rutten, who came to the Tigers from an at times rigid environment at Adelaide (under the famously systems-driven Neil Craig) was also intrigued by the level of control.

It didn't happen overnight. Livingstone arrived at the club in January 2009 as manager of player development. His first day was the first training session for Ben Cousins, the wayward Brownlow Medal-winning midfielder from the West Coast Eagles—and an ill-fated messiah recruit for Richmond, in Terry Wallace's time.

"It really was amazing how many people came for that training session," Livingstone says. "I knew the crowd wasn't there to see me arrive." Six months later, senior coach Wallace was given the sack, and by August the club had appointed Hardwick. The new coach quickly asked Livingstone to manage the coaching program, which has grown now to include 10 staff, coach included, something the dictatorial McHale could never have foreseen. The "football performance" part of his title relates to everything from dealing with the property steward to the facilities team and to AFL compliance.

The schedule is also his domain—developed hand-in-hand with Hardwick and physical performance manager Peter Burge. And it is a relentless and unruly beast, too. Meetings upon meetings. Pre-meetings and post-meetings. But Livingstone makes sure every gathering has value.

What is a given meeting about?

What is it trying to achieve?

How is that measurable?

The role is management and administration but also—four times per year if possible—he makes an evaluation of the performance of the coaches.

"I've got a database of their key actions. If they're a development coach, maybe it's an opportunity to present in front of the whole playing group. Maybe it's match committee, and the suggestions they make about new drills or adjustments. Their voice on the track. And their core work—making our players better."

There's a series of vertical magnet lines on his whiteboard—each one a strip of players with a coach at the top. He points to the magnet for coach Xavier Clarke, who is responsible for the magnets of Corey Ellis, Jacob Townsend, Nathan Drummond, Jack Graham and Ivan Soldo. "None of them is a core senior player. They're kids. But how's this guy getting better, and this guy?"

Just as the development of players is attributed to specific coaches, the development of coaches is owned by Livingstone. Take the assistants who were let go last year.

"We take it as a reflection on ourselves," he says. "You wonder 'What could I have done to help them coach better?' It's got to be a reflection on you as well."

Those coaches, however, sat through feedback sessions that were honest and at times tough in 2016. Brendon Lade left to take up a long-term offer with Port Adelaide, an offer Richmond could not match. But for the others, Livingstone imagines being let go was no surprise. "It was *not* a good time to be out of contract and have a year like that."

Livingstone wishes the evaluation process could be more formalised. He met with new club sponsor Swinburne University only this week to ask about their teaching programs.

"I want to see if they can help us with some evaluation here that's regular and ongoing and measurable. We're elite at giving weekly feedback to our players—we've got to strive to do that with our coaches."

Timetables. Reports. Feedback. Evaluation. It makes sense that his background is teaching and education. And he is not alone. Jake Niall of *The Age* wrote in 2015 about Hawthorn and its glut of educators-cum-coaches. At the time, Rob McCartney, Chris Fagan, Brendan Bolton, Damien Carroll, David Rath and senior coach Alastair Clarkson himself all had a teaching background. "AFL clubs would do well, thus, to re-imagine their football operations as a small school," wrote Niall, "or a classroom in which there are about 10 teachers and 45 pupils, plus support staff."

Niall noted that while the Hawks' perceived edge over the competition in both kicking and the needs-based recruitment of players had been mimicked, no copycat rival had emerged in valuing and hiring teachers. Richmond though, already had a group of coaches with a teaching pedigree.

Development coach Ryan Ferguson, along with McRae, and Livingstone himself, have all spent time in charge of classrooms. Even facilities and integrity manager Steve Wyatt, a long-time policeman, finished his career as an instructor at the Police Academy. Former forwards coach Greg Mellor, senior development coach 'Choco' Williams, and past leadership boss Gerard Murphy were all teachers. (Even the club's recent Punt Road Oval naming rights deal with Swinburne University is as much an alignment of values as a sponsorship.)

"For a long time, our work has been about putting a curriculum in place," says Livingstone. "You maintain your strengths, but our core subject matter is our areas of improvement. From the start of training until the finish, you don't do a drill unless it's helping us play the way we play, and play better."

Livingstone taught in Dandenong throughout the 1990s, and was then appointed director of sport at Xavier College, a role he held for eight years. He didn't want to be a school principal and so already had what was, in effect, the ultimate job in his field. He was approached a couple of times by AFL clubs but didn't make any overtures himself until the head of football position came up at Richmond. He wasn't qualified for the gig but applied anyway. Interviewed by then-president Gary March, the Tigers offered him the lesser position of manager of player development.

"I remember those wise words, sometimes you've got to go backwards to go forwards," he says. "So, I thought 'Oh well, I'll give it a go'."

Seven years later, he is still like a teacher with a red pen, only now he gives grades and scrawls feedback into the margins for AFL coaches, based on what their player-pupils are achieving. As the team trains, Livingstone has interns collecting information on every drill they do, creating databases and collating it all for reports that can help coaches address any of the issues raised in those endless staff meetings.

You say we need to get better at ground balls? Well, how many times have we trained that? And have they got better? If Brandon Ellis needs to get better at picking up ground balls, then one would expect that the amount of times he practises that skill is greater than average compared to the whole team, or at least compared with other midfielders. "And if he's not getting better, we either can't coach it, or he's not good enough."

The players benefit from this data as well. Last season, the players received an update every Monday, like a school report card—and it was thorough. Were they nailing skills work? Or flunking GPS tracking? Each weekly report came with comments from coaches. Sometimes the players followed up. A few players would call Hardwick shortly after the report came out, to talk through any area in which they felt they had been marked hard; not all players needed such regular discussions, but the information was all there, served up every Monday morning, welcome or not.

In 2017, however, this information is contained to the coaching group, used for internal tracking, rather than being handed back to the players every week. "That said, no one at any given time can claim they don't know how they're tracking," Livingstone says. "Anyone who is delisted by us, it's not a surprise. I would suggest they saw it coming."

⁂

Like many coaches who are largely anonymous backroom boys, Livingstone was nevertheless a talented footballer, playing high-level suburban footy, then VFA. His prime was perhaps at 24, when he played for Box Hill one week, followed quickly by a midweek VFL representative game, a game with Melbourne reserves the following weekend, then he was taken in the mid-year draft and played a game with the Richmond reserves one week later—four different jumpers in a fortnight. He remembers meeting the legendary Allan Jeans, who was coaching the Tigers in a short-lived (single season) stint in 1992. But Jeans didn't rate Livingstone, and told him so: "OK laddie, we'll give you a chance. They tell me you're okay. We'll soon see."

Eventually one day Jeans called Livingstone at school, where he was teaching physical education, and the tone was the same: "Hello son. It's Allan Jeans here, Yabby. Just ringing to let you know you've got a game. We're going with you tomorrow. Still think you're too slow, but we're going to play you anyway."

Livingstone was delisted at the end of the year, then did pre-season with the club in 1993 and was drafted again. John Northey was the new coach.

Livingstone dominated at Reserves level but struggled to get past midfielders Matthew Knights, Craig Lambert, Tony Free, Wayne Campbell and Stuart Maxfield. Eventually he got picked and played Friday night football against Adelaide, tagging Craig McDermott. He played eight games in two seasons but never managed to play in a winning side. His AFL career though was over by the end of 1993.

It was 16 years before he left teaching to return to Punt Road, and he was shocked by what he found. The gym was the same. The offices spaces were antiquated. He chaired match committee in a small office where two recruiters were trying to work at their desks. There was no modern Swinburne Centre. No Korin Gamadji Institute. The whole club existed in the bowels of the old grandstand. The football department had a bin in the middle of the room to catch leaking water when it rained.

At the time, the Richmond Cricket Club also shared the facility, so the oval had a hard pitch in the centre—a turf table around which the rest of the field had fallen. A heavy downpour always blocked one drain, making a lake in a forward pocket. Brendon Gale walked into the water after one torrential storm in 2011. The former-player now CEO wanted to see how deep the stagnant pool had become. It was up to his waist. And this was not 1979, 1989 or 1999—it was 2009.

"I'd get here early in the morning and chase possums out, clean off possum shit and piss," says Livingstone. "And this was meant to be an elite training environment. We'd meet potential recruits off site, even some coaches, because we didn't want to take them through here and put them off the place. Now our facilities are a competitive advantage."

Still, Livingstone always has facility envy. He has toured training centres at major American universities and NFL teams. He's seen massive auditoriums and entire theatrettes devoted solely to, say, a defensive line. "And then the line room is branded that way," he says. "You can put your pictures and plays and messaging on the wall, and it creates this learning space."

Livingstone oversaw the reconfiguration of the football department rooms at Punt Road over summer. They brought in bean bags and couches. They made sure the line rooms radiate off a central eating and recovery hub, so the players can have a coffee or a chat while they wait to see their line coach. They put the massage rooms back downstairs, allowing the players to go directly from the track to massage and vice versa. They didn't make these adjustments because of some kind of *footy feng shui*. Greater space and better facilities allow teams to maximise their most valuable commodity: time.

"If we can put eight weights racks in instead of four, it means the players can get through their weights program in three fewer hours every week, and maybe that means the players can spend more time with their coaches," he says. "There's a reason Hawthorn are moving to a bigger and better facility in Dingley."

That comic on the wall with the peaks and troughs and storm clouds and obstacles may be labelled "Reality", but if Livingstone has anything to do with the way the rest of the season unfolds, 2017 will more closely resemble the smooth track in picture one—the straight and steady incline from go to goal.

"You can't afford to ride rollercoasters, not in this business," he says. "You reflect, review, and then you move on."

That's what they did in the off-season. Livingstone wonders what Jeans would have thought of their changes—the mindfulness sessions and emphasis on connection and vulnerability. He recalls a famous quote from the Hawthorn and St Kilda great: *"Coaching is like cooking sausages. You can boil them, fry them, curry them, but they are still sausages."*

Livingstone sees the changes made at Richmond in a similar way. The core business of producing great footy players hasn't changed. They still teach skills, and drive fitness, and refine strategy, and demand commitment. But the flavour of the way things are framed this season seems somehow different.

"People came back and said that it just feels … *not the same*. They feel refreshed," he says. "And maybe some of these things are just minor changes to how you cook that sausage, but it all helps."

31

GAME WITHIN A GAME

B lake Caracella stands in the midfield meeting room, walking a cross-section of the playing list through the key points to remember for the upcoming game against the Giants. Kamdyn McIntosh is there, on a beanbag, as are Brandon Ellis, Nathan Broad and Oleg Markov. On a couch at the back of the room sit Jason Castagna, Daniel Rioli and Ivan Soldo. Trent Cotchin leans forward in a chair, as do development coaches Ryan Ferguson and Xavier Clarke.

They're staring at a chart projected on to the wall. It's titled "Pre-Clearance Contested Ball Differential" and refers to the ability of teams to win contested football *within* the stoppage—before it emerges into that hint of open space on the edge of the pack.

"Look at that screen," says Caracella.

Greater Western Sydney is ranked first in the competition, the Tigers, fifteenth.

The midfield coach pushes a button and a new chart appears. It's titled "Post-Clearance Contested Ball Differential" and refers to each team's ability to fight for the football on the fringe of the action, *outside* the immediate crunch of the scrums that form at ball-ups and boundary throw-ins.

In this metric, the Tigers are fourth in the league, the Giants, fourteenth.

"What's that telling you?" asks Caracella.

McIntosh: "They're good inside the contest, but not on the outside?"

This is precisely what the midfield coach wants to hear. If the Tigers are to beat GWS at the MCG on Sunday, they will need to match GWS inside the contest with an arm-wrestle between equal numbers, where the Giants are at their best. But they cannot afford to take extra numbers inside the whorl of the pack, because the goal is to beat them elsewhere—to stop them from spreading and breaking away in space.

"They've got a lot of ball hunters," says Caracella. "High draft picks, very good players, but they all hunt the footy—they all want the ball in their hands. We match them inside—*or beat them*—then control the outside, and we might expose their defence."

To prove the point, Caracella shows another chart—this one displaying the results of Giants games throughout the season so far. The Giants wins and losses, it seems, are strikingly aligned with Post-Clearance Contested Ball. Caracella has basically isolated the single factor—*or at least one important factor*—that correlates most closely with all GWS victories.

"When they win that stat, they win the game. When they lose that stat? They tend to lose the game. The results are right there," he says, pointing at the wall. "So, what's the takeaway?"

Cotchin: "Match them on the inside, beat them on the outside."

The young coach now begins showing "edits"—action clips from the last time Richmond played GWS, when the Tigers lost in Western Sydney after a last-minute goal to Jeremy Cameron. Edit after edit shows Richmond players staying around the contest, blocking exits and stopping runners. Caracella murmurs approving commentary as the tape rolls.

Watch this. Trapping them. This is us at our best.

They hunt the footy—we're going to hunt them.

Giants midfielder Dylan Shiel wins the ball in close and dishes a short handball to the outside runner, Tom Scully, but there is a Tiger waiting to pounce. Caracella keeps talking.

You don't need to be perfect.

Perfect is just a bonus.

Work hard.

Use your numbers.

Execute.

Rugged clearance player Callan Ward fights through a rolling maul and farms the Sherrin out to Josh Kelly, but Richmond is there in numbers.

Caracella points to the Tigers circling the stoppage.

Get from contest to contest, and control them on the outside.

You know the stats.

Can we expose them inside defensive 50, one on one?

Again and again he shows footage of what he wants to see, along with gentle reminders about how to succeed. It all seems so simple. His messaging has a calming, repetitive cadence.

Get numbers to where the ball is going.

Get numbers to where the ball is going.

It's a game within a game.

A game within a game.

////////////

In his office later, Caracella reiterates the plan, but also explains how he came up with it—and how he then teaches it to a couple of dozen footballers. You begin with the basic desired outcome: kicking more goals than the opposition.

"Now take that back a step, and you've got to get good scoring opportunities," he says. "Go another step back from that, and you've got to get the ball in your hands."

To do that this week, Caracella looks at how the Giants win the ball and how they move the ball—examining their strengths and preferences. "It's not really about exposing a weakness. They don't have a weakness," he says. "They're great at some things and less great at others, so it's more about exposing their *way* of playing."

Loosely speaking, Caracella is the midfield coach at Richmond, but in truth he is responsible for how Richmond attacks, with a focus on the structure and shape of the 18 men on the field. The notion of a "game within a game" is something he explains well in basketball terms.

The Cleveland Cavaliers, for instance, might position a trio of long-range shooters on the three-point line not because they want to take the shot, but because it will open up space for LeBron James to run at the hoop, playing only against his direct opponent. That one-on-one is a game. A post-and-screen might be a two-on-two game. "But the other guys are allowing that game to happen, because they're in dangerous positions in the wider game," he says. "Game within a game."

Caracella handles much of the macro level strategy within the team—the patterns and mechanics at play. Again, we're talking about those mysterious footy 'structures' spoken of in press conferences and post-match interviews and talk shows and feature articles. But how are they trained?

"You break it right down, as simply as you can, and build it up from there," Caracella says. "We might train something one-versus-one, then two-versus-two, then three-versus-two, or four-versus-three. You train it on the ball. You train it *near* the ball. But you also start training it *away* from the ball. You train those three-point shooters, who allow LeBron his one-on-one, or the post-and-screen two-on-two."

I've seen them training such movements on Punt Road Oval, the coaches calling out the exact plays they want to see, then watching the players set up and move as each of the commanded passages unfold, one after another.

"Next one!" Hardwick will roar. "Centre forward stoppage!"

And so, the midfield group moves as one, shuffling together to a forward flank where they contest a ball-up, although "contest" is not the right word, because there are no opponents. Sometimes there are no witches' hats. There are no assistant coaches occupying space, pantomiming resistance. There is only the unencumbered movement of the senior players, gliding through drills, and the coaches walking their players through every tap to handball to kick to mark to goal they want to see.

One play yesterday began with a defensive tap from Nankervis to Cotchin, who handballed to Grigg, who kicked short to the leading Riewoldt, who quickly turned and snapped to Rioli, sprinting towards the goal mouth.

There was no resistance. No-one feigning a tackle. No-one giving even mock chase, or even manning the mark. The players were all alone, showing them what perfection looks like. It is almost like shadow boxing—a chance to embed each movement into their minds without distraction. Automation through repetition.

Later they do the same thing with coaches blocking their field of vision. Then they do it against an opponent—yellow guernseys versus orange bibs, perhaps—and slowly but surely with instruction and correction, explanation and reiteration, the pattern will sink into the psyche, like muscle memory.

Such structures seep into their understanding of football all week long, in match reviews, in opposition analysis, in training meetings, in line meetings.

They learn what ideal structures look like through footage of perfect and imperfect set-ups, from all different angles, and from diagrams. Senior players guide younger players. There is also the "walk through", where the players assemble inside the gym, in rows, exactly as they will line up in the team on the weekend, at which point the coaches will walk amongst them and ask: *Forward 50 stoppage, what are you doing, Jack? Kick in, fast play, where are you Grigga? Protect the game scenario, what should you be doing at the centre bounce, Cotch?* Then they talk through the answers amongst themselves, while standing in their positions, set to scale on a basketball court.

Training structures is something that happens in large part by osmosis, the game plan gradually settling over the playing group with every one of these interactions at the club.

Caracella says the vernacular is crucial, too. As a coach, you don't want to have to explain again and again the long-winded concept of players guarding against the opposition's attempts to switch play by foot from one pocket to the opposite wing, and how Richmond players need to be close enough to their opponents to discourage such passing—not when you can simply say, 'We need to watch our Uranus cover'. "The terminology helps sink the message into the players' minds," he says. "So, we use that language at all times, so it spreads across the club, so they get reminders of concepts and real familiarity."

Caracella sees the changed game style this season as being one that allows players greater freedom to choose within a broad strategic framework.

"Previously, I think things were more coordinated, and decision-making was more structured—*If the ball's here, you do this, if it's there, you do that*—whereas now it's more open—*You can do this, this and this, or that*. You're not wrong or right. You have options, make the choice, figure it out."

This mindset was evident only 10 minutes earlier, in a meeting with Justin Leppitsch, in which he showed a series of edits from previous games, and then asked the players to sit in pairs and consider various questions.

What did Astbury do well with this kick?

Watch this stoppage, and rate the positioning of Dustin Martin from 1 to 10?

Did McIntosh run the correct pattern here?

How could Butler have avoided this loopy handball?

Take the last question, for instance. Cotchin says that Butler could have delivered a short kick sideways into what they call a "passing lane", which is correct. Markov says he could have taken a shot on goal, which is also correct. Rioli says he could have taken on the tackler, tried to step him, or spin past, which is also right.

"Yes, yes, yes," says Leppistch. "These scenarios are all about 'How?' What are the options? What are the percentages? What can you choose? What *will* you choose?"

Caracella says this is how an AFL team teaches decision-making. Footballers want to express themselves on the field, by how they play the game. And they want to have fun. Understanding the many options open to them does this. Whether you're an attacking half-back flanker, or a full-forward, or a defensive back-pocket, you want to bring your desired form of ascendancy to the contest.

"And when you're all showing some part of yourself, you're expressing yourselves as a team," he says. "I think our trademark would be pressure. We've got an identity. The players have an identity. And when you have that, you can work to match and complement each other."

In that sense, little has changed since when Caracella joined the AFL. He was drafted by Essendon in 1994 and played 126 games there, including the 2000 premiership. That Essendon side was recently dubbed by experts at *The Age* as the greatest flag team of the new millennium, eclipsing those of Brisbane, Geelong and Hawthorn. He moved to Brisbane later, where he played 34 games, including the 2003 premiership. He finished up at Collingwood (27 games), and coached there for three years. He came to Tigerland in the off-season, fresh from a seven-season coaching stint at Geelong, including the 2011 premiership.

"I started at 17, drafted out of school, and it was amateur," he says. "I got to training the first day and most players were working full-time. But that was when things changed. By 1997, no one was working anymore."

Still, the players lived within a different kind of in-season rhythm than they do now. After a game they would go to the social club and pick up their drink cards, then have a meal. "Then you would kick on afterwards and go somewhere else, and go out. You'd stay at a teammate's house, and get up and your clothes would stink of smoke, and then you'd head to rehab."

It was, he says, a great life experience. And there are elements of that era that remain crucial within football clubs. "You still want them to have fun," he says. "A lot of those nights on the grog built that camaraderie. The game's a bit more professional now, and the players can get in a bit more trouble—

with cameras on phones, for example—but they're still young, still learning about life."

Freedom, he says, is essential.

"Not many people like being controlled every second of the day," he says. "And it's the same on the field—you want to make a decision or two for yourself."

//////////

The game is a wet one. Jimmy Bartel, the Geelong champion and wet weather specialist, discussed such games earlier in the season. He said you must go for the ball with one thought in mind: never assume you will take the footy cleanly.

You must assume it will slip through fingers, off hands, and skid along the wet grass—that it will ricochet off shins but always move in the direction it was first propelled. The waterlogged ball will confound you with its sheer inability to be grasped—but it will be more predictable than ever. Bounces will not surprise.

Late in the third quarter, Dion Prestia demonstrates the theory in practice. The tiny rover (175 cms) stands behind GWS tall forward Rory Lobb (205 cms) in perhaps the biggest height disparity on the ground. A long kick comes toward Lobb, sailing through a driving grey rain. In dry conditions Lobb would swallow the mark. In these conditions though, Prestia knows Lobb might drop it, and so Prestia does not even contest the mark. He doesn't stand next to Lobb. He puts no physical pressure on Lobb. He just stands and waits for the tall man to drop it. Which, of course, he does, leaving Prestia to scoot away with the footy. Goal.

Richmond wins playing hard football but also smart football. They tap the ball to advantage. They kick long to the top of the goal square. They handball long and forward. Wet weather forces teams to minimise exchanges of the ball and maximise the return for every possession. Richmond does this. GWS does not.

The Tigers also stick to their plan. Everywhere you look, the team sticks to the defensive guidelines laid down during the week by Ben Rutten.

For instance, the casual supporter might notice that GWS—when kicking in after a point—has no trouble finding a short target to the left or right, deep in the pockets. The casual supporter might be frustrated by this. The casual supporter might scream at Richmond to "man up" or "zone up", but these kicks are exactly what the Tigers want. Rutten had shown footage of them days earlier—mulling over how "enticing" they want that option to look to the Giants. "This kick has got to be so *juicy* for them," he said. "And then we fly in, and man the mark, and press."

Nathan Wilson, the speedy Giants halfback and runner, is having little impact on the game, and that is important, too. Wilson was identified during the week and the forwards were given the task of thwarting his attacks, being ready to counter and chase. "He'll smell a turnover," Rutten said. "He'll smell you switching, and he'll go." He doesn't "go" at all this day.

Nick Haynes is down on form, too, which is a significant win for the Tigers. Although injured for much of the season, Haynes has established himself as a perfect mid-sized defender insofar as he trusts himself to leave an opponent and take intercept marks. "Very, very good player," said Rutten. "If they get an outnumber in defence, they'll want him loose." Richmond's forwards though equalise in the air, neutralising his impact.

Steve Johnson cannot seem to get into the game up the field, or find the ball running back towards goal. The former Cat has lost his mojo of late. Richmond can't afford for him to find it now. "Not in great form, but he'll slide out the back, slide out the front," warned Rutten. "He'll play tricks on you."

The Richmond defenders are also running hard to camp in the space behind every Tiger foray forward. The Giants like to counter-attack by running quickly into a paddock, moving the ball early. "Give them access to the space, they will take it and run," said Rutten. "Give them access to the space, they will cut you up." They run. But the Tigers are there, countering.

All of that glosses over the fact that Richmond's first quarter was terrible. The Giants kicked three goals to none. So what happened? What changed that led the Tigers to victory in the remaining three quarters?

Livingstone offers the basic explanation. In the first quarter, the players at the coalface simply weren't winning the ball. "We weren't touching it," he says. "Then Dusty and Cotch have 12 touches each in the second quarter, and suddenly the game is being played on your terms, being played at your end, and you're able to set up."

Caracella points out that there were also some structural shifts. They switched from playing five forwards to six. They made subtle changes to the positioning of certain midfielders. They abandoned a couple of match-ups and experimental tactics that weren't working.

"Just like that you get back on top," he says. "It was good to reverse the game. I thought we had *intent* all game. But once you get the structure matching the intent, then you start to get traction. Then you get it done."

The players also stuck to the maxim set by Caracella during the week: *match them on the inside, control them on the outside.* Time and again throughout the contest the footy was farmed out towards a lurking Giant, on the move or in space, but Richmond always had someone there to check the imbalance. The "orange tsunami" was never given the chance to crest, instead constantly crashing against the bulwark of Richmond resistance.

That all-important "Post-Clearance Contested Ball Differential" actually ended on a modest +9 in the Giants favour. But as Glenn Luff of *Champion Data* explains, the contested ball victory for GWS meant little in the end, because the Giants were under so much pressure that those post-clearance contested possessions almost never translated into quick ball movement. *Champion Data* has a statistical measure for everything, it seems, including ball movement. It examines turnover chains and clearance chains—the way all possessions interconnect, and how far those interconnections travel. According to these measures, the Giants are the best team in the competition at moving the ball—144 per cent *better* than the League average. "It's their one wood," Luff says. "But Richmond restricted them to 334 per cent *lower* than the League average."

The Tigers gave them no space, no ability to move the ball from the back half. Take the statistic known as "basic defensive chain conversion". GWS had 53 chains of play starting in their defensive 50, and only three of those got inside their attacking 50. "That's 5.7 per cent. The AFL average is more than 20 per cent," he says. "Statistically, it was the worst ball movement the Giants had all year."

The value of this victory is hard to overstate. Before the game, there was a sign on the walls of the Richmond rooms that read: *All roads lead through GWS.*

A win would keep Richmond in the top four. A win would confirm their credentials as contenders. A win would give Richmond breathing space, a game clear of a nipping pack led by Port Adelaide.

In the warm-up, Hardwick had said that the Giants were a team stocked with lavish talent—that they were premiership favourites for a reason.

"And us?" he asked, pausing for a second. "No-one thinks we can do it. No-one thinks we can go all the way. No-one thinks we can beat these blokes today, on our home deck."

The win proves them all wrong. The win is vindication. The win is everything.

32

THIS IS STANDING STILL

All is dark and quiet on Bridge Road in Richmond. Very few cars roll along this thoroughfare at 6:15am on a Tuesday in winter, and so the only shop lit up inside is the Little Bridge Café, just up from the corner of Punt Road. Lina Haidar is in there now, not so much getting her store ready for the day as prepping a special order—breakfast for the weekly coaches' match review meeting at Punt Road Oval.

Haidar was born in Lebanon and came to Australia in 1974, when she was 11. She has been a Richmond supporter ever since. She grew up in Richmond, drifting once or twice as far out as Kew or Balwyn, but was always drawn back to the inner suburb. The first matches she attended featured Francis Bourke and Kevin Bartlett. "You were able to walk on the field then," she says, hunched over the coffee machine. "Great days."

Her shop is a now something of a club fixture. Ben Rutten and Blake Caracella stop in for a wrap from time to time. Neil Balme enjoys her home-made pasties. "Benny Gale comes in for the lamb soup. Bachar Houli comes in and loves my cooking." Haidar makes slow-cooked lamb and baklava, *moghrabieh* (Lebanese couscous) and *rez bedjaj* (chicken and rice), *maghmour* (Lebanese moussaka) and *loubieh* (green beans in oil). Each recipe was passed on by her mother, all of which might make the risk-averse order placed by the men from Tigerland once a week just a little galling—but she finds their taste endearing.

"They like toasted Turkish rolls with butter and Vegemite. Fifteen of them," she says, grinning. "Sixteen donuts, jam and Nutella. Cheese and spinach pastries. Little meat pies."

She fixes 13 coffees, too. Most are standard flat whites and lattes, but a few get special orders. Livingstone likes a cappuccino with one, which Haidar labels "HANDSOME". Hardwick likes a strong flat white, and so she makes that one last, then takes a black marker and draws on it a love heart and "XOX".

"I get up extra early for them. I do make that effort," she says. "They're an amazing lot. And they're Richmond."

////////////

Inside the war room on August 1, the first day of the last month of winter, sit a dozen men, huddled around the large oval table marked up like a football ground. They dive into the rolls and coffees, and then into the match review of the Round 19 clash against the Gold Coast Suns three days earlier, which Richmond won by 33 points.

Such is the weekly pattern within the club. A game is played. The next day—while the players rest and recover and decompress—the coaches code hours upon hours of tape. Sometimes it takes a day more. The day after that, they all come to this early morning meeting armed with observations and questions, and moments within the game they want to highlight.

The coaches are joined by list manager Blair Hartley, opposition analyst Jack Harvey, pro scout Nick Austin, General Manager of football Neil Balme and tactician Hayden Hill. It is 7am, four degrees outside, and there is little chit-chat. Blake Caracella begins by screening the best attacking clips from the game against the Suns, uttering phrases as he goes—little fragments of the football department lexicon that would make sense to these men but few others.

Shape, shape, shape, and lengthening.

QB, lateral, overlap.

Speed, options to shape it, or look for the fat lob.

The clips have titles like "Review Attack Foundation Mechanics" and "Scramble to Set Defence". Much of it is baffling, but some of the terminology becomes apparent as the footage rolls. A player takes a mark and turns immediately, giving a short handball to a player streaming past from behind, and so the term "Using the trailer" makes sense.

They examine both the macro and the micro. Someone sees a scrubby short kick from Dustin Martin, for instance, and wonders whether it was too ambitious an option—whether that particular chip is ripe for turnover. Justin Leppitsch thinks it was fine. "He's a high risk, high reward player," he says. "It's not a black and white option. He plays well in the grey."

They find things they *definitely* don't like. Players inside the forward 50 not reading the cues off their midfielders—or at least not reacting to them quickly enough. Players who are "trudgers"—or at least are playing this game like trudgers.

Hardwick frowns over one such offender. "This is where this guy has got to get better. The intensity is not there," he says. "Did he have a tackle? Might need a shot across the bow this week."

Leppitsch questions the skills errors of another. "He's got enough evidence over the past few weeks that pinching off short kicks doesn't work for us. Individually these guys need to know what's best for them."

Rutten looks forward to the next game—against the Hawks at the MCG—and doesn't like the way the team is setting up without the ball: "We need to get better at defending these shorts. Hawthorn will find their options and kick better than Gold Coast."

They all watch now as footage backs up that notion: Tiger jumpers fill into the required space, but with too little proximity to their opponents at half-forward.

"*This*, against Hawthorn, will kill us," adds Hardwick, pointing even to the little things, like players not running in quickly enough to man the mark. "No power-manning the mark here. Just gives him five metres. Just hands it to him."

In a full ground view of the field, there are two spare Suns players on the far side of the ground. To the layman it might seem risky for Richmond to leave those Gold Coast players loose, but watching the footage unspool with the coaches, you understand why they are allowed to remain free. As long as Richmond defends well against short kicks, those unmanned Suns are irrelevant, because they can only be reached with a penetrating 50-metre kick—and 50-metre kicks hang long and high in the sky. They can be cut off, spoiled, turned over in space and galloped down the ground. Guarding against long kicks is not a priority.

"Hawthorn is AFL number one for backwards kicks," says Hardwick. "So first and foremost our mids and forwards need to get on these short options."

Leppitsch: "I think the message to the forwards is, 'Look what's behind you', because better teams will go back, use these shorts, and go right around us." Leppitsch now looks at a passage of play during which all the Richmond defenders—or at least a few of them—appear to be looking for space of their own, each one seeking a chance to be the loose man in defence: "Leigh Matthews used to say it all the time: 'Let the spare be the spare—you play on your bloke!'"

They talk about the Gold Coast defenders, too, and judging when to leave their spare backman alone, and when to equalise and man up. Hardwick says it's fine to leave some Suns players spare: "But this guy—Jack Martin—can never be free."

On the wall of the war room is a handwritten statement in whiteboard marker: *We are building an athletic, competitive, smart, tough, skilled, character-based football side that consistently competes in finals and challenges for premierships.*

Hardwick is not looking at that statement, but at times during this meeting—poring over errors of judgment and lapses in concentration—he does seem to be referencing it. Like now, as he walks up to the screen as the edits continue to roll, and isolates a player who looks tired, or distracted, or just uninvolved.

"If we want to go all the way, we must get better at this," he says, finger pointed. "Hands on hips. Resting. Resting. This is standing still—not stalking. It's the wrong mentality."

///////////

A group of senior players enters the room next. Alex Rance, Trent Cotchin and Jack Riewoldt of course, but also Sam Lloyd and Ivan Maric and Bachar Houli. As a group, they say they were pleased with the clinical nature of the game, with the ability of the team to shut down switches of play, and to never allow the Suns' running game to get going.

They talk about a few individual player issues that need to be addressed.

How to provide that feedback is always a quandary. Some players need to be taken aside and spoken to in private. Others respond well to having their mistake highlighted in front of the group—while still others can handle that but need to be forewarned.

The focus switches to a positional error made by an experienced player, one who should have done better. "I don't think it's a bad clip to show, so long as you word him up," Hardwick says. "We can't pussy foot around this stuff."

Riewoldt: "He might be one of these guys—you give him five positives but he comes out of the meeting with that one negative in his head going round and round and round… But if it's there, he needs to be told."

McQualter: "Is it an individual chat, rather than a group one?"

Hardwick: "I think it's worth approaching him and saying, 'This is what we're going to show', to give him a chance to put his hand up."

Riewoldt: "It'll be good for him to own it. A little self-cleansing."

Hardwick: "Yep, if he drives it, it becomes easier to accept."

They talk, too, about young ruckman Ivan Soldo, who battled hard and had the better of Jarrod Witts—one of the surprise form ruckmen of the competition this season. But Soldo was nevertheless dirty on his own game. Rance says he tried to praise him immediately after the match, but the second year player wouldn't hear anything—talking down his own performance because of low possession numbers.

Hardwick sees this often. It can be a problem with players on the fringe— who go in and out of the side often due to structure and size or match-ups rather than their effort or output. "It's horses for courses, because sometimes we just might need more speed," he says. "But he might read it the wrong way."

McQualter says not to let that chatter happen—to get on the front foot with positive reinforcement: "Shut that talk down," he says. "Immediately."

Riewoldt: "I was proud of his fire. He gets down and dirty."

Hardwick: "He'll get better every game he plays. He's 21, not played much footy either. There aren't many 21-year-old senior rucks running around."

They talk about goalkicking, and the misses that have plagued the season so far and were again on display. Jason Castagna kicked three goals, but could have kicked six. Perhaps someone needs to calm him down before he kicks?

Riewoldt says all the younger players need is a senior player to walk up and offer a quick, soft reminder—"Routine, mate"—before leaving them alone. They don't need instruction on technique during the week. Each player needs to learn what works for them, develop their pattern, and own it on game day.

Balme asks if maybe a specialised goalkicking coach could help the list as a whole, because missed set shots and poor conversion is not confined to one player or to one game. Hardwick isn't convinced.

"At the end of the day, players kick how they kick. You find your routine. I once saw Jason Dunstall trying to teach Buddy Franklin to kick," he says. "Most horrific thing ever."

McQualter points out that time spent on repetitive goalkicking does work for some, Dan Butler for example. "He has become a very good set shot for goal now," he says. "Eighteen months ago, you wouldn't back him that often. But he's become a very, *very* good shooter."

They debate the merits of snapping set shots at goal. They talk about the way players line up and come in on an arc, almost running at the point post to drag it back across the line to goal. The issue is when players should receive guidance on all these things.

It's a ball drop issue.
It's a run up problem.
It's all about visualisation.
What's your routine?

Leppitsch: "I reckon you'd rather no voices than four voices."

Riewoldt has a final word before they leave. The games now, he says, are becoming more and more important. And one of the big strengths in the coaching group is the "calmness" they bring to work every day.

"It's so important, and it's been such a notable change this year," he says. "The environment that's been set up on game day, in meetings—the players have been feeding off that. It brings an air of confidence. Keep it up."

////////////

As the players depart, the coaches soon go back into the minutiae of positioning and structures. They talk about layering and crushing and squashing. They talk about good numbers and the outnumber. They talk about traipsing and triangles. Connections and double threats. Perfect, almost perfect and *perfect*-perfect.

That's a good look for us.

That's a bad look for us.
How do we look here?

Most of the time—as the edits roll and they switch between camera views—they are not even looking at the ball. Seemingly always they are drawn to what happens *around* the ball, in larger and larger concentric circles. Watching them dissect the game you begin to understand that tracking the footy—as viewers do in the grandstands and at home—is not really following the game. What happens to the ball is an outcome—following its path has more in common with watching the scoreboard than the contest. The contest is everywhere else, on the edge of the pack, the fringe of the bubble, the players in the distance rolling forward, and those behind them running to set up the defence. Most of the action—the business of winning and losing football games—is on the periphery.

By 9:40am, 160 minutes into the meeting, the group switches to player ratings and that colour-coded ranking system devised by Hayden Hill. Rioli was a dark green. Butler was a brown. Brandon Ellis was light green. "I think a pump-up for him would be good," suggests Rutten. "His improvement has been significant."

They look at Corey Ellis, and note that he got pushed off the ball a little easily a few times, but he also remains poised and clean when he has it in hand. Then there was that courageous mark he took, flying back into a rising pack, face first.

"I don't think he shirks it—that's not an issue," says McQualter. "Just physically he's not quite strong enough yet."

"He's another guy who's almost there," says Rutten. "I reckon if you give him a pump up it could go a long way."

"I reckon it's his run," says Leppitsch. "If he can get those first three explosive, quick steps right, he'll fly."

They talk about the younger players who might be suffering fatigue at this point of a long season. Do they drop one or two for a week, for a rest? (It could diminish their confidence.) Do they give them a rest during the week instead? (Perhaps a training session off?)

They talk about reminding players who aren't playing a starring role that they are still working for the good of the team. Butler, perhaps the most improved player on the list and a critical component of the forward pressure brought to bear by the team this season, has been quiet for a few weeks. He hasn't had the same output in kicks and handballs and goals. But he has—just this past weekend—registered 40 pressure acts, more than some opposition players register in a month of football.

"He's running to all the right patterns, and he doesn't always get the reward," says Leppitsch. "It's helping us win, but he doesn't get the result personally. He could use a reminder of his value."

They also spend time debating their own system, including those colour-coded ratings. Sometimes, the reds and greens and browns spat out by the formulaic approach don't tally with what they think, or believe, and so they adjust them manually.

"Let's be honest, Grimesy's defensive game is his strength," says Hardwick. "His one-on-one work and positioning is elite. *Absolutely elite*. And he's probably in the top six of our best and fairest. So, we can't always look at the stats sheet."

By 10:09am, the VFL coaches—McRae, Clarke and Ferguson—run through their report from the match against North Ballarat. They look at scoring and tackles, and the form of first-year player Jack Graham, specifically his contested work, his spread, his ability and willingness to equalise.

"You should see some of his defensive stuff. He just charges," says McRae, eyes alight. "He's as ready as an 18-year-old is going to get. The sooner we get him into the senior team the better."

Ferguson mentions Jayden Short: "He looked a cut above, right from the start. Oleg (Markov), too. He's played some really good ones, especially in the air."

They talk about Connor Menadue. How can they find a role for him in the senior team? What job can they create? Can they train him to use his speed and endurance and "find the outnumber" more often? Only a year ago, the shorthand annual feedback for Menadue offered a positive and a negative. The positive: his sheer running power. The negative: *cannot survive on 13 possessions*. They see in him an Isaac Smith-type player, if he can double his possession rate. "I really like this kid," says Hardwick. "I might have to catch up with him this week."

They talk about stalwart ruckman and club talisman Ivan Maric, and how his mother came into the VFL rooms after the game on the weekend, in tears. She is about to go overseas, and with Maric retiring at the end of the season, she knew it was the last time she would see her son play.

"He played like that," says McRae, smiling. "He played like he wanted to do it for his mum. You could feel it meant something to him."

It's 10:30am when they finish up, three and half hours after they began. The players are already warming up on the ground, ready for training. The coaches have some selection decisions to make in the coming days, but haven't made them yet. Houli, Miles, Ellis, Graham and Butler are the five players they have on the bench right now, but they can only take four into the next game.

The coaches look up at that board for a few moments. They move magnets one way, and back. As they turn the decisions over in their heads, they grimace. As they apply their minds to the task, they stare. As they realise the futility of deciding right now, they sigh and pack up. They leave the room and head down to the oval. In five days, Hawthorn awaits.

33

TURN OF THE WHEEL

T he usual material is scrawled on the whiteboard in the rooms at the MCG before the Round 20 match against Hawthorn.

Play to your strengths.

Celebrate.

Fight.

But also the words "connection", "belief", and "happiness".

Wait, *happiness?*

There it is, the change at Richmond in 2017, spelled out in one word. And Hardwick isn't talking about the happiness in winning but the happiness in playing—the pure gratitude for the game and the joy in its application—the chance to compete and create with close mates in front of mammoth crowds. His eyes sparkle as he speaks. He seems to be without worry or fear.

"Today is a Richmond man sort of game," Hardwick says. "What does that mean?"

"The Hawks are in form," says one player. "They're a good side."

"Yeah, and what are they playing for?"

"Survival," says someone.

"Their life," says another.

This is what Hardwick wants to hear—that Hawthorn's season is on the line. And it is. Lose today and the likelihood of this great club reaching finals all but vanishes. So where lies the weight of expectation?

"It's on them," Hardwick says. "We expect to bring our game, our process, but they've got the weight of the world on their shoulders."

He praises the players in front of him now, and reminds them that they are unique. They are the youngest side in the eight. They are the fastest. They have the best defence. They play with strength and work ethic and connection. "That's what makes us *us*," he says. "There's not another side like us."

He loves the way they celebrate, for example. He loved watching vision— only a few days earlier—of a Richmond goal being kicked, and Dylan Grimes at the opposite end of the field, pumping both fists. But you know what? "When Grimesy spoils a ball that's an inch from being a mark—our forwards should be doing the same thing, because it's outstanding. Celebrate everything we do."

He asks Daniel Rioli to flip the A3 picture for the week. Hardwick then admits that what the players are seeing on the wall is his "inner geek" brought to life. It is a picture of eight book jackets, all of the "Choose Your Own Adventure" variety, a popular children's series in the 1980s and 1990s. Each book made the reader the protagonist in the story, and offered a series of choices that would dictate the narrative: Go through the cave, or take the mountain pass? Hardwick used to read them as a child, and there they are all on the wall in front of the 22 footballers.

By Balloon to the Sahara.
The Third Planet from Altair.
Who Killed Harlowe Thrombey?

Hardwick talks about peeking over the page to see what might happen next, and turning back to his starting point if the outcome was bad (like being eaten by trolls, for instance, or murdered by trail bandits).

Hardwick has brought up the subject because his cousin sent him an article during the week with the headline: The Perils of Choose Your Own Adventure Books. The contention of the thinkpiece in the US monthly, *The Atlantic*, is that these books train people to think that our choices are always either right or wrong, life and death. So you know what he learned about decision-making from reading those books?

"Nothing," he says. Because in life—and in football—you don't get to peek over the page and see what will happen. Nor should you make choices based on fear. "All we have is the path we're on," he says. "It's about the next contest, the next moment, the next time you run, the next time you hit the ball."

The next time they play.

////////////

W ithin the hour, they take the field. And they win, handsomely.

They win through smothers and tackles. And through jagged, overlapping handball chains.

Brandon Ellis lays powerful bumps.

Kamdyn McIntosh surges across the field in a full-bodied sprint so that a solitary outstretched fingertip reaches the ball before his opponent.

Daniel Rioli, Dan Butler and Jason Castagna crouch on their toes all game long, in front of their men, and it gives them an advantage in the moments that matter, when the ball is hacked out of congestion and skids forward, allowing them to swoop and scoop it up from their heels.

Kane Lambert runs and runs to hunt the man and the ball, helping himself to 15 kicks and 15 handballs, in a season that keeps getting better for the honest onballer. Having earned the right to cheat a little—to gamble on his teammates, to drift into the dangerous space—he ghosts forward so that when the ball is won he is there waiting, alone, with only the goals in front of him.

Josh Caddy marks strongly, and swaggers and bustles, and kicks goals around his body and from long range set shots. He plays his best game for the club. Four goals. 28 disposals. After his first major—the first of the game, a goal square rocket into the third tier of the Great Southern Stand—he high fives a woman in the cheer squad on the boundary.

Nathan Broad shows a willingness to sprint and cover contests that are not his, rather than guarding his own man, showing a kind of bravery in playing to win and not to save.

Dion Prestia, returning after injury, sets his small frame up against the highest possession winner in the League, Tom Mitchell, who still gets 35 touches—more than any player on the ground—but few are effective, and fewer still are damaging, and in fact many of his looping handballs end up in the arms of hungry Tigers. Mitchell's impact is blunted and muted by a player who has 31 of his own touches, and a goal, too.

Shane Edwards sees gaps others don't, and finds space where there is none, and ends the day with a handful of goal assists to his name.

The backline is as stingy as ever, David Astbury undefeated in one-on-one contests, spoiling and blocking and taking a game high 10 marks, Alex Rance continually running through the onslaught of opponents to drive the ball back, and Dylan Grimes is flint-hard, knocking opponents more fiercely than ever, and grabbing marks with an angry stiffness.

Dustin Martin has 32 touches and two goals, customary this season for an elite player becoming a champion.

The game is won all over the ground, but again the small Richmond forwards are the catalyst. They move so quickly without the ball. It is as if the spaces between them are imperceptibly but immediately narrowed, closed without warning, as if there was never any space for Hawthorn—none worth trying to run through, at any rate. This form of pressure has only recently been given an unofficial moniker by commentator Gerard Healy, who calls it "The Tiger Tornado", and it wreaks havoc as it swirls on the MCG. And so the Hawks try to kick or handball or tap the ball through the gaps in the Richmond net, but the gaps seem to move with them, too, and so the next man in the escape plan is cornered. Whether it's Jack Gunston or Brendan Whitecross or Blake Hardwick or Ryan Burton, again and again they are caught in a tangled skein of yellow and black.

//////////

Hardwick has a sure smile in the rooms afterwards. He tells the players he believes, and that something about the way they played suggests to him that they, too, believe.

"There are wins within footy clubs that make you think…there's another one, more proof," he says, holding up his hands. "We just grow and we grow and we grow. Winning's great, isn't it?"

Thirteen wins in the season is a good result, but winning starts somewhere, and right now, he says, it starts with "prep"—and so the players boo and hiss as high performance manager Peter Burge takes the reins for recovery.

The players now must split into three groups for seven-minute rotations designed to assist recuperation and revitalisation. Group one goes into massage, just flush rubs as needed, with the intention of stimulating blood flow, rather than deeply kneading sore muscles. The second group eats and drinks, gulping down *Up & Go* and *Gatorade* and water, and snacking on pretzels and rice crackers and muffins, or perhaps a banana or protein bar. The final group lies down on the floor to do stretches, using large rubber bands to help control each movement as they gently shift and rotate their limbs.

The fitness staff float throughout the groups. The mood is light, as they exchange pleasantries while extracting little bits of information. "Dion has pulled up really well, for instance," says Burge. "And he played really well. So that's great, because he's a professional and he's been sore. He got a great result because of the way he prepared."

Soon after they go back to the club, trudging there in tracksuits. Again, they need to eat. The post-match menu at Tigerland tonight is meatball subs, heavy on the melted cheese and sauce. Kylie Andrew, the club nutritionist, says this dish has been popular of late, but she knows to keep the menu revolving or the players will get bored. One week she will offer a make-your-own-burger bar. Or a steak sandwich. "They're dehydrated," she says. "So they crave salt and also something a little 'fast foodie'—something tasty they really want to eat."

Afterwards, they complete a water-based active recovery, which means that while happy supporters meander through Yarra Park singing the club song in the falling darkness, the players dip down into the 25 metre lap pool beneath the complex, and walk or jog up and down, up and down, for ten minutes to a quarter of an hour. It allows them to keep moving without weight on their joints.

The dreaded ice bath is the last thing they must do. Richmond's baths are set low, at 11.5 degrees, meaning the players should only spend one or two minutes in the water before jumping out and then into a warmer, ambient spa. They get in and out, in and out, alternating between the two in what is called a "contrast bath" (or "hot/cold immersion therapy").

Grimes cringes as he enters with one quick plunge. No use edging in slowly—it only prolongs the discomfort. There is nothing worse than the ice bath, he says, especially after a game in cold, wet weather, when you are already chilled and waterlogged. "But at least you're not doing it alone. Some of our best times are in the spa after the game, laughing about what happened on the field."

Recovery, he says, is a necessary evil. You want to put your feet up and celebrate, but you know the work will be better for you in the long run. It's good for the mind, too. "It gets you thinking about what's coming," he says. "It's the first turn of the wheel towards the next game."

By 7:30pm, a little more than 90 minutes after the game, most of the players have departed, gingerly hopping into their cars to drive home. Most will stop off somewhere on the way for a little more food. Playing a game of football is effectively skipping a meal, so it's never long until they need something else in their bellies. "Normally the players use the game as an excuse to treat themselves, and head to the golden arches or to see Colonel Sanders," says the grinning Grimes, knowing that, in particular, Burge would hate to hear this. "I crave salt, so chips and a thickshake would be my ideal cheat food."

By the time they get home they want to collapse, but they also know they must continue icing their injuries, to settle the ligaments and fibres from where this joint was twisted or that flesh was bruised. The ice packs go on and then off, often throughout the night and the next day. The first shower in the morning is exquisitely painful, as the hot water seeps deeply into every scrape and cut and gouge in their skin, torn by turf and boots and fingernails. They check and treat each wound. They apply and re-apply compression bandages.

There is no long easy rest on the couch, either. The players need to move, walk, maybe do some more water work, or an extra ice bath. A gentle stretch. A light jog. The day after a game is critical for setting up their week. The Hawthorn game was Sunday, the first recovery day is Monday, and, because of the six-day break, they will be needed back at the club for a light training session on Tuesday.

"And we want them in reasonable condition to do that," says Burge. "They're not going to be training hard, but what they're able to do in our main session on Thursday is determined by what they do in the 48 hours immediately after a game."

At this part of the season, says Grimes, he is usually limping—feeling an overbearing accumulation of niggles and fatigue. This year he feels better. Right now though, after victory—after all the maintenance and convalescence of the recovery regimen—he just wants to be home, outside the city back to Mount Macedon.

"It's good to get out there. You're in the country, so you wake up for breakfast in all that space, and you don't have to think about footy at all. Whether I play a good game or bad game, win or lose, that's the best thing for me: switching off completely."

34

IT'S PART OF THE GAME

I t's Friday afternoon at the Bilal Bin Rabah Masjid, a new $14 million mosque in Newport, designed by renowned architect Glenn Murcett. The café and library within the modern Islamic complex are still being finished, and so there is construction fencing all around, but the main hall of worship is complete, and resplendent. A plaque on the wall offers the words of the Prophet Mohammed: *Whoever builds a mosque for the sake of Allah, Allah will build for him a house in paradise.*

Standing outside, in a fitted black Puma tracksuit, is Bachar Houli, the Richmond half-back and devout Muslim. He smiles widely as his brothers approach and softly shake hands, and greet one another, opening each dialogue with the phrase *As-salamu alaykum* (peace be upon him) and closing each little insight into their lives with the words *Insha'Allah* (God willing).

Houli is proud of the mosque—not so much the edifice itself but the potential it has to attract new followers to the faith, particularly young ones. He notes that if the cavernous concrete space with high glass walls on all sides is not inspiring or appealing to young people, then it is not serving its purpose.

"We want to bring them here, to bring them close to the religion, because the whole purpose of the religion is happiness and peace—that warm feeling," he says. "Our Imam says if our hearts are not present in a beautiful mosque, then there is no reason to have a beautiful mosque."

He runs into one such young man now. His name is Bader Ismail, and he is

15. He plays footy for Newport Power, and is a member of the Bachar Houli Academy—a program Houli runs to attract Muslim kids from multicultural backgrounds to the game. In the program are kids from Lebanese, Sudanese, Turkish, Iranian and Indonesian backgrounds; the Academy teaches them leadership and resilience, as well as football development.

"We want to get them drafted, or at least playing at their full potential," Houli says. "We've got 25 in the Academy now, and been running it for five years. We haven't had anyone drafted yet, but we think it will come—if they implement good habits and discipline and hard work."

He says the teenage Bader, from Altona North, is one who could use such traits: "The kid is a jet, but I'm trying to get him to lose 30 kilos," says Houli, smiling. "Full-forward. Absolute jet. A machine."

He approaches now.

"All good, brother?" asks Houli.

"Bad news," says Bader. "Played on the weekend. Sling tackle. I go to the tribunal. They hear evidence from the players. I get four weeks. But they drop it back to two. I'll miss out on the Grand Final."

Houli looks him in the eye: "It's a test, yeah?" he says. "In life we'll be faced with tests. But we stay strong, insha'Allah."

Both men move into the mosque now, out of the cold, with dozens upon dozens of others. They know it is time to enter when the *adhan*, the call to prayer, is sung. Barack Obama said the Muslim call to prayer "is one of the prettiest sounds on earth at sunset", and indeed its lyrical undulations are haunting, each note stretched and joined in solemn but soaring musicality.

It echoes under the cathedral ceiling here, which is supported by hulking steel beams, and decorated with triangular light wells—cavities in the roof that are coloured red and blue and yellow and green. The floor is soft beige carpet, and all the men are in socks or bare feet, assembling along lines marked on the floor, facing the front of the room. Every line fits 50 or so men, and today they fill 10 to 12 lines, or 500 to 600 males, with a similar number of women in a separate space upstairs. Houli's father, Malek, is here. So is his mother, Yamama. The Friday speech is the equivalent of a Catholic Sunday Mass, and so the congregation turns out in force.

There are older men who can no longer kneel and bend and rise, so they sit in chairs. A smiling toddler wears a warm felt panda hoodie—white with black ears. There are teenagers in *taqiyahs* (scull caps) and others in Nike baseball hats. There are men in cargo pants and men in *thobes* (ankle length full-body robes). Some worshippers wear high-vis fluorescent orange vests—on a break from the building site. Others wear collared blue shirts with the telltale epaulets of the taxi service.

Most have already performed *wudu*, their ablutions—an act of ritualistic cleansing in which they sit and wash their mouth and face and neck, and arms and feet and toes. Now purified, they can stand and then kneel inside the mosque, bending forward in supplication, touching their foreheads to the carpet.

The sermon, or *Khutbah*, is delivered first in Arabic, then English, and today the subject is apology—finding the strength and courage to say sorry. The Imam says only arrogance and ignorance will prevent a person from saying they are sorry. The best of sinners are the ones who seek repentance. "When you make a mistake with a human being, you must swallow your pride," he says. "You must make an admission of guilt, and seek forgiveness of the other."

///////////

B achar Houli knows something about seeking forgiveness. That's what he did after a Round 14 game, more than a month ago now, against Carlton at the MCG—a mostly unremarkable match except for an incident involving Houli and Carlton utility Jed Lamb.

The ball was moving toward the Richmond goal, and Houli was rolling forward, parallel to the play, but Lamb was with him, grabbing at his jumper and tugging at his body. "I remember the whistle was blown," says Houli. "Prior to that I remember very little. I wasn't angry."

Angry or not, Houli threw his left arm back behind him, and it collected the trailing Lamb flush in the temple. Lamb fell limply forward through the air, unconscious before he even hit the ground, where he remained.

"I was trying to cause separation, to get a run at the ball. I had no intention to strike him in the head, but unfortunately I hit him sweet," says Houli. "I've never hit anyone on the field, or off the field. I've never thrown a punch in my life."

"Before I knew it I had players coming at me, telling me it was a shocking act, and I agreed. I lost my patience—a virtue I'm taught by the *Quran*—but

I didn't mean to hit him in the head. Still, there is absolute regret, because I did hurt him."

Afterwards, before leaving the ground, he sought out Carlton leaders Marc Murphy and Bryce Gibbs: "I said 'You guys know me, and that's not my character'. And they accepted my apology."

He reached out to Lamb, too. Leaving the rooms he saw a Carlton assistant coach, and asked for Lamb's phone number. He texted Lamb that night and got an immediate reply: "It's part of the game, mate. I know you didn't mean it. All good."

Still, the strike became an issue. Houli had already been in the headlines that week, meeting with Prime Minister Malcolm Turnbull, who described the work Houli does with Muslim youth as being of "extreme and extraordinary importance". When the hit was referred to the AFL Tribunal, such remarks—as well as written character references from celebrity journalist Waleed Aly, former Tigers assistant Mark Williams, and AFL diversity manager Ali Fahour—were tendered by Richmond. Then Houli's counsel, Michael Tovey, successfully argued that Houli should not be convicted of an intentional strike to the head, "but an intentional strike, resulting in contact to the head".

The 29-year-old running defender was given a two-match suspension— a sentence that inflamed the football public. Hundreds of column centimetres, hours of talkback and thousands of social media posts and comments—more than a few of them tinged with Islamaphobia—flooded Melbourne in the aftermath, as perhaps only a full-blown AFL "scandal" can.

Depending on your perspective, the League listened or the League blinked and—in an historic about face—appealed its own penalty. It sent the case to the AFL Appeals Board two days later, on the grounds that a two-match suspension was "manifestly inadequate", and that neither Houli's standing in the community nor the glowing references should have had any bearing on the outcome. As board chairman Peter O'Callaghan QC put it: "A blow from a person of exemplary character has just the same impact of a person of bad character."

Houli's suspension was doubled to four matches. He would miss games against Port Adelaide, St Kilda, Brisbane and Greater Western Sydney. He left silently, turned up for work the next day, and continued to train—his mind on the month ahead.

"I had a choice. How do I accept it? Am I going to be a sook about it? Am I going to blame others, or am I going to cop it on the chin like a man and move on, and continue to show who I am? I didn't mean it, but I accept whatever is thrown at me."

Was this a trial of his own—like that being faced (with rather less scrutiny) by young Bader Ismail?

"Yes, it was a test. And I was prepared for it. Our beloved Prophet tells us that life is full of trials. He was tested. He was tortured by his enemy while trying to bring harmony and peace. I want to be like this person, so I do my best."

Houli has been tested more than once. As a proud Muslim man, with a thick beard and a willingness to promote multicultural causes, Houli has been a lightning rod more than once—never by his own design.

In 2015, there was the episode in which 3AW breakfast show presenter John Burns was said to be overheard referring to Houli as a "terrorist" at a pre-match function at the MCG. One year later, a member of the anti-Islamic "United Patriots Front" unfurled a banner at a Richmond match with the words: "Go Pies! Stop the mosques!"

Even after the strike on Lamb, well-meaning pundits with grave intonation expressed their fear that Houli might become a victim of "merciless" booing upon his return, the kind that would drive Sydney champion Adam Goodes from the game. Houli wasn't sure what would come his way, but he was prepared to accept whatever that was.

"I was going to smile," he says. "You can throw whatever you like at me. You can take football away from me. I don't care. My true purpose in life is to worship God."

Such statements speak to his commitment to his faith, something that is often lost in the shorthand description of Houli as "devout". He prays five times a day—including those morning prayers in winter when it means rousing from slumber at 4:15am. He has twice performed the *Hajj*—the annual pilgrimage to Mecca, Saudi Arabia, the most holy city in Islam—and once the *Umrah*, a lesser pilgrimage to the same place.

"I'd love to go every year, if I could. It's a beautiful place. Holy. And as strange as it sounds, it's 'me' time. You get away from people, the world. You focus on yourself spiritually. You come here," he says, sitting on the floor of the now deserted mosque, "and sometimes your mind is still on your work."

Balancing his work as a footballer with the demands of his religion is not without challenges. Some obstacles are easy to overcome.

So that he can pray when he should, Richmond has set aside a tiny room for Houli, just off the race at Punt Road Oval. On game day at the MCG, he prays in the AFL drug testing room—using the compass app on his iPhone in order to face Mecca. In the big boxes of food brought to the rooms for digesting before and after the game, the club always supply Halal options.

Ramadan can be difficult, given the need to fast between dawn and sunset, between the *suhur* (the pre-dawn meal) and the *iftar* (the post-sunset dinner). How Houli copes with this is perhaps the most common question he fields about Islam.

"Fasting is one of the five pillars of Islam, but honestly it's not as strict as the need to pray five times a day. If you're sick, you can still pray. If you can't stand, you can sit and pray. If you can't sit, you can pray lying down. If you can't move your body, you can pray with your eyes. We pray five times a day to maintain our connection with God, to bring us back onto the path."

With fasting though, he says, there is some flexibility. If you are sick, you can break your fast. If you are elderly, or on medication, or travelling, you don't have to fast. But you need to offer a form of compensation— perhaps feeding the poor and the needy. Mostly, on training days, he just deals with the hunger and lethargy.

"If I think I can't handle it, if I think I'm going to faint, then I break my fast. God will judge. Not my Imam, not my friends," he says. "If I'm breaking the fast for a game—and the game is my work, my livelihood, my means of supporting my family—God will forgive."

Houli grew up in Altona North, the middle child of seven siblings (five boys, two girls). He played footy for Spotswood and his brothers played, too, but the game wasn't encouraged at home. Houli hid football from his parents at first. When he was 11 he was caught sneaking in the back door at home, with a best and fairest trophy smuggled under his jumper.

"My parents felt that footy was a vehicle that might drive us away from education. They had no love or affection for the game," he says. "They thought life was only about hard work, but sport is such a great way to keep your mind active, build relationships, get kids off the streets. Young people aren't engaged in sport enough—they're unoccupied and inactive, and it's a cancer."

Within a few years, however, his parents saw him play, and saw his growth, and became his biggest supporters and followers. "There was genuine care," he says, smiling. They celebrated his rise through the Western Jets, and the day he was drafted by Essendon in 2006 (pick 42). He played only 26 games there in four seasons, and that lack of senior football was what convinced him to come to Richmond in late 2010.

"I just wasn't getting an opportunity," he says. "I was guaranteed more games and security by James Hird when he came on board, but by that point I had made a commitment to Richmond. Dimma showed so much faith and wanted me here." Since joining the Tigers he's hardly missed a game, taking his tally to 165 when we spoke.

He says he has no regrets about the move—perhaps an understatement given what followed at the Bombers. The infamous supplements saga— or, as reported in a governance review by former Telstra boss, Ziggy Switkowski, an environment that combined to create "a disturbing picture of a pharmacologically experimental environment never adequately controlled or challenged or documented within the club"[14]—began just before the 2012 season, around 18 months after Houli had departed.

"Good timing for me," he says. "I treat that moment as showing God loves me, by putting me in a safer environment, because I probably would have taken what I was given, like everyone else did. I would have trusted my doctors and the hierarchy at the club. I was a young player, making my way. A lot of those guys were."

He is not a young guy now—in football terms at least. He is 29, and has played 11 seasons, and is entering that period in his career when football managers begin suggesting one-year deals every time a contract is due to expire. Houli is happy to play each game as it comes and sign up for each season under those terms. He feels better than he ever has, in both body and mind.

"Maybe that comes from winning," he says. "Winning is such a beautiful thing. All I want now is that pure success—a flag."

Such statements might sound obvious or expected from a footballer, but it was not always this way for Houli. "My mentality really has changed.

---

14 http://www.essendonfc.com.au/news/2013-05-06/dr-ziggy-switskowski-report

Early on in my career, I felt I needed to make a name for myself, to get as much of the ball as I could, to get involved and stay involved and be noticed. It's beyond that now."

In his eyes Richmond, too, has a different mentality. Hardwick, Houli says, has created an environment this season in which the players can relax. He can scarcely recall a tense moment at Tigerland in 2017.

"At the end of the day you're here to play footy—something you love—and that's what Dimma encourages. If you know what you must do to play your best footy, you have a clear mind. We're truly in contention. We're a chance to take that Cup home. And if we don't, we move on. That's footy—there are no guarantees."

35

A GOAT OR A HERO

The big brother, Simon, picks up his little brother, Dave, from a hotel on La Trobe Street in Docklands, adjacent to AFL HQ and Etihad Stadium. Simon is driving an old and slightly banged-up Ford Territory, and so Dave mocks him, as little brothers do. "If you're going to bag my car you can piss right off," says Simon, helping his sibling with his bags. "Bloody walk to Geelong."

Of course, it doesn't come to that. They're joking and they're professionals—heavy hitters, in fact. The big brother is Simon Matthews, the General Manager of Communications and Marketing at Richmond, and the little brother—now in the back seat and on his phone—is David Matthews, Chief Executive of the Greater Western Sydney Giants.

They're not the only brotherly pairing in football administration. Leaving aside the many siblings on AFL lists, there are the likes of Rob Auld, CEO of AFL Tasmania, and his brother Travis, the League's GM of clubs and operations. The most prominent pair would be Channel 7 announcer Hamish McLachlan and his brother Gillon, CEO of the League itself.

The Matthews boys are headed to Sleepy Hollow today to see their parents, and watch the Tigers take on the Cats. It's a little homecoming. They grew up there in the suburb of Highton and played the game, though mostly school footy. On the highway passing Point Cook, Simon has his right hand on the steering wheel and his left on a coffee, and explains that footy was big at their *alma mater*, Geelong College. Former Bulldog Nigel Kellett was there. *Who else, Dave?*

"Oh, there have been a heap since," he answers. "(Will) Schofield at West Coast. (Lachie) Henderson at Geelong. The Curnow brothers, Ed and Charlie."

Most of the trip David is making phone calls or sending emails. Right now, he has his earbuds in, listening to a 3AW radio discussion of an incident involving Giants forward Toby Greene, who was cited one night earlier by the match review panel for rough play, after lifting his leg in a contest and putting his boot studs into the cheek of Bulldog forward Luke Dahlhaus. The football media was quickly in a frenzy, and David isn't impressed with the treatment of his star player.

"Tim Lane's making it sound like he's killed someone. Dahlhaus is still alive, isn't he?" he says, shaking his head. "It's a split lip."

That's just one situation to monitor. The other is a request the Giants lodged with the AFL this morning, to investigate an incident immediately following that spiteful clash, in which a Bulldogs fan poured a full beer on Greene's head as he left the ground. "Can you believe that?"

And with that, he returns to his phone, to the business of putting out spot fires, which is also a large part of Simon's job, as the media gatekeeper and controller of all "messaging" circling within and around Tigerland. His pathway to the role was unusual. At university, he majored in genetic engineering and industrial microbiology but decided a life in a lab was not for him. He did a graduate Diploma of Education instead, then took a year off and worked in a pub as a barman. A friend, Mark Hayes, was writing a weekly column for the *Geelong News*—a free weekly newspaper—and when he went overseas asked Matthews if he would fill in, so he did, and eventually became the paper's sports editor. The sister paper was *The Geelong Advertiser*, which is where he ended up for a handful of years. As a Geelong fan, it was a dream job.

"I got paid to go and watch and write about Gary Ablett," he says. "I won't hear anyone say he's not the greatest player the game has ever seen."

In mid-1999, his friend Matthew Drain, who was Football Manager at Essendon, brought him to the Bombers as Media Manager. He was there for 11 years, including half a dozen in senior management. Then Brendon Gale called and brought him to Richmond in mid-2010, the final season of the troubled Brownlow medallist Ben Cousins.

Day one in any job is a nervous experience. Matthews remembers he had only just made a coffee and sat down at his desk when he saw Gale coming his way. He had just turned his computer on, when the boss knocked on his door with a message.

"Cousins is unconscious, in an ambulance, on the way to hospital," he said. "Welcome to Richmond."

In such situations, says Matthews, the first step in issue management is to gather the facts. He put out a holding statement, noting the club was aware one of their players was in hospital. But there were complicating factors—in this case a private admission to hospital, a matter between doctor and patient. Cousins said he had taken sleeping tablets, which was passed on to the press. "Then we told Ben he could front the media and tell them the same thing, if he wanted."

Matthews still remembers how the wayward star got out of his car at Punt Road, coffee in hand, and grinned as he told the cameras he needed a little caffeine. "And of course, the media was just lapping it up," he says. "Before we went out to talk to them he was doing this stretching routine, and I'm sure he didn't hear a word I was saying. But he walked in and just had that capacity to make people eat out of the palm of his hand. He was very charismatic."

Much of what is produced by Richmond's communications team though is far more workaday. The club has a strong digital presence, for instance, and today they will have a small team at Simonds Stadium producing streamed audio from the VFL curtain-raiser.

"We analyse all our online numbers, and people would be surprised at the content consumed around VFL level—they really want to know where the next stars are coming from. We always want to ask, 'how are we building an emotional connection with our fans?' 'Connection' just seems to be a word coming up all over the club right now, particularly in football but everywhere. It's the stories we tell."

The story today is not from the curtain-raiser, but the main event—the two best midfielders in the competition going head to head. The reigning Brownlow medallist Patrick Dangerfield and the man most likely to take that mantle in a month or so, Dustin Martin. The latter—perhaps as notable for his football ability as his enigmatic nature and public silence—must make him an interesting entity to manage.

"It doesn't take any managing at all, because he doesn't do any media, and I can understand where that comes from. I can understand Dustin's complete frustration and disappointment with the way things around him have been covered and portrayed. So many things have just been written about him without any facts. He doesn't feel the need to help sell newspapers, or help TV stations to grab eyeballs. This year in particular we've given him as much space as we can, and judging by the way he's playing his football we're not going to change much."

With Martin, there is a balance the club needs to strike, even when it comes to internal media. The club wants his workload to be light, but the fans adore and consume anything and everything featuring the midfielder. For example, in the match against Hawthorn, in Round 20, the players wore jumpers with a purple trim—the colour of club partner the Alannah & Madeline Foundation, a not-for-profit set up to protect children from violence and abuse—and then the club auctioned the guernseys to support the Foundation.

"You flick through the sale list and there are the winning bids for this one and that one. 700 bucks here. 900 bucks there," says Matthews. "You get to Dustin Martin... $8100."

The fact that the player remains unsigned by the club, and is fielding an immense contract offer from North Melbourne, and is playing by far the best football of his career—in a year during which Richmond has never been outside the top eight—and you have a perfect storm. Matthews shakes his head. "There must have been 5000 stories on his contract. We thought about cutting a video together with every time Dimma and the players and the CEO have been asked a question about his contract."

The club's messaging, as directed by Matthews, has been consistent: *The process will take as long as it takes. As a free agent, Martin is entitled to take his time, because it's a big decision. We love having him at our footy club, and he clearly loves being part of our footy club.*

"But I was standing with Leppa (Leppitsch) after we beat Port Adelaide (Round 15), and the look on Dustin's face was just jubilation. Pure jubilation. He was more excited than anybody. He loves winning. To me, he doesn't look like a person who doesn't want to be at Richmond."

After almost two decades in football, Matthews says he now couldn't work in another industry. Not any more. He loves that the business he serves is so vibrant every week, and the way all the contests count in some way. "I'll be driving back up the highway tonight—win, lose or draw—thinking about what we want to tell our fans. How has the coach performed in the press conference? What is the media going to pick up?"

He turns his head now towards his brother, who was a member of the AFL executive before he joined GWS in 2011. He performed a range of roles over 13 years there, including an executive position as GM of game development.

"You worked at head office, Dave. Would you struggle to *not* work in the cut and thrust of a club now?"

"Yep," he answers. "Club life is far more addictive."

The two talk regularly throughout each season, sharing tips, seeking advice. *Who would be ideal to spearhead this project? How do the fans view this controversy?* You wonder what Dave Matthews sees when he looks south from Blacktown to Richmond.

"The main thing that we've seen and that our Board has talked about with the Tigers is that, over the years, Richmond has been characterised by instability. But that's well gone," he says. "When we started the Giants, we talked to (Geelong entrepreneur and long-time Cats president) Frank Costa about what is important, and he said, 'You've just got to get your key people in the right spots and back them in'. Geelong was close to sacking Mark Thompson (in 2006), and he goes out and wins a flag. I imagine the Tigers have had some difficult discussions about Hardwick, but what would the Richmond of the mid-1990s have done?"

Simon chirps up now. The way the club remained steadfast and refused to crack or splinter during a difficult 2016 is a point of pride for him. "It's a time when we were really, really strong. Because the rank and file were grumpy. They really were, and with good reason."

The coverage, however—of everything from the players to the coach to the Board and Board challenges—frustrated and dismayed him, particularly the idea that Richmond might be criticised for its stability—as if seeking certainty meant finding comfort in complacency. "Stability actually *enables* change, because change without stability is chaos," he says, voice rising a little. He is proud of the way club president Peggy O'Neal stared down all the critics and held firm to the club's process—even as outsiders lambasted the club for stagnation. "I have absolutely no doubt that some of the sentiment towards her is because she's female, because this game still hasn't got that right."

The message presented by O'Neal and Gale, he says, was consistent throughout the post-season: *The club has done a lot right, but had a bad year on the field.*

We enter Geelong now, pulling off the bypass road, wending through the more picturesque part of town. Before the trip is over, we pass Geelong College.

"There's the old school," Simon says, looking out his window at the Newtown campus. "Kicked three goals on that ground in a house match. Gun."

//////////

Richmond is almost favoured to win today. The Cats are higher on the ladder, but were beaten soundly at the venue only a week earlier by Sydney. They are missing their captain and star midfielder Joel Selwood due to injury, as well as onballer Mitch Duncan and key forward Tom Hawkins to suspension.

But this is still a hostile environment, and still one of the most statistically significant home ground advantages in football. Neil Balme, who was football manager at the club for eight years, said only a week earlier—in the MCG rooms shortly after Richmond had defeated Hawthorn—that the Tigers need to embrace such challenges. His time as a player at Richmond was characterised by a thirst for such encounters. He thinks it crucial to prime all players to have that mentality.

"We want these games. We deserve these games. These games are why we play. These games are who we are," he said. "After all, a bit of grass is a bit of grass. The crowd can't get a kick."

The wind swirls, and the ground is narrow, and one team trains here every day of the week and the other plays here irregularly. Since 1980, the Tigers have played at Simonds Stadium 24 times for three wins, the latest in 2006. That win, by 20 points, is Richmond's latest over Geelong, followed by a run of 12 straight losses.

Statistics aside, on this day Richmond is placed under enormous pressure. The Tigers pride themselves on tackles and forward-half turnovers and corrals and chases and closing down space, but Geelong is the number one pressure team in the competition. Today it shows. The Tigers go down by 14 points, but the loss feels more like a 40-point margin.

The siren sounds. The skies darken. Rain falls. And the television presenters do interviews with victorious Geelong players on the field, under umbrellas held by production assistants. Matthews stands and watches from the race as the Tigers trudge from the field.

The outcome is soured with the news that Josh Caddy has pulled a hamstring, and the loss effectively eliminates Richmond's chance of finishing inside the top two, and even places its top four hopes in jeopardy, with a rampant Sydney Swans sitting fifth, waiting for a single slip up from those ahead of them in the run home.

Hardwick gives his presser, but Matthews doesn't stay to listen. He is long since past managing or monitoring the coach's rapport with reporters. He has known Hardwick since the coach's playing days at Essendon. "I think he gets a bad rap. In most of his press conferences he's good fun. He's pretty human, too."

Matthews also knows that criticism of coaches following compulsory post-match press conferences is mostly just filler. Get beaten, he says, and all the coach's comments get picked apart, spun around, turned upside down, taken out of context, amplified and magnified and sent out into the world with a news story, then news analysis, then opinion piece then think pieces then hot takes until it's all a hot mess.

He saw it happen when Richmond lost an early game in 2016, and Hardwick uttered the following: "This side isn't the same as last year. We are trialling some blokes in some different positions. We might have to take a little half step backwards to go two steps forward, but I'm very confident we will take the two steps forward."

The three words "half step backwards" became an issue for many in the commentariat, particularly after Hardwick claimed the Tiger list was the best at his disposal during his time at the club.

"Everyone says that's a mixed message, but it made perfect sense," says Matthews, taking clear umbrage. "He's just saying, 'The list I've got is the best I've worked with, but we're looking at a few things that might take us back a step to take us two more steps forward'. But because you're getting beaten, the whole world wants to make it into a 'rebuild' conversation."

"That comment became a storm, but now it rings reasonably true. He pumped a heck of a lot of games into young players, and trialled players in different positions, all of which was a 'half step backwards' as they adjusted.

You'd be hard-pressed to say we haven't now taken those 'two more steps forward'."

Matthews can get his back up, but he is pragmatic. He knows there is a certain futility in attempting to keep his club out of the news.

"Did you ever see *The Natural*?" he asks, talking about the Robert Redford film about a preternaturally gifted baseball star. He is remembering a specific scene. It's an exchange between the athlete, Roy Hobbs, and a hard-bitten journalist, Max Mercy. Mercy believes he is there to protect the game, by making or breaking the likes of Hobbs.

Hobbs: Did you ever play ball, Max?

Mercy: No, never have. But I make it a little more fun to watch, you see. And after today, whether you're a goat or a hero...you're gonna make me a great story.

"That's Richmond," says Matthews. "We're a story either way."

In darkness now, as the Ford Territory comes over the West Gate Bridge into Melbourne, Matthews talks passionately about his wider purview, which is now much more than media. He has a large staff, around 25. He might be working today on messaging but tomorrow—for instance—he will be in Canberra for meetings with Indigenous Affairs Minister, Nigel Scullion and the Minister for Trade, Tourism and Development, Steven Ciobo, about some developing opportunities in India.

Richmond is a diversified sporting club. Matthews needs to tell the story of *Aligned Leisure*, their fitness and recreation business, along with their sports leadership institute through Swinburne University, the *Korin Gamadji* Institute, their *Next Generation Academy*, their connection to the Alannah & Madeline Foundation, and the Bachar Houli Academy, and a partnership with *VicHealth* on gender equality.

"The story is so much broader now than football," he says. "The shape of the business has just changed. But it all speaks to us being a strong and bold club."

In many ways this peripheral work is what gives him the most pleasure in the role—not being a spin doctor or crisis manager. He likes the way all those employees and charity partners and community groups, and the fans they bring in to meet the players all wear the colours and all feel as though they are part of the same endeavour.

They all ride the result on the weekend, sharing a common goal that percolates throughout and beyond the organisation. They are all trying in some small way to win that next premiership. They are all working toward that cup. Together.

36

THE UNTAPPED
COMPETITIVE ADVANTAGE

A short distance southeast of the Punt Road Oval, across the Yarra River and along its brown banks, sits an office and a person crucial to the Richmond rebirth of 2017.

The office is perched in a tall building in South Yarra, and its lobby is filled with personalised sporting paraphernalia: cricket boots, signed by Shane Warne; a mini Malibu surfboard, given to the business owner by Kelly Slater; a soccer ball autographed by the entire Barcelona Football Club, a gift to a friend.

His name is Ben Crowe, and although well known within clubland he is unknown to the average AFL fan.

The sports marketing expert was once the youngest ever director at Nike, co-founder of sports entertainment group Gemba, and now current co-founder of *Unscriptd*, a company that helps athletes around the world (through offices in Melbourne, New York, London and Barcelona) tell stories directly to their fans. Those short confessional video clips released this year featuring Trent Cotchin admitting his foibles and fears and his love for Dustin Martin? That's *Unscriptd*. The company has worked with Cristiano Ronaldo, Virat Kohli, Steph Gilmore and Cathy Freeman, but that's not why Crowe has been important to Richmond this season.

Crowe is also a professional mentor, who has worked with AFL executives, the AFL Coaches Association, with his close friend Andre Agassi and for many years with another close friend, Hawthorn coach Alastair Clarkson. (While we chat his phone rings multiple times, and the name "Clarko" appears on the screen.)

Crowe has also worked with Peggy O'Neal since she became Richmond president, and in late 2016 he was asked by CEO Brendon Gale to work closely with some of the Richmond football department leaders. Ever since then, he has become an influential voice in the ears of both Damien Hardwick and Trent Cotchin, and a regular presence inside the club and occasionally on game day.

Today he wears black pants, a thin black jumper with the sleeves pushed up to the forearm, and black leather Campers, and offers first his smiling elevator pitch for *Unscriptd*. "The idea is to educate, inspire and enable athletes to become storytellers," he says. "It's about finding out their own story first—*who they are*—so they can show up in the world with more authenticity and purpose, and planned confidence."

The company's offering is not unique in this space but in fact part of a wider trend. In the United States, for instance, there is LeBron James' Uninterrupted and The Players' Tribune, founded by former New York Yankees shortstop Derek Jeter. More recently in Australia there is PlayersVoice, offering the "unvarnished" ruminations of everyone from Israel Folau to Nick Kyrgios, Jeff Horn to Joe Ingles. Each site promises to "deepen the connection" between sportspeople and their fans. They promise "raw" storytelling, often in the first person, through articles and videos and podcasts, although Unscriptd is the only global player that also uses technology to connect athletes with content from their teams, leagues and sponsors.

Take the boast of PlayersVoice: *"We created a community where sportspeople can share their thoughts, hopes, dreams and fears. A safe space with no gambling ads, no banner ads and no keyboard warriors. No beat-ups. No clickbait. No agendas."*

These portals become a place where AFL Women's star Erin Phillips can share her views on the gay marriage debate ("Plebiscite: A platform to discriminate"), and where Collingwood forward Alex Fasolo can share the candid details of his battle with depression ("Death was an escape fantasy").

Such tales are both admirable and brave, but in some ways these sites also represent a threat to traditional journalism, leaving the stories of athletes in the hands of marketers and ghost writers - contributing to a kind of echo chamber in which public relations masquerades as journalism.

US website Deadspin (company slogan: "Sports news without access, favour or discretion") likens these sites to celebrity trash magazines, seeing little difference between Derek Jeter opening up about "feeling guarded" to an "In her own words" piece from Taylor Swift on the cover of People. The athletes themselves, unsurprisingly, see the new channels for communication as a way of correcting an imbalance, and giving them ownership and control of their identity.

Either way, that's Crowe's day job, and the work he is doing with key Tigers dovetails neatly into the narrative at Tigerland this year, in that Richmond has become an entire club of storytellers, led by the two bodies around which any playing group orbits—the coach and the captain, the sun and the moon of any side. Crowe works mostly one-on-one, whether catching up for quick coffee, or guiding a series of longer meetings to construct a "Life Plan" (which he did for both Hardwick and Cotchin).

The process covers four areas initially - authenticity, vulnerability, connection and storytelling - and starts by unearthing values and beliefs, behaviours and passions. "What's their legacy going to be? What's the eulogy at their funeral? How do they make people feel? Do they stand for something?" Crowe says. "It's extraordinary what happens when you put your purpose together on paper: the world just organises itself and bizarrely comes back to you."

The work with Crowe is hard, too. It is mentoring and guidance but also self-examination and therapy. Sometimes there are tears, but in shedding them they also shed worries and fears. It has an impact. "They've done all the heavy lifting here and they deserve all the credit for investing so much time and putting themselves through such intense self-exploration," says Crowe. "It takes insane courage to be so vulnerable. My job is just to organise their thinking but they've done all the hard work."

When I first interviewed Cotchin a year earlier, at the start of the 2016 season, there was little in the way of easy back and forth. The exchange felt guarded, and trained. His answers were neither dishonest nor frank. He was saying all the right things, but holding back. Interviewing Cotchin this year revealed a changed man. Crowe points out that the captain has admitted this year that he did not feel entirely comfortable with his leadership.

"He's said a few times publicly he thought he had to be this perfect person," says Crowe. "And that's not uncommon in professional athletes. It's called *'perform, perfect, repeat'*. They think their connection with others or love for them comes from being the perfect athlete. It's flawed, and it's messed up. But it's common. The alternative is 'I'm imperfect, and I'm full of struggle, but that's okay because I'm still worthy'."

Crowe says this was the first and most crucial change in Cotchin this season: a sense of self-compassion. In the alpha-male world of sport, he says, the more common default stance is being defensive and closed off, preventing curiosity and creativity and even courage. Crowe recounts the moment earlier in the season when Cotchin stood in front of his peers, and told them his fears.

"He told them in his own words and own way that he was imperfect, full of struggle, shit-scared, emotional—'I don't have all the answers, and I cry a lot, but I believe I am worthy to take you guys on a journey'—and the whole room goes 'Thank God', because he's just given permission for everyone else to be imperfect and open and real and raw. The team worked out that their imperfections are what connects them. Those nuances are the magic."

Hardwick was similar. Amid the frustration and confusion of the calamitous 2016 season, the coach clung tightly to process and analysis and exhaustive examination.

"I think he thought he had to have the answers," Crowe says. "He spent more time watching more games, more training, more reports, and yet the answer was never in the tape or on the training track. The answer isn't always in the data." He points to a quote often attributed to Einstein: Not everything that counts can be counted. Not everything that can be counted counts.

This year though, Hardwick has "dialled up his right brain", tapping into a sense of curiosity and playfulness and a newfound appetite for storytelling. The former is on display before every game, Hardwick opening almost every address to his players with a silly anecdote, apropos of nothing.

Before one game, he explained to the players that he doesn't really understand the technological mechanics of social media, but that one night earlier—all of a sudden—his wife's phone had gone crazy, with dozens upon dozens of alerts, and then he heard a scream. Someone had hacked her account and replaced her profile picture with a provocative image of a scantily clad young woman. "She got more than 100 friend requests. And you know who one of them was? Connor Menadue! Connor Menadue!"

Before another game, he explained why a small patch on his forehead was a little red. It was because Hardwick is a germophobe, and he wanted to thoroughly rinse his gym bottle, so he added boiling water then shook it up. "The heat expanded it, and BOOM, it explodes as I take off the lid, and now I've got this bloody great scalding blister at the top of my noggin!"

The tales he tells sometimes contain no specific message the playing group needs to absorb. They do not segue into the next point he wants to make. They are not ripping yarns or incredibly funny moments he just had to share, and yet he offers a new one at every game. He did no such thing in 2016. In his highly-controlled messaging last season there was no room for an anecdote about stopping his car late at night to help a drunken man cross Nepean Highway. But there's method in his madness.

"Why would you possibly tell that story?" says Crowe, posing the rhetorical question. "The purpose of those stories is distraction and levity, because you've almost got to fight against all that seriousness and anxiety and information."

Then there are the planned stories Hardwick tells—the ones meant to educate and inspire. The metaphors and allegories vary in tone and seriousness, and always they are built up from a prop specific to the 2017 season—an A3 picture, pinned to the whiteboard at the front of the room.

Sometimes he draws on the animal kingdom. Before the game against the Bulldogs, for instance, the A3 picture was of a badger. Specifically, a snarling honey badger—a creature described as the fiercest on earth. "You know why?" Hardwick asked. "Because it has no fear. It embraces the fight. It has got tough skin, sharp claws, and teeth like knives. When it fights a lion three times its size, do you think it goes for the head or the gut? It goes for the gut. Because it's *smart*. This thing is not the biggest, not the toughest, but it is the *meanest*. This thing is never afraid of the fight. It might die, but the thing it takes on dies a slow, painful death. Tonight, we have twenty-two fierce, smart animals out there, scratching and ripping at the Bulldogs' underbelly."

Sometimes he draws on the past. Before one game, the picture was a sepia-toned photo of Richmond players rejoicing on the field after the 1967 premiership, 50 years ago, because that victorious side fits the template of the team today. It was Royce Hart and Francis Bourke's first year at Punt Road. Kevin Bartlett and Michael Green were in their second year.

"They've spoken about that season, and they reckoned they weren't the most talented side throughout the year—but what they had was belief. You work, you believe, and suddenly it starts to roll."

Sometimes the picture is comical. Before the game against Adelaide, which no expert or fan or punter or betting market gave Richmond a chance of winning, the picture was of Homer Simpson and a speech bubble that read: "Kiss my arse!" The point was his defiance of what the football world believes. "What do people think about us? They're waiting for us to fail. Today, we play the way we want to play, and they can kiss our arse. We walk off the ground today and go, stuff you blokes, we know we're the real deal. Only one team walks off tapping their backside, and that's us."

Later in the season, as the wins mounted and Richmond began to gather respect—as well as a place in the top four—the theme turned to dreams of success. The picture before the GWS game, Round 18, was a photo of Hardwick himself, standing in the hallway at home in plaid pyjama pants, holding up two thumbs and a smile. He looked like The Fonz, except for the spearmint green jumper he was wearing—one with the words "why not?" printed on the front. His wife, Danielle, bought it for him.

"When you're in a good position, and you're elite athletes, and you're up the top, you can't help asking yourself, are we quite ready?" he said. "Are we old enough? Are we good enough? As soon as I feel that doubt, or we have a loss, you know what I do with that jumper—I put it on, and I remind myself 'Why not us? Why not this year?' What I want to see out there today is something that makes people on the outside start to wonder...Why not this side?"

Crowe is one of the only people outside of the direct football department who sits in on such briefings, and he vividly remembers the story Hardwick told in the first pre-season game of the year. It was about Hardwick as a junior basketball player (in the B team), who one night was promoted to the A team but played it safe, and forever regretted it. He encouraged his players to do the opposite, to play with dare, with joy, without fear. "I was watching Jason Castagna's eyes, and he was *lit*," says Crowe. "Dimma had him in his hands. Castagna kicked three goals in the first half. He ran riot. That's the power of telling child-like, light-hearted, magical stories."

It all stems from a renewed thirst for learning. Hardwick is watching more movies and reading more books, and thinking about the messages within them. Cotchin, too, has been receptive to a new approach to leadership, coming off what he described as the worst year of his life. "You know that old eastern philosophy, 'When the student is ready, the teacher will come?' Well, they were ready," says Crowe. "They were sponges. I can work with a CEO or coach for six months and not crack them. But Cotch and Dimma were ready, and all credit to them for doing all the hard work."

What it has led to on field is a battle framework better known as "In command, out of control." The phrase comes from a Malcolm Gladwell book *Blink*, in a chapter about US Lieutenant-General Paul Van Riper, a Marine Corps leader who took command of a team during an enormous 2002 war game known as the Millennium Challenge. Van Riper's role in the war game was to assume control of a small rogue company, and fight against a much larger force, which he successfully managed by empowering his troops— offering them guidance but encouraging initiative. The philosophy was to create a shared purpose, and then let them go to work.

"It's freedom within a framework—looks random, but it's not," says Crowe. "It's spontaneous but deliberate. Instinctive, really, like the Bulldogs last year. *How the hell did he know that guy was going to be there? How did he know to tap that forward?* You watch the Grand Final—their play is seemingly blind, based on faith."

Crowe admits he has been surprised at how quickly Richmond has been able to embrace the model: they all seem to have grasped that if you show care for your teammates, they will perform more strongly as individuals.

"Because if you lose all sense of ego and self, you'll dial up the little things—talking, shepherding, running, blocking. The great outcome? You'll play better. Connection is the last untapped competitive advantage."

Crowe speaks like this, and says this kind of thing often. There is virtually no element of sporting excellence for which he does not have some slick bromide, expressed with a play on words, or alliteration, or via a catchy rhyme.

What corrupts our performance is often not skillset but mindset.

Replace expectations with appreciations.

If you give 10 times more than you get, you'll get 10 times more than you give.

It might sound like corporate speak, like the sporting equivalent of weasel words, or like a motivational poster come to life, but there is merit in his messages. The tone may be smooth but perhaps the power to soothe is the balm this playing group needed – especially after the stinging failure of the season before. Consider the alternative, for instance. Take the words of someone who looked at sport in the old way. Think of the legendary Notre Dame football coach Knute Rockne, and his blunt view on losing: "Show me a good and gracious loser, and I'll show you a failure."

Last season at Richmond this worldview was made manifest. Anger and embarrassment and dismay and desolation followed any bad loss—but this season? A loss is examined. A loss is considered. A loss is addressed. And then put behind them. Players and coaches leave the briefing room after a defeat with the hint of a smile and a pat on the back, each man seemingly safe in the knowledge that they know the way forward—that they are stronger for understanding their faults and flaws, and why sometimes they fall or fail.

GRAND FINAL

ADELAIDE	4.2	4.7	5.10	8.12	(60)
RICHMOND	2.3	6.4	11.8	16.12	(108)

WHY NOT US?: The game couldn't produce three players as different as Dustin Martin, Jason Castagna and Kane Lambert, but the determined and intense Grand Final performances of all three typified Richmond's effort to swamp ladder-topping Adelaide. Lambert transformed himself from VFL afterthought to third place-getter in the Jack Dyer medal during the club's remarkable flag season.

FOR POSTERITY: In recent seasons, each team has come together for the official team photo. For the Tigers, the photo shows a group relaxed and ready to play the game of their lives.

BACK ROW (L-R): Shane Edwards, Kane Lambert, Jason Castagna, Jacob Townsend, Nick Vlastuin, Alex Rance, Bachar Houli, David Astbury, Nathan Broad, Jack Graham, Toby Nankervis, Josh Caddy, Daniel Butler, Kamdyn McIntosh.

FRONT ROW (L-R): Dion Prestia, Dustin Martin, Dylan Grimes, Brandon Ellis, Damien Hardwick (coach), Trent Cotchin (captain), Jack Riewoldt, Shaun Grigg, Daniel Rioli.

ECSTASY AND AGONY:
Exhausted Tigers players embraced each other in scenes of unbridled joy following the final siren, while vanquished Adelaide opponents slumped to the MCG turf. The Crows had been run ragged all day and failed to adapt to Richmond's incessant pressure. From left: Shaun Grigg, Jack Riewoldt, Kamdyn McIntosh, Toby Nankervis, Dustin Martin, Nick Vlastuin, and Nathan Broad.

ABOVE: Soon the Tiger celebrations had begun in earnest, beginning with the traditional podium photo. **Back row:** Dan Butler, Dustin Martin, Nick Vlastuin, Shaun Grigg, Daniel Rioli, Trent Cotchin, Jack Riewoldt, Jacob Townsend, Kamdyn McIntosh, Jack Graham, Josh Caddy, Toby Nankervis. **Front row:** Kane Lambert, Dylan Grimes, David Astbury, Alex Rance, Dion Prestia, Nathan Broad,

BRAIN'S TRUST: The inspired and stable leadership of club president Peggy O'Neal (above with Dustin Martin), CEO Brendon Gale, (right with Martin and Jack Riewoldt) and coach Damien Hardwick (below getting an ice bath from Martin) was a cornerstone of Richmond's first Grand Final success in 37 long and often difficult years in the AFL wilderness. O'Neal weathered an attempted board coup in the off-season to become the first female president of an AFL premier.

CUP OF LIFE: Players and fans alike could hardly contain their glee at finally grasping football's Holy Grail. Soon, and well into a memorable night, the local streets of Richmond were a sea of yellow and black jubilation. Clockwise from top left: Daniel Rioli, unable to make the lap of honour after a late in the game injury to his ankle, hitches a ride with captain Trenth Cotchin, Jack Riewoldt enjoys the moment and the Premiership Medal, Bachar Houli takes the Cup to the Crowd; the players rejoice as one; and Kamdyn McIntosh and Nick Vlastuin pose for selfies.

WINNERS: Alex Rance ponders the moment he's a premiership player, in his 175th game, after nine seasons; Defensive coach Ben Rutten celebrates with Trent Cotchin, and another Medal for Dustin Martin, this time the Norm Smith Medal.

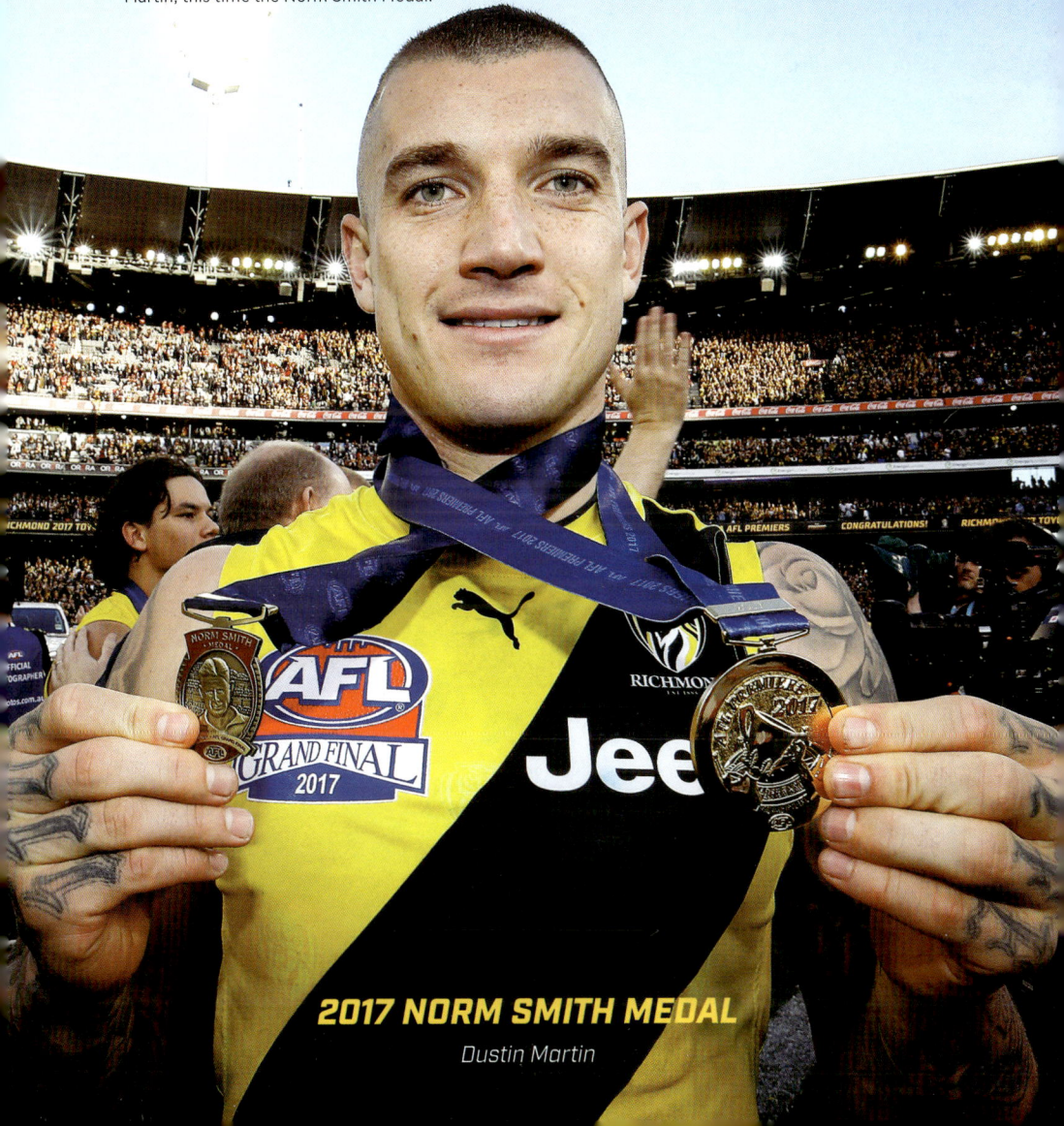

2017 NORM SMITH MEDAL

Dustin Martin

ALL IN: Throughout 2017, the dictum at Richmond has been it takes "all of club" to win a flag, and, when it was all over, senior players and VFL players joined together for a memorable photo.

37

A DOUBLE-EDGED SWORD

The first time Ben Griffiths suffered a concussion, he wasn't sure what had happened. He was perhaps 10, and he woke up lying on the ground at home in Mitcham, confused and sore. Moments earlier he had fashioned a rope swing in his backyard, gone sailing through the air on the improvised piece of play equipment, until it snapped. "I knocked myself out on a tree root," he says, brow furrowing just a little, resting on a couch in the forwards' meeting room at Tigerland. "That was the first one I can distinctly remember."

It would not be the last. Griffiths, 25, was drafted to Richmond in 2009 (Pick 19, from the Eastern Ranges in the TAC Cup), and to say his career has been interrupted by head injuries is an understatement. There was a heavy knock to the head in a VFL game in 2013. In Round 6, 2015, he collapsed, face down, after a concussion against North Melbourne. He barely moved after a knock during a 2016 pre-season game against Fremantle, his head colliding with the shoulder of Aaron Sandilands—the Docker man mountain who weighs in at around 122 kilograms.

The worst hit though was one of the first—during his time at Richmond—in the final quarter of the final round of the 2012 season. That day in Perth, Griffiths flew into an innocuous rucking contest but found his body tunnelled. As he tipped in mid-air the ground beneath him rose at speed. His temple struck the Domain Stadium surface and his body crumpled.

On replay you can hear the concern of the callers: "Oh no. Is there any movement? No, there's zero movement. That boy's in a lot of strife."

Griffiths was applauded as he was taken from the ground but does not remember the clapping. He remembers only that from there he went to hospital. "That one was bad," he says. "I was out for a while. And after that one, it sort of felt like it took less to feel the effects of a hit."

All of which is context for what happened to the tall forward in 2017. In Round 2 against Collingwood, under lights, he flew for a high mark but came to ground awkwardly, and came away with another concussion. After two weeks off, he made his return to the field in a Round 5 VFL game, and was concussed again. Scared and confused, he took immediate, indefinite leave from a game that had suddenly gotten serious.

///////////

It wasn't supposed to be like this. Griffiths started playing football when he was eight years old, and loved it as much for the McDonald's meal after each Auskick session as he did the goals and tackles. He quickly understood that he could kick the ball a great distance, leap higher than most, and pluck marks from the sky—but he played only for fun with his friends. That's all he wanted from the game. "You don't think about it much then," he says. "You play because it's playing."

The great shame of the 2017 season for Griffiths is that Richmond became a place where it *is* fun to be playing. Not only that, but with the departure of tall forward Tyrone Vickery to Hawthorn, Griffiths knew he would have his clearest run yet at a full year as the second tall target beside Jack Riewoldt. He was excited about the changes he saw at Punt Road before pre-season had even begun.

"I was really pumped as early as late last year," he says. "The young guys all got back a couple of weeks earlier than they needed to, and that filtered back to the older guys—just how hard they were training, and how well they were running. Straight away there were guys who stepped up, setting new standards. Dan Butler and Ivan Soldo really stood out to me. Kane Lambert and Nathan Drummond are really good all the time, and even they were improving. Coming out of Christmas and into the New Year, it was a polar opposite of last season. Last year this was a really hard place to be."

This year, Punt Road is an easy place to be. The Tigers are in the top four, and headed tomorrow to Perth to face a Fremantle side with little motivation. Beyond that they play St Kilda, and then finals beckon. Griffiths should be a part of this, but instead he has played a solitary full game and two halves.

"It's so frustrating. You want to be playing, and you have to go watch all the games, and there are just these times where you think 'Shit, I could be helping there'." Wanting to make an impact but not being able to stings. Rehabilitation is often done in isolation, too. "They work you hard. You get tortured," he says, laughing ruefully. "It's almost prison."

In the middle of it all was the nagging concern about his long layoff as he coped with the after-effects of concussion, an issue that has demanded examination and reform from the game itself, and nervous trepidation from those affected.

"This year was really tough. It was hard to open up about it. I didn't feel like I could talk about it that much. I didn't know if anyone was going to understand what I was feeling, or going through," he says, sighing. "It's complicated."

///////////

The one other person at the club who best understands the complications surrounding concussion is the club doctor, Greg Hickey. The assessment process today is heavily proscribed by the League, he says, and strictly regulated.

This is how he describes it: imagine a player goes down in a contest on the outer wing. He is sprawled on the ground, moving a little but clearly not well. It is not immediately clear what happened in the collision. Hickey first sprints onto the ground, and talks to the player right there. He asks questions.

Who are you playing on?
What team are we playing?
Who did we play last week?
What's the score?
What day is it?

But mostly, at this stage, he is looking for obvious red flags. Was the player unconscious, even for a moment? Is he disoriented? Can he stand up?

If he sees any such warning signs, or if the player complains of any other telltale symptoms, then another layer of action is required, such as reviewing footage of the incident on the bench—replaying the hit from different angles to check for force and connection. They do this for all incidents on the field, whether a twisted knee or a shoulder collision. A second doctor employed by the club on game day, Dr Andrew Daff, looks over the video so they can then assemble all available knowledge.

As part of the new protocols for managing the problem, any player suspected of sustaining concussion is then taken into the rooms to perform the SCAT-5 (Sport Concussion Assessment Tool, Fifth Edition)—a formal diagnostic process that takes around 15 minutes to complete.

Firstly, they look for obvious symptoms like double vision, vomiting or convulsions. They check for signs of confusion, headache, fatigue, nervousness and irritability. "It can be difficult. If you're asking a player questions in the middle of an AFL game, of course they're going to feel fatigued and nervous," Hickey says. "But usually you can tell pretty quickly if someone's not quite right. You know these guys well, so you can tell if they're responding appropriately."

The form that Hickey fills out then has a series of 'Yes' or 'No' boxes to be ticked.

> Lying motionless on the playing surface? **Y / N**
> Blank or vacant look? **Y / N**

Then come more of those questions from the field.

> At what venue are we playing today?
> Which half is it now?
> Who scored last in the match?

These are called the "Maddocks questions", because they were devised by Dr David Maddocks of the University of Melbourne. Maddocks published them in 1995, in a thesis titled "Neuropsychological recovery after concussion in Australian rules footballers", but they have since been edited and augmented and adopted. Hickey has usually covered most of these kinds of questions on the field.

Next, he performs a set of varied evaluations, including the Glasgow Coma

Scale and the Cervical Spine Assessment. There is also a cognitive screening process looking at immediate memory and recall. Hickey reads aloud six sets of words, each of which need to be repeated back to him, in any order.

Finger. Penny. Blanket. Lemon. Insect.

Dollar. Honey. Mirror. Saddle. Anchor.

Baby. Monkey. Perfume. Sunset. Iron.

Concentration comes next, starting with short lists of digits, which Hickey recites and then asks the player to recite back to him—in reverse order.

Four-Nine-Three becomes *Three-Nine-Four*, which sounds simple enough, but they must perform the task more than a dozen times, and the string of numbers grows longer and longer. Could you remember *Eight-Four-One-Nine-Three-Five*, and the recite it in reverse? Could you recite the months of the year in reverse order? Because that's what comes next.

After that, a neurological screening is required.

Can the patient perform the finger/nose coordination test normally?

Then there is a balance examination. One test starts with a line on the ground in the corridor, about nine metres long. The player has to walk along it, heel to toe, and see how quickly they can get to one end, spin around, and come back.

Another test requires them to stand on one leg, while Hickey counts how many times they stumble or sway within 20 seconds. "You see plenty of guys who pull all the numbers and words out, who look like nothing's wrong with them," says Hickey. "Then you do some balance testing and they're quite wobbly."

The testing regimen is not perfect. Neither Hickey, nor any other club doctor, for that matter, possesses established baselines against which to assess the players. Testing a football side on all measures in pre-season would take weeks to organise, and would likely be ineffective because it wasn't done during game conditions. "The testing is more about getting a subjective read on them," Hickey says. "These guys all have great balance, so you can tell if someone is poor."

Hickey concedes concussion has become a far greater issue in the game than it once was, but he cautions that the ongoing debate about its effects—short-term and long-term—does not necessarily mean it is more common, or even more insidious.

"Management of concussion was completely different even 10 years ago. Players often used to return to the game with minor concussions, but we're far more conservative now. Far more conservative," he says. "Times have changed."

///////////

The effects of any concussion vary depending on the individual, and their history, and the nature of the collision, but what Ben Griffiths went through in 2017 would be familiar to anyone in the aftermath of a heavy head knock.

He couldn't sleep. His sensitivity to light was extreme. He suffered constant, splitting migraines. His moods were bad, and shifted swiftly. He didn't feel like himself, but had trouble even gauging what that meant.

"I was at war with myself," he says. "I was trying to work out 'Is this what I'm like, or is it because of the knock?' It's a tough one because everyone reacts differently." He repeats the point he made earlier: "There wasn't really anyone I could talk to."

Griffiths ended up turning to one person he knew would understand: Justin Clarke, the Brisbane defender who retired in 2016 at just 22, following a severe concussion. It happened to Clarke at pre-season training, when he entered a marking contest, caught a small shove in the back and then tumbled forward, where his forehead caught the knee of a player sprinting in the opposite direction. Clarke dealt with an array of debilitating symptoms in the months that followed, but the seriousness of the hit and the hopeless feeling of being lost was perhaps best surmised by the opening passage of a profile by Michael Gleeson in The Age back in March:

> "Justin Clarke left home to drive to university. He got halfway and stopped. He had driven the road hundreds of times but suddenly he had no idea which way to go."

Griffiths was glad to talk to Clarke. It was worth the time, and the contact, if for nothing else than to reconcile the notion that the recovery process would probably not be quick, or linear, or immediately conclusive.

"It's not that it gives you clarity," Griffiths says. "It was just good to talk to someone who had gone through a really bad one."

Retirement was a very real possibility for Griffiths, who will turn 26 in September, the week of the Preliminary Final. He thought deeply about what life without football might look like, and, early on, didn't know whether he wanted to play footy again. "But in thinking that, I also knew I was not in a good head space to consider the decision. So I tried to suppress those thoughts, and focus instead on just getting better, feeling better, feeling *me*."

He had brain scans, and saw a neuropsychologist. A complicating factor was the unique nature of the concussion sustained against Collingwood. In that incident, Griffiths' body hit the ground but his head did not. Nor did his head make contact with an elbow, or fist, or forearm. As his 99-kilogram frame slammed into the turf, his head merely shook. That prompted him to also see a vestibular physiotherapist, who assessed his inner ear function and spatial awareness and visual processing.

"Turns out I was going at half of what I should have been. My left eye wasn't working as well as it should have been. So that could have been an underlying issue that made me more susceptible."

Griffiths never went down the late-night rabbit hole of his own online research. He never turned to Dr Google, and he has never seen the Will Smith film *Concussion*, about the disturbing consequences of concussion in the gladiatorial NFL.

Had he wanted to, he could have read stories about the scandal surrounding the treatment of NFL athletes, and the legal strain it has placed on that sport. Journalists across America have written searing articles on the issue. He could have read *The People V. Football* or *The Future of Football* or *The Concussion Diaries*. Or he could have read individual accounts, like *What Ever Happened to Joseph Randle* or *Did Football Kill Austin Trenum* or *Dave Duerson's Secret Life and Tragic End*.

But Griffiths doesn't want to get caught up in what one writer or filmmaker thinks about the issue, preferring to listen to specialised medical opinion. The media, he says, has done a great service in making people aware of concussion. "But at the same time they've gone a little bit too far, so that everyone is scared of concussion or instantly thinks that it's unresolvable and definitely has long-term impacts. And there's really no definitive proof of that."

Here it is worth mentioning Chronic Traumatic Encephalopathy, a degenerative brain disease often found in people who have suffered continuous repeated blows to the head, like the many NFL players dealing with such horrors as early onset dementia.

People often mistakenly equate the single blow concussions dealt with by AFL players with the catalogue of constant hits accrued by gridiron players. The latter can be described as "subconcussive impacts"—hits below the threshold for concussion.

One way to think about them is offered by the Concussion Legacy Foundation, which likens concussions to cars hitting pot holes on the road. Bad pot holes might cause a burst tyre or cracked axle. Smaller ones won't, but drive over them a dozen times a day, every day of the year, for more than a decade, and pervasive wear and tear will reveal itself. Griffiths understands the distinction.

"There are certain parts of the US experience that are comparable, but they're almost on two different spectrums. They get these constant smaller hits, which is different from those big irregular hits."

At the end of a long process—more than three months off football—Griffiths says he felt he had all the facts in front of him. He felt recovered, too. He felt positive about there being no long-term effects. "I also wanted to play footy again," he says. "So I came back."

Unfortunately, he injured his shoulder upon his return, and so had to wait again. It is just days before Round 22 of the AFL season, and Griffiths has not played a full game since Round 1. "This week I'll play three quarters in the VFL. The week after that I'll play a full game. I just want to have an impact. It's been pretty sucky watching on from the sidelines when everyone's playing so well."

Of all the players in the VFL team right now, Griffiths has earned an acute sense of missing out. His best makes him an immediate selection in the Richmond 22. The Richmond small forward set up has worked in 2017, but that does not mean it is the only way or the best way. The Tigers would love to have a key forward who runs as well as a powerful endurance athlete like Griffiths, not to mention one who can play second ruck, relieving the burden on the overworked Toby Nankervis.

"That's probably the hardest part for me, where I'm thinking, 'If I was there I could really help the team'. But you look past that—it's not about me, is it? It's about all of us."

The environment at Richmond this season has at least been an ideal recovery space for Griffiths. The compassion and honesty and humour bubbling throughout the Punt Road Oval complex has sustained him well. "It's not forced. It's genuine. We can open up to each other. It's definitely helped me this year. There was a three-month patch where I was really struggling, and the guys were unreal. *Unreal.* But it's a double-edged sword, too. It's awesome to watch and I love sharing the emotion of what they're going through. But at the same time, I feel this great sense of jealousy, because I'm not part of it."

"It really is amazing what can be achieved. You come into the year with no expectations. Certainly no one outside the club gave us a chance to play well, or win. But that comes back to the culture here that's been created. We express our individuality, instead of having dozens of the same guy. And when you get a group of blokes on the same page, who want the same thing, who all work hard for it, watching them express that on that field is pretty special."

38

SHOPPING FOR PRODUCTS

A man sits in the rain on a folding chair, next to an oval in Craigieburn. He has a thermos and packed lunch. A frigid breeze blows, and through binoculars he watches some of the best teenage footballers in the country slogging away on damp grass. It's the start of a triple header between the six Victorian metropolitan TAC Cup teams—the Northern Knights versus the Western Jets, then the Oakleigh Chargers against the Sandringham Dragons, and finally the Eastern Ranges versus the Calder Cannons.

The watcher is Matthew Clarke, the National Recruiting Manager for Richmond (and not the former Adelaide, Brisbane, St Kilda player). He has a spiral notebook on his lap, and occasionally writes a thought on one of the dozen or so players he expects to shine today—and even a few who bob up with a surprise flash of talent. "You have to go along with an open mind," Clarke says. "You go along with preconceived ideas about what you're going to see and you're likely to get it wrong."

Clarke is not watching alone, either. Two part-time Richmond scouts are here. Anthony Fagan, who works at the club in membership, is sitting nearby. Rob Draper, whose day job is managing the Brighton Recreation Centre, is on the other wing. All AFL clubs have such people on the payroll. Richmond, for instance, has around a dozen.

They're here in such foul weather, watching the game live, because doing so offers them an insight that a video camera cannot. "On tape, we can't see why a forward isn't getting to the right spot," says Clarke, "or if a midfielder isn't running defensively."

He points to a light bodied boy in orange boots—potential father-son recruit Patrick Naish, son of 1990s Tiger goalsneak Chris Naish, who played 143 games with Richmond and a further 18 with Port Adelaide. "Watching live means we can see everything we need to see," says Clarke. "Is Naish positioning himself correctly? Is he using his voice to help teammates?"

Clarke and Fagan and Draper aren't the only professionals watching. There are perhaps four dozen recruiters here. He points them out. There's Stephen Conole from Brisbane, near the flank. The guys in front of the scoreboard are from North Melbourne. In the pocket are the St Kilda boys. "That's West Coast over there," Clarke says. "I think I saw Mark McKenzie from Hawthorn on the wing."

Clarke points to a Jets player under scrutiny from all the scouts. "Number 19, there, in the middle, green boots, see him? That's Cameron Rayner, potentially the number one pick," he says. Rayner is an explosive player already likened to a frightening hybrid of Christian Petracca and Robbie Gray. "Big-bodied, strong, fast. It'll just depend on who has the first pick, and what they need."

////////////

C larke grew up more on cricket than football. Raised in Mt Gambier, he went to the University of Adelaide to study economics, but had really moved to the city to play grade cricket. He never quite reached Sheffield Shield level, instead finding himself going along to football games with Geoff Parker, a friend from cricket, who is now recruiting manager for Port Adelaide. Clarke became a part-time scout for Melbourne, and did that for eight years. He joined Richmond in 2009 and took over as National Recruiting Manager this year. "I love footy. I watch a lot of it. Too much, to be honest. I enjoy identifying talented kids and watching them succeed— even at other clubs."

He has a soft spot for those players who earn their career through hard work and quiet application. "A lot of boys out there don't work hard enough," he says, looking at the field. "They just bob along and think they're going to make it on talent. I love watching the hard workers succeed."

Today his notes are brief. He doesn't need to produce an essay because most players are well known to the watchers. Naish, for instance, has spent time training at Richmond, so there is no point in writing that he is a fast, slight player with foot skills.

Written next to his name today: "Ball handling OK".

Next to tall prospect Mark Baker of the Knights: "Not much ball, wandered a bit".

Next to Knights speedster Ethan Penrith: "Better poise".

Clarke keeps an eye on Alex Federico of the Knights. He watches clean Jets midfielder Lachlan Fogarty, who could go in the top 30. He notices Knights half-back Ben Wiggins: "I haven't seen him before. But he has good defensive intent. Maybe worth another look."

Rayner now seizes a moment, kicking a goal from 50 metres—a left foot snap across his body. It is breathtaking, but the recruiters are also here to watch him a few minutes later, when Rayner runs out of breath on the wing. He is hunched over, hands on his knees. "See? While the others are all spreading from the contest he's blowing up, walking, because he's given everything. And he'll be like that for a couple of minutes. AFL footy is going to be a shock."

Rayner will still be selected in the top five, perhaps still pick one. But the recruiters will know that he runs an 11 on the beep test (which is poor), and that he may not develop the endurance required to run, for four quarters, through an AFL midfield.

Scouting talent is mostly a thankless task but it has its joys. Like the moment last year when Jack Graham slid to Richmond with pick 53, despite winning the Larke Medal, awarded to the best player at the National Championships. Graham makes his senior debut this weekend in Perth against Fremantle, and Richmond win by 104 points. He acquits himself well, too, running hard and amassing a game high 11 tackles. He looks entirely comfortable at the level. He fell so far on draft day, says Clarke, because of his mature body. The questions asked were all along those lines: Was his junior form the result of being a "man child"? Could he replicate that success against grown men? Did he have any physical development left?

"But he was a guy we really rated and needed. He needs to work on his kicking a little, but that's another thing about Jack. You tell him he's poor in an area, and he'll get the shits for a minute and then go, 'All right, I've got to fix it, so what do I do?' He's driven."

It makes you wonder what it must be like to study a draft pool for years on end—to develop a ranking of every promising junior footballer in Australia, and then watch as your first pick in the draft is traded away—as happened in 2016 when Richmond parted with pick six for Dion Prestia.

"It's tough," says Clarke. "But you don't really know what's going to happen until the trade period, so you have to be across everything. There's also an element of learning. Regardless of who you pick, you come up with an order and you can look back in a handful of years and see whether you got the order right or not, and question why. It's like studying for an exam, but you don't get your marks for five years."

The research Clarke does is also crucial intelligence for trade week. The club needs to know what kind of player is likely to be available with pick six, for example, to compare its potential against the known value of Dion Prestia.

Ultimately there is a frightening amount of uncertainty in the draft. For comparative purposes, look at the US college football system, which feeds the NFL. In university those players live the life of professional athletes for four years. They play in a series of wildly popular, televised, graded conferences, too, meaning recruiters can assess the very best against the very best. AFL recruiters, by contrast, need to examine Victorian players in the TAC Cup, then Western Australian boys playing in the lower quality WAFL Colts system, South Australian boys playing school football, or sometimes senior football, and then players from marginal football states.

The rules in junior football are also different from the AFL, which becomes a factor. Take the density rule, which demands that two players from each team are required inside each 50-metre arc at stoppages, along with an additional three in each forward half. The rule was created to alleviate congestion in junior football, to give the teenagers a chance to showcase their skills. "But it also means you don't get to see the key forwards and key backs using their endurance, because they don't need to," says Clarke. "In fact, they can't, because they have to stay in the arcs."

The US college system also has the advantage of teams with fierce rivalries desperately trying to beat one another. The collegiate competition there is a way of life—a quasi-religion. It is in their interest to play with ruthless defensive intent. In the AFL feeder teams there is little adherence to structure, and midfielders are often not tagged.

The biggest factor is age. NFL players enter the system at 22—fully matured. "I was at the Tampa Bay Buccaneers 18 months ago, and when I told them we draft kids who are 17 and 18, they just shook their head," Clarke says. "One guy laughed and actually called a friend over: 'Hey! This guy takes high school kids to play in the pros, all of them! How stupid's that?' But that's just our system."

Clarke has been in the recruiting game for around 16 years now, and has learned a few lessons. He cautions coaches when they say they don't want small midfielders, for instance, because he remembers how he once felt about Fremantle ball magnet Lachie Neale.

"He was one I thought was a really good player, but I had this little bird on my shoulder saying 'Nah, he's too small'. Rory Laird is the other one. They both got through every club in the draft, and were selected as rookies," he says. "Little boys who can't win contested footy are still a risk, but those boys could both win their own ball. And they've become All Australians."

Selections not working out as expected are harder but not impossible to reconcile. Clarke tries to be as analytical as he can. "You have to stick to your guns with the coaches, because you've often seen these players for years. But you also can't be a dog with a bone and just hang on thinking you're right when it's clearly not the case."

The biggest recruiting shift Clarke has noticed is the recent emphasis on character. Ten years ago, he says, talent outweighed most considerations, but the pathways are much stronger now and so the most skilled players tend to be pooled together early. In telling them apart, psychological analysis is crucial. The players do four different psychological tests and then Richmond has a consulting psychologist, Kim Stephens, examine those reports. Stephens attends 99 per cent of draftee interviews and is in fact on the road now, interviewing boys in Melbourne, Perth and Adelaide—maybe 25 home visits this month.

"We need to drag together their background. Who they are. Who their parents are. What environment they're in. What support network they have. Trying to predict what these boys are going to be is so difficult," Clarke says. "The game is so tough, we need to find out which guys can handle that—not just for a year or two but for a career. Resilience is huge."

They look of course at attributes and abilities—everything from decision-making to standing vertical reach—but endurance is the big one. It wasn't that long ago that players who had strong endurance had a big advantage over everyone else; now endurance is almost a given. "You *have* to be able to run. With the speed of the game and capped rotations, if they don't have legs they won't be able to survive."

Clarke is in many ways like a pathologist, examining specimens to determine how they came to be in front of him. Tracing where they came from is the only way to assess where they might be headed. "Have they played for a long time? Have they been in a pathway program? Have they had many pre-seasons? Did they come from another sport?"

A brawl breaks out on the field and he sees one player in the thick of the melee—not a black mark but noteworthy nonetheless. "There's Penrith on the bottom of it, which is not unusual," he says, smiling. "He likes to get involved in that stuff."

The game ends, the Jets beating the Knights by 16 points. For Clarke, that's one match down, two to go. Then he'll head home, thaw out, watch the Wallabies, get a decent sleep then hit the road early for a trip to Ballarat and another triple header. He'll spend Monday writing reports and adding notes to the Richmond database. It sounds exhausting but by this time of year, he says, it's simpler. Most players on their radar already have a few dozen reports written on them. Their GPS data, fitness testing results and personality profiling is in hand. Now all Clarke and his team must do is choose from a carefully narrowed pool.

"In this game, you've funnelled the 44 out there down to a few," he says. "Six months ago, at the start of the year, you're looking at everyone."

///////////

Three days later, five men sit in the list management room at Tigerland—the only group office within the football department. There's recruiting officer Luke Williams (who has previous experience at Geelong and Carlton), pro scout Nick Austin (who has also spent time at the Western Bulldogs and Port Adelaide), long-time Tigers recruiting chief Francis Jackson (now in a part-time role looking at future drafts), and head of player personnel and list management Blair Hartley (also from the Power, and the Bombers before that).

They've been spread all over the country this past weekend, from regional

Victoria to suburban Adelaide and outer Perth. This Tuesday morning meeting is a chance to share what they saw—who they liked and who they didn't.

There are also those they make allowances for—overlooking an obvious deficiency because of one convincing strength.

> *No footy IQ. But when the footy is in his area, he's powerful and can win at stoppage.*
>
> *Little run or flair. Despite all that, defensively he was really strong. Went back with the flight, showed courage.*
>
> *He can't run. The most running he did was for a rotation. But he is a beautiful kick. You can hear it—snap!*

They talk in depth about the households in which the players are raised—the overall circumstances of their lives—particularly when this is a concern. Their summations of character are precise but informative.

> *He's really introverted, but you sense he's just humble. You can't imagine him talking himself up.*
>
> *His dad was putting all sorts of pressure on him. He basically had a breakdown. You just sense he's carrying this weight.*
>
> *He's a solid kid. Works hard. He's not a dickhead at all.*
>
> *He's a naughty boy. A freak on the field—but you can't draft him.*

Their one line summations on football talent are even better—colloquial but incisive—creating a complete mind's eye picture of each player with a few quick words. Sometimes they are harsh and dismissive, because they must be.

> *The big boy? Not good enough. Can't run. Full liability on defence.*
>
> *He's got an electric cut and go—true flash.*
>
> *He's a conduit—he's not the bear in the square.*
>
> *Can't play in traffic—he's a tackle bag.*
>
> *So quick. Deadly over those short distances.*
>
> *He doesn't read the dirty ball. If it isn't in his lap, he can't get it.*
>
> *He's a big softy. When it gets really hard, he turns his toes up.*

For seemingly every player they have multiple inputs, too. Each man in the room has a considered offering, a rebuttal, something to note, something else to remember. One quotes his statistics. Another saw him play a week earlier.

One questions his listed height: *Has he grown that much since last year?* One recalls a moment: *You remember that goal in the first quarter against Western Australia?*

The walls of the room are covered in whiteboards with dozens of names on magnetised strips. One wall breaks them into positional roles. Another wall divides them up by League, including the smaller Division 2 teams of NSW, Tasmania, Queensland and the Northern Territory. Nine teams from Western Australia. Eight in South Australia. Six from Vic Metro, and six from Vic Country. Even the big schools in Melbourne are listed, from Carey to Xavier, Haileybury to Scotch.

The most important board is divided into three sections. The names in the bottom section are grouped under the heading "Late Rookie", the middle section are "Definite" and the top crop are "First Round".

They move magnets between these groups based on meetings like this. They discuss one player they have loved for a long time, for instance, who has just come back from injury. His stunning return performances have seen his stocks rise.

"He. Is. A. Beast," says Clarke, who watched him on the weekend. "He could have put an All Blacks jumper on and not looked out of place. He's massive—and has massive upside."

The others agree. And so Clarke stands, walks over to the whiteboard, picks up his magnet, and moves it from Definite to First Round.

///////////

B lair Hartley, in his office afterwards, says the point of having so many eyes on football fields around the country is not really about seeing more players in more places—no great players will go undiscovered. Of greater importance, he says, is having *different* eyes watching the *same* players. "It eliminates bias," he says. "It's a check and balance."

Hartley started in football at Essendon in 1999 as a part-time opposition analyst. He was 18 and had no idea what he was doing. He turned full-time in 2000, the year of the Bombers' last flag. Over time he moved into video analysis, game analysis, pro scouting, and helped run Essendon's VFL team.

The late Dean Bailey went to Port Adelaide and brought Hartley along. There he did opposition analysis, then became National Recruiting Manager, and stayed five years before Hardwick asked him to come to Richmond. He is now responsible for recruiting, trade, free agency and the draft. It's a big job, as he describes it: "The ins and outs of our list. Staying in touch with managers to find out who's in and out of contract across the competition. Having knowledge of player worth. Coming up with trades."

Tall players are a consideration right now. The form and fitness of Rance, Astbury and Grimes masks a relative lack of depth in the Richmond key defensive stocks, while up forward Riewoldt stands alone, and will be 29 going into the next season. Riewoldt needs a foil—but also a successor.

The Tigers have two first round picks in the draft, one of their own, and one courtesy of trading out Brett Deledio last season.

They might look for a tall target at the trade table. Or in the draft. Or rely on the nascent talent of their younger players. No decisions have yet been made, but Hartley nevertheless has scrawled on a board in his office the names of all the key forwards in the competition, and next to them the number they were taken in the draft.

Jack Riewoldt (13). Nick Riewoldt (1). Tom Lynch of the Suns (11). Tom Lynch of the Crows (13). Jon Patton (1). Tom Boyd (1). Josh Kennedy (4). Jarryd Roughead (2). Lance Franklin (5). The list goes on and on, and they are all low picks.

"With key forwards you don't get something for nothing," says Hartley. "There are certain places you go shopping for products, and you don't go to Savers (the recycle store) for tall forwards."

Another consideration is the form of young Paddy Naish, which is both a blessing and a complication. AFL Media draft guru Callum Twomey recently ranked Naish as high as Pick 10. Former Hawks champion and list manager Gary Buckenara—only today—ranked him as Pick 7. His strong form is a conundrum, which Clarke puts best: "We'd love to have him, but we just need to make sure we rate him appropriately. We can't get caught using our hearts and not our heads."

It is difficult for Hartley—for anyone in recruiting, for that matter—to digest the blunt external responses to their moves at the draft and trade table. Take the 2004 National Draft, and the top five picks—1. Brett Deledio, 2. Jarryd Roughead, 3. Ryan Griffen, 4. Richard Tambling, and 5. Lance Franklin—then consider the sheer column centimetres dedicated to dissecting the order of those selections, all done with 20-20 hindsight.

Yet every club has a top ten selection that didn't pan out. Melbourne has one (Cale Morton, Pick 4, 2007). The Western Bulldogs, too (Jarryd Grant, Pick 5, 2007). Port Adelaide (John Butcher, Pick 8, 2009), and the Gold Coast (Daniel Gorringe, Pick 10, 2010). Hawthorn is not immune (Mitch Thorp, Pick 6, 2006), nor Adelaide (John Meesen, Pick 8, 2004), Geelong (Kane Tenace, Pick 7, 2003), North Melbourne (David Trotter, Pick 9, 2003), or Essendon (Pick 10, Jason Laycock, 2002).

"The reality is it's an inexact science," says Hartley. "You're trying to make judgments on kids who are 17 years old. They come into clubs and all sorts of things can derail or divert a career: injury, death in the family, personal issues, clashes with coaches, homesickness," he says. "The scrutiny can take a toll on them, too, so it's really important for us to get around those players and make sure they're ready for the experience. It's part of why we judge character so closely now."

Looking at one selection in isolation also ignores the depth of changes on any AFL list—especially at Richmond. Hartley joined the Tigers at the beginning of 2010. From the entire 2009 list at the club, only four players remain. It is one of the most complete overhauls in football—only Brisbane has turned over more players in that time.

Hartley has a final thought on the nature of success in football—not just for teams but for individuals (including recruiters and scouts): choosing a player is one small part of the football program. Fitness staff, the medical team, welfare officers, development coaches and leadership programs all contribute. Often it is difficult even for insiders to tell which element has played a greater or lesser role, he says, yet the media, he says, have a "pass-fail attitude" to player selection. "They treat recruiting like a win-loss column, when it's really a long game. A long unpredictable game, affected by many, many factors."

The stakes are high, too. Hartley has in his memory a list of missed opportunities he would prefer to forget. He shakes his head now, thinking of the clearest example, from the 2007 draft when he was at Port Adelaide.

"Our last pick was 49. And we talked ourselves out of taking David Zaharakis as a bottom-age kid. I *loved* him. I went to his house and interviewed him. And the week leading into the trade period and the draft, I sat at home for three nights coding every single one of his kicks, and I ended up convincing myself that he needed to improve his kicking, and needed another year in the TAC Cup. No one drafted him. He improved so much that he went next year at Pick 23—we could have got him as cheaply as you want."

The biggest win he's been involved in was the selection of Robbie Gray. The brilliant, balanced forward was out of condition when Hartley (and the older and wiser Mick Moylan) first saw him. "But we delved in and found out he was working at a meat packing plant, and getting up at ridiculous hours, working all day, going to training at night, and his groins were gone. He was eating chicken parmigiana. He hadn't been through the academy or pathway system, and had no idea what he was doing. But there was one game where he played a little at half-back and went through the midfield, and *wow*. We walked away thinking there might be reasons *not* to pick him, but we wanted him anyway. We got him at Pick 55."

The information Hartley has at his disposal now is broader than it was then. He remembers visiting the New York Jets with Hayden Hill, and seeing how the NFL team had three software writers building their system. The Tigers haven't reached that level but the depth of information they possess is getting there. Every player, for instance, is rated on such traits and abilities as competitiveness, kicking, football smarts, football character, ball-handling, potential improvement, tackling, contested footy, uncontested footy, endurance, marking, leg speed, defensive intent, agility, and more.

Hartley brings up the file on Jack Graham, to show me how he rated in his draft pool last season. Endurance: fifth overall. Tackling: third. Ball-carrying: second. Contested footy: first. Competitiveness: first. "In this file, we can look at his psycho-motor testing, his family history, sporting history, his education history, his employment history, his psych reports, his stats from every game."

They have such reports for every player they might consider taking, whether the first pick in the national draft or the last choice in the rookie draft. All that is left is to make a choice. "And so, we sit and we argue. For hours," he says, smiling. "It's good fun."

39

CHEST TO CONTEST

I t is mid-morning on a Friday, two days before Richmond's final home and away game of the 2017 season, against St Kilda at the MCG. More than likely, it will be the veteran Nick Riewoldt's last game for the Saints.

In the Graeme Richmond Auditorium at Tigerland, Blake Caracella gives the group his key messages about the Saints—about connection, and working from contest to contest, and one other thing: against this team, they must move the ball off the line. Go lateral, go short, and go quickly. "Limited risk, and we gain 20 metres while bringing the ball more central, into space. We are the best running team in the comp. Speed all over the place," he says. "Long down the line is our last option."

Ben Rutten wants the Tigers to watch out for St Kilda players streaming past for handballs: to get in the way of these "trailers" at every opportunity; put a bumper bar on them, run them down, corner them, blitz'em. His most important point is to counter the Saints' strength as intercept markers. He shows an edit of their captain, Jarryn Geary, running into a gap and taking an uncontested chest mark between two sets of wrestling talls. "What's your responsibility here, Butts? *Stop. Him. Jumping.* Worry about your ground stuff later—we *must* bring that ball to deck."

Justin Leppitsch, in his inimitable comedic style, conveys to the players that they must run hard toward goal, to make the St Kilda forwards accountable. He jokes that the Saints won't do the running required to keep up. "Membrey won't do it. Billings won't do it. Riewoldt—*maybe it runs in the family*—won't do it. Gresham—*he'll be off writing a novel*—won't do it. We took 20 uncontested marks inside 50 against them last time, in a smashing, and it's because of this. We equalise, and we'll get nice open shots."

The best presentation of the day though is given by Andrew "Mini" McQualter, the stoppages coach and former St Kilda utility. He has two messages for winning the all-important contested ball on Sunday, and they are written in big blue capital letters on the whiteboard: FIGHT and CHEST TO CONTEST.

"These are the most important things this week," he says. "What do you think I mean by FIGHT?"

Shane Edwards answers: "Fight through the tackle."

"Correct," says McQualter. "We don't want to go through their hands. They will bring pressure from all angles. They'll spoil kicks. They'll smother handballs."

He shows an example, of Melbourne half-back Michael Hibberd, surrounded by four Saints. Not one of them sits off the Demon. Instead they converge at once, laying a group tackle. It is their method, and McQualter sees it as an opportunity.

"They want to hunt the ball. They want to hunt the man," he says. "So, what's Hibberd's responsibility? He must fight through these tackles, knowing there will be people to help on the outside. Give me an example of how you fight through these tackles Oleg (Markov)…"

Arms up.

"Yep."

Step through.

"Yep."

Drive the legs.

"Yep."

Side step laterally.

"Yep."

Sell a story.

"Yep."

Cotchin has a point to make, and so offers a question to the room: "What's the worst-case scenario?" he asks. "When we fight?"

Shane Edwards answers: "We get tackled."

Cotchin: "And if we get caught holding the ball, is the turnover slow or is it fast?"

Edwards: "Slow."

The moment the players are describing right now is instantly recognisable to any football fan. A player absorbs a tackle, knows he is caught, goes tumbling to earth and allows a pile on to begin. The player is then slow to get up, and slow to release the ball. Perhaps he leaves it on the ground and hovers over it—or maybe he clings to the ball and rises at a glacial pace, turning and tossing it back with a loopy underarm throw. He does this because every half second counts. Because if those half seconds add up to three or four or five *full* seconds, then every Tiger on the field can run 25 metres or more into position, into their niche within a structured defence.

As a single play, a free kick against the Tigers for holding the ball might look like a morale-sapping moment, but the players know it is far, far better than an errant, panicked handball that ends in the waiting arms of a fast-moving opponent. McQualter loves that his players understand this. "Yes," he says, nodding. "We want to be willing to cop some holding the balls this week. Absolutely. We cannot afford to cough the ball up. You've got to be really strong and fight through these situations."

This is also where CHEST TO CONTEST is relevant. If both teams have seven players around a given contest, for example, and four Saints run at one Tiger, logically there will be three Tigers only a few steps away. "They might collapse in on you from all sides," says McQualter. "Which means if we fight through, we will find someone on the outside."

The three remaining Tigers on the outside, however, must be involved in the contest, or *ready* to be involved. McQualter shows a handful of clips now from the flogging delivered to Richmond by St Kilda last time they met, and in each clip he freezes the frame, and points to Tiger players on the periphery. To the untrained eye there is little to see. But look closer and you notice that one Tiger is sneaking goal side. Another has turned towards his opponent. Another is running parallel to the ball, in the direction he hopes it will move. None has his body turned to directly face the ball. None has CHEST TO CONTEST.

"Look at this, where are we?" says McQualter. "We're off to the races. We're not on the job. So if we don't win this contest, good luck defending the turnover. That was us last time. But we can fix that."

He shows clips now that illustrate what he is after—edits from subsequent games, after the club addressed that issue and began training it every week. "Look at this, the ball hits the deck and we *adjust*, we change our body angle. We hold. We are much, *much* better at this now. We've coached it, you've trained it, you know it."

He shows another clip, and freezes the frame again to point to all the players with their eyes and body focused on the football. A Richmond player fights through the tackle, and there are yellow and black guernseys all around to help.

"That's how we want to play. When the ball is in dispute, we've got numbers in the TV screen," he says. "Numbers in the TV screen—that's what we want our fans to see. We're already better prepared for this. It stacks up. Doesn't it?"

⁓⁓⁓⁓

It is Sunday, 3:20pm, and the AFL ladder is in flux. If the Tigers win, they will finish third, with the all-important double chance in finals, and will likely play Geelong at the MCG in a qualifying final. If they lose, they will finish sixth and likely play an Elimination Final against Essendon—an old rival in a cut-throat game.

The Richmond coaches and players tell waiting media what they have told them all week—all season, really—that the results around them do not matter. They are right. Their fate is in their own hands.

But still, 90 minutes before the bounce, the coaches sit in their briefing room beneath the arena, watching the Bombers play the Dockers, knowing a Bombers victory will knock the Saints out of the finals—removing the greatest motivation of all for the Saints to win today.

"What about an eight-goal third quarter from Essendon?" asks Peter Burge. "That's the best-case scenario."

"Yep," says Hayden Hill. "A few St Kilda boys in the rooms knowing they won't play finals could be handy."

They also talk about West Coast, and how the Eagles need to win by 25 points at home against the Crows to sneak into the finals. The Adelaide captain and full-forward (Taylor Walker) and full-back (Daniel Talia) are already out. The Crows don't need to win either—they have first place and a home final secured. Hardwick jokes that the Eagles should play a debutant, and tell him to hit a few key Crows, just to make things easier.

The coaches love these moments before the game, when small talk takes over. It means they're prepared. It means every contingency plan has been formulated, and every decision ratified. It means they can waffle on in comfort about short studs versus long, and how in their day they used the pre-game warm up to sprint and jump and test the turf with twists and hard cuts. It means when someone says the word "cut", that they can remember that episode of *The Simpsons* in which Homer is a pee-wee football coach, and relishes the process of cutting his players. The coaches now re-enact the scene, one by one delivering the lines they have memorised.

Leppitsch: "Now it's time for the easiest part of any coach's job. The cuts. I wasn't able to cut everyone, but I have cut a lot of you."

Hardwick: "Steven, I like your hustle. That's why it was so hard to cut you."

Livingstone: "Congratulations, the rest of you made the team."

Hardwick: "Except you, you and you."

Leppitsch: "The rest of you can hit the showers. Rod, you don't have to. You're cut."

They carry that smiling sense of calm throughout the entire pre-game schedule, through line meetings and individual meetings and the coach's address. Today the A3 picture on the whiteboard is two pairs of RM Williams boots, old and new, and the message is about "preparation", and all the little things you need to do to put the shiny new boots on without sustaining bloody great blisters—and there are more jokes and caring smiles and impassioned pleas to enjoy the day, enjoy each other, and enjoy the game.

///////////

The game begins and the afternoon sun is high and bright. The curved blade of the grandstand roof leaves an arc of shade over half the field, and into the other half sprints Nick Riewoldt on a long run, near the end of a career built on long runs. His blond hair catches the glow from above and his predominantly white uniform is almost iridescent. If his Saints lose today, this will be his 336th and final game of League football.

Tributes have flowed for him all week, the words of former player and columnist Timothy Boyle perhaps the best, describing Riewoldt as one who took the game too seriously but knew this about himself, and one who made a career of exhausting himself again and again and again. His piece quoted retiring Bulldogs captain Bob Murphy: "I always thought of him as a giant, pumping heart on horse legs, willing himself to the ball again and again to satisfy a deep sense of hunger in his soul. It was intimidating to witness up close."

The first kick to the long blond Saint goes out on the full. The second lands at his feet. The third is too high – lofted and slow and simple to spoil. It is his day but it is not. By the end of the first quarter Richmond is three goals in front and the rain is sheeting down, and Essendon has beaten Fremantle, and so St Kilda has nothing left to play for but pride—and for the outgoing champion with the number 12 on his back.

Richmond extend its lead, and the Saints look lively only once, as they fight through the third quarter, switching the play, streaming past for handballs, kicking three goals and clogging every Tiger thrust for just one against the flow. Early in the final quarter, the Tigers lead by 24 points, and something strange happens.

The crowd at the Punt Road end of the ground stands and claps and cheers, despite there being nothing of note to applaud. It is the work of a social media meme, circulated on Twitter amongst Richmond fans, with a plan to send a message to Dustin Martin that he is loved, and that his fans are desperate for him to stay with the club. The idea was simple: cheer for number four in the fourth minute of the fourth quarter.

And so that minute arrives, and they do, and it feels contrived, hokey even, and then something serendipitous happens. Martin steps into the moment. As they chant his name in the cheer squad, he bustles and gathers and fends, and then curls a banana through the goals, sapping energy from St Kilda and snapping any illusion of resistance.

He attends the next centre bounce, too, and seizes the Sherrin from Cotchin on the wing, and he could easily handball over the top of the player in front of him, or kick long, but instead he storms past Dylan Roberton, pushing him away as though he were no obstacle at all, and with the outside of his boot he chips lightly and deftly into the arms of Jacob Townsend, who calmly converts. With a 38-point lead, the game is won. Martin leaves the field and by the time he reaches the bench, the Olympic Stand has become one big tiered standing ovation. The crowd is 69,104 but it feels like more.

Richmond wins by 41 points, and Nick Riewoldt is chaired off the ground by team mate Josh Bruce, and his cousin Jack Riewoldt. Martin wins the Ian Stewart Medal for best on ground, and is presented with the award in the change rooms afterward.

Standing nearby is a quiet player, who has just kicked five goals, after kicking six goals the week before. His name is Jacob Townsend.

He grew up in Leeton, near Wagga Wagga in NSW, and played Rugby Union as a child. That's how he tackles, too. He was preselected by the GWS Giants in 2011, and played a handful of games in four seasons there. Kevin Sheedy thought he was the toughest player on their list, and that is why he was brought to Richmond in October two years earlier—as a bullocking midfielder. The club posted a video of his highlights at that time. A nervous goal. A clumsy mark. A few snaps. A few clearances. And then the video turns to his real strength—his attack on the ball and the man. The commentators tell the story of each simple play.

Look at Townsend! Hard head. Tough as they come.
Townsend likes to tackle—brilliant!
Gee he likes it rough.
Fantastic tackle!
Big tackle!
Thumping tackle!

But playing senior football at Richmond didn't come easily. Last pre-season every player was given an assessment, with a positive "green" summation and a negative "red" summation. Townsend's green: *Attack on the ball.* Townsend's red: *Do you think you really belong here?*

As then assistant coach Brendon Lade said at the time, Townsend has (or had) enormous self-doubt. "People need to get around him and reinforce the positive," Lade said. "He's one of those guys who needs it."

None of this is surprising. In 2016, Townsend played only four senior games. In 2017, until a fortnight ago, he had played none but was on the cusp, brought up as a subject of discussion in the coaches' match review. Townsend had been dominating at VFL level—so much so that by the end of the season he would win the Liston Medal for the best player in that competition. He had worked on everything asked of him by the coaching staff. High-speed running. GPS numbers. Tackling. Offensive manoeuvres. Marking. Goalkicking.

He texted McQualter that week with a simple, plaintive message: *What more can I do?* Hardwick nodded. He understood. "The hard thing is, Jacob needs to see himself the way we see him," says Hardwick. "More like Caddy than Cotchin."

As fate would have it, a hamstring injury to Caddy is ultimately what it took for Townsend to get his chance. He was brought in for his first game of the season against the Dockers, to win the footy but also curb the influence of Michael Johnson, and then to do the same against the Saints, this time muting Jake Carlisle.

He stands now in the rooms, muddied and bruised, happy to have done his job on the tall Saint. "He's a big man. He moved me around like a rag doll," Townsend says. "But that was my job. Just to stop him from going for his marks—play on the best third-man-in marking player. Then when the ball comes to ground, try to out-pressure them and get my hands on the ball."

It is clear as he speaks that Townsend has a stutter. He always has. It stops him from speaking his mind in meetings, or even chatting casually with friends. Most of the time he knows he will stutter before he speaks, and so he does not speak.

His wrist is wrapped in strapping tape, and on it are the words *Anchor* and *Next mom* and *Work*. They are his key word prompts from mindfulness training sessions with Emma Murray. "It's all about staying in the game," he says. "They're the words I need whenever I'm drifting."

Anchor is a reminder to centre himself with big deep breaths, and a lift of the shoulders. *Next mom* means next moment: "Because if you're thinking about the past, you're not thinking about what's next." The final word, *Work*, is the bedrock of his game, and always has been.

He leaves to stretch now, but not before giving his mum and dad, Denise and Peter, a hug. The pair had planned this trip to Melbourne for a month. Until recently, Townsend was unsure if he would be given a new contract, and in fact had begun looking for a suitable apprenticeship placement, turning his gaze from a career in football to one on building sites. His parents booked this trip assuming they would be here to see his last ever VFL game.

"Instead we're here watching him in the ones, kicking five goals," says his mum, almost crying. "I can't believe it."

"We're so impressed with his determination," adds his father. "He hasn't given up. He's just stuck in there, hung in there. He's taken his chance. We're just very proud of him."

"We've been proud of him since he was born though," says his mum, sniffing.

"He's never disappointed us," says his dad. "Never given us a day of grief."

"We just feel so happy for him," adds mum, beaming. "So happy."

///////////

Hardwick is happy, too. He congratulates his players. They have finished third on the ladder, inside the top four. He tells them this is something the club has not achieved in 16 years. He says it was based on hard work, on setting standards, paying the price in pre-season and reaping the rewards now.

"This side sitting in front of me has got pure grit," he says. "Not many other sides have gone through what you've gone through this year. Too small. Not good enough. Can't win big games. Or close games. You know what? You've proved them all wrong."

He says they have perseverance and resilience, and that these are traits in common with teams that go all the way.

"You play for each other. You play for the fans. You've been nothing short of sensational," he says. "As a coaching group we can't be more proud of you."

But, he concludes, the journey is just starting. It is exciting, he says.

So be excited.

"I don't want you to hide from it—I want you to embrace it. When you walk down the street, love it—enjoy all the energy. And when we're back in our four walls," he says, slapping the cinderblock wall of the briefing room, "we get to work."

40

ALL FOR ONE

I t is 8:30am on Thursday, August 31, when the Tigers meet for the first time after the end of the home and away season. The players have all enjoyed a three-day break, and are ready to work towards a Qualifying Final against Geelong in eight days' time.

But first, the room applauds Dustin Martin and Alex Rance, for their selection in the All Australian team the night before. Rance was named captain, and while it might sound unlikely for a full-back to be named skipper, West Coast defender Darren Glass did receive that same honour as recently as 2012. Credit given, they move on to nominations for the Francis Bourke Award.

The players do this every week—openly recognising candidates for the acts they perform on and off the field. People might imagine that awards selected "by the players" tend to involve macro-level anonymous voting at season's end, but in fact they routinely examine and discuss little gestures and deeds, always of a selfless nature.

Jake Batchelor says Steven Morris is worthy. Batchelor sat in the VFL coach's box on the weekend and was shocked by how hard Morris ran in all directions, and by what it produced. "His ability to turn a one-vs-two against us into a two-vs-two, or a one-vs-one into a two-vs-one—out of pure work rate and speed, getting from contest to contest—was just so noticeable."

Cotchin speaks next. He has two nominations, the first for Martin.

The way the star midfielder began the final quarter against St Kilda, he says, determined the way the entire team played that quarter. "I know he's been doing that all year, but that's why I love playing with him."

Jack Graham was Cotchin's other standout. The first-year player had an astonishing 70 pressure points for the second week in a row. (The AFL average is 43.) "You're not going to be left out of too many games at senior level bringing that kind of intent."

Riewoldt puts winger Kamdyn McIntosh up for recognition, for protecting Jacob Townsend. Townsend battled St Kilda defender Jake Carlisle all day, and then in a tackle on the wing found the tall Saint's forearm in his face. "And Kamdyn has come sprinting in and manhandled Carlisle to get him off Towna. To run in from so far away to take care of your mate—that's a pure team act."

Rance had two examples of "fight" that he wants to highlight. One was Nathan Broad, who was unhappy with Saints champion Nick Riewoldt after a contest, and showed him as much. "I just love that you flew the flag," Rance says. "I love seeing blokes stand up for themselves."

The second was a mental fight. Dylan Grimes lost his boots during the week—a pair made with custom orthotics. Rance says you might scoff, but he was impressed that the once injury-prone Grimes just strapped up his ankles and played as he always does. "He played another cracking game. I just think that's a sign of mental resilience."

Rance has one more person to note—not a nomination but praiseworthy nonetheless—for Craig McRae, and the demeanour of the VFL coach when he sits on the AFL bench—remaining calm and letting the players be, even when frustrated. "I know I was pretty filthy when I got dragged for running forward and being undisciplined. I was fuming, and you calmed me down and I really appreciate that calm you bring to the bench. It's not always a word—it can just be that hand on the shoulder that brings us back."

Morris nominates first-year forward Shai Bolton, and the strides he has made in recent weeks at VFL level. Morris has been "blown away" by the defensive edge to Bolton's game. "There's been a massive spike in that area of his game. His game is so far above the level it's not funny. Not really kicking goals—just putting people in better spots. It's that Spurs mentality."

The Spurs reference goes back to a film Hardwick showed the playing group during the season, about the San Antonio Spurs basketball team in the

NBA. The short documentary was called "The Beautiful Game", and centred on a share-the-ball mentality that produced a championship-winning team. The Spurs saw greatness in making your teammate great.

Their best was not bombastic dunks, or long range jumpers that fall like water, but the humble act of passing. The ball simply moved from Spur to Spur to Spur with electric speed, without touching the floor, leaving opponents flat-footed, rooted to the spot, chasing an orange blur with their eyes, heads swivelling as they succumbed to a thoroughly unglamorous but devastating mode of play.

Led by revered coach Gregg Popovich—and players including Tim Duncan, Manu Ginobili and Tony Parker—the Spurs were notable for their willingness to sacrifice gaudy individual statistics in the name of the team. Their mantra: "Pass up a good shot if a teammate is open for a great shot."

The players at Richmond took this to heart. They adopted the philosophy as their credo. In the change rooms before games, blank spaces on the walls between lockers are now filled with laminated pictures of Spurs players, and none of them are shooting from the perimeter or enjoying hang time en route to the basket—they are passing and tipping and setting screens. This is how Richmond wants to play.

Josh Caddy mentions that 'Spurs mentality', too, in his praise for Jason Castagna—remembering the small forward charging forward into space but handballing over an opponent to a loose Tiger in the goal square: "He could have blazed away and had a shot, but the composure he showed, early in the game, set the standard for the day."

Embracing the Spurs credo is not the first time the team has taken cues from other codes this season. The playing group also watched "Chasing Great", about All Blacks champion Richie McCaw, and constantly refer to his calculated menace and uncompromising desire. They love the bluntness of his quest—his straightforward rejection of any half steps or lapses in commitment.

Hardwick also found wisdom in the message of NFL coach Jon Gruden, whose Tampa Bay Buccaneers won the 2002 Super Bowl. He showed the playing group a documentary on their victory—"America's Game"—narrated by the Hollywood actor Laurence Fishburn. The Buccaneers were a club a lot like Richmond, possessing a powerfully unenviable history of recent failure and humiliation; decades of disappointment, in fact. The year they finally won was the season in which they adopted a new philosophical ideal: "POUND THE ROCK".

The term represents the constancy it takes to wear an opponent down. It was a favourite catch phrase of Popovich and the Spurs, too, but Gruden went as far as to bring a 35-kilogram slab of granite into the team locker room, as a visual aid and reminder. Hardwick did the same thing this year, too, having Giuseppe Mamone lug a lump of stone the size of a basketball down the highway to Geelong in Round 21. He brought it into the briefing room before the game that day, and let it sit on a table in front of the players. Although the presence of the prop didn't have the desired effect—Richmond lost by 14 points—the concept nonetheless lives on within the group.

The coaches and players may not know it, but "Pound the Rock" did not come to light 15 years ago with an NFL coach in Florida. It was the work of a Danish-American journalist and photographer named Jacob Riis, who documented the tenement slums of New York City in the nineteenth century. "The Stonecutters Credo" was a statement attributed to Riis, about the laborious and at times seemingly fruitless grind of social activism. He said that when nothing seemed to help, he would go and look at a stonecutter hammering away at a rock perhaps a hundred times, without so much as a crack for his reward.

"Yet at the hundred and first blow it will split in two and I know it was not that blow that did it, but all that had gone before".

////////////

The clubs turns to new media for new inspiration constantly, and they do so again today. In the theatrette Paul Wiegard, managing director of the Madman Production Company, is introduced. Madman produced the films Kenny (2006) and Animal Kingdom (2010). Wiegard walked here this morning from his office in the old Pelaco shirt building in Richmond, to show the team his latest documentary, in the hope that something might resonate.

"All for One" is the story of the Orica GreenEdge cycling team, shot over five years and built from 4000 hours of footage at European races including the Tour de France and the Giro d'Italia. It won the audience award for best documentary at the Melbourne International Film Festival this year.

"It's about trying to establish who they are, and what they stand for, and how they compete," Wiegard tells the room. "What are the things that connect and help build team culture."

The players step out for a few minutes to hit the bathroom, gather water bottles and a cushion or two. Half a dozen players walk back into the auditorium with bean bags, then recline freely in the darkness at the front of the room, on the floor beneath the screen. They settle into the quiet space, and Wiegard speaks again. Many documentaries, he says, are made to investigate and demonise—to find an abuse of power, or look for the things that drag people apart.

"Rather than focus on the black spot on a white page, we wanted to look for the things that bring people together," he says. "What was their group DNA? There's all manner of metaphors and parallels here for your professional careers. Hopefully in the next 90 minutes we can also extract a few 'man tears' out of you."

And indeed, as the film delves into the biographies of the riders and the team that supports them, players and coaches do wipe at their eyes. They laugh a lot, too. As they meet each cyclist, whether culture drivers like Simon Gerrans or work horses like Svein Tuft, they see a little of themselves. They see colonels in charge of the team. They see unglamorous role players. They see players recruited who might seem a risk physically, but who embody the desired values of the group. They see team members coming together slowly, feeling one another out, faking unity until they find a groove then finally form a connection that becomes tribal.

They love the little Colombian hill climber, Esteban Chaves, whose interviews are often subtitled to make up for his pidgin English, but who always presents as funny, relaxed, full of life and humour and love in the face of misfortune, isolation and horrific physical pain. "Enjoy the ride. Enjoy the day," he says in his singsong South American accent. "Because you never know what will happen."

The players applaud and then go into rotations and gym work and eventually training on Punt Road Oval. Immediately following their departure, Hardwick stands with Tim Livingstone, Dan Richardson, Ben Crowe, Shane McCurry and Craig McRae. Hardwick thinks they should use the film in a few leadership and culture sessions in the coming weeks—to tease out its themes and messages, and let them filter through.

"Did you notice that word in there?" asks Crowe. "Grit".

"I heard a beautiful line," adds McCurry. "Something like 'We're cyclists, we're athletes, we're humans'."

"And all those setbacks," says Richardson. "The blood and the sadness, but the humour."

"They celebrated life, celebrated imperfections," says Hardwick. "That's us."

Later, the players discuss their key takeaways, too.

Shaun Grigg sees in the Orica GreenEdge team the Spurs mentality made manifest yet again: "They recruited blokes who fit the culture," he says, "just like us."

Caddy says he loved the way they enjoyed one another: "We have a good time, at the right times," he says. "We have a laugh, but we flick that switch and work hard."

Grimes liked the way the riders did everything they could to make life easier on their leaders: "That's us—we value our roles so much," he says. "We do what's required in our bubble to make it easier for someone else."

Cotchin focused on the diversity of the team, in race and age and personality: "They're a team with all different backgrounds, and they embrace it. I love that about our group. We're all different and we enjoy that for what it is."

Riewoldt noted the way they celebrate: "They talked about the yellow race leader's jersey, and how there's something special about yellow. It rang true for me. There is something special about our jumper, too."

Rance recalls the story of one rider, who fronted up after breaking his arm, to ride in the most brutal sprint race of the season, and won: "He did something he had never done before, because he had the evidence in his training that he could do it," he says. "A lot of players here in this room have never played in a final, but we've got the evidence that we can perform."

David Astbury applauds the way the riders weren't segregated by experience: "We've allowed the young guys to express themselves as much as they can—and they've brought an energy to the group that's crucial. That's essentially what Esteban did."

McRae, too, valued what Chaves brought to that group—even that beaming, gigantic grin clad in big steel braces. He sees the same thing in more than a handful of young players at Richmond. It reminds him of the book "How to win friends and influence people", and a factoid he clings to every now and then, when thinking about the best teams.

"You know the number one thing that influences people?" McRae asks. "Smiling."

⁄⁄⁄⁄⁄⁄⁄⁄⁄⁄

Hours later, Brendon Gale sits in the beer garden of the London Tavern on Lennox Street in Richmond, nursing a lemon, lime and bitters, and picking at a steak sandwich. It is the eve of finals, the eve of spring, and he wears sunglasses. He never really spent much time at this Tigers local, even as a player. When he was Richmond's centre half-forward (rather than now, as CEO) he was too recognisable to front up to the bar, but he would love to know what the place is like during a big Richmond fixture.

"They reckon when we beat Sydney in the last game of 2014, to make the finals, the guys working here were just scared. It was this mass of civil unrest and euphoria, the hordes taking to the streets," he says. "Part of me would like to experience that. A day of drinking pots and being a supporter."

He talks now about what he sees as the greatest transformation at Richmond this season, but, for the sake of context, explains what it was like 12 months ago. "Put yourself in the environment of last year. The club's under siege. By early July, the season was gone. People were worried about their jobs. Media speculation ramped up about who's going to get the sack. So, we decided to hold up a mirror and take a look. You're looking for answers. You're looking to make certainties out of uncertainty."

The now famous football department review, supported by Ernst & Young, was well underway months before its existence was made public. They knew they had an issue, but equally they knew it wasn't talent, or fitness, or facilities. "It was our lack of connection," Gale says now. "Between our coaches. Our players. And perhaps more importantly, our player leaders with our coaches."

Gale says it slowly became clear that the club had not placed enough value on relationships. "Have you heard that saying, 'People don't buy what you do—they buy why you do it'?"

This is a famous marketing line. It was uttered by British motivational speaker Simon Sinek in a 2009 TED Talk titled "How Great Leaders Inspire Action". It is the third most popular TED Talk of all time and has been viewed more than 33 million times.

"I think a few years ago we knew who we were, what we were and why we were a little better. We were the jumper. We were yellow and black. Chris Newman led that, and we drifted from that idea," he says. "I think we lost a sense of purpose. But the good thing was that once we sat down, landed the helicopter and said, 'This is what we've found out', it felt like confirmation. It was like the footy guys were going to arrive at that conclusion themselves, but the review helped."

Earlier in the year Gale made a wistful off-hand remark about his admiration for Western Bulldogs coach Luke Beveridge. It was only a few months after their premiership, and Gale was enamoured with the way the Dogs seemed to play for the coach, and for one another, with an affection bordering on platonic love. It made Gale envious. The quirk of the 2017 season then is that Richmond's narrative has unfolded in such a similar style. People outside the club have noticed the high-pressure game plan, the small forward line and the premiership drought, but they haven't noticed that other quality that Gale keeps returning to, and what he saw in the Bulldogs: connection.

"The AFL environment is very competitive. It's dog eat dog. And our club is a tough club to be involved with, because there's such huge interest in our ups and the downs. We wanted to say to our guys 'You can be who you want to be, and be supported and be trusted'."

Perhaps the most interesting facet of the cultural shift at Tigerland is its deliberate and methodical nature. Stories of cultural revolution in clubland tend to follow an almost accidental plotline—always as if by luck or fate. Think of the dynastic Cats and you think of a timely alignment of stars and club leaders, with Bartel and Kelly and Johnson and Ablett brought together in a single draft (2001). Think of Sydney and you think of a solitary uncompromising leader around whom all will orbit, in the form of Stuart Maxfield, and the Bloods culture he created for all Swans since to follow.

But with Richmond the shift was premeditated and planned. They brought in a professional mentor (Crowe), a new leadership and culture expert (McCurry) and then ramped up their mindfulness training program (Murray). Backed by key pillars of influence including Gale, Hardwick and Cotchin, the rest of the club simply fell into line. The process was not organic but organised—not fortuitous but forensic.

Even cracking Hardwick open was choreographed. It was Gale who offered to send the coach late last year to Harvard University, for a week-long course on "authentic leadership". Gale has studied there, too, and sensed that Hardwick would derive something of meaning—some quiet contemplation or introspection—just from his time in Boston, walking Cambridge Common and Harvard Square and along the Charles River. But Hardwick was reluctant. He wanted to visit a range of professional American sporting clubs.

"That just sums up his mindset back then," said Gale. "He was a little defensive last year. The coach was coaching but he wasn't really present because he wasn't fully present. But he changed his mind. Dimma's always been a really curious thinker. He's got an insatiable appetite to learn. I knew he could go and learn more about game plans or preparation, but his next true voyage really was self discovery: 'It's about you—about understanding and unleashing the power of you'."

By the time the beginning of the 2017 season was upon the club, says Gale, an eerie calm had enveloped Punt Road Oval. "I remember the week before round one, sitting, having a beer on a Friday night with Dimma and just saying 'Mate, there's something wrong with me, because I've never felt so composed on the way into a season'. Dimma said he felt the same way. Dan Richardson, too. We were just … relaxed."

Gale would be telling fibs if he said he thought then they could finish in the top four. Last year was, after all, not The Year of the Tiger but an undeniable year of horror. It was, perhaps, the season Richmond had to have.

"Maybe it was important and instructive for our mob to go through that, to know we didn't meet expectations," he says. "But you don't shit yourself. You don't start making rash, kneejerk responses. You go again, and you hold the line."

41

IT CARRIES YOU ALONG

Four years ago, Nick Vlastuin was the subject of a feature article that was almost 5000 words long. It was written by Emma Quayle, an award-winning football writer at The Age and now a recruiter with the GWS Giants. The piece was one of five, each examining a full season in the life of a footballer, and each one had a label. "The Veteran", for instance, or "The Star", or "The Young Gun".

Vlastuin was "The Debutant", and his debut season—2013—ended in an elimination final against Carlton at the MCG. The article ended shortly before that game, however, with a hopeful quote from the young defender.

> "It's going to be the biggest game in my life. It's going to be the hardest game, the most competitive game. Things will happen that I haven't been through before, I'd say. It's like everything that's happened up until now doesn't really matter. I think I'm going to like it."

He didn't like it, as it turned out. Not after what happened. Not after the Tigers had allowed a 32-point lead to become a 20-point loss in front of 94,690 people. But the quote was accurate in other ways. It *was*, then, the biggest game of his life. "It was so loud," he says now, sitting downstairs at Tigerland, one day before a Qualifying Final against Geelong. "I remember running out, and looking around in the initial warm up. It felt like the ground was literally shaking. Pretty cool."

He's also right that the game was one of the hardest. He knew it would be, going into the match battling the slight but persistent ache of hamstring soreness. "The plan was to be subbed out at half-time, but Reece Conca tore his hamstring off the bone in the first ten minutes. I was struggling near the end of the game," he says. "Carlton had started rolling the dice, and sometimes that pays off. We really stopped playing."

Playing was different then. It is now almost five years since he was drafted (Pick 9, 2012) and he is a crucial cog in the Richmond defence— an interceptor with perfect balance in the air, who flies for marks without looking to see what or who is around him. On the ground, he repels the ball in straight lines, picking gaps in oncoming traffic and hitting the seams of packs, breaking them open at their binding. In his early years in the League, however, Vlastuin felt constantly fatigued, shot in both his muscles and his mind. He was far from cocksure, physically.

"I remember my first year, after 13 or 14 games you were pretty much done. You wanted the year to end. Second year, you push it out to 16 or 17 games. This year is different. I'm older, and I had 10 weeks off in the middle of the year with injury, so the body is fresh[15]. Mentally you're getting a bit tired, but it's finals, so you suck it up."

Four years ago, he was also unsure of his place in the side. Hardwick has since taken to pointing out Vlastuin in front of the group, extolling his virtues and saying "That's why this bloke is one of the first magnets picked every week". But Vlastuin still has selection nerves, still questions himself after a poor play or a quiet game.

"I've always been a really harsh self-critic. Even at the start of this year I doubted my spot. I was playing in midfield and rotating through half-back, and you would get switched around, and as they flip you you're wondering 'Did I get switched because I'm not playing well?' And then you go back, and you need to reset your mind to defending again."

Externally, Tiger fans suspect that Vlastuin—who was drafted as a midfielder—is champing at the bit to play on the ball, and being held back from some stifled ambition to follow the Sherrin into tight skirmishes at centre bounces. But perhaps they are projecting, because Vlastuin loves

---

15 In Vlastuin's first season, he made his debut in Round 5, and then missed only two matches, through injury. In 2014, he played 20 of 23; in 2017, he was injured in Round 7 with a fractured scapula, and would not resume until round 17.

defence. "I just want to help out my teammates, to be honest. I'd rather get someone else a goal than kick the goal myself," he says. "I want my team to have trust in me. I want to create two-on-ones by work rate, to help a teammate out, to make his day that little bit better. That's what I want to be known for—not being 'hard' or 'composed' or anything like that. That stuff doesn't matter."

Vlastuin used to retreat inside his shell at the club, particularly in those early seasons. He was scared to talk to senior players. Now he is confident in the environment. He has a kind of carefree grace. He has a gigantic bushy red beard, which makes him look like a character from Game of Thrones—the Wildling warrior, Tormund Giantsbane. He gets that a lot. Comfortable in his own skin, he now tries to pass that on to the younger players around him.

"Jack Graham made his debut in Perth a few weeks ago, and that was the same ground where I made my debut. So, I tried to take him under my wing a bit, tried to relax him. Told him AFL's easier than the VFL in some ways, because if you play your role and everyone else does as well, you don't have to make things up. If you're in the right spot you'll get the ball, because people aren't going to stuff up their kicks as often. I just tried to keep his confidence up as well, because we all know he's going to be a good player—it's just whether he believes it or not."

Vlastuin recognises that he needs to perform this kind of role, because he has the talent and respect to make any small sermon stick—and because the time is right. "I'm in my fifth year at the club now, and when I got here Cotch was in his fifth year, and he was captain. Looking at that, I can't hide. I don't have an excuse not to lead."

For the first three years of his career, Vlastuin lived at home, in the outer suburb of Eltham, with his parents. Then he moved to South Yarra where he lived with Western Bulldogs forward Tom Boyd. The pair had played together for Vic Metro in under-18s. Now he is in Albert Park with Corey Ellis. Moving out was the right call.

"I just like my freedom. Mum used to ask me so many questions, and she doesn't know that much about footy. She might ask what drills we did at training, but it'd be impossible to explain even if I tried. The traffic, getting back to Eltham, was bad. Planning my day was bad, too."

Boyd is his surfing buddy. That caper began when Vlastuin was 18, on a gap year before being drafted. He had a car and a licence, and Boyd had a beach house near Anglesea. They started going on surf trips and never stopped. The past two weeks, in fact, Vlastuin has surfed five times, at Phillip Island and on the west coast at Johanna, Torquay and Lorne. He was in the cold water two days ago at Anglesea, 10am, floating on his board, looking up at grey skies.

"You're just by yourself. You can't look at your phone. Every wave is different," he says. "You can still have fun even if the surf is shit, just mucking around, talking in the water. I always get out feeling heaps better than when I went in. Even when you're sore the day after a game, you forget about it in the first 10 minutes. It's like my meditation, when I'm feeling mixed up in the head."

Vlastuin has no long-term goals. He never really did. As a teenager he wanted to be drafted. Then he was, and he wanted to play a senior game. Then he did, and he wanted to play more. And he has. "And then you just float," he says, stretching one hand out in front of him, a comment that makes it hard to imagine his head ever getting mixed up or muddled. "You're just so busy. You *can't* dream ahead. It carries you along. I'm in my fifth year and the average AFL career is three and half years. I just want to be in a winning team, to win a flag."

He thinks the Tigers can beat Geelong tomorrow. And if they do that, he says, they should have a good chance to win the premiership. "Just depends on whether some blokes can get over their demons from previous years," he says. "It's on your mind a little bit, because we've played three finals and should have won two of them, against the Blues and the Kangaroos. The other year we were lucky to make it. This time we have the double chance, and it's at the MCG, and we saw the VFL side win last week. It all helps."

This year, he says, has been like no other at the club. He puts it down to freedom—both around Punt Road Oval and during matches. Last season, Vlastuin says the club's strategic decision-making was too regimented, and it showed. On field the Tigers were playing two steps behind because they were too busy thinking two moves ahead. "It just wasn't natural. You'd go to do one thing and realise 'That's not right'—then you go to do the *right* thing but it's too late. It's like we were playing with the handbrake on. Now we just get the ball and make it up."

During that period he felt over-coached, too, with so many structures and plays and positions and responsibilities and key words. It was as if the depth of analysis and preparation built and built each year until the players finally collapsed under the groaning weight of it all. "There was this layer of work. Then we'd add another layer, and it got to this point where you couldn't remember it all. Now they've just thrown everything out and said, 'This is what we're doing. That's it'."

He says the players grew weary, too, of the homework they needed to do via an app called Playerlink, watching tape at home. Vlastuin didn't mind the weekly assignments but he says it made others nervous. Ten minutes on our kick-ins. Ten minutes on *their* kick-ins. Ten minutes on stoppages. Ten minutes on transitions. All in a Keynote presentation with the voices of coaches talking over the top of the vision.

"They could tell when you hadn't watched it, too, and blokes would get stressed," he says. "They'd put it up on the board in meetings—who had and who hadn't watched."

As much as Vlastuin sounds like a relaxed adult, back in school he was the tough kid. He had an older brother and the pair fought. "As a kid I always loved the rough stuff," he says. "Probably used to hurt other kids, just by tackling them."

Now he is a collected presence within the Richmond backline. He spends his time organising the "high three" of Ellis, Houli and Broad. He plays often as the spare defender, too, meaning his role is to get into the right positions and help the "deep three" of Grimes, Astbury and Rance—whether with intercept marks, or spoils, or mopping up the mess at their feet. He only likes playing loose sometimes.

"I like beating a man, because you feel like you've done something," he says. "When you're spare, you come off sometimes and you've played well but you're like 'Shit, I haven't been near a guy all day'. Have I really beaten the other team, or just mopped up? You watch the vision and everyone's busting their arse tracking a man, and I'm sitting out the back, guarding space. I kind of feel guilty."

He's happy enough though, doing his job, plying a specific trade with his very specific skill set, while all those around him perform their role with their own talents.

"The analogy we use around here is puzzle pieces," he says. "We're not all square blocks in a pile—we're bits of a jigsaw. We're all different."

Upstairs, minutes later, the team goes into a morning meeting. Despite the relaxed feel at Richmond this season, structures and setups are still important, and so they discuss "the junction" and "the numerical" and "the deep zone adjust". But, Hardwick says, nothing is as important as their individual strengths. "It really is the core part of our game," he says to the players in the auditorium. "It's the 90 per cent."

They talk today about chasing the "desire to succeed", instead of running from the "fear of failure". They need to believe.

"We set ourselves a challenge, didn't we?" Hardwick says. "Reaching the top four, and we got it done. But the big challenge now is the second part of the season. The most exciting part. We put what we've done in our back pocket, and we start again."

He points out also that after the loss to Geelong they could have gone two ways, into "Post Traumatic Stress" or "Post Traumatic Growth".

On the screen now sit four images. Hardwick wants to know if they can figure out what each one has in common with the other.

A Fremantle logo. A GWS logo. A St Kilda logo. And a picture of the Adelaide Oval.

No-one quite nails the connection, so Hardwick explains. In each case they were beaten at their first meeting this season, but they learned something new from each encounter, and when they returned they were better.

The Dockers beat the Tigers in Round 8, but Richmond demolished them in Round 22. The Giants won in Round 9, but they lost in Round 18. The Saints embarrassed the Tigers in Round 16, and Richmond ended their finals hopes in Round 23. At the Adelaide Oval, Richmond was utterly overwhelmed by the Crows in Round 6, and so on their return to that forbidding stadium in Round 15, they beat Port Adelaide.

"We learned from every game, and we grew. That obstacle became an opportunity," Hardwick says. "Every time we've asked you to raise the bar, you've done it."

Next the players enjoy a "pump up" tape—a few minutes of vision of what they do best, set to music. Between the clips they read quotes from Matthew Lloyd and Isaac Smith, Garry Lyon, Jonathan Brown and Jobe Watson. The last is from Wayne Carey: "The pressure they apply is astronomical. Their brand stacks up in finals."

The clips are ugly football. A Tiger grabs the footy and forces it forward, it bobbles, and another Tiger charges in, and it ricochets, and another yellow and black jumper is there, and the ball is hacked forward by foot, but no mark is taken, and it is soccered along the ground, bashed in the direction of the Richmond goal, and as a viewer you realise that you are holding your breath, that at no point in the long chaotic chain does Richmond have complete control. The ball is always in dispute, until it finally squeezes free into the arms of a Tiger, who gives it to another with a little space and time, and it becomes a goal, and there is a moment of primal release for the men on the field and for everyone watching them. You realise that this is the way Richmond has won all season long.

"All heart, all effort, all intent," says Hardwick. "It's that red line, that grey area, that in between. I've never coached a side like this—that makes me just sit in wonder."

But the first slide of the presentation sends the message the coach wants the group to absorb most. It is a photo of Geelong footballers, muscular and moving, and it reads: "What stands in the way becomes the way".

Hardwick looks up at the photo, then back to the group, and then at Vlastuin.

"Nick," he says, "you look a bit like a philosopher. What do you think that means?"

Vlastuin looks up at the screen, leans back, crosses his arms and replies.

"Simple," he says. "We know we've got to go through 'em to go through 'em."

42

MOW THEM DOWN

Brunton Avenue is empty this evening but for the quick, cold breeze blowing up the road toward the MCG. It whirls through the trees, kisses the bronze statues of Dick Reynolds and Haydn Bunton, and nips at the necks of the people pouring into the stadium. And it dances through the gaps in the towering steel sculpture known as *The Legend*.

This hulking 20-tonne work of art has been called, by various critics, "a climax of exuberance and energy" and "a steel drawing of a full crowd going berserk". The artist, Anthony Pryor, never saw the work assembled. He was 40 when he died of cancer, only months before it was unveiled. His widow, Jutta, says her late husband had wanted the piece to be a grand statement—an arch worthy of a great meeting place. "It could be a wave," she says. "It could be a man leaping up to strive for the ball."

The sharp zig-zags might be the frozen movement of two opposing teams, like the Tigers and Cats. The tripod legs may be the limbs of great athletes like Dangerfield and Cotchin, entangled in the contest, the crossed lines perhaps an almighty collision, on a cold night like this one, under lights, suspended in time and space.

Not far away, all is still and warm in the coaches briefing suite, way down the back of the Richmond change rooms. The men gathered there are smiling, not long before the 2017 second Qualifying Final between the Cats and the Tigers. They are prepared and ready, and so all that is left is to fill in time. They chat about Las Vegas and bourbon and "the footy gods", and Dennis Rodman and Anthony Rocca and did Vincent van Gogh really cut his ear off while he was drinking absinthe?

They amble about and chit-chat and the patter is no different from before any game—not one bit—yet there is an edge. There is a flinty, yet flighty feeling in here. There are more deep breaths than normal. More sighs. More comings and goings from the room itself, whether to grab a little triangular jam sandwich on white bread, or to ask a question of the medical staff, or just to lean on a wall somewhere else, away from the collective wait, instead of clustering together like a family in a basement shelter, wary of the tornado about to envelope them all.

The backs have their line meeting and Alex Rance speaks up: "Just a quick one," he says. "We've all experienced this with the Anzac eve game, but with the national anthem, make sure you use that as an opportunity to reset and not be overawed by the occasion," he says. "There's a crowd, and another team lined up on the other side like soldiers. Lower your gaze, and think about your strengths, and the brilliance you've accumulated— *we've all accumulated*—over the year. Put a hand on the guy next to you. Bit of touch, bit of love, then we're ready."

Jack Riewoldt, in the forwards line meeting, says something similar: "Accept that there are a few people out there watching a game of footy. It's a fact," he says. "But remember that our one wood is our chase and tackle. *Every single one of them* will hesitate at some point, and then we are just going to mow them down. Let's run these guys off their feet."

At 6:53pm, Hardwick addresses his men. He jokes with them about his usual game day routine, and how his wife Danielle and daughter Isabelle upset his habitual process today by wanting to ride into the game with him, instead of allowing him his standard solo drive. There is no more important game this season so far, but Hardwick again maintains a lightness of mood with such stories. It is his point of difference in 2017.

In 2016, when he needed a lift from his players before big clashes, his speeches toed a certain line. They were impassioned. For all Hardwick's everyman schtick in press conferences, for all the statements that begin with "The reality is…", and for all those "Mrs Hardwick" jokes, the coach is a born orator. After his speeches last season, assistants and administrators— on more than one occasion—smiled as they held out an arm, showing off the goose pimples and chills he could coax from grown men. The speeches were all laced with profanity, but felt profound in the moment.

"This side is a bully," he said before one game. "It's what they are. It's what they do. But at some stage you've got to stand up and go, you know what, I'll whack you back. So, what are we going to do? We're going to go right up to that bloke, and put him *down!* You put him *DOWN*, and you see how it goes from there. No backward steps today. We are smashing that bully in the mouth."

Another time, as the season slipped away, he wanted a show a force. "The first 10 minutes of this game is a dead set ambush," he said. "Because this is a side you can *break*. You can break them in half by being hard, being tough, being physical. We're over 'em, over 'em, *OVER 'EM!* … And then they're done, looking to get out of here."

That was then. Now, he offers jokes, and hokey homilies, and the weekly laminated A3 picture, and the only man in the room who has not turned over one of these images is Bachar Houli, so he strides to the front of the room and flips the laminated paper to reveal a craggy mountain peak—an arrowhead capped in snow, framed in the thinnest deep blue sky. "This is the tallest mountain in the world," says Hardwick. "Mount Everest. And this part right here is called The Hillary Step. Eighty percent of people who die on this climb die here. It's the death zone."

The Hillary Step is only 12 metres high, but it is a difficult Class 4 rock face to scale—and it sits 8,790 metres above sea level. The danger on one side? A three-kilometre vertical drop. The challenge is said to have pushed Sir Edmund Hillary to the limit. A body was found there only recently, hanging from a rope. Hardwick riffs now on this deadly precipice.

"The climbers die because they're focused on that point above, the outcome, the goal, the top, instead of *rope here, footstep there*—process and progress," he says. "The summit is there. It'll *always* be there. But you've got to pay the price, and the price is the work—and our work is our focus on what got us here. We are *small*. We are *powerful*. We are *quick!* We know what we do makes sides quiver. So, let's get it done, step by step."

///////////

The Tigers settle quickly into the game. They tackle hard and often, and in pairs and trios. They rush the ball forward in mad scrambles and speculative taps and hacked kicks, all of which is the directive tonight—but it doesn't pay off as often as it could. Although there is a gentle drizzle the ball isn't quite slick enough to bomb blindly, and so the Geelong backs prove big enough and good enough to block for their spare men and take easy marks. They win aerial contests all over the field.

Fumbles are costly, too, whether it's Prestia on the breakaway, or a double grab by Riewoldt, or a missed scoop by Rioli. Fumbles afford the opposition a precious half second, and, in a half second a four-metre gap on your man vanishes. Half a second is all it takes to turn a clean run through a clear field into a wrangled pack of players clattering to earth—an untidy jumble that swallows the football, until it is held tightly among limbs and trunks, until the whistle is blown and the yellow ball is thrown up again into the black satin night.

By the end of the first quarter, Richmond has two goals, and Geelong none.

In the second quarter, the Tigers apply ever more pressure, but they squander the open field, squander inside 50s, and squander shots on goal. Still, they are four goals up, and two minutes from half-time Geelong has not kicked a major. The Cats respond in a flash with two, including one from Patrick Dangerfield on the run—a goal so close to being *too late* that the siren sounds as it drifts through the middle.

The Tigers enter the rooms at half-time only nine points up, knowing they should lead by three or four or even five goals. Their pressure rating for the two quarters was 1.9 (elite) and 2.2 (rare), but their lead is flimsy. Have they missed their opportunity?

Hardwick tells them that the game plan remains intact this night—that if the short options Inside 50 aren't ideal, aren't obvious, aren't on, then go long to the square, because if the ball is turned over there, what happens? The Cats will have to fight their way out through the entire field—all 18 Richmond players. So, kick long, boys, even to an absence of Richmond jumpers.

"Grass is our friend," he says. "We kick it to space, our pace will take over. Won the first half? Great. We put that in the pocket. We move on. The game demands we start again."

The half-time break is just that, a lengthy separation of play—a 20-minute chance to sever one passage of football from the next, to snip the continuum. But sometimes after the restart, it is as if there was no gap at all, as if the play had continued, the momentum leaping the void, skipping time. Geelong throws their energy at Richmond early in the third quarter, and for all the talk of 'The Tiger Tornado' and the forward-half turnovers caused by the Richmond smalls, Geelong is statistically the best pressure team in the League, and they show those wares now, pushing and cornering and kicking truly until, improbably, halfway through the term, scores are level.

This is the moment when the game hangs in the balance, when the Richmond of late might have stumbled, tripping over the chance in front of them. Yet this Richmond responds, unbowed by the gravity of the situation. Before, their back would have snapped under the weight, but this Richmond straightens its knees and shrugs off that downward expectation, and so the Tigers begin pressuring again, closing down space, forcing it forward, finding shots on goal and missing them at first, but then a long range set shot bomb from Vlastuin sails through, and then Dustin Martin speeds away from Tom Stewart on the wing, and kicks low to Riewoldt, who bustles and gathers and spears his own shallow kick to the goal square, and all throughout each moment of the play the roar of the crowd grows until the ball lands in the arms of Dion Prestia, and he rams through the goal and the stands are delirium, and pandemonium, and Richmond goes into the huddle 13 points up but it feels like much, much more.

Prestia grew up barracking for Melbourne, and the biggest game he saw as a Demons fan was the 2000 Grand Final, played in front of a crowd of 96,249. He remembers being one of thousands pulling a cloth banner in Melbourne colours over his head and down onto the field as part of the cheer squad. He remembers the high hit by Essendon wingman Michael Long on Demons ruckman Troy Simmonds, which saw Simmonds stretched off, sparking a 25-man brawl. He remembers that his Dees lost by 10 goals. He remembers little else.

Later, he won't remember much of this contest either—the biggest game in which he has played, in front of 95,028. He will remember walking up the race and thinking "Take it all in—take in as much as you can." He will remember the crowd going wild as he stepped onto the playing surface. And he will remember this goal and the roar that immediately followed, and stretched, and rose. "In the moment, you don't notice the crowd because you're zoned in—or zoned out—but you kick the goal, and you're walking back to the centre of the ground, and people are going crazy. That's the kind of thing you want to take in."

//////////

The stadium is full. Perhaps two thirds or more are Richmond supporters, and so the arena becomes one flickering, fantastic wall of Tiger support, a giant curving cliff of yellow and black, colour and noise.

It is the largest crowd for a Richmond game since the 1982 Grand Final. It is the largest Qualifying Final crowd ever. It is 4122 days since the club beat Geelong, and it is 5837 days since the club won a final. But the Tigers win this one, and are headed to a Preliminary Final in two weeks—16,072 days since the last time they played in one.

The final quarter is pressure, pressure, pressure and, finally, *release*. Sweet release. Martin steps into the moment again, to shrug two tackles, turn, and kick 60 metres off a step into the waiting arms of Shaun Grigg, alone in the goal square. Dan Butler surges out of the forward line in pursuit of two Cats, and sticks the tackle.

They are 28 points up! 34 points up! 40 points up! Caddy goals—46 points up! Cotchin flings his body forward at a contest, spinning and swooping and splitting a pack like a sharpened axe on a hollow log, and he lobs the ball on his left foot and the floater sails through, and the crowd dances and the stands heave.

The roar they offer now is like a wave that has built and built and finally risen, this season, into something monstrous. The fans sing the song and are let loose on the city now, a true horde—unbridled and unchained.

//////////

Hardwick smiles as he enters the rooms, unable to contain his glee and his pride. People pat his back and shake his hand and clutch him by his shoulders, until it becomes too much and he deflects and dismisses the attention: "I didn't play!" he yells. "I didn't play!"

There are so many hugs. Dustin Martin and Emma Murray. Tim Livingstone and Andrew McQualter. Brendon Gale and Matthew Clarke. Ben Crowe and Peggy O'Neal.

Then in the briefing room there is nothing left but grins and ruddy faces. Justin Leppitsch talks about the crowd noise, and starts laughing. "It reminds you of our Brisbane days," he says, mocking the memory. "Especially those early Bears years."

Craig McRae shakes his head: "When Geelong ran out, they got booed. Did you hear that? The boo for them was louder than the cheer for us. I've never heard that."

They talk about the pressure they saw, a staggering average of 2.1 over the course of the game. Hardwick writes the stats he likes most on the whiteboard. They laid 92 tackles. They had 33 forward-half turnovers, from which they created 7 goals 3 behinds.

"That pressure—I've never seen anything like it," says Gale. "It just kept coming in wave after wave after wave. Extraordinary."

Tony Singarella, a game day assistant, was shocked at the level and persistence of both the physical and mental aggression thrown at Geelong: "It's like the boys were just *willing* them to give up."

The last of the players then enters the room, the door is closed, and Hardwick looks up at them. He pauses a long moment. His voice is soft: "How good is it?"

And the room erupts: *YEAHHHH!!!!!!!!!*

Fists are held high. Players put one another in headlocks. The coaches applaud. Hardwick speaks. "That was as *brutal* a game as I've seen," he says, shaking his head back and forth, back and forth. "Just *fierce*. It's how far we've come. People have always challenged us about the way we play. But the courage and the relentless nature of your performance was nothing short of outstanding. Sides are going to fear us."

He goes over what went well—the standard post-game examination, which can only skim the surface. Good balance at stoppages. Good use of their long down-the-line contest method. The shape they created. The space they guarded. He congratulates the players—they're into a Preliminary Final.

"Job well done. We've given ourselves a chance. But we're still in that death zone, The Hillary Step, where we can see the summit but we've still got to take *every little step* along the way. Enjoy the win. I'm so proud of you."

The players all sit back, happy, enjoying a golden silence. Riewoldt, in the back row, opens his mouth and speaks to the dream they all now see could be real.

"Why not us?" he asks. "Why not, hey?"

43

THE WIN WE'VE WANTED

Three men sit at a plastic picnic table covered in a Tiger-striped tablecloth, in a cramped, ramshackle nook upstairs in the old grandstand at Punt Road Oval—now the club's museum—chatting about all things Richmond. The three are Digital Marketing Manager Josh Berriman, Editorial and Research Manager Tony Greenberg, and Roar Vision Producer (and former Tigers' champion full-forward) Matthew Richardson.

Today they are simply "JB", "Greeners" and "Richo", and together they are "Talking Tigers", a club podcast that has run for five years. Around 5000 people listen online every week, and another 6000 or so download the episodes through iTunes or audioBoom.

There are standing microphones and cables, cameras and sound mixing consoles, and the boys sit down to talk. They'll do this for a couple of hours. "Testing one-two," says Berriman. "Test, one, two."

In this week, in the lead-up to the first Preliminary Final the club has contested since 2001, there is no such thing as too much 'Tiger Talk' for the hordes to devour. More than 3000 people are outside now, attending an open training session, and even in those moments when the club gates are closed and the players and coaches are at work indoors, the fans linger. They stand outside the front doors for hours on end, waiting for a glimpse of the coming and going stars, and of course they file into and out of the

Tigerland Superstore to buy jumpers and beanies and all things yellow and black. Since the finals series began, the club has sold more than $200,000 worth of merchandise.

Perhaps one day a portion of those goods will end up here. The exposed brick office looks more like an attic filled with overflow memorabilia. It is bursting at the seams with paraphernalia, from big outdoor signs with outdated logos to framed caricatures of Kevin Bartlett, signed photos of Paul Broderick, dusty and cracked Ross Faulkner footballs, and dozens of vintage hats and scarves. In front of one wall sit a row of disused lockers with names like Dean Polo, Kayne Pettifer and Cleve Hughes inscribed on the swinging doors. There are plastic tubs and cardboard boxes, filing cabinets and Saratoga trunks, all crammed with Richmond teddy bears and Richmond gym bags and Richmond drink bottles—it's a trove of Tiger trash and treasure.

One of the better items hangs on the wall. A gorgeous framed poster from 1972, with an etching of a prowling Tiger and then a message in stacked deck headline format, in varied font sizes. It looks like an old circus poster.

The
GREAT
and remarkable
TIGERS
adored and beloved by thousands everywhere
WILL PERFORM
Great Feats of Football Skill and Dexterity
and
Bedazzle
Their Opponents
With Their Skilled And Adroit Handling of the Leather
AND BE THE DESPAIR
of all those who would dare
to enter the Tigers' lair
EAT'EM ALIVE

It was designed by Joe Greenberg, then an artist at *The Herald* and uncle of the Greenberg seated here. Tony Greenberg is a font of Tiger lore and passion, and that's what this podcast is—a chance to share the love. The trio runs through a VFL report, and the notable players and moments from the latest win at the lower level. That team is headed to a Preliminary Final on the weekend, too. They read out emails and tweets, including from one fan who thinks he has "broken the code" to getting his messages read out on air, usually by insisting he is writing from some far-flung place. (This time he writes from outer Mongolia, although in truth he is on the NSW south coast.)

They interview Nathan Broad, and he shares jokes about the locker room behaviour of quirky wingman Kamdyn McIntosh, part of a running joke on the show informally known as "The Chronicles of Kamdyn". Richardson takes a pot shot at the media (or social media) for beating up a story around the behaviour of Richmond fans during the win over Geelong, as part of a regular segment called "The Richo Rant". Greenberg tells dad jokes in another regular spot titled "Greeners' gags".

Where does a fish go for money? A loan shark.
I was gonna tell a joke about boxing ... but I forgot the punchline.

Then there's "Chief Watch", a segment in which they poke fun at Richardson's former teammate, club boss Brendon Gale. (Last week they had nothing to tell, so they made up a tale about Gale attending the recent VFL final and reclining on a hill like Caesar or Nero, while his children fed him grapes and massaged his feet and fanned him.) Most of these moments end with mocking laughter and braying guffaws and the three men shaking their heads at their own obsession. "Oh, my God," says Greenberg. "We truly have spoken some rubbish this year."

But their devotion to Richmond also shines through, and their deep knowledge of the club now, and of the Tigers of old. Greenberg tells them that this Saturday against GWS will be 50 years to the day since the 1967 premiership, which ended a 24-year flag drought. "It was against Geelong, a magnificent game and a beautiful day," he says. "I was nine years old, and I remember being on the edge of my seat. The lead changed all day and I vividly remember when the final siren sounded—I was standing on my seat and cheering madly. It was a team like this Tigers team. None of them had played a single finals match until that year, and they were up against a team of superstars. Farmer, Goggin, Wade, Marshall. Fred Swift kicking drop kicks to the centre from full-back for us. 'KB' kicked the sealer."

They sigh, and are silent, and Richardson signs off: "Good to be here, lads. What an exciting time to be alive."

///////////

Richardson doesn't like looking back too often, and this is wise. It has been said before that Richmond is a club in many ways paralysed by its success in the 1960s and 1970s, one that for too long has navel-gazed instead of looking forward. Richardson played in that 2001 Preliminary Final, as did Gale, in his last game. So did the forward line coach, Justin Leppitsch, and the VFL coach, Craig McRae, they for the rampaging Brisbane Lions, on their way to a famous treble.

Richardson recalls little of the match. He does remember beating Carlton in a dour match a week earlier, just days after the September 11 terrorist attacks in the United States. He remembers that Ansett Airlines collapsed that week, and so thousands of Richmond fans had to bus it to the Gabba. "We came across a side that was about to be one of the greatest teams of all time. We travelled to their home ground, which was imposing then. They were a class above—they played in four straight Grand Finals."

The difference he sees this year—that which allows him to not merely dream but also believe the Tigers can reach the Grand Final—is the team's consistency. "They're not getting too high and not getting too low. I just see a level of effort and personality from the whole group. I think most winning groups in the history of sport have that—a kind of evenness. You've got to be level, and they just seem to be on the same page."

He watched them from the boundary line in the Qualifying Final against Geelong, in his special comments role for Seven. What he saw as the play unfolded was a team that set up strongly in front of and behind the ball— who moved together as a group. "It was so noticeable. All over the field they were well organised and seemed to know their role," he says. "Isn't that what makes great teams?"

He is happy for the fans, too, in particular for the style of play brought by Richmond this season. The club, he says, has not been known in any recent incarnation for its pressure or tackling or ferocity, and now it is their defining trait. He has heard this all year long: the new brand, built on strangling the opposition, is driving supporters up out of their seats. "It's exciting to watch," he says. "You know what you're going to get every week, and as a supporter of a team you turn up and pay for your membership or your ticket, and if you know you're going to get effort, and hunger, and intensity, then win, lose or draw you walk away going, 'They brought it, yep, they brought it'."

The fans themselves also get to feel a part of the contest—that their frenzied cheering is a spur or a lift or a literal support. Richardson suspects "the 19th man" can be a factor, something to feed off. He saw it against Geelong, not in helping the Tigers break the game open but in helping that crack become a chasm.

"Sometimes, when you get a roll on, and you sense the opposition falling, it helps," he says. "If the game this weekend is close, and we get out to a little lead, and the crowd is roaring, then you can feed off that energy and go to another level. It contributes to momentum, but it's not going to get the job done. It's the icing on the cake."

///////////

Hours later, in the Maurice Rioli Room, on level three of the Punt Road Oval complex, a few dozen people have gathered. They're spread out in the large space, mostly on the floor, which is all green carpet except for one long, crooked, diagonal section of brown parquetry. The wood functions as the dance floor, but also represents the nearby Yarra River, with the green carpet its banks.

The room fills with the sound of thick, clear packing tape ripped from fat rolls, and the snips of people kneeling with scissors, cutting out the edges of 22 painted players, each one numbered and correctly scaled, with the right hair colour and body shape.

"How are you doing?" a boy asks a woman, as he cuts around the shoulder of the paper Dion Prestia.

"Absolutely flying," says the lady, shearing the elbow of the paper Daniel Rioli.

These are the diehards. When we think of Richmond supporters we think of the Tiger Army, the mass of supporters, the 75,000-plus members and the way they can fill a stadium, and scream "yellow and black", and envelope Swan Street and Bridge Road after a victory, but the supporter base has a core, and this is them. They are the ORCS—the Official Richmond Cheer Squad.

"You've got people who, in normal life, probably wouldn't look at one another in the street," says cheer squad leader Gerard Egan. "But during those four hours at the MCG during a game, it's friendship, it's family, it's home."

It's also a responsibility they take seriously. If you sign up and want to sit in their section, for instance, you are required by charter to support the team with "colour and voice"—at least according to their official welcoming letter:

> If you choose to sit in the cheer squad then you will be expected to use flags, floggers or patty dukes (plastic pom-poms). We also expect you to join in chants when they are started. If you choose not to participate then you may be asked to vacate your seat for someone who will.

I joined the cheer squad for a week once, a handful of years ago, as part of a magazine story. I remember building the banner in an old community hall in nearby Coppin Street, and holding it aloft at the game, lugging gear across the stadium hours beforehand, and then barracking like hell as Richmond was comfortably handled by Collingwood. The novelist Nick Hornby once described the natural waking state of all long-suffering fans as one of "bitter disappointment", and although he was writing about his soccer club, Arsenal, I chose to believe he was writing about Richmond.

Most of these people, they tell me now, were born into Richmond. Their dad went for the Tiges. Or their mum was a Tiggers fan. Or pop lived in Richmond. Or nan always worked in Struggletown. It is something handed down, and a reminder of the Bruce Dawe poem, Life Cycle:

> When children are born in Victoria
> They are wrapped in club colours
> Laid in be-ribbonned cots,
> Having already begun a lifetime's barracking

Many studies have been done in an attempt to explain what causes us to latch onto various teams, and why those connections are so hard to break. Dr John Cash, a social scientist at the University of Melbourne and Carlton fan, once remarked that clubs are "vampiric" in this regard: "Once they sink their teeth into you, it's like an infection of the blood."

Attachments to football clubs can be formed for any number of reasons—geography, parentage, performance—but then our subsequent biographies are framed through the game itself, and the club we choose.

Every match throws you back into the nostalgia of your own personal history, from every painful loss (the 1995 Preliminary Final in the rain at Waverley against Geelong, when Richmond supporters began singing the song in the final quarter of an 89-point thrashing), and every delirious victory (the 1995 second semi-final against Essendon at the MCG, when Matthew Knights kicked three goals in the first half, all from long, loping, bouncing runs through the middle of the ground). None of us is immune.

"Your own life story gets entangled with the life of the club," said Cash's colleague, Joy Damousi. "The more you talk to anyone about their team, you realise they're actually talking about themselves."

She's right, of course. Think of those friendships you have with people who barrack for the same team. Ask yourself: would your bond be as deep, would it be as enduring—*would it even exist*—without your shared passion? Historian Manning Clark, a passionate Carlton fan, called our allegiance to club colours a "strange infirmity", and "an emotional bath of agony and ecstasy", and, in Tiger supporters at least, it is one that produces a distinctively Melburnian mixture of melancholia, mourning and flickering hope.

Not right now though. Not for Brett Beattie, otherwise known as "Trout from Woodend", also known as that guy in the Richmond cheer squad with the curly yellow wig—the Tiger equivalent to the renowned Collingwood Magpie fan Jeff "Joffa" Corfe. "Up here you've got a lot of people who know the club more deeply than me," Beattie says. "I always say 'I'm a fan with a big mouth'. That's all."

Right now, as the sun sets and a VFL training session begins on the oval downstairs, Beattie is working the room with his colleagues. There's a quiet, industrious buzz throughout the place. Adults and children are painting black stripes on a pair of mammoth yellow Tigers, pouring liberally from two-litre bottles of Washable Poster Paint. Their eyes are alight. Is the lid off?

"The lid is never off," Beattie says. "Last week was a release—it was relief. We got the win we've wanted. This week it's about, do we go further and demand respect, or let people say we fluked the win? I think they'll go in hard. You can't go in cocky, but you've got to go in believing you'll give it your best shot. And if we get over the line, if we take the win, then the lid will be *right* off. It'll fly up past Kim Jong-un's rocket!" Beattie was raised mostly in Kyneton and took his love for the team from his father, Terry, and uncle, Paul, but for many years before that he grew up in

Richmond. "In those streets," he says, pointing out the window at the modern apartment blocks casting shade on the little terrace houses and narrow streets of the former suburban slum. "I used to ride my bike past the church there, St Ignatius on the hill, and then down those streets past the pubs. I'd ride the trains and walk the boulevards and the gardens. This is my town."

He passed his love of Richmond down, too, to his son Beau, who was 10 years old when he asked his father if they could sit for an afternoon with the cheer squad. "I said to him, 'If we go over there, you can't just sit in the seat. You've got to commit'. He's never looked back. We made our own banners that we bring: *Cop that!* and *Miss it!* and *The tribe has spoken.*"

I met Beau once when he was a university student. He said something that stopped me cold—something that makes you grasp just how similar following a football club can be to nationalism, or religion, or the blind devotion and connection to any imagined community or cause. "I would actually die for the club," he said. "If they said someone had to die to save the club, I would do it. It sounds crazy, but if you knew how much it meant to people, it would make sense. I'd do anything for Richmond."

"Trout" has been a solid cheer squad member for around 16 years. His family holds six memberships. He goes to all the games, of course, but also to the banner-making and other functions. He used to be a committee member. It will be 9:30 tonight before he gets home to Woodend. "It's a community. You help each other. You care for these people. We all give up family time for this. When the kids were growing up, it was hard to keep it up, and hard to keep them in it, because the team wasn't going so well. But there are so many families who have kept their kids true," he says. "At three-quarter time last Saturday, to see my son jumping up and down and cheering the Tigers, and after the game to see my daughter smiling for two straight hours after the game, chatting outside gate four, it's something special. I feel like I've passed the baton—that they'll never leave now."

As for the rest of the football fans around Melbourne, he suspects most of them want to see Richmond fail. "Not because they hate us, but because they love giving it to us," he says. "But it's funny, we just don't care about the jokes any more. That's all over. They said we'd be terrible this year: we're great. They said we wouldn't make the eight: we did. They said we couldn't stay in the four: here we are. They said we couldn't win a final: there it is. They say we can't beat the Giants: we don't care what they say. Not any more."

44

WE'RE SOMETHING SPECIAL

I t is two hours before the Preliminary Final against Greater Western Sydney, and the coaches are in their MCG briefing room, affixing magnets to the whiteboard. The key starting match-ups are all there.

Daniel Rioli on Brett Deledio. Kane Lambert on Heath Shaw. Dan Butler on Nathan Wilson. Jacob Townsend will be responsible for stopping Nick Haynes and his damaging intercept marks. The laconic Kamdyn McIntosh will have his work cut out, running with the League's marathon man Tom Scully. Dion Prestia will be the nominal opponent of star midfielder Josh Kelly. Dylan Grimes will be responsible for young gun Toby Greene. Alex Rance will not float across the backline today, but instead manage big Jon Patton.

The board is almost set when AFL chief executive Gillon McLachlan enters the room. He looks every bit of a ruckman, the position he once played as an amateur footballer. "Good luck," he says, shaking Hardwick's hand. "You've done a hell of a lot of work to get here. You deserve it."

He leaves and they return to the board, and now some guesswork. Giants captain Phil Davis is sure to go to Jack Riewoldt. Aidan Corr will likely sidle up to Josh Caddy. Shaun Grigg will need to run with Callan Ward.

The remaining messages are familiar. Give the Giants "No time"—by blitzing. Give them "No space"—by stalking. Remember sometimes that there are "No perfect plays"—and so, judge the heat of the moment and scramble if needed.

Match them on the inside.

Control them on the outside.

Stay connected.

The coaches sip lattes. They eat tiny Vegemite sandwiches, and devour donuts with bright yellow icing. Tim Livingstone paces the room, bouncing and catching the little red rubber ball he brings to all games. *Pock. Pock. Pock.*

They stare at the TV screen, where a *Fox Sports* host chats to a Rugby League coach. Hardwick shakes his head: "Jeez, that's a terrible game," he says. "I'm amazed anyone watches it. They don't, I suppose, if you count crowd numbers."

Opposition analyst Jack Harvey sits in the corner, back against the wall, flicking through a play book and poring over statistics. Harvey was sitting in the top level of the Adelaide Oval the previous night, watching the Crows (just in case Richmond wins today). "It didn't feel like 50,000 supporters," he says. "It was so loud. Their fans are up, too."

Justin Leppitsch appears on the screen next, from an interview filmed a day earlier. The television sound is turned down, and so the other coaches mimic what he might be saying.

Yeah, I played in three premierships, was kind of a big deal…

Yeah, I've clearly changed everything at Punt Road this year…

Of course I'm the difference this season—who else would be?

Leppitsch joins in on the joke, too: "Yeah, last time Richmond played in a prelim final I was there. Played on Richo. I was clearly the difference that day, too."

They talk about how the conditions outside are blustery, which should suit the chaotic playing style of the Tigers. It has just hit 31 degrees in the sunshine, making today, September 23, 2017, the fourth hottest September day on record in Melbourne. They are joking about the need for sunscreen when Jack Riewoldt, the fair-haired, light-skinned full-forward enters the room. "Sunburn *and* windburn out there, Jack," Hardwick yells. "The double whammy!"

Quickly though they rehash the serious elements of this deadly serious game—raising a series of points that were made in the opposition analysis two days earlier.

They talk about conversion, which was a problem in both games against the Giants this year. "Back then we were AFL number one for shit snaps," Hardwick said. "How do you reckon our scoring has been since then? Yeah, *elite.*"

They talk about dangerous players, who were raised specifically by Ben Rutten in the same Thursday morning meeting. "Wilson's *really* dangerous. He gets the ball and runs *straight* and *fast* and kicks it a long way," he said. "Scully, wherever the space is, he'll run into it. Up and down. Up and down."

They talk about maintaining width, and managing the Giants away from the collision zone inside stoppages. "We *must* take care of the outside, guys," said Blake Caracella. "Having a 'plus one' inside the contest is of no use to us. They want access to the space."

They talk about the importance of running to fill that space. Hardwick shows a clip of Nathan Broad, sprinting 100 metres across the ground not to guard a man but to occupy an open field. Do you ever wonder how a side just *happens* to have that spare player ready to mark the blast kick out of defence?

Broad's selfless running is how.

"No kick, no mark, no handball. No stat at all," said Hardwick. "But a big pat on the back from the coach. Terrific play. *Terrific.*"

They talk also about the need to work hard and roll forward. It's an interesting point. Attention is often given to players who run hard into defence, as if that were the ultimate team act.

He's such a two-way runner.
What a great gut runner.
Runs so, so hard to help out the backs.

But being willing to run forward is just as altruistic. Hardwick shows a recent clip of Kane Lambert and Shane Edwards surging forward. Neither received the ball, or even called for it. Nor did they spoil a contest. But by running hard into the forward 50, the spare defenders of the opposition were forced to be accountable, meaning Jack Riewoldt could be left one-on-one— able to win a 50/50 contest and score.

The final talking point is a reminder they have made clear all week. The key part of the GWS game plan is *offence*—which, for effectiveness, relies on the defensive intent of their opponent. The key part of the Tigers game plan, said Hardwick, is *defence*: "It's dependent on no-one but us. This is our advantage."

A little over an hour before the first bounce it's time for line meetings. First come the defenders. Rutten asks how they're feeling. He looks at Dylan Grimes. "What did you do this morning?" he asks. "Milk the cows?"

Grimes: "Well, they're male cows, so no."

They all laugh and Rutten takes them into their mental preparation, talking about playing the game "breath by breath" and "moment by moment", always knowing that if things turn bad they have their abilities, their willingness to contest, and their understanding of one another. It's written on the board: *Strengths, Fight, Connection.*

"When you drift out, come back to this," he says. "You've got more than enough evidence and tools. Brando, you don't need to have all the tools, because what you haven't got Nick's got, and what Nick's missing Dave's got, and what Dave goes without Rancey has. And Bachar. And Broady."

Rance tells them they need to communicate out there: "Even if you think it's useless, make sure you chat today—*Dave, I've got your back!*—and say it bloody loud. We don't want anyone to feel alone out there. We want to be connected. Let a mate know you're fighting this battle together."

The midfielders meet a few minutes later, and Andrew McQualter looks serious. "Let's talk about the elephant in the room," he says. "Who saw *The Age* today?"

He's talking about a back page spread on Kamdyn McIntosh, and they all laugh.

"Did you see that photo? Twirling that bloody moustache. *Shameful.*"

Grigg talks about something else he saw in the paper—an article that described the Giants versus the Tigers as the "billionaires versus the battlers".

"I loved that," Grigg tells the group. "That's us."

"Great," says McQualter. "Our mindset has to be that we're the hunters. We are the hunters, boys."

Next come the forwards, and they talk about making the Giants defend, about celebration, about creating a ground level advantage, about making sure every GWS disposal is made under pressure. They discuss the crowd and its likely impact, a talking point all week.

Perhaps 4000 Giants fans will make the trip to the ground, and the crowd predicted is 94,000, meaning there will be a potential support base of 90,000 for the Tigers—even the neutrals won't be neutral on this day. It will be the largest partisan crowd in the history of Australian football. The players need to drink that in. Riewoldt, sitting next to Shane Edwards, tells them to enjoy the experience: "Have *fun!* Don't push back on the emotion. The crowd—they're out there for us. Embrace it! I've been waiting 12 years for this. So has Shane."

Josh Caddy offers his own thought. He wants his teammates to remember the connection they have developed all season long: "The Giants can't see it, they can't hear it, but it's there and I guarantee you they don't have it—and they can't defend it. So, let's use it, and play with passion."

Soon all the players are gathered.

Hardwick tells a story.

This one is about his former teammate, Essendon forward Dean Rioli. He met with him the night before. Rioli was a gifted forward who missed the 2000 Bombers' premiership with an injury suffered only a few rounds before the finals. Hardwick says seeing his old teammate triggered a memory.

"I remembered the time he went back to the Tiwi Islands," says Hardwick. "He'd had enough. He said, 'I'm gone, I just need a couple of weeks off'. So Kevin Sheedy sent Robert Shaw and Mark Harvey up there to go get him, and bring him back." Apparently, Shaw and Harvey arrived, and Rioli quickly told them he was always coming back to Essendon—he just needed a few weeks away.

"They said 'Really?' He's like, 'Yeah, definitely, without a doubt. I'm coming back'. So Shawry gets on the phone to Sheeds and goes, 'You're not gonna believe it, but he's not coming back'. And Sheedy says, 'Well you blokes bloody well stay there and make sure he comes back!' So Shawry and Harvs are up there for two weeks yabbying and fishing, the bastards!"

Again, Hardwick has the room in brief stitches, and then he turns immediately to the game at hand. He starts with the A3 picture, which is turned over by Nick Vlastuin. It is a drawing of a stork, eating a frog, but while the frog is in the mouth of the stork, its green arms are stretched out and its hands are strangling the big bird.

"All year we've heard, 'You're too small, you've got no forward line, you can't win it, you can't get it done'. We get no respect from anyone. We've been the underdog all year. People have just been *waiting* for us to fall over. But we're something special, boys."

"We know there will be moments where we're the stork, and we're strong, and we've got them in our mouth. But they're also going to come at us, and then we're the frog, and when we're the frog we've got our hands around the neck, choking them."

"I love the way we play. I love what we represent. And today we get to show it off in front of 95,000 people. So, I ask you, why not? *Why not us?* Believe in the simple premise that finals are won on one thing: team football. Believe in yourself. I believe in you."

///////////

Richmond opens the game with the biggest of moments. A clearance from Cotchin, a ball spilling to Martin, who handballs to Lambert, who barrels the goal through from the square. It takes 21 seconds and the MCG shakes with aural and visual fury. That goal is followed by another, and a near miss, and Richmond looks like the game is a runaway, but the Giants coolly respond.

They scoot and skate and run. They get outside. Josh Kelly is a sublime footballer and he has a sublime start, gathering the ball at will, scything through and darting around opponents. In close, he takes remarkably quick evasive short steps. Cornered, he has a beautiful short baulk that makes his opponents look foolish. In space, his legs are long and his pace at full stride is daunting. He is balanced, composed, and kicks goals. Richmond leads by one goal at quarter-time but is flattered by the margin. In reality, the Tigers should be two goals down. Should the game continue in this fashion, they will not win.

By half time their lead is only a point, and the coaches' briefing room is an uncharacteristic flurry of questions, and analysis, and diagrams drawn in a hurry in blue whiteboard marker.

There is tension in the air now, and at times silence but for the loud click and bang of the heavy black door to the room opening and closing as one assistant after another enters and leaves, conferring with Hardwick then with the players under their watch.

Boys, is it a low stoppage game?
Seems to be ping-ponging a bit.
Pre-clearance contested ball, mate, down by five.
Jesus, post-clearance contested ball, down by seven!
Hit outs to advantage, guys, down 1 to 11.

They're having problems defending the GWS kick-ins. They're having problems clearing their own kick-ins. They're having problems at ball ups; and at throw-ins.

Contests long down the line are proving an issue, as is the Giants "OTL movement" or ability to shift the ball Off The Line.

They go through various solutions. A block here? A spare there? The options they want players to take. The plays they want them to avoid. Conveying all of this information—in addition to the whispers of the line coaches as the players get their rub downs—is not their goal. Offering every insight and discussion—every statistic and structure—can be not only confusing for the players, but confronting. Telling them everything tells them that something is wrong, something serious. And so, the coach cherry-picks and he softens.

Only two minutes earlier—in the privacy of the coaches' room—those kick-ins were causing Hardwick perhaps the most consternation. He describes them as something he wants to tweak a little; nothing dramatic, a little adjustment, just something to remember.

He tells them he wants them to move the ball around a little more—shifting the ball with lateral handballs and short diagonal kicks, working the angles to work the advantage and work their way through the field.

The only point he states bluntly, with obvious disappointment, is something he expects his players to know already—that they are being beaten at the coalface, both inside and outside of the clearances.

"But why is that exciting for us?" he says, eyes now open wide. "Upside! The upside is *enormous!* If we just win a couple of those contests, catch a couple of those shit bounces we've had, things will change in an instant. The challenge is to stay in the moment."

He points to the whiteboard now, at two words he wrote earlier in the day. Two words that he writes every week: *STAY CONNECTED.*

"This is *exactly* the game we want against this side—the arm wrestle," he says. "Because what we do know is that we're one of the fittest sides in the competition."

He taps another note on the board, this one that says they have only used 40 rotations so far today. He puts his finger near the letters in red marker: *50 LEFT!!!*

"We start early. We start hard. We start again. And it all starts up here," he says, tapping one finger to his temple. "We know the strength of our individuals, and we know what we do together. You don't have to win the game off your own boot. You don't have to win the game right now. You've just got to grind them down."

//////////////

I t's hard to tell when exactly the match is won. The process begins with a snap from Daniel Rioli in the pocket, a moment of individual brilliance that nonetheless begins with the prized 'Spurs mentality' of the team—a tackle from Jack Graham, a kick to Riewoldt who beats two opponents to bring the ball to ground, where it is roved by McIntosh, handballed to Castagna, then to Lambert and finally to Rioli, who leans back to curl the kick high and across his body.

A typical Tiger goal comes next, the team forcing the ball forward, punching, tapping and tumbling it their way until Townsend kicks from close range. It is ugly and effective and the commentators say so: "There was nothing pretty about that at all! It was just surge momentum, scrappy footy!"

Rioli, knocked off balance, kicks his fourth goal to add to his six tackles. Nobody else comes close to those numbers.

Three Tigers pounce next on a short Giants kick, Lambert gives to Castagna, who finds Riewoldt, who could kick for goal but instead kicks back to Lambert. He could kick for goal but instead kicks to Edwards. He slots the shot and they lead by 20 points.

Lambert, so often the common denominator, again finds Graham, who finds Townsend, who lobs a towering kick that tumbles into the arms of Martin, who snaps his first goal of the game with three minutes left in the quarter.

Martin is not done. With just 16 seconds left, the ball again comes to the bull midfielder now stationed at full-forward, and a spooked Heath Shaw tugs just a little at his jumper, pulling the fabric up near the chest. Free kick. Goal. Thirty-one points up. If the roar of the crowd at the beginning was unprecedented, the roar at the last break was unheard of, but heard loud and clear.

Early in the final quarter, just more than a minute in, a series of skirmishes ends with a loose ball bouncing toward the goal mouth, and it is of course Martin who sprints to meet it, and the callers need only call his name to call the play.

"Dusty!" they cry as he gathers.

"*Dusty!!*" they cry as he spins.

"*DUSTY!!!*" they cry as a banana kick curls off his instep and through the tall white posts at the Punt Road end.

There are other wonderful Richmond moments and goals throughout the last term, but with a 37-point lead and less than a quarter to play, the game is over, and it is Martin again who has ended it. He is a match-winner, yet again. Sometimes people receive that designation by dent of sheer possession numbers, plus a handful of tackles, and perhaps the most metres gained, or some other cold metric. Martin though, for the third match in a row, has kicked goals either side of three-quarter time, effectively ending the contest, demoralising opponents, and winning the match. He doesn't do these things alone, but they are things he alone can do.

As with all things Richmond—at least in recent finals—there are some heart murmurs ahead, as the Giants answer with goals to Patton and Himmelberg, to draw the margin back to 23 points. But, the murmurs dissipate within moments, as Riewoldt, and Butler (twice) put victory beyond doubt. If the Qualifying Final victory was a release, then this is something else. This win is an awakening, as if something has been cast off and forgotten. If week one of the finals was a relieved sigh from a tense body, then week three was a wail. Halfway through the final quarter, the mass of Richmond fans gathered know now they have reason to dream.

The grandstands throughout the last moments of the quarter are not just thunder but a vast expanse of yellow and black caps, scarves and guernseys. There are air punches and flecks of spittle and grown men sprinting up and down the aisles and around the concourse, letting loose 35 years of pent-up energy and excitement and hope. One man stands wearing an old woollen guernsey with an Esso logo, and as Dan Butler snaps his first goal across his body, with ten minutes to play, the man simply hunches over, fists clenched, forearms flexing, upper body shaking, eyes shut, mouth open—*wide open*—screaming.

Each moment is thoroughly drunk by the fans and each, in turn, communes with those closest, and not just family and friends. There are handshakes with strangers, hugs with strangers and high fives with strangers, some of which ring out with a triumphant *SMACK!* and some of which miss altogether because the nerves are just too jangled, too filled with giddy energy and too little coordination or control; or even care.

In the change rooms, where the doormen and the massage staff and the physios have watched the game on a television in a darkened room, there is more of the same. Knowing the game is won, Media Manager Nicky Malady and her lieutenant, Georgina Cahill, and Bronwyn Doig, all sprint together from the flat screen and through the change rooms, and around two corners. They giggle like kids as they run up the black rubber race, so they can be near the field and feel a part of the moment when the Tigers beat the Giants by six goals to advance to a Grand Final.

///////////

The song is sung in the rooms, and there are tears. So many tears, and so many smiles, and so many breathless interviews given to waiting media. The players, as one, are gleefully incredulous at the position they are in: given the chance in seven short days to play for a premiership. The coaches applaud but then quickly assemble in the briefing room for their initial post mortem.

Livingstone enters the room: "Any injuries?"

Nothing serious. The game was played fiercely and so there are cuts and bruises and sprains, but nothing severe. "Any tribunal issues?" he then asks.

In most post-match press conferences, coaches are asked about whatever incidents have taken place during the game. If something happened in the first quarter, for instance, it has likely been replayed on various platforms, and been thoroughly dissected and assessed by experts, often accompanied by a certain verdict. The coach, however, almost customarily responds to any questions about this jumper punch or that high bump by saying "I haven't seen the incident". Many in the media believe this is an automatic deflection—the simplest way of not answering any question about any infringement. Sometimes though, such as when you have a Preliminary Final to win, it is the truth.

Answering Livingstone's question, pro scout Nick Austin tells the room there is one potential tribunal issue: "Cotch, on Shiel."

The entire coaching collective looks up from the whiteboard with quizzical bemusement, heads cocked sideways.

McQualter: "What?"

Rutten: "When?"

Livingstone: "Where was it?"

Hardwick: "Really?"

Caracella: "Was he going the ball?"

Not one of the coaches has seen the passage of play in which Cotchin dives at the football and collects Giants playmaker Dylan Shiel. Shiel plays the rest of the quarter, but after the break he fails a concussion test and is out of the game. The mobile phone reception in the rooms is failing, so they can't even see the clip. They turn to discussing the potential outcome anyway.

Was it a bump?

You can't suspend him. He's the captain.

Surely, he plays. It's the Barry Hall rule.

Only a moment later, Cotchin, who has carried two fines into the finals— another fine will see an automatic suspension imposed—is the first player to enter the room, and the captain asks the coach immediately and directly: "Am I in trouble?"

Hardwick still hasn't seen the clip, but answers anyway: "Nup. Nup," he says. "Going the ball. All good."

Two days later, with the AFL community equally divided over the nature of the collision—with media experts certain, both ways—Cotchin is cleared. So too is Brandon Ellis, who caught Giants wingman Lachie Whitfield with a high bump that received significantly less media scrutiny, but could just as easily have ended in suspension. Now though, they gather as a group to hear the coach once more. The familiar booming voice of team manager Mark Opie echoes down the hall—"*LET'S GO!*"—calling them all inside.

The room is at capacity, filled with players, coaches and many others. Blair Hartley and Matthew Clarke and Francis Jackson and Luke Williams from recruiting. McRae, Xavier Clarke and Ryan Ferguson from the VFL. Gale and Richardson. Murray, McCurry and Crowe.

Hardwick looks up at them all with that same placid smile he wore after their last victory. He waits for them to fall silent. To make eye contact. He lifts his hands from his side, palms upturned.

"Who likes playing in Grand Finals?" he says with smile.

And they scream in response: *YEEEEAAHHH!!!*

"Unbelievable," says the coach. "Terrific effort. The game itself, first half, we were a bit off. But there were bits of play in the second half, you go to the tape and it's just that surge mentality. It's brilliant to watch. There's a bit of play in our defensive-50 and it's just *bodies* flying *everywhere!* You *just weren't prepared* to give up a goal, and that's what makes sides great."

He adds his now standard finals-time message, about embracing the moment, loving the hype, enjoying it all for what it is, the big week ahead that they don't need to worry about or fear. It will all be organised for them.

What they need to do is put their mind to the Adelaide Crows, a team that beat them by an embarrassing 76 points earlier in the year. Hardwick has not forgotten. He wants his players to remember, too.

"I've been waiting since round six to get back at these guys. I bloody have," he says. "I was doing cartwheels when they won their prelim, because you know what? Every time we've had a second crack at a team this year, what's happened? We've won. Put the Grand Final aside. I want these guys on a skewer."

45

A GOOD JOURNEY

As Richmond revels in the glory of a long September run, the club's VFL side has also assembled an impressive post-season. They have beaten Collingwood in an Elimination Final, then Casey in a Semi-Final, then Box Hill in a Preliminary Final, and now they are here, at Etihad Stadium on a Sunday afternoon, playing in a Grand Final against Port Melbourne.

This side has been a second shining light for the club all year, headed by the calm, convivial presence of Craig McRae. The former Lion has been there every week, taking training at night, long after the AFL staff have left for the day. He has been there on the sidelines for games in Coburg and North Ballarat, Williamstown and Werribee, always with club polo shirt tucked into black slacks, hands in pockets, yelling phrases—often on repeat—into the swirl of action on the field.

"On your toes! On your toes!"

"No tease! No tease!"

"Stalking! Stalking!"

McRae is sincere. He points at Connor Menadue as he comes to the bench, shaking his head with respect at what he has seen from the young running player. "Gong, breaking the lines mate," he says, rolling his hands over and over one another. "Playing to your strengths."

Jayden Short comes off next, chest heaving, blowing hard, totally gassed after several straight line surges through the middle of the oval. "Onya Shorty, I can hear you from *here*, on the other side of the ground. It says you're interested in the game."

Ruckman Shaun Hampson comes to the sideline and goes straight to a seat, having taken a handful of strong contested marks. "Love it when you jump at the ball, Hammer! Damn. You look like a good player when you're jumping at it."

He claps Mabior Chol as he comes off, after several marking contests deep in the Richmond backline. "You are growing into a man right before our eyes, Marbs," he says. "As tough as I've ever seen you."

The senior listed players have come to watch the three VFL finals as well, and are now here to see this one. Ordinarily, in the crowd at such games, they are constantly stopped for autographs. They sign jumpers, and the front cover of the Footy Record. They sign hats, and boots, and many, many footballs. They sign printed caricatures and laminated photos brought to the ground in plastic pockets by fans seeking a keepsake to frame. A son begs his father to let Alex Rance sign his regular grey hoodie, and the dad relents. A man approaches, and all he has that can be signed is a $20 note, and so Rance signs that, too. They pose for selfies, wave after wave. The moment one fan sees another fan approach, the rest begin to line up, too, as if a single selfie granted has an unrelenting gravitational pull. "On a slow day, in a quarter of footy, I might do 25," says Rance. "On a busy day, maybe 100."

Today, after the Preliminary Final victory over the Giants, the players can enter through the basement of the stadium, and take the goods elevators up into a pair of hospitality suites. They are there to support their mates, but the game ends badly.

It is a close match, and Ben Lennon takes a set shot after the siren, a shot to win the game by a point. His kick drifts to the right, and instead the Tigers lose by four. In the change rooms afterwards, there is a sad finality in the air. The senior team has come down too, some of them carrying niggles from the day before: Lambert has a compression bandage on his ankle, Vlastuin with a limp from a mean corkie to his behind. They hug their crestfallen mates, mentally noting a scene they hope to avoid in the AFL Grand Final next week.

McRae speaks. He is proud of what they have achieved, and how far a once struggling football program has come. He thanks them all—the VFL listed players, the coaches, the staff, and the tireless volunteers.

"We don't say, 'That's it, all done'. We've got a great mindset and we strive to get better. We talk about developing a culture, well that's what we've done," he says, nodding. "We stand here disappointed—but as a club united. We haven't arrived, and this is not the end."

//////////

But it will be the end for some. There are VFL listed players who will not be asked back next year. And there are AFL listed players who will face difficult exit interviews in a little more than a week. For most, right now, their fate is uncertain.

But not for one player.

When we think of great careers ending, we often think of choreographed tearful goodbyes. There have been more than a few this season. Nick Riewoldt carried from the MCG. Luke Hodge and Bob Murphy and Matthew Boyd, finishing in the same game. All were chaired off the field, all were the subject of profiles and photo spreads and an outpouring of social media congratulations and television interviews and heady tributes.

Some careers end without any of that. They end here, on a cold afternoon in the Docklands, under a domed roof in a kind of false halogen twilight.

At the start of this day, Ivan Maric looked happy in the rooms.

He lay on the blue carpet, stretching his back beside Oleg Markov and Ben Griffiths, for the last time. He bent on one knee, to stretch his hamstrings next to Ben Lennon and Callum Moore, for the last time. He ran through handball drills behind Anthony Miles and Taylor Hunt, for the last time. He took off his warm-up top and pulled down the Richmond guernsey, walked onto the field with Reece Conca and Tyson Stengle, and slid in his white mouthguard and did his run-throughs and practised his ruck duels, for the last time.

A few hours later, after the final siren, he shook hands with all of his opponents. He hugged one of them. Number 28. Robbie Nahas, with whom he played at Richmond for two seasons.

Then he trod his way across the field, over divots of a kind of wet, sandy loam, his wrists strapped as always, his socks up, as ever. He listened dutifully to the speeches as the Port Melbourne victors were presented their medals and their Cup. He stood tall the entire time, placid and immovable, as his teammates sat on their haunches. He walked from the field and down the race, between Shaun Hampson and Sam Lloyd. He did not wave to the crowd and they did not wave to him.

Ivan Maric played 77 games with Adelaide, and 80 with Richmond, and while he was valued at the former club he remains truly beloved at the latter. And so, this is how a storied career sometimes ends, with four kicks and five handballs, one mark and four tackles, 21 hit outs and one painful loss.

It ends with a gentle giant in a tiny room, lying on a cushioned bench, body flat, back set up at an angle, hands in lap, eyes closed, while a blinding orange surgical light sits inches from his face. Dr Sachin Khullar, the club's VFL doctor, sutures a slight wound just below his right brow—two stitches with a band-aid on top—and uses a flat piece of paper to daub the blood, which runs down his cheek and spills in drops and smears on the yellow of his guernsey, under his neck.

"It's been a good journey," Maric says, smiling serenely a moment later. "I suppose when I was young I was like, 'I really want to give this a crack'. I always believed that I could, that I was good enough. Then, I reckon last week, I realised that really—*really*—what I was searching for in my career, was to be part of a team where everyone was willing to give to one another, completely, at any time, and I feel like I was part of something with this team. It would have been really nice to have that premiership medal, to show evidence of it, but I'll still never forget being part of this group."

Rance sneaks up behind the smiling ruckman now, and hugs him deeply, the champion defender resting his head in the crook of the ruckman's neck. "You can be pretty proud of the culture you've built here," Rance says softly. "Really proud."

Rance is not the only one, either. McQualter hugs him. As does his cousin, Ivan Soldo. Conca comes by for a cuddle. In fact no one who sees Maric in the medical room shakes his hand—they all embrace the big man. Rance explains why.

"He's brought this incredible human quality," he says. "Where sometimes football clubs are professional environments, and it can be sterile, and cut and dried, and 'You're not good enough, piss off mate', Ivan's just been a person. We all want to be loved and cared about, and he has those little things that not everyone is gifted with. He has an ability to connect with people, and make them feel like they're a better person than when they woke up."

"Thanks mate," Maric says, quietly chuffed. "That's pretty nice."

He will miss football, this man mountain with soft brown eyes and a softer voice. "I absolutely *loved* just coming in and doing the work to get better," he says, his eyes closing on the word *loved*, as if he adored that work out on the track. "Training hard, doing the extras, it gave me the opportunity to compete at a really high level against the very best. I *loved* that. My alarm always sounds in the morning, and I'm up straight away, trying my very best never to hit snooze."

When he trained, Maric did far more than going through the motions. He would always do his drills while considering the other ruckmen throughout the League, wondering if *they* were training as hard, if *they* were looking—like him—for little ways to be better. On the field though, he adored nothing more than going head-to-head with a serious opponent.

"I liked looking for ways to grind him down. Running past him with really strong body language. Then backing that up with fierce aggression, so when he walked off the field he didn't have to say anything but I knew that he was sore, and he was going to feel it all week. I love the respect between ruckmen all around the League. You love looking them in the eye, and shaking their hand. It's a personal thing for me. I'll miss that."

Playing with the team, for the team, is what he will miss most. "I wish I could do that forever. Fighting with my teammates to the end, no matter what the scoreboard says. But, unfortunately, you can't, just because of age."

Time outruns all athletes. The American sportswriter Red Smith, covering the inevitable destruction of an ageing Joe Louis by a young Rocky Marciano in 1951, wrote about visiting the old champion in the dressing room afterward, while a trainer applied ice to his cut and cauliflowered ear, his head pillowed on a rolled-up towel. It was a fight in which Louis was knocked down, and knocked from the ring, and out of the fight—and out of boxing forever. Maric was not hit by some upstart junior today—his bloody brow was the result of an accidental head clash. But the words of Smith still ring true. "An old man's dream ended," he wrote. "But the place for old men to dream is by the fire."

Maric is not going to sit by any fire. He will work for the club in a player welfare role and perhaps some ruck coaching. He is excited by the prospect of guiding footy players through the twilight zone from a professional athlete into standard citizenry.

"I think it's a skill that needs to be practised. We're all boys when we come into the League," he says. "And when you get to 29 or 30, you need just as much love and guidance, because you just don't bounce back as well as you did when you were younger."

Maric lost his spring in 2016. He injured his back early in the year, and couldn't train as hard as he liked. He tried, but never regained the dynamism that made him—and his long flowing mullet—a cult figure in his first years at Richmond.

He leaves the game not having won a final. He leaves the Tigers nonetheless having made an indelible mark on the club.

"I loved being part of a team. If I had wanted to be an individual athlete, I would have done that. All I ever wanted to do was contribute, do my job, and help others do theirs. I'm happy with my career. But I'll miss everything about it."

46

THE LION

The Yarra River sparkles in this moment, on this night. Its little ripples catch and reflect the orange fireballs exploding from the towers lining the Southbank promenade, outside Crown Casino. Inside, the vast Palladium function room is full, and all are upstanding, as Dustin Martin walks to the stage to accept the 2017 Brownlow Medal.

All night, he has sat at the Tiger table with Sam Lloyd to his left and Daniel Rioli to his right, as he amassed a record 36 votes, including a record 11 best-on-ground performances, and now he stands and moves and shakes hands with his teammates while en route to the podium for the standard winner's interview with Channel Seven stalwart Bruce McAvaney.

He looks uncomfortable up there, pursing his lips over and over, poking a tongue into his cheek, holding his hands by his side, behind his back, in front of him and then on the lectern. He offers little nods to McAvaney's prods, and the barest of smiles. He is self-effacing and honest and at times funny, but in all his answers tonight and at the next day's all-in press conference—indeed always—brevity is his friend.

"It's interesting."
"It's unique."
"It's surreal."
"I'm a bit nervous."

He looks and sounds fidgety and unsure of himself. On the field he is anything but. Dustin Martin is the most dominant football player in the land. He has just won the most prestigious individual award in the game, after being named in the centre of the All Australian side, on top of winning the AFLPA MVP award, also known as the Leigh Matthews Trophy, all of which prompted Matthews himself to suggest that no player in the game's history has compiled a better season of football. To the people at Tigerland who know Martin's game so well, none of this is surprising.

Martin grew up near Castlemaine, on a big block of land, with two brothers, Tyson and Bronson. They made their backyard into a football field, complete with makeshift goal posts at one end. He played Auskick at six. He left school when he was 14, and moved to Sydney to live with his father, Shane. He played for an under-18s team there, in Campbelltown, when he was 15. He drove forklifts for his father's transport business, and worked also at the apparel business of Shane's wife, Adriana.

He missed his friends though, and so came back to Victoria, and lived with his mum, Kathy. He worked three days a week for an electrical contractor in Bendigo, and then a short stint as a stonemason in Castlemaine. He played senior football for Castlemaine (in the Collingwood colours) as a 16-year-old, and a little cricket, as a fast bowler for Guildford, before finally playing a handful of games for the Bendigo Pioneers in the TAC Cup, the stepping stone to the AFL.

Those are the dot points of his life, before he was noticed.

It was in 2008 when Francis Jackson, Richmond's long-time recruiting manager, first saw Martin play. It was his "bottom age" year—the year before he was old enough to be drafted—and he was rampaging across a football field in Golden Square, just outside of Bendigo. "I remember his power, his ability to surge, and his skills on either side of the body. It seemed there was nothing he couldn't do," says Jackson. "He had that ability to keep his feet, but even more so playing against boys. He just had so many modern-day attributes."

The following year, those attributes were on show for all to see. Matthew Clarke, who was in his first year as a recruiter at Richmond, was taken aback. "What stood out then stands out now. Natural size, ability to kick the footy, strength. He said he was born to play AFL, and he's shown that. He always had the tools," Clarke says. "His running wasn't super but it was good enough, and by the end of the year he went to the Draft Combine and ran a 14.3 beep, which is excellent for someone who hadn't been in the pathway system long."

What Clarke and Francis (and by then most of the football community) saw was power, which is different from brute strength. In many ways, Martin's physical dominance has little to do with his upper body. His force comes from the sheer brawn of his legs, paired with perfect balance. Martin almost never falls over. "You look for that—whether boys can stand up in a tackle and shrug and move, and Dustin could always do that," Clarke says. "The fend was there, but more important was being able to hold his ground under physical heat, and not to collapse."

That prodigious kick was on show early, too, but in some ways even that has been misread. When Martin barrelled the ball 78 metres in round one against Carlton, all anyone could talk about was his ability to kick the ball long and flat, but his accuracy is devastating as well. "It's his ball drop," says Clarke. "Dustin guides it down *so far* that he almost puts it on his foot with his hand. It means the margin for error is really small, so his short chips are exceptional, too."

The recruiting team saw all of this as they assessed the country boy who is one day certain to become an "Immortal" of their club. They wrote down everything. After interviews, for instance, it was clear that he was "extremely coachable" and had a "strong desire to succeed". Psychological evaluations revealed, "Very good mental toughness" but also "Scores above average for worrying." His stated aspiration at AFL level was "to win a premiership and be a one-club player", and the three personality traits Martin named as his best were loyalty, commitment and strong character.

When Clarke and Jackson were convinced that Melbourne would select Tom Scully and Jack Trengove with their first two picks in the 2009 draft, they made the trip to Bendigo to tell Martin, then 18, they were going to take him with pick three. "This was the only time we've told a kid we were going to pick him, but we wanted to make him feel comfortable," Clarke says. "It's funny, but he hardly said anything. You tell some kids, and they give you high fives or they break down in tears. He was like 'Yep, that's good, no worries'."

They all played a round of golf together at Eaglehawk Golf Club, labouring through a very slow nine holes. Martin was not a golfer. "He was like Happy Gilmore—he took a run up swing once," Clarke says, laughing. "It was a strange morning. Dustin was wandering around with one club on his shoulder, hitting balls and not saying much. He was just like he is now in a lot of ways."

Arriving at Richmond, he was just as withdrawn. Tim Livingstone says his shyness stood out immediately. He keeps a photo of Martin from the night of the draft. He is alongside his father, Shane. The kid in the picture looks frightened, perhaps lost. "I use that photo in presentations sometimes," he says, "alongside a photo of Dusty on the MCG, at his best, to talk about how we have to take these kids from being shy and nervous to performing in front of 85,000 people. We do it by looking after them like family."

The transformation of the club's newest son took time, but the captain, Trent Cotchin, saw his friend mature immediately if incrementally. "Simply put, he came into the AFL environment as an 18-year-old, but he seemed much younger in some of the ways he behaved," he said. "Yet for every year here, I think he's grown three, if that makes sense."

His maturation was not an uninterrupted ascension. Brendon Gale recalls not only the time in 2012 when Martin was suspended by the club—after dabbling with sleeping pills and missing training—but also a pre-season training session in 2010, when Martin was sent from the training track. "He had had a big night, and he wasn't right to train. We had to have a serious chat with him about his future. But he was young, and the spoils of AFL are great, and it takes time to work it all out and understand the professionalism required at this level."

There was also that anxious time in 2013 when Martin flirted with the notion of leaving the club—for the first time—even going so far as to tour the facilities at Greater Western Sydney. Jackson remembers the moment well, and his immediate conversation with Dan Richardson. "I just said 'We can't let Dustin leave—he's a Brownlow medallist.' We just needed to help him past that stage of his life. There was a little immaturity—maybe a lack of worldliness." Many have helped him in that regard. Former club President Gary March, former player and administrator Wayne Campbell (now head of football at GWS), former development coach Mark (Choco) Williams, as well as Cotchin and his only senior coach, Damien Hardwick. Through it all he has also drawn a raffish collective of friends, from Dane Swan to Michael Gardiner and Jake King.

Martin has been no stranger to headlines this season, as the 'Will he stay or will he go?' contract discussion became saga. The negotiations dragged on and on, but this was a contract Martin had to make count. No matter where his brilliant career goes from here, Martin will not retire and make a living in football media, and he is unlikely to coach. Leveraging the best deal for his services in 2017 was compared by some to LeBron James in the NBA, but it was perhaps more reminiscent of Dutch soccer player Johan Cruyff, the star of the Netherlands in the 1970s. Like Martin, Cruyff knew his own talent, and its worth, and how that worth would one day vanish: "When my career ends," said Cruyff, "I cannot go to the baker and say, 'I'm Johan Cruyff, give me some bread'."

Gale was the CEO of the AFL Players' Association when free agency was being introduced, and so he sees the irony—now he's at Richmond—of player bargaining power coming back to "bite us in the arse". Nevertheless, he was a champion of Martin's right to choose. "It went longer than we wanted, it was drawn out, and it was announced probably not the way we would have preferred. But it had no impact on us as a footy club."

He was happy, as was Richardson, and Neil Balme, and Martin's manager Ralph Carr—and Martin himself—that they could reach a deal on the eve of the finals. They shook hands at Carr's home in Hawthorn on a Thursday afternoon, after all had headed there separately from Tigerland. "There was media outside expecting an answer, so we figured if we all walk out together they'll follow us," says Richardson. "So, we split up. It was a really good way to finish it all. We had a hug, and said a few words, and had a couple of Coronas each."

All of which allowed Martin to return to what he does best, and what gives him the most joy. People inside the club describe the football field variously as his "home", his "sanctuary", his "safe space."

"Dustin is at his happiest when he's out on the footy field," says Livingstone. "Even when he comes to the bench, he sits down for a minute and always wants to get back into it: *Get me on! Get me on!*" he says. "And out of all the guys who come to the bench late in the game when we're about win, he shows the most excitement."

Hardwick thinks Martin is "free" when he plays the game—that he is one of the gifted ones—those savants who just pick up the ball and know exactly what to do. "I'll use Matthew Richardson as an example," he says. "People say, 'Why don't you get Richo to come down and coach?' Well, Matthew Richardson was a freak. A *freak*. He just played the game on instinct—you can't teach that. You can't teach what Dustin can do either."

Perhaps this sells short the depth of work done by Martin not only to improve his game but to understand the total team game. Andrew McQualter, who began working with Martin this year as the stoppages coach, says the bull-like centreman is a quick study. Some players need hours of vision to make an idea concrete. Not Martin. "What I've learnt with Dus' is that I can tell him something once—*in this scenario, if this happens, you need to do this*—and straight away he goes, 'Yeah, got it', and the next time he'll do it perfectly. He's as smart as anyone I've seen in that regard. I probably didn't realise he had that nous about him."

Martin also speaks up now more than he ever has, which, granted, is still not a lot. But what he says has an impact on the playing group. "From the outside, you might suspect that he's quite simple in his approach to footy," says Cotchin, "and while he does just go out there and play, I think he sees the game a lot better than people imagine."

Martin means a great deal to Cotchin. When the captain sat down at the start of the season with Ben Crowe to write a life plan, one of his goals was specific and personal: *I will do everything I can to help Dustin Martin win the Brownlow Medal.*

"I think that just shows how much care and love I have for him as an individual, but it's also about how far I've come myself, in terms of where I fit and what I want for our group. I don't think the medal is anything Dusty has strived for, but by me focusing on someone else—instead of myself—I think it helps the group. Dusty would be the same. He's incredibly caring."

Caring is indeed a word that continually comes up in relation to the superstar. The first comment I heard Martin make in any group setting at Richmond was about standards. The coaching group was soliciting the players for suggestions, and Martin spoke up in the faintest murmur: "I think it would be good if guys could be more respectful in the players' lounge, cleaning up after themselves."

Martin is known amongst friends for his enormous heart, too. The people closest to him see it as a defining trait. McQualter recounts a story about his daughter, Emily, who is 13 weeks old and was recently found to have a cancerous growth, a rare neuroblastoma. She had to have surgery on her adrenal gland when she was seven weeks old. The cancer is now gone, but it was an understandably wrenching time for McQualter, a first-time father, and his wife, Jane. "It's been brutal, and Dustin was one of the first people to consistently ask me how things were going. Not many people see that caring side, but it's one of his most important traits."

Hardwick, too, sees this in his star midfielder. He remembers being as curious about Martin as anyone when they first met. "He's got that hard exterior. Chiselled. Tattooed. He looks like he means business. But as time went by the real Dustin came out. I'll be sitting on the couch at 10pm after a win, watching the TV, and he'll send me a picture of him with a beer and the words 'I love you, coach'. You wouldn't think he would be that guy, but that's who he is. It makes me feel better just knowing he's around."

Martin is of course quiet, but he is not uncommunicative. He has 198,000 followers on Instagram. He preferred to remain silent for this book, even though he was aware of my presence and purpose at the club this season and last. Yet while his famous fend—the "don't argue"—might apply equally to opponents on field and to the media, it is far from analogous in his private dealings with most people. Especially his teammates. He sends a message out to the midfield group every game day: *Can't wait for the game today, love playing with you boys, let's get it done.* "He's a connector," says McQualter. "He's the one driving that bond and energy."

He is perhaps the opposite to what people might expect, too, in terms of his willingness to help. Martin is in fact a born pleaser, a "yes man" who has only recently learned how to say no. "Everyone wants a piece of Dusty, and he feels genuine guilt if he doesn't uphold a commitment he's made," says Cotchin. "He gets quite insecure about letting people down."

His reluctance to speak in public might also suggest Martin is guarded about what he says because of how it might be construed, or twisted, but Cotchin suggests he is far more comfortable with himself than anyone he knows. "Dusty is what he is. He doesn't care what people think. He's taught me the value of that," Cotchin says. "But sometimes I wish he would do some media, because I'd love people to know the real Dusty, which is this genuine person who wants the best for everyone that he loves."

Martin it seems is full of contradictions. His favourite movie might be the paean to gangster rap, *Straight Outta Compton*, and his favourite musician might be hip-hop star Drake, but his life is not all bombast and gold chains.

"He's got a presence off the field that almost doesn't suit him," Hardwick says. "He loves fine restaurants. He loves fine wine. He loves seeing places he hasn't seen, moving through Argentina or Brazil. He's a rare beast, but he's our beast."

Fitness boss Peter Burge has spent a lot of time with Martin, and says people would be surprised to learn how curious he is about the world. When Martin was still adjusting to the physical rigours of AFL footy, he and Burge used to walk and jog Yarra Park and the Tan Track together, and Martin was always full of questions. "He's inquisitive about how things work. Why are people fighting about this? He'll look at a building and go, 'It's amazing to think someone built that—I wonder how they did it?' He watches documentaries about the cosmos, and what's going on in the universe."

Martin is, of course, famously durable. He has missed only one game through injury in his whole career—now 178 games in eight seasons, since his debut in Round 1, 2010. "He hates missing training," says Burge. "There are times we have to tell him to have a light session. We should do it more often, because he won't come to you if he's tired—he'll want to please everyone. We have to say, 'You're due, mate. Take a rest'."

Physically, he has found what works best for him through trial and error, accounting for his exceptional drive. His current formula includes extra boxing sessions each week, which he does in Port Melbourne with Sam Lloyd. Time in the ring has improved his body composition but also his footwork and aggression. He has experimented with different diets and ways of eating, too, whether high fat or low carb or some other fad. "He reads up on this stuff," says Burge. "He's reading a book now about minimalism, and there's a chapter in there on diet, around portion control and cleaner food. He always wants to learn."

His meal the night before every game, however, is set. It is a ritual. Shaun Grigg comes over to his spotless apartment, where Martin cooks them both honey mustard chicken and rice. That quiet space is better than eating out. The day of the first VFL final, with the Tigers up against Collingwood, Grigg got a glimpse of what life is like for Dustin Martin in public. The pair sat together at the back of the old Port Melbourne grandstand.

"I was right next to him, and I felt awkward. There were hundreds of people in the seats in front of us, and they were just turning around—one by one—to look at Dustin. They barely stopped the entire game. It comes with the territory, I suppose, but that would happen everywhere Dustin goes, every restaurant, coffee shop and street. It would be so tough. You can sense when someone is sitting over the other side of the room watching you." Many at the club suspect this is part of why Martin lives his life the way he does, flitting between the homes of friends in a perpetually busy state. "Even when he comes over for dinner," says Cotchin, "he gets there, plays with the girls—hide and seek, puzzles, drawing—has dinner, does a little sitting around, and then he's gone." The homes of others in his circle of friends are perhaps the only spaces outside of his own home that he can exist without being tracked by the constant public gaze. "People look at him and might suspect he has a crazy lifestyle, but I can tell you where he is on a Saturday night," says Hardwick. "He's at home watching Netflix."

The 26-year-old footballer is wealthy. He is healthy. He plays a game for a living. And he is preternaturally gifted in that game, and so he is served a constant stream of adulation and praise. People often say to Hardwick that they would love to be Dustin Martin, and Hardwick thinks he might, too, at least for two hours every weekend. "But then when it comes to your actual life, and you realise you can't go anywhere without someone looking, pointing, taking a photo. Can you imagine doing that every day for years on end? It must be exhausting. If you're Dustin it's like you're in a zoo. And you're the lion."

Gale uses a different animal to describe the player: "He's a lamb," he says. "He avoids confrontation—except on the footy field." Gale believes he also has a special kind of intelligence: "There is a particular kind of focus—and it's quite rare—in applying a free and unfettered mind to the task you're performing, to your full potential, whether you're a QC, a surgeon or a footballer," he says. "Dustin has some amazing physical gifts but he brings those gifts fully to bear because he is so present."

Some of that can be attributed to his faithful adherence to mindfulness. Emma Murray remembers her first meeting with Martin in 2015. He texted her. He hadn't had a great start to the season. He said there was a lot of "noise in his head", and so Murray had him close his eyes and imagine what his best football looked like. He felt like his shoulders and chest were important when he played well, and then over time he came up with specific words to focus on during games.

Many of the players on the list have words of their own that they have unearthed while working with Murray. When Cotchin finds his performance slipping, he repeats to himself: *Strong, Clear, Calm, Jokey.* Shane Edwards, when he needs a spark, has a different three: *React, Run, Angles.* Whenever Brandon Ellis feels as though his game is slipping, he returns to a single phrase: *Strong clean running machine.* Murray winces when people summarise Martin as a freak, or as one of those players who by nature "wills himself into the contest"—because it sells short the large body of work he puts into both his physical game and his mental game. She drilled this notion into the fleet of young forwards earlier in the year:

"Dusty is doing this work every single day," she told them. "I see him every week. I have multiple conversations with him every week. Straight after the siren he's reflecting on the thoughts he had, what state he was in, how did it affect his performance: 'When I thought this, what did that make me do?'"

Murray then asked the mosquito fleet to think about the words that represent their best football. Martin has his. "Dusty has got three things in his mind the whole game," said Murray. "*Strong. Aggressive. Unstoppable.* That's all he says. Any time something goes wrong he says 'strong'. Anytime he does something that's weak he says 'aggressive'. Anytime he tries to do something and someone blocks his way, he gets up and says 'unstoppable'."

Murray also introduced Martin to meditation, which he trusted and now finds indispensable. It makes him feel clear of mind. "He's got an impressive connection with his own emotional intelligence and what he needs," Murray says. "His self-awareness is incredible. If you measured intelligence around that self-awareness, his understanding of his headspace and what's going on around him, he's off the Richter Scale, more so than any athlete I've ever worked for. It's phenomenal."

On the field, she doesn't see the rampaging beast that others do. She sees something that transcends football, seeming closer to art. "I just see magic on the field. I see someone who has tapped into an energy. So many players are playing with layers of stuff that they're thinking about. If you could look into their minds they would be so busy and full. If you could look into Dusty's mind, it would be this white, bright, light of energy."

There is one final anecdote that might help illuminate the best yet most enigmatic player in the competition. Gale decided to get fit earlier this year, and so he began swimming in Port Phillip Bay, and he kept going even into the winter months, effectively joining those fanatics who swim in water so cold you need to wear a hat made of wetsuit material to avoid an ice cream headache. Gale was talking with someone from the group only recently, and learned something that was unknown even to the fitness staff at Richmond.

Dustin Martin does the same thing—on occasions—alone, at night.

"It makes perfect sense," says Gale. "It's quiet. No one bothers him. It's a peaceful place, and I think he would probably enjoy that solitude."

Martin uses a steam room first. Then he steps across the sand, enters the frigid black water of the bay and swims out in the darkness, with the city lights in the distance blinking back at him. It is beautiful, and tranquil, and silent, and it reminds Gale of one final animal analogy.

"You look at images of footballers—action shots, getting the ball, anticipating contact—and you know how they've got that startled, panicked look?" he asks. "You look at Dustin's eyes in those moments, and they give nothing. They reveal *nothing*. He's like a shark. Like a great white, just cruising through the water. And then he strikes."

47

BURN THE BOATS

Something is rumbling inside the old community change rooms in the Jack Dyer Stand at the Punt Road Oval.

Can you hear it?

That low thunder growing louder and louder?

A door swings open and then the percussive thuds ring out with a blast, and every player on the list—and every coach—steps into the concrete space with the low ceiling, and the noise is deafening.

Four drummers are at work, moving and shaking and pulsing, smashing what look like bongos. One rattles a *shekere*, a hollow gourd covered in a net of beads, and another belts a *dunun*, a big cylindrical drum played with a stick. They are dressed in bright-patterned billowing pants and shirts, and they sway with a beat that fills the room.

The standard equipment meant for this space—all the free weights and stationary bicycles—has been pushed into corners. All that is left is enough seating for around 60 people, in concentric circles, and in front of every seat is a drum—one for every coach and player and administrator.

Boubacar Gaye, who first picked up a drum in Senegal when he was 14, explains now that everyone is about to become part of his drum circle. He tells them how the men need to play the drum. He shows them how to do it, too, holding it off the ground, pinched between the legs, tilted at an angle. He guides them through various patterns, and shows them how to switch between hitting their own drum and the drum of the person next to them. Then he yells: "One, two, three *and GO!*"

Gaye plays a small combination of taps and thuds, and the players all mimic him a moment later. They are grinning, and their shoulders roll and bounce, and awkwardness quickly gives way to abandon. They are smiling and tapping and flinging flat hands onto the stretched skin. They patter and whack and scratch their fingernails across the surface. It grows warmer in there, too, and so their faces grow red. Sweat pours down Gaye's neck. And then he stops them.

The drum they are playing—a rope-tuned goat skin tightened across a hardwood base, shaped like a goblet—is called the *djembe*. "It means 'gather in peace'," Gaye says. "It was used in West Africa to bring the community together, to call out. Before we had the telephone, this is what we used. Today it is a musical instrument."

He walks the players through the various strikes they can make, and he hits the drum slowly—*boom, boom, boom*—and at first it sounds like the rhythm inside the dank hold of a ship powered by oars.

"Now," he says, grinning, "you guys feel the vibes, close your eyes, and *hit the DRUM!*"

And the men in the room dressed in yellow and black sneakers and tracksuits, singlets and shorts, let their arms and hands fly wildly. Hardwick laughs while sharing a moment with McIntosh. Grimes and Griffiths exchange smiles. Riewoldt and Rance bang each other's drums and grin. Rutten and Rioli. Graham and McQualter. Caddy and Martin. Even Dan Richardson and Neil Balme are laughing and drumming as the sound fills the room. All of them are drumming and beaming together.

It is cacophonous, and so finally Gaye has them stand on their toes, and reach for the sky; then stoop low, in squats and stretches. Then they shuffle, two steps left—*clap!*—and two steps right—*clap!* They wave their arms in unison. They take a knee, and open their arms wide, and they repeat after him.

"Go, hey!"

Go hey!

"Go, hey!!"

GO HEY!

"Go, Richmond!"

GO RICHMOND!!!

Shane McCurry, who runs the leadership and culture program for the Tigers, stands for a moment and pauses. This is the final session of The Richmond Man for 2017. He says he wanted something different for the players—a celebration and a message.

"Just want to say boys, whether we're playing drums or playing footy on the field, connection is really important. When you play together it's so much easier, so much louder, and so much more fun, so keep going on that journey, and get that prize you've been waiting for."

The session is over, and they are ready to leave, but Bachar Houli is not quite finished. A few players begin to stand but Houli sits and hammers the drum with speed and touch, and he gets faster and faster, and there is a perfect and hypnotic off-beat rhythm, and so Oleg Markov dances next to Houli, moving his hips and hands like a young man at a warehouse dance party. He shimmies and shakes while Houli hunches over and smacks and pummels that drum, and the two of them are in a frenzy and the room is clapping in unison, and, as the beat finds its peak they all roar, and leave the space grinning, ready for lunch in the players' lounge. It is Tuesday, September 26, and Grand Final week has begun.

⁄⁄⁄⁄⁄⁄⁄⁄⁄⁄⁄

There are light, casual moments throughout this week, as the big game approaches. The club presents framed pictures to all players who have notched milestone games this season. 50 each for Lloyd, McIntosh and Lambert. 100 to Grimes, Prestia and Caddy. 150 to Houli. 200 to Edwards.

One morning they do their final round of voting for the Francis Bourke Award—each week the playing group votes on a 3-2-1 basis for the players who best uphold values of "awareness, united, relentless and discipline"—and Steve Wyatt, the former policeman and integrity officer at the club, comes in to collect the voting slips. He looks different today. He is wearing his old VicPol uniform, and carries a silver case like an Armaguard officer—and he has a gigantic German shepherd on a lead, which fills the auditorium with one of those powerful big dog barks. (It is the pet of one of the administrative staff, and later it runs through the Punt Road complex, licking footballers' legs and panting.)

Events demand attention all week long inside and outside the club. Beyond Monday's Brownlow there is the Coach of the Year award, won, this evening, by Hardwick. A new round of AFL Women's licences is announced, and Richmond will enter the League in 2020, a project already being led at the club by Richardson and former Collingwood AFLW player Kate Sheahan.

The foot traffic around Punt Road Oval is plentiful and constant, and so a temporary chain link fence is erected around the Swinburne Centre. Inside, little guided tours of the facility trickle through.

In the administrative wing of the building, people are working in a kind of fever dream, marketing events and planning merchandise, not from a sense of false confidence but because, should Richmond win on Saturday, the club needs to be ready to capitalise.

Richmond is on every front page and dominating TV news broadcasts, the club colours in shop windows and painted on fences and doors and windows. A mural of Dustin Martin goes up in a nearby alley. The speed limit on Punt Road is dropped to 40 kilometres per hour, to accommodate the influx of pedestrians throughout the precinct.

The space between Punt Road Oval and the MCG is filling, too, with a slowly growing city of marquees, and the constant arrival and departure of trucks with labels like Coates Hire and Black Tie Toilets and Harry The Hirer. Balme foreshadowed this moment straight after the win against the Giants.

"It will be a big week. There are only two teams left, and only one of them is from Melbourne, so the media's going to be all over us. That's ok. Soak it up," he said. "But everyone needs to buy into it—we can't have all the same guys doing it. So, when we ask you to do something, ask some advice about what they'll want to talk about, then buy into it."

The message the players and coaches offer to the media is that it's "business as usual" once they enter the club—and, despite scepticism from some, that is absolutely correct. When the players go downstairs to the change rooms, and the gym, and the pools, and the massage tables and the medical quarters, they switch on.

They are aided by a visual reminder, there always. Marked on the floor near the entrance to the lower level is a white line painted near the bottom of the stairs. The team has a policy of stepping onto a "virtual playing field" when they cross the white line. No mobile phones. No guests. Cross that line and they are at work.

"Upstairs, people are looking for their tickets, and car park passes, and people are passing through the office and there's all this action," says head trainer, Matt Pearce. "But downstairs we put all that aside. Even if I'm completely anxious inside myself, you've just got to straight bat everything this week. Getting strapped, doing prep, nothing changes. It might be Grand Final week, but down here it could be Round 12."

Indeed, the weekly schedule emailed to all staff by football compliance manager Jenna Earle remains full, each item listed on the expected day at the expected time. Medical screenings. Wellness reports. Strength training. Massage. Recovery. Rehab. Conditioning extras. Injury prevention. Mobility. Walk throughs. Selection. Review. Captain's run. Nothing changes.

The opposition analysis is as important as ever. Picking apart the Adelaide game plan and personnel is trickled out to the playing group in various meetings.

The Crows, Rutten says, score heavily from turnovers. They have set plays but they don't rely on them. "They'll make it up," he says. "They want it fast."

Like most teams, he says, they get beaten when they face enormous pressure. Like most teams, they get beaten when they get smashed in contested ball. The Tigers *must* spread the Crows, they *must* separate their defenders, and they *must* bring the ball to ground.

And they need to track their defenders as they try to clear the ball by foot: "We *must* chase out of our forward line. We've got to empty out and come with them. We have to slow them down."

When the Tigers are manning the mark, they need to *sprint* at the mark, using their hands to point at that imaginary line on the ground, letting the Crows know their space and time is limited. They need to get in their faces with movement—to "take their eyes" and limit their vision. "Get right up on it *to the centimetre*," says Rutten. "That gives us two seconds. Two seconds is gold. We can cover 20 metres in two seconds. We can block an outlet in two seconds. In two seconds, we can stop their movement completely."

He shows clips of games in which the Crows were beaten. The first was against Hawthorn. He shows how the Hawthorn defence simply worked back and handed their opponents over, from defender to defender, preventing any overlap chains. "Look at the Hawks," he says. "Not working hard, but they know exactly what they're doing." Organisation is everything.

Leppitsch speaks about preventing Adelaide's back six from taking marks.

He shows Jake Lever taking an easy mark, while a Crow and a Hawk wrestle. "We are *not* letting them do that," he says. "We *cannot* let them get extra numbers behind the ball. That's how they set up their attack. We can do this—the MCG is much bigger than the Adelaide Oval, so the gaps on the field are going to be foreign to them."

Caracella shows a clip of another Crow, Jake Kelly, the son of Magpie full-back, sports agent and entrepreneur, Craig Kelly, picking up the ball and running, under pressure from a Hawk in pursuit. All Australian defender Rory Laird runs for Kelly, offering to receive the handball. Then Jack Gunston enters the frame, and he has two options. He can charge at Kelly, or he can stay with Laird. He stays with Laird, choosing to guard rather than blitz.

"See that?" says Caracella. "Kelly can't release because Gunston is on Laird. Kelly holds onto it for a second, gets tackled, holding the ball, shot on goal. Gunston has created that with his positioning."

There are more reminders throughout the week. The Crows are zero and five when they score fewer than 45 points from turnovers. In eight of the past nine games, the Tigers have held their opponent under this critical number.

Hardwick points to individual players, too, and how they need to be curtailed. All Australian ball magnet Matt Crouch is one of them. "Cotch, I need you to crash into this bloke all day. Make him earn it. Get physical. He's a very, very good player—we can't let him have it easy."

He points to ruckman Sam Jacobs, too, who he considers perhaps the best big man in the game. But this message is for everyone. "Anything you can do to help Nank, do it," Hardwick says. "Just get in Jacobs's way. Block his path. Make him move an extra metre to get around you. By the last quarter, I want Jacobs to have run further than he ever has. I want him tired out."

Much of what they discuss relates to the obvious clash of styles this weekend. Adelaide possesses frightening offensive ability. Richmond, a strong defensive method. This, says Hardwick, is an advantage. "We can control what they do," he says, nodding. "We can. But they can't control us. Remember that: our one wood takes away theirs."

The day before the Grand Final, people begin lining up outside Punt Road Oval—sleeping out, basically—from 4am. They aren't after tickets, or autographs. They're waiting for the gates to open for a 10am open training session. By 8 o'clock the line has stretched from the front gates down Brunton Avenue, around the corner and up Punt Road itself, all the way to Bridge Road, almost a kilometre.

Choppers chitter in the warm spring sky as the squad of 25 slides across the field, and the crowd chants "Dus-tee! Dus-tee! Dus-tee!"

Columnist and TV host (and former Tiger mascot) Waleed Aly is here. Greens leader Richard di Natale, too. Caroline Wilson of *The Age* has even removed her objective journalism hat—just for one day—to write a long and heartfelt column about her Richmond upbringing. The sleeping Tiger, it seems, is stirring. Some 16,000 have paid for tickets to watch tomorrow's game on big screens at Punt Road Oval, and 30,000 are expected at the family day on Sunday, win or lose.

The Grand Final parade comes next, and the AFL estimates a record 150,000 people attend, watching the players sitting on wooden chairs in the back of Toyota HiLuxs, rolling through town from the old Treasury building in Spring Street, into Yarra Park, to a stage near Gate 3 of the MCG, where the crowd wears scarves, and more than a few hastily trimmed "Martin Mohawks" are dotted through the mob.

There are Adelaide flags, too, and some fans who sing along to their song, to the tune of the official hymn of the United States Marine Corps. But the Tiger song rings out next, and the crowd comes alive, and the television cameras, carried on big metal boom arms, swing low over the masses, and the air is warm and heady, with expectation, anticipation, and impatience.

/////////

Back inside their training complex, Hardwick has one final message for the players, before they leave to go home and rest, and perhaps snatch a few hours of fitful sleep and vivid dreams.

Again, it is a video clip of their best football, set to music. But the entire clip is about tackles. Nothing but tackles. And roars. And he tells the playing group the last story he wants them to consider this season.

This one is about Hernan Cortes.

The story takes place in 1519, and the Spaniard adventurer has landed on a Mexican plateau. He has sought gold, and jewels, but knows that with only 600 men against the Mayan forces, the odds of a successful conquest of the Yucatan Peninsula are not in his favour. Cortes, says Hardwick, made impassioned speeches, and roused his troops, but ultimately delivered victory on the back of three words. These three words, it is said, inspired his men but also made them understand that there was no exit strategy, there was no second prize—that the choice before them was between fighting and dying.

"'Burn the boats', was what he said," says Hardwick, staring out at the room. "We cannot turn back. We have only one trajectory.

"What have we said all year? Our best footy is in front of us, and that has been true *all year long*. Too small? Too young? Not good enough?"

He stands now in front of a black slide, with another gigantic three-word phrase in tall white capital letters: WHY NOT US?

Then he stands back for a moment, saying nothing, letting it sink in. Letting them mull over the message they have heard now for months.

"We've backed in our process since day one—*day one!*—and it's been a fantastic season, a great celebration. But there's one piece of silverware we want to get," he says. "No going back. Fight or die. We give everything.

"We burn the boats."

48

40 FEET TO GO

G rand Final Day arrives, and the MCG, and all about it, is overrun. You could be forgiven for thinking the game is incidental to the scene, such is the circus that envelopes Yarra Park. Not just the private functions and long breakfasts with celebrity MCs, but the food trucks and the sound stages and the radio booths where former players and coaches and commentators are sharing their analyses, and guessing who will win and why.

This sporting contest has become an annual festival around which a gigantic peripheral celebration unfolds. It is like The Masters, or Wimbledon, or the Super Bowl, or the Melbourne Cup. It is an outsized full city event, and today it will be attended by 100,021 people, with millions more watching on TV or online. Who knows how many more are gathered in pubs, in backyards, and at community gatherings. It is the grandest stage, and a stage that no player from either team has ever graced. It is the first time that has happened since the first decider, in 1898.

Down in the Richmond rooms before the game, a little after 1:30pm, the defenders step into a tiny room, no bigger than a spacious walk-in closet, ready for their line meeting. Rutten calmly explains what they already know—slowing Adelaide down will be the overriding principle that governs their afternoon. "Today is about expectation and responsibility," he says. "What do you reckon I mean by that, Tigger?"

Vlastuin: "Play your role. Same as every week."

Rutten: "Exactly. Bring your strengths, bring your fight, bring your celebration.

Dylan, your role's no more important than Broady's. Rancey, your role's no more important than Dave's. Bachar, your role's no more important than Brando's."

He tells them a leader is as important as a follower. He tells them to trust the way they play. He tells them to trust their teammates.

Rance claps his hands together as they leave the little space. "The Hillary Step, boys. Foot by foot," he says. "The summit's always there."

The midfielders roll into their line meeting next, and McQualter speaks first.

"Hey there boys," he says, as casually as if he were saying hello in the street. "Remind me what's important at stoppages today?"

They murmur the answer he wants: manage the outside.

"Bloody oath," he says. "And why? It means we'll get to where quicker?"

They answer as one: the next contest.

"Exactly right. We'll be able to get out quicker. That's our strength—getting to the next contest. So when you're at stoppages, be really aggressive with your body work. What else? Josh?"

Caddy holds a footy in his hands and answers: "Just focus on the process. The Hillary Step."

"It's a great analogy, isn't it?" says McQualter, smiling. "I love it. It's easy to look up there at the top, but the process is what's got us here. The process is fun. Who's had fun doing it this year?"

They all have.

"It's been unbelievable watching you blokes grow, the enjoyment you get from playing with each other, the trust and belief you have in each other. I don't think I've ever seen a group like it. Blake?"

Caracella nods, too. He says he has never seen this kind of group—not as a coach, not as a player. It makes him proud to be part of it. But he wants to talk about something else for a second. He points to a line he has written on the whiteboard: Game of Mistakes.

"Grand Finals are games of mistakes," he says. The more we stay connected, the more we get to the ball to help each other out and fix our mistakes, the better we're going to be. Chest to contest. Win the ball early. As the game opens up, take it off the line. Enjoy the day."

Cotchin has a final word before they leave. He says the team has evidence now. They've talked about it all year, this notion of earning respect from others for what they have done. Now he wants them to respect themselves.

"We talk about confidence," says the captain. "It's because of the way we've been focused, from before the season even started. You should be really confident in your individual abilities, but also what we do as a team. We have all the evidence."

A moment later the forwards occupy the same tiny room, and Leppitsch points to the whiteboard, and the words Game of Mistakes, and he cocks an eyebrow and shakes his head. "OK, so don't look at that. That's Blake. I don't know what that is," he says, and they all laugh. "I have no idea. A new TV show? A Game of Thrones spin off maybe?"

He points instead to his own mnemonic device on the board, the word MUSIC. He asks them to tell him what it means.

Riewoldt answers: "It's the cornerstone of how we play. It's the non-negotiable of what we bring. They can't take this away from us."

The word does stand for something—a list of reminders that Leppitsch has been drilling into the team all season long.

M is for Movement.

"Use your feet, don't get stuck, don't get planted, get moving," he says. "Make them defend."

U is for Unity.

"We drive celebration, we kick goals," he says. "We use the Spurs' mentality."

S is for Structures.

"We know what we do at stoppages. With LDLs (long down the line kicks), we make the call. If your opponent's got the best position, we get to him, and we lock him down. If we've got the best position, we make him pay."

I is for Impact in the air.

"We've done this really well this year, given our size and shape," he says. "Take a body, manage the third man in."

C, finally, is for Chase and tackle.

"This is what we score off. We're the best front-half turnover team in the competition, guys, because we do this really, really well. Every week everyone talks about how you've just got to move your way through Richmond, but they can't do it. They just can't do it."

Within minutes each of the lines has filed into the larger briefing room, for their final pre-game address of the season. As always, Hardwick has a story to tell. His kids are home, because it's school holidays, and they're driving him a bit insane, particularly as he sits there trying to affix his player magnets to a board. His daughter sidles up and asks a question: How does he decide who starts on the bench?

"And I said, 'Well, Imogen, I'm glad you asked that. As you might know, I was named coach of the year during the week, and these four selfish pricks…'—he points to the magnets of Ellis, Edwards, Graham and Castagna—'…not one of them sent me a bloody text of congratulations!'"

They all laugh then, and talk about how much fun the week has been, how they have not shied away from the limelight, but also how nothing has changed. Despite the moment, it is another week for getting down to business. He talks about the big things—like setting the ground up behind the attack—and all the little things they can do to stifle the Crows.

"All we're asking you to do is buy your mate three seconds. Standing on the mark, blocking a run, making a guy hesitate with the ball—that's all we're asking," Hardwick says. "It is so important. You cannot underestimate the smallest of things. Today, it's all about the inches."

He has Rance turn over the final A3 picture of the year. It is a series of mugshots. Six rows of four. Twenty-two players. One coach. One Richmond logo. But the mugshots look, well, ridiculous. Each photo is as unflattering as the next. The faces are blowing air, or being hit in the head with a ball. Noses are mashed by elbows. Lips are drawn as they brace for impact. Eyes are half open or half closed, squinting or rolled back in the head. Tongues are out. Teeth and gums are bared. Cheeks are sucked in, or puffed out like a blowfish. The coach calls the pictures "munted heads", and the players just sigh and smirk.

"There is a reason we've brought out the munted heads," says Hardwick. "It's because we've embraced imperfection this year, haven't we? We all understand we've got strengths, and we all understand we've got flaws. The game today is going to be based on imperfection. We're asking you to embrace those moments."

He looks up at the whiteboard now, where there is one last thing written in blue—40 FEET TO GO—and then he turns back to the group.

"Everyone, from pillar to post, has said you can't do it. We've proven them wrong. We are quick. We are powerful. We celebrate what we do," he says. "We are on the Hillary Step. The summit is there, but we've got to walk each foot to get there. I love what we've done, but we've got 40 feet to go."

The players walk out into their preparation area, and begin their leg swings and windmills and warm up drills. And Neil Balme whispers: "This is the easy bit. Now we've just gotta play."

///////////

The game is a game of moments, as all games are, but such snippets of time seem so magnified here, so elongated and important. The goals and tackles and marks on this day will be replayed again and again, over and over, at least by the fans of those who win.

Rory Sloane nails the first goal of the game from a set shot. Vlastuin fumbles soon after, and Eddie Betts swoops in the goal square. At the other end, the Tigers pressure the man and contain the ball in the space they want, but Riewoldt takes a screamer and then misses, he takes a mark on a lead and misses, and takes a shot on the run and misses. The Crows are up 26 to 15 at quarter time, yet it does feel as though the Tigers are on top. They've won more clearances, more contested ball, had more time in their forward half, but goals win games and they are kicking behinds.

The rain comes now, only the barest trickle, but it feels like an omen—a reminder that this Richmond side has prevailed in the wet. Riewoldt has a set shot snap, and sneaks the ball over a strangely vacant goal line; there's a whisker in it. A little more rain comes now, in slow grey drifts, and Townsend kicks a goal from long range, and the Crows lead is cut to two points. Graham powers through traffic, turns and steers a fast drop punt on the run, and Richmond is in front. Martin wins a one-on-one from a Prestia clearance, drives home his kick and the Tigers are up by nine points going into half-time.

"Ground zero! Ground zero!" screams Cotchin on the way into the rooms. "Start again! Start again!" Each of the groups meet and they talk while they recover. "Remember to rotate," says Caracella to the midfielders. "Stay fresh.

Don't think you have to stay out there and do it all yourself."

McQualter asks for all eyes on him. "What do you think happened with all of Adelaide's finals?" he asks. "At half-time in both games they were up by 40 points. Now they're down by nine. They have not had a look at this. This is their unknown."

Grigg is enthusiastic. He talks about the final moments of the first half, when Richmond refused to yield the lead: "We can hold them, boys. Those last three minutes they were just pressing, pressing, pressing, and we just didn't give it up."

Each player continues with his own separate routine in the gap. Dion Prestia takes a quick shower and changes into a fresh jumper, as always. Martin sucks down an energy gel shot. Broad wipes a cloth at a fat bloody lip. Riewoldt, lying stomach down on a massage table, inhales a banana. Rance pats Bachar Houli on the back: "Super start, mate, super start. Courage mate, courage." Simon Reinsch, the football technology coordinator, sits with Toby Nankervis, holding an iPad and showing the young ruckman every one of his ruck duels at stoppages, allowing him to see first hand what will win against Jacobs and what won't. Then Rob Innes, the rehabilitation coach, reminds them all that this is a Grand Final, and so the half-time break is slightly longer than normal. Connor Menadue is outside on the MCG, winning the Grand Final Sprint, but in here they can take it easy a few minutes longer: "Still got six minutes! Suck it in! Plenty of time!"

Hardwick stands in the briefing room and marks his messages. A pressure rating of 1.94 is what he wanted. Richmond kicking five goals from turnovers is what he wanted. "We've got the game in a grind, exactly what we wanted," he says. "Really simple philosophy for the second part of the game: stay in the contest. I reckon a couple of times we've gone early and stepped through, but we want to stay chest to contest. It's a highly contested game, so the more you stay around it the better we look."

He looks up that Hillary Step message on the board and wipes away the number four, replacing it with a two: 20 FEET TO GO.

"Stand up. Everyone get a touch on someone," he says. "There's 20 feet to go to that summit. Stay within the framework. Have the desire to succeed. One foot in front of the other, one step at a time."

///////////

In the third quarter, the Tigers do as they have done all year. They run in groups and knock the ball on, and spill it free in scragging co-operative tackles. They punch it and shovel it and farm it forward in numbers, all as one, like the teeth of a plough, ripping up the field in front of them.

Graham kicks a set shot goal, and the score is 46 to 31.

Grigg nails his own clutch bomb: 53 to 31.

There is a contest and a spoil in the goal square and Lambert runs forward, knowing this is where his teammate will handball—even blindly—and so he receives the gift with open arms and snaps across his body into the wall-to-wall Richmond crowd at the Punt Road End: 59 to 31.

The Crows work themselves into the game, but only at times. Their captain and spearhead, Taylor 'Tex' Walker, lines up for goal, and the crowd begins to sound like a time capsule, like barrackers of yore, yelling "BOOOOO!" and "Chewy on yer' boot!" But he steadies and delivers.

Then Graham, the fifth gamer, the only teenager on the field, who has played in more finals than regular season matches, steps in and kicks his third goal. A South Australian boy, he grew up a Crows fanatic, and worshipped Sloane. Now he is comprehensively tagging the star blond midfielder out of the game, and helping himself to a scoreboard haul—and a place in Grand Final folklore.

Soon Martin marks, and handballs to Castagna, who snaps and goals, and the lead is 72 to 39. Richmond has won "the premiership quarter" in emphatic fashion, and lead by 34 points with perhaps half an hour to play. Adelaide has kicked just one goal in two quarters.

The stadium lights come on as the afternoon fades, and Riewoldt marks and kicks what for many feels like the sealer: 80 to 40. Lambert runs and runs and bounces and bounces, and handballs to Prestia, who slams the goal across his body into the Adelaide cheer squad at the city end, and the score is 86 to 40, and somehow Richmond is delivering an utter rout. It is around this time that Greg Baum of The Age, writing on deadline, sums up the moment and the day: "It was the slick of Adelaide versus the stick of Richmond, and the stick won. The Crows aim to be exact, the Tigers exacting, and they were."

Adelaide does peg back two goals and perhaps a few Tiger hearts—weakened and wearied by the years—flutter a little, but only barely so. A set shot from Townsend is the salve, and it makes the score 94 to 54. Another from Butler: 100 to 54.

Fittingly it is Martin who stamps his frame on the game with a high snap. The red Sherrin soars up into the sky as he pivots, shooting up almost vertically, far above the height of the goal posts. The ball hangs there in the last blast of sunshine, covering the few metres between him and the goal line almost in slow motion, giving the fans a chance to wind up, to stand up, to take a deep breath, the time to set themselves for that moment when that tumbling football falls down and through the posts and they can then exhale a heavy, hot breath of yellow and black fire.

At the fence in the Richmond race, the VFL players sprint up in suits and pink wristbands, awaiting the end, and the chance to join their friends, and their smiles are wide. League boss Gillon McLachlan steps through them, waiting with the Premiership Cup in his hands. Fans are applauding every chip kick and mark as the clock winds down, and Connor Menadue is impatient: "Come on!" he screams. "Blow the bloody siren!"

And they do.

Martin and Grigg and Riewoldt collapse together as one. As do Cotchin and Houli and Edwards. The Richmond Football Club has won the 2017 AFL Premiership, the 11th flag for the club, and its first in the national competition. The Tigers won it by a resounding 48 points, and 11 players kicked a goal. In breaking a 37-year drought, it is as if a great spiritual and psychological—almost physical—weight has been lifted. They have come from 13th on the ladder in 2016 to first in 2017—the greatest year on year leap in the game's history.

The song plays and as the lyrics ring out and the horns of the tune toot, the crowd seems to be bouncing. There is no fury in them, only disbelieving delight, and deliverance. Laughter and incredulity. Happiness.

On the ground, a Richmond pack rolls across the turf, a chaotic amalgam of presidents and players, captains and coaches, forwards and trainers, recruiters and rovers, waterboys and wingers. In the background, the Adelaide players slump on the turf. Their coach, Don Pyke, seeks out Hardwick to congratulate the winners, and Cotchin dashes away from his teammates to offer his hand to Walker.

Ralph Carr, the manager of Dustin Martin, stands in the race, and fields a congratulatory text message from another client, the singer Kate Ceberano, as he high fives people over the fence.

"Norm Smith Medal, what do you reckon? I think Rance or Houli," Carr says. "Rance was supreme."

And in that moment, former Essendon champion, James Hird, the winner of the 2000 Medal makes the announcement: And the winner of the Norm Smith Medal is, Dustin Martin. Carr, doubly delighted, continues high fiving the crowd. "And that doesn't even matter!" he says. "That won't matter to him at all. Not one bit. For Dusty it's always been about the premiership."

The players now take their victory laps, premiership medals in hand, or hanging loose around their necks, shining in the reflected light from the towers above, like little golden winks in the shaded parts of the field.

The Board members are all out there, too, all feeling overjoyed and sustained by their resolve, and they assemble for a group photo on the 50-metre line.

Leppitsch and McRae are together on the wing, posing for their own picture, holding up four fingers each—for their three flags with Brisbane and now one more.

Tim Livingstone is there. He looks dazed and confused, his head filled with wild thoughts: "What am I doing here? How am I in the middle of the MCG, celebrating a premiership?"

Francis Jackson is with him. He is the man who sat in his car at a little oval in Ballarat on a rainy night 10 years ago, secretly and silently watching a 16-year-old Dustin Martin. He helped recruit 16 of the 22 members of this team, including Cotchin and Martin, who, he predicted from the outset, would each go on to win the Brownlow Medal.

Cotchin carries Daniel Rioli on his shoulders. The small forward was injured late in the game, and will need ankle surgery. The victory means everything to him and his family—and to his people, as described in a story later by Hardwick. "At the start of the finals series, a turtle swum up onto the Tiwi Islands, very near where he grew up. Normally there, they capture turtles, kill them and eat them. But this one came ashore in a place they normally do not, and the elders said, 'No. The turtle is Daniel's totem.' And so, they kept it alive. They fed it and cared for it. When the flag was won, they let it go."

Rex Hunt, a Richmond premiership player in 1969 and 1973, stands at the edge of the field, tears in his eyes. "It's all about the fans," he says, looking up at the revelry. "People who have got troubles in the world, they've been eased just a little by this. This is what football clubs do—they have the power to make you feel better about life."

Bronwyn Doig and Steve Wyatt come jogging up from the rooms next, each with one of Cotchin's daughters, Harper and Mackenzie, in their arms. They carry the kids to the skipper at the Punt Road End.

Hardwick's teenage daughters, Imogen and Isabelle, fly out onto the field soon after, sprinting to maul their father in a double hug on the half-forward flank. The now famous "Mrs Hardwick"—Danielle—arrives in time to join them.

In the rooms, Martin is the one who brings the entire playing list into a massive circle. Rance is the general creating space to make it happen. "This is surreal," says development coach Ryan Ferguson, "but it makes perfect sense, too."

They sing the song and it is a defiant scream. There are family photos and champagne bottles and beer bottles and pizza slices and the room seems as full and welling and warm as the eyes and hearts of all those there. The players and coaches and footy department staff cram into the privacy of the briefing room next, away from the media, away, even, from their families and friends. Only players, coaches and direct staff are here now, and Mark Opie, the team manager, holds up the Premiership Cup and they roar as one.

Brendon Gale is drenched in beer. Matt Pearce is drenched in beer. Opie wants a drink, too, so Martin removes his left boot and pours a Crown Lager into the sweaty blue and yellow footwear, and Opie gulps deeply from it and they roar again. They call on Cotchin to scull his drink, and he takes a few little sips and smiles. They call on Bachar to down his drink next, and so the devout Islamic man takes his bottle of water and holds it high and pounds, pounds, pounds it and the players dance and chant Ba-char! Ba-char! Ba-char!

Gale steps to the front of he room to speak. He was in tears throughout the final stages of last quarter, but has composed himself now. "Can I be serious for one second? I'm so proud of us and you in all aspects. It takes a club to get to a Grand Final. It takes players to win premierships. To answer the fiercest questions of all, in the fiercest contest of all, my heart is just bursting with pride. I'm just so, so happy. And I think the key to all of this is unity. Unity is strength. Unity is power. And the way you guys have connected this year and opened up and built trust with each other, the way you've played for each other, and your coaches…. You're a unified group. And we're all behind you, aligned from the top down. We've unlocked something that teams can't compete against. And we've got massive upside, massive upside. I'm so proud."

Cotchin, in socks, with a medal around his neck, thanks everyone in the room. "I couldn't be more proud of the way you've come together. Embracing imperfection—I think that's what's bound us so tightly. We've talked about a journey. Mine's been 10 years long. To Dimma, all our coaches, staff, our playing group—from number one (Vlastuin) through to number 47 (Soldo)—I couldn't be more proud of the energy, effort and connection you've brought all year. It didn't just happen, you made it happen."

Hardwick refuses to drink and so the players boo him, and instead he pours a beer on his own head. Then he looks up, and waits for them to fall silent, as he has done after every victory in this finals campaign, now historic. He smiles.

"Who likes winning premierships?"

And they roar! And they leap to their feet! And more champagne bottles are opened and sprayed on the group. And they shake up beer bottles and blast the frothy booze over the whole room. And Hardwick waves them down. He has a few words left. One more story.

He is proud of the playing group, he says, but he wants to acknowledge all of the players here, particularly the VFL guys in the room. His story is about a guy who played US college basketball with the immortal NBA champion Bill Walton.

"It's a great story," Hardwick says. "This guy, I forget his name, he got recruited to UCLA, effectively to make Bill Walton a better player, to do everything he could to make this star player better. There's 22 blokes here who played today, but there's 22 more who didn't play. But through all your training, and all your effort this year, you've made this side great."

And he's right, of course. To his right is Anthony Miles, who will soon win the Paddy Guinane Medal for the best and fairest player in Richmond's VFL side this season. He is the kind of performer who drives competition for spots every week. To his left is Jayden Short, the perpetually bubbly, ambidextrous backman who played 16 senior games this year, and kicked the long range sealer in the Tigers' close win over Port Adelaide. He looks at Taylor Hunt, who has been praised all year for leadership and work rate. He looks at Jake Batchelor, who will finish second only to Miles in the VFL voting, after an outstanding season. They are all applauded.

Hardwick thanks the trainers and fitness staff: "You're the best in the business. The premiership tells us that."

He thanks his assistant coaches: "You're outstanding. I certainly gave you free rein, and that's because of the trust I've got in you. And I commend you."

He thanks the entire group now, for doing something that hasn't been done at this club in almost four decades: "The manic nature of the way you played the game, it's just so exciting! I feel like you guys can have your thing tonight, all your celebrations—I'm going home to watch the tape!"

And then: "We burnt the fucking boats!"

They sing the song once more. And they stamp their feet and the beat rings out as they belt it out. Martin stands and has his hands on Graham's chin as he screams. Riewoldt stands with two fists in the air. Astbury and Lambert have their arms around each other. The Premiership Cup sits on the floor in front of them all. And someone throws a deflated plastic shark down on top of it—the shark they fought over in the warm Queensland water, back in January, on pre-season camp, when they learned that first important lesson about playing with joy and abandon.

They depart the room soon after, headed for the showers, and their suits, and to sing the song again in the centre of the oval, and so Riewoldt can join The Killers on stage at the post-Grand Final party in a most unlikely, yet typical, cameo. Then they will be in buses, headed to Crown Casino to see their families and celebrate some more. As Hardwick leaves behind them, Livingstone slaps him on the back.

And then Livingstone, alone now in the space, walks to the whiteboard.

The Hillary Step message is still up there.

It still reads: 20 FEET TO GO.

He holds up his thumb, and it hovers over the text. In a single stroke he wipes away the number two, and leaves the room smiling.

ROUND BY ROUND

ROUND 1

CARLTON
4.3   7.4   12.4   14.5 (89)
RICHMOND
7.3   13.5   15.11   20.12 (132)

GOALS

Carlton: Weitering 3, Wright 3, Kreuzer 2, Silvagni 2, Casboult, Gibbs, Armfield, Thomas

Richmond: Martin 4, Castagna 2, Butler 2, Nankervis 2, Rioli 2, Caddy, Edwards, Grigg, Riewoldt, Cotchin, Lloyd, Prestia, Vlastuin

BEST

Carlton: Murphy, Weitering, Gibbs, Docherty, Marchbank, Kreuzer

Richmond: Martin, Prestia, Cotchin, Castagna, Butler, Conca

BROWNLOW MEDAL

3: Dustin Martin, 2: Dion Prestia, 1: Marc Murphy

ATTENDANCE: 73,137 at the MCG

ROUND 2

RICHMOND
2.4   5.5   9.8   14.15 (99)
COLLINGWOOD
2.4   5.10   7.13   11.14 (80)

GOALS

Richmond: Riewoldt 2, Cotchin 2, Martin 2, Rioli, Lennon, Houli, Ellis, Edwards, Caddy, Butler, Grigg

Collingwood: Hoskin-Elliott 3, White 2, Treloar 2, Moore, Broomhead, Mayne, Grundy

BEST

Richmond: Cotchin, Rance, Grimes, Houli, Lennon, Martin, Nankervis

Collingwood: Grundy, Hoskin-Elliott, Pendlebury, Treloar, Adams Brownlow Medal

BROWNLOW MEDAL

3: Adam Treloar, 2: Trent Cotchin, 1: Will Hoskin-Elliott

ATTENDANCE: 58,236 at the MCG

ROUND 3

RICHMOND
2.2   5.6   9.8   11.10 (76)
WEST COAST
2.6   5.13   7.14   8.17 (65)

GOALS

Richmond: Martin 2, Butler 2, Rioli 2, Lambert, Houli, Castagna, Grigg, Riewoldt

West Coast: LeCras 3, Kennedy 2, Hutchings, Darling, Cripps

BEST

Richmond: Martin, Cotchin, Conca, Butler, Castagna, Riewoldt

West Coast: Gaff, Shuey, LeCras, Priddis, Masten, Nelson

BROWNLOW MEDAL

3: Dustin Martin, 2: Trent Cotchin, 1: Alex Rance

ATTENDANCE: 42,523 at the MCG

ROUND 4

BRISBANE LIONS
3.2   4.3   8.6   10.6 (67)
RICHMOND
5.6   10.9   13.14   17.17 (119)

GOALS

Brisbane Lions: Hipwood 2, Zorko 2, D. Beams 2, Bell, Schache, Taylor, Robinson

Richmond: Riewoldt 4, Castagna 4, Rioli 2, Grimes, Nankervis, Menadue, Cotchin, Grigg, Caddy, Butler

BEST

Brisbane Lions: Rockliff, Martin, Robinson, Mayes, D. Beams, Gardiner

Richmond: Cotchin, Riewoldt, Grigg, Prestia, Castagna, Rioli

BROWNLOW MEDAL

3: Shaun Grigg, 2: Stefan Martin, 1: Jack Riewoldt,

ATTENDANCE: 21,669 at the Gabba

ROUND 5

RICHMOND
3.1   6.6   7.11   12.16 (88)
MELBOURNE
3.4   7.6   11.7   11.9 (75)

GOALS

Richmond: Riewoldt 6, Castagna, Butler, Grigg, Rioli, Martin, Caddy

Melbourne: Hogan 3, Garlett 2, McDonald, Watts, Petracca, Salem, Hibberd, Hunt

BEST

Richmond: Riewoldt, Nankervis, Martin, Houli, Grigg, Caddy, Cotchin

Melbourne: Oliver, Hibberd, Hunt, N Jones, Frost, Petracca

BROWNLOW MEDAL

3: Jack Riewoldt, 2: Toby Nankervis, 1: Dustin Martin,

ATTENDANCE: 85,657 at the MCG

ROUND 6

ADELAIDE
5.0   11.6   18.11   21.14 (140)
RICHMOND
6.3   7.3   8.3   10.4 (64)

GOALS

Adelaide: Walker 5, Lynch 3, Sloane 3, Cameron 2, Jenkins, Betts, Douglas, Jacobs, Smith, M.Crouch, Otten, Milera

Richmond: Rioli 2, Riewoldt 2, Markov 2, Butler, Martin, Lambert, Houli

BEST

Adelaide: Sloane, M.Crouch, Jacobs, Lynch, Walker, Laird

Richmond: Cotchin, Martin, Lambert, Nankervis

BROWNLOW MEDAL

3: Rory Sloane, 2: Matt Crouch, 1: Taylor Walker

ATTENDANCE: 51,069 at Adelaide Oval

ROUND 7

WESTERN BULLDOGS
1.1   4.6   8.11   11.14 (80)
RICHMOND
5.3   7.6   9.7   11.9 (75)

GOALS

Western Bulldogs: Smith 4, Adams 2, Stringer, Picken, McLean, Bontempelli, Hunter

Richmond: Riewoldt 4, Martin 2, Butler, Miles, Lambert, Caddy, Grigg

BEST

Western Bulldogs: Dahlhaus, Bontempelli, Hunter, Smith, Macrae, T.Boyd

Richmond: Martin, Riewoldt, Rance, Grigg, Caddy, Houli

BROWNLOW MEDAL

3: Marcus Bontempelli, 2: Luke Dahlhaus, 1: Dustin Martin,

ATTENDANCE: 46,387 at Etihad Stadium

ROUND 8

RICHMOND
2.1   5.1   5.5   10.10 (70)
FREMANTLE
2.3   5.6   9.11   10.12 (72)

GOALS

Richmond: Riewoldt 3, Caddy 2, Cotchin, Castagna, Martin, Rioli, Ellis

Fremantle: Taberner 2, Kersten 2, Mundy 2, Hill, Fyfe, McCarthy, Pearce

BEST

Richmond: Rance, Martin, Grigg, Cotchin, Grimes

Fremantle: Walters, Hill, Johnson, Langdon, Hamling, Mundy

BROWNLOW MEDAL

3: Michael Walters, 2: David Mundy, 1: Brad Hill

ATTENDANCE: 31,200 at the MCG

ROUND 9

GREATER WESTERN SYDNEY
1.2   4.5   6.9   11.12 (78)
RICHMOND
6.3   7.8   10.10   10.15 (75)

GOALS

Greater Western Sydney: Cameron 3, Reid 2, Scully, Lobb, Williams, Greene, Taranto, de Boer

Richmond: Riewoldt 2, Menadue 2, Cotchin 2, Castagna 2, Grigg, Lloyd

BEST

Greater Western Sydney: Kelly, Shiel, Wilson, Whitfield, Scully, Davis

Richmond: Rance, Martin, Grigg, Nankervis, Cotchin, Houli

BROWNLOW MEDAL

3: Dustin Martin, 2: Josh Kelly, 1: Alex Rance

ATTENDANCE: 10,677 at Spotless Stadium

ROUND 10

RICHMOND
4.4   6.9   9.12   11.15 (81)
ESSENDON
6.0   8.1   10.3   10.6 (66)

GOALS

Richmond: Riewoldt 2, Edwards 2, Caddy 2, Lloyd, Elton, Martin, Ellis, Nankervis

Essendon: Daniher 3, Goddard 2, Fantasia, Heppell, Green, Stewart, Zaharakis

BEST

Richmond: Martin, Ellis, Rance, Cotchin, Houli, Nankervis, Grigg

Essendon: Zaharakis, Goddard, Hurley, McGrath, Parish, Watson

BROWNLOW MEDAL

3: Dustin Martin, 2: David Zaharakis, 1: Brandon Ellis,

ATTENDANCE: 85,656 at the MCG

ROUND 11

NORTH MELBOURNE
2.4   7.6   8.9   9.12 (66)
RICHMOND
3.4   6.10   12.13   14.17 (101)

GOALS

North Melbourne: Wood 2, Atley 2, Brown, Waite, Higgins, Gibson, Hansen

Richmond: Riewoldt 2, Martin 2, Butler 2, Lambert 2, Castagna, Cotchin, Edwards, Ellis, Grigg, Rioli

BEST

North Melbourne: Gibson, Dumont, Macmillan, Tarrant, Hrovat

Richmond: Martin, Riewoldt, Prestia, Rance, Houli, Lambert, Ellis, Cotchin

BROWNLOW MEDAL

3: Dustin Martin, 2: Trent Cotchin, 1: Bachar Houli

ATTENDANCE: 36,100 at Etihad Stadium

ROUND 12 – BYE

ROUND 13

RICHMOND
5.3   7.6   9.7   10.11 (71)
SYDNEY
0.4   3.5   7.6   12: .8 (80)

GOALS

Richmond: Riewoldt 2, Martin 2, Bolton 2, Cotchin, Castagna, Edwards, Lloyd

Sydney: Reid 2, Franklin, Hewett, Lloyd, Heeney, Parker, Hayward, Papley, Kennedy, K.Jack, Rohan

BEST

Richmond: Rance, Houli, Cotchin, B.Ellis, Astbury, Martin

Sydney: Lloyd, Newman, Heeney, Kennedy, Jones, Mills, Hannebery

BROWNLOW MEDAL

3: Josh P Kennedy, 2: Jake Lloyd, 1: Alex Rance

ATTENDANCE: 58,721 at the MCG

ROUND 14

RICHMOND
3.3   5.10   7.13   11.18 (84)
CARLTON
4.1   4.2   6.6   8.10 (58)

GOALS

Richmond: Riewoldt 3, Butler 2, Castagna 2, Ellis, Lambert, Bolton, Nankervis

Carlton: Casboult 2, Kreuzer 2, Wright, Thomas, C. Curnow, Cripps

BEST

Richmond: Rance, Houli, Martin, Lambert, Castagna, Riewoldt

Carlton: Kreuzer, Cripps, Docherty, Gibbs, Casboult, Jones

BROWNLOW MEDAL

3: Patrick Cripps, 2: Alex Rance, 1: Dustin Martin

ATTENDANCE: 64,448 at the MCG

ROUND 15

PORT ADELAIDE
1.6   5.11   6.14   8.15 (63)
RICHMOND
1.4   3.8   7.10   11.10 (76)

GOALS

Port Adelaide: Powell-Pepper 2, Ebert, R.Gray, S.Gray, Trengove, Neade, Dixon

Richmond: Butler 3, Stengle 2, Cotchin, Rioli, Martin, Riewoldt, Lloyd, Short

BEST

Port Adelaide: Wingard, Ryder, Wines, Westhoff, Jonas

Richmond: Martin, Ellis, Lambert, Butler, Rance, Grigg

BROWNLOW MEDAL

3: Dustin Martin, 2: Kane Lambert, 1: Chad Wingard

ATTENDANCE: 39,979 at the Adelaide Oval

ROUND 16

ST KILDA
5.3   14.8   19.8   21.12 (138)
RICHMOND
1.3   1.4   4.9   10.11 (71)

GOALS

St Kilda: Membrey 5, Riewoldt 3, Bruce 2, Stevens 2, Gresham 2, Montagna 2, Ross, Billings, Longer, Steven, McKenzie

Richmond: Castagna 2, Cotchin, Caddy, Grigg, Martin, Butler, Lloyd, Ellis, Riewoldt

BEST

St Kilda: Ross, Steven, Riewoldt, Montagna, Stevens, Steele, Membrey, Sinclair, Longer

Richmond: Lambert, Grigg, Ellis, Edwards, Astbury

BROWNLOW MEDAL

3: Seb Ross, 2: Tim Membrey, 1: Leigh Montagna

ATTENDANCE: 47,514 at Etihad Stadium

ROUND 17

RICHMOND
4.4   5.8   9.13   16.16 (112)
BRISBANE LIONS
1.3   4.6   6.8   12.9 (81)

GOALS

Richmond: Riewoldt 4, Butler 3, Martin 2, Castagna 2, Edwards, Cotchin, Prestia, Rioli, B Ellis

Brisbane Lions: Keays 2, Schache 2, Hipwood 2, Cutler, Zorko, Bastinac, Mathieson, Walker, McCluggage

BEST

Richmond: Martin, Prestia, Cotchin, Riewoldt, Butler, Short, Miles

Brisbane Lions: Witherden, Andrews, Taylor, McStay, Rich

BROWNLOW MEDAL

3: Dustin Martin, 2: Jack Riewoldt, 1: Trent Cotchin

ATTENDANCE: 28,188 at Etihad Stadium

ROUND 18

RICHMOND
0.2   4.6   8.8   9.10 (64)
GREATER WESTERN SYDNEY
3.4   3.5   4.5   6.9 (45)

GOALS

Richmond: Riewoldt 2, Martin, McIntosh, Lambert, Castagna, Rioli, Caddy, Nankervis

Greater Western Sydney: Haynes, Patton, Greene, Whitfield, Kelly, Ward

BEST

Richmond: Martin, Cotchin, Vlastuin, B.Ellis, Rance, Lambert

Greater Western Sydney: Ward, Davis, Shiel, Wilson, Williams

BROWNLOW MEDAL

3: Dustin Martin, 2: Alex Rance, 1: Callan Ward

ATTENDANCE: 33,467 at the MCG

ROUND 19

GOLD COAST
4.2   5.3   8.4   10.5 (65)
RICHMOND
3.4   8.8   11.11   14.14 (98)

GOALS

Gold Coast: Lynch 3, Miller, Rosa, Wright, Saad, Fiorini, Martin, Lonergan

Richmond: Rioli 3, Nankervis 3, Castagna 3, Grigg, Caddy, Cotchin, Martin, C. Ellis

BEST

Gold Coast: Hanley, Hall, Swallow, Martin, Fiorini, Witts

Richmond: Martin, Cotchin, Rance, Rioli, B. Ellis, Miles

BROWNLOW MEDAL

3: Dustin Martin, 2: Aaron Hall, 1: Alex Rance

ATTENDANCE: 16,207 at Metricon Stadium

ROUND 20

RICHMOND
5.4   6.8   9.10   13.15 (93)
HAWTHORN
1.3   2.5   4.8   9.10 (64)

GOALS

Richmond: Caddy 4, C.Ellis 2, Martin 2, Rioli, Cotchin, Soldo, Prestia, Nankervis

Hawthorn: Miles 2, Breust 2, Schoenmakers 2, Roughead 2, Mitchell

BEST

Richmond: Caddy, Prestia, Martin, Lambert, Nankervis, Rance, Grimes

Hawthorn: Sicily, Mitchell, Smith, Howe, Roughead, Gunston

BROWNLOW MEDAL

3: Josh Caddy, 2: Dion Prestia, 1: James Sicily

ATTENDANCE: 58,342 at the MCG

ROUND 21

GEELONG
3.2   8.5   8.9   11.14 (80)
RICHMOND
3.4   4.5   7.9   9.12 (66)

GOALS

Geelong: Taylor 4, Menzel 2, Motlop, Stanley, C.Guthrie, Mackie, Simpson

Richmond: Martin 2, Riewoldt, Houli, Butler, Caddy, Cotchin, Rioli, Edwards

BEST

Geelong: Taylor, Dangerfield, Menegola, Kolodjashnij, Motlop, Tuohy, Smith, C.Guthrie

Richmond: Lambert, Martin, Cotchin, Prestia, Grimes

BROWNLOW MEDAL

3: Patrick Dangerfield, 2: Harry Taylor, 1: Dion Prestia

ATTENDANCE: 32,266 at Simonds Stadium

ROUND 22

FREMANTLE
3.4   3.5   5.7   7.9 (51)
RICHMOND
3.0   11.2   17.5   25.5 (155)

GOALS

Fremantle: Bennell 2, Crozier 2, Fyfe, Deluca, Ballantyne

Richmond: Townsend 6, Riewoldt 4, Lambert 3, Butler 3, Martin 2, Rioli, Houli, Edwards, McIntosh, Nankervis, Rance, Graham

BEST

Fremantle: Fyfe, Hamling, S.Hill, Mundy

Richmond: Martin, Grigg, Townsend, Ellis, Lambert, Houli

BROWNLOW MEDAL

3: Dustin Martin, 2: Shaun Grigg, 1: Jacob Townsend

ATTENDANCE: 34,204 at Domain Stadium

ROUND 23

RICHMOND
4.1   11.5   12.7   19.8 (122)
ST KILDA
1.2   4.3   9.9   12.9 (81)

GOALS

Richmond: Townsend 5, Riewoldt 3, Grigg 3, Prestia 2, Martin 2, Butler 2, Graham, Cotchin

St Kilda: Gresham 5, Billings 2, Membrey 2, Bruce, Riewoldt, Longer

BEST

Richmond: Martin, Grigg, Prestia, Cotchin, Townsend, Vlastuin, Nankervis, Houli

St Kilda: Steele, Gresham, Billings, Sinclair, Ross, Dunstan

BROWNLOW MEDAL

3: Dustin Martin, 2: Shaun Grigg, 1: Trent Cotchin,

ATTENDANCE: 69,104 at the MCG

QUALIFYING FINAL

GEELONG

0.4   2.4   4.9   5.10 [40]

RICHMOND

2.4   3.7   6.10   13.13 [91]

GOALS

Geelong: Motlop, Dangerfield, Parsons, Hawkins, Taylor

Richmond: Townsend 2, Caddy 2, Butler, Vlastuin, Edwards, Prestia, Grigg, Lambert, Castagna, Cotchin, Riewoldt

BEST

Geelong: Duncan, Tuohy, Dangerfield, S. Selwood, Lonergan, Smith

Richmond: Martin, Prestia, Rance, Cotchin, Vlastuin, Lambert

AFLCA VOTES [GARY AYRES MEDAL]: Martin 9, Cotchin 8, Vlastuin 7, Prestia 4, Lambert 1, Rance 1

ATTENDANCE: 95,028 at the MCG

PRELIMINARY FINAL

RICHMOND

4.3   5.7   11.11   15.13 [103]

GREATER WESTERN SYDNEY

3.3   5.6   6.10   9.13 [67]

GOALS

Richmond: Rioli 4, Martin 3, Butler 2, Lambert, Caddy, Castagna, Townsend, Edwards, Riewoldt

Greater Western Sydney: Himmelberg 4, Ward 3, Kelly, Patton

BEST

Richmond: Cotchin, Rioli, Martin, Grimes, Rance, Lambert, Prestia

Greater Western Sydney: Ward, Kelly, Tomlinson, Scully, Davis, Himmelberg

AFLCA VOTES [GARY AYRES MEDAL]: Martin 8, Rioli 8, Cotchin 7, Ward 4, Rance 2, Tomlinson 1

ATTENDANCE: 94,258 at the MCG

GRAND FINAL

ADELAIDE

4.2   4.7   5.10   8.12 [60]

RICHMOND

2.3   6.4   11.8   16.12 [108]

GOALS

Adelaide: Sloane 2, Walker 2, Betts, Greenwood, B. Crouch, Cameron

Richmond: Graham 3, Townsend 2, Martin 2, Riewoldt 2, Caddy, Houli, Grigg, Lambert, Castagna, Riewoldt, Prestia, Butler

BEST

Adelaide: M. Crouch, Jacobs, B. Crouch, Sloane, Laird

Richmond: Martin, Houli, Rance, Edwards, Prestia, Graham, Astbury, Grimes

NORM SMITH MEDAL VOTING: Martin 13, Houli 10, Rance 2, Edwards 2, Prestia 2, Graham 1

AFLCA VOTES [GARY AYRES MEDAL]: Houli 10, Martin 8, Rance 6, Edwards 4, Graham 1, Riewoldt 1.

ATTENDANCE: 100,021 at the MCG

471

HERO: Dustin Martin did it all in 2017, winning every award available, but the one he sought was the premiership medal, and Cup, here celebrating with the tiger army. On the fence are his former teammates, Nathan Foley (left) and Jake King.(rigth).

2017 AWARDS

ALL AUSTRALIANS
Alex Rance (captain),
Dustin Martin

BROWNLOW MEDAL
Dustin Martin

AFLPA MVP
(Leigh Matthews Trophy)
Dustin Martin

NORM SMITH MEDAL
Dustin Martin

GARY AYRES MEDAL
(best player in finals)
Dustin Martin 25 votes
ahead of Trent Cotchin 15.
Bachar Houli polled
10 votes to finish equal fifth.

JACK DYER MEDAL
*(votes awarded on a 0-5 basis
for every player)*
Dustin Martin, 89,
Alex Rance 80,
Kane Lambert 76,
Trent Cotchin 73,
Dylan Grimes 69.

AFL GOAL OF THE YEAR
Daniel Rioli

AFL COACHES ASSOCIATION COACH OF THE YEAR
Damien Hardwick

J.J. LISTON TROPHY
(fairest and best VFL)
Jake Townsend

FRANCIS BOURKE AWARD
*(Each week, the playing group votes on a
3-2-1 basis for the players who best uphold
their trademarks values of awareness,
united, relentless and discipline)*
Dylan Grimes

BILL COSGROVE-HARRY JENKINS BEST FIRST YEAR PLAYER AWARD
Dan Butler

MICHAEL ROACH MEDAL
(leading goalkicker award)
Jack Riewoldt (54 goals)

GUINANE MEDAL
(VFL Best and Fairest award)
Anthony Miles

DAVID MANDIE COMMUNITY AWARD
Shane Edwards

THE PLAYERS
Season 2017

PLAYERS	GAMES	GOALS/BEHINDS
Astbury, David	25	
Batchelor, Jake	1	
Bolton, Shai	6	3.4
Broad, Nathan	10	
Butler, Dan	23	30.15
Caddy, Josh	22	21.22
Castagna, Jason	25	26.20
Conca, Reece	6	0.4
Cotchin, Trent	25	17.8
Edwards, Shane	20	11.16
Ellis, Brandon	25	7.4
Ellis, Corey	6	3.0
Elton, Todd	6	1.5
Graham, Jack	5	5.0
Griffiths, Ben	2	0.1
Grigg, Shaun	25	15.13
Grimes, Dylan	25	1.2
Houli, Bachar	21	5.9
Hunt, Taylor	2	

ARM IN ARM: There was much discussion pre-game as to how the Tigers would face down the Adelaide 'statue stare'. They did it with a minimum of fuss, standing as one.

PLAYERS	GAMES	GOALS/BEHINDS
Lambert, Kane	24	13.13
Lennon, Ben	2	1.0
Lloyd, Sam	8	6.6
Markov, Oleg	7	2.1
Martin, Dustin	25	37.29
McIntosh, Kamdyn	24	2.5
Menadue, Connor	9	3.1
Miles, Anthony	5	1.0
Morris, Steven	1	
Nankervis, Toby	24	11.7
Prestia, Dion	22	10.12
Rance, Alex	25	1.0
Riewoldt, Jack	23	54.37
Rioli, Daniel	25	25.13
Short, Jayden	16	2.1
Soldo, Ivan	7	1.0
Stengle, Tyson	2	2.1
Townsend, Jacob	5	16.2
Vlastuin, Nick	16	2.1

Epilogue
A PREMIERSHIP CAPTAIN

After the celebrations and frivolities and the private gatherings, as players and coaches and staff shared the joy of winning a premiership, there is a final, official, bit of business to tick off. On Monday afternoon, two days after the premiership was won, Punt Road Oval is quiet. There is refuse strewn about Yarra Park from the celebrations during and after the game. The scissor lift cranes, stage scaffolding and port-a-potties are being hauled away on flat bed trucks. Supporters linger, with plastic bags of fresh merchandise. As they leave, they pose for photos in front of the bronze statue of Captain Blood, Jack Dyer.

The training facility is not yet empty. In the immediate days following and throughout the flag victory, many players come back to the club. In the heat chamber downstairs, Corey Ellis and Todd Elton and Kane Lambert are all powering through a session on the stationary bike. "That's pretty common," says Brendan Fahrner, known as "Breezer", the sports scientist who, among so many other things, places the GPS trackers into the jumpers of the players every game. "They've been out having a big couple of days, and they're professional athletes, so they get the guilts, start feeling sluggish, and come back in to sweat it all out."

Above them, in the war room, the exit interview between Trent Cotchin and Damien Hardwick gets under way. Every player will have one. Some will have better reviews and news than others. Also there are Justin Leppitsch, Tim Livingstone, Andrew McQualter, Blair Hartley, Craig McRae, Dan

Richardson and Peter Burge. You can imagine, in different circumstances, this would be rather an intimidating experience.

Not today: there are coffees and waters and all are in casual clothes. Cotchin wears black skinny jeans and a grey long sleeved T-shirt, a black hat and blue Chuck Taylors. The people looking at him have a mix of pride and respect in their eyes.

"How did you go, Trent, talk us through," says Hardwick. "How has your season gone?"

Cotchin laughs, and they all do, too.

"Individually? Relatively consistent. I remember speaking to Mini (McQualter) and Cara (Caracella) earlier in the year, and I just found a new value in our group not being about possessions. I think I led that."

McQualter agrees: "At the start of this year, you said 'All I want to do is make my teammates better'. And I think that's how you played, all year. And I think it made you a better player as well."

Hardwick says Cotchin's finals series epitomised his entire year. "You were just a battering ram," he says. "I look in my mind and wonder what I want our captain to look like, and that was you. It was unbelievable watching that. There was a contest on the wing… Who was it?"

Livingstone remembers: "Sloane. By rights it was Sloane's ball."

"And you just came in and smashed the footy," says Hardwick. "As soon as I see you playing like that, I know we're going to win. That's the best form of leadership. It inspires. It's not only inspired our players—it inspired our whole fan base. I think you've found your niche. You don't have to get 25 or 30. You won a Brownlow, but this was by far your best season."

Blair Hartley nods: "One hundred percent. One hundred percent."

Cotchin says it feels funny, because while he felt like he played well during the year, finals were a revelation to him. "I feel like in finals I really understood what works for me. I just grew in confidence. I know I can impact the game with 17 possessions, by throwing myself at everything."

Hardwick says the captain has also done wonders for the coaching group. "You've been a great conduit between us and the players. It was a pretty tough year last year, and that's an understatement. But you've led the club."

McRae says he saw how the season would unfold for Cotchin the moment he stood up in the early Triple H sessions, and spoke with such rawness and honesty. "You were authentic, and it just opened the door. Everyone else had their chance, but when you showed who you were and where you'd been, it was like they all could, too."

Cotchin nods. He says he thought he had good relationships with people in the club before this season. He thought he knew what that meant. But he didn't. He says he'll never forget the moment Ben Lennon reached out to him, in the days immediately after that session, just to have a coffee.

"You don't realise the impact that sort of stuff can have on everyone. 'Lenno' said, 'To know that the captain has had the same thoughts as a second or third year player means everything'. It's been good fun though. I'm grateful for everything we've done together."

McRae wants to ask about the future. How is he going to handle success—what does it look like? "We can be really comfortable, or we can be hungry again. It can be like a drug for us," McRae says. "And you've got a massive part to play in that. And it's not on November 27—it's in little moments that pop up between now and then. And then well into the pre-season."

Cotchin nods vigorously. He has already thought about this. He has already assessed the year and seen what went right and wrong, and where he wants to take the side from here. "I'm genuinely dissatisfied, and I honestly think that the majority of the group is," he says. "The conversations we've had all year have been about the journey, and our best footy being in front of us, and this just feels like part of our journey, not the destination. That's what's exciting for our footy club."

McQualter returns to the individual: "I reckon one area you can get better, and it'll prolong your career, is as a one-on-one forward. I reckon if we do a shitload of work against Rancey and some of the defensive guns on your marking work, you can become a greater player. It was probably an area you didn't do much of in the last part of the year."

Cotchin: "It's funny you say that. I kicked more goals this year, but they were goals as a mid. I want people to treat me like Dusty when I go forward."

Leppitsch agrees: "It's really important for you, too, because you do all that battering ram stuff so well. We want to give your body a break every now and then."

They all shake hands, and Cotchin gets ready to leave the room, and head out into the corridor, and then out through the foyer, where there are the ten premiership cups the Tigers have won since 1920, in glass cases with team photos behind them. There is one empty case, soon to be filled with the cup he held up on stage the MCG two days.

He will need just a little time after this campaign to escape, and not to reflect but to lose focus, to gaze in wonder for a while.

Before he can go though, Hardwick grabs him. He gives him a hug, and leaves him with a thought.

"Two things, mate, just to finish off on. One, continue to have fun," he says. "And two, remember, you are a premiership captain."

ACKNOWLEDGEMENTS
AND AFTERWORD

There are so many people to thank for making this book happen. I'd like to first thank my mother, Dorothy, and father, Keith, to whom the book is dedicated. As parents, they juggled four sons but never missed a match of our junior or senior footy. Growing up, they gifted us an appreciation of both sides of this great game: my mum for its beautiful lairs, and my dad for the value of a player with a bit of mongrel in him.

My wife, Nikki, has been my everything these past two years, taking care of our little son, Charlie, when I was too busy for drop-offs or pick-ups, or when I needed to sit, alone and pre-occupied, typing all day and into the night. You have been a constant support and reassuring presence, ever encouraging and comforting. I love you and could not have done this without you.

To the publisher and editor, Geoff Slattery. Your quick initial faith in me to write my first book will not be forgotten, nor your willingness to take on this project two years in a row. You have been a constant guiding voice, helping direct the narrative, helping me kill my darlings, and helping me write what the readers want. (But really, mate, you could have let me keep a few more swear words.)

Simon Matthews, Richmond's corporate conscience, was the first person I reached out to at the club, way back in late 2015, immediately after the Tigers' devastating loss to North Melbourne in an elimination final. I'll be forever in your debt for taking that first meeting, having a coffee and a chat, believing in the idea, and then selling it to the footy boffins.

To Richmond CEO Brendon Gale, President, Peggy O'Neal, and the entire Board, I thank you for not just approving this idea, but endorsing it, no matter what the consequences of 2017: who could have known, at this stage last year, the end result? That decision is testament to your belief in not just the football department, but also the strength of the entire football club. I am also grateful that a book of this nature allows all fans to understand the truth of a modern, professional sporting club. There is so much more to it than coaches and players.

I'd like to thank all the players on the Richmond list. I didn't interview you all, nor even get to know most of you that well. I apologise if at times I was a lurking presence, leaning on walls and scribbling madly, but I never wanted to interrupt you at your work. Thank you for graciously accepting my lingering presence, and, in particular, thanks to Trent Cotchin, Jack Riewoldt, Dylan Grimes, Kane Lambert, Shaun Grigg and Bachar Houli, for remaining constantly welcoming and helpful. A special thanks also must go to Brandon Ellis, for sharing his unvarnished life story in what is usually a closed session for players only. And thanks also to Ben Griffiths, who was so accommodating and frank in a season so affected by injury.

I'd like to thank all the assistant coaches—Justin Leppitsch, Ben Rutten, Blake Caracella and Andrew McQualter—for their help explaining the finer points of modern football, and for being such good company. The VFL coaches, too, including Xavier Clarke and Ryan Ferguson, led by the always positive Craig McRae, deserve a mention for their warmth, openness, and for what they achieved this season.

I would also thank the coaches who came before them. I spent less time at the club in 2016 but I learned much from each of Brendon Lade, Ross Smith, Greg Mellor, Mark 'Choco' Williams and Mark 'Wilba' Williams.

Thanks also to Hayden Hill for his company and reassurance, and to Jack Harvey for the clarity of his tactical explanations. (I would not have understood much of what was going on in match review or opposition analysis without the help of this intelligent pair.)

Thanks to Dan Richardson and Neil Balme, for their help within the football department, for clearing up confusion and for steering me in the right direction on more than one occasion.

Thanks to Peter Burge, Rob Innes, Luke Meehan and Brendan Fahrner for continually explaining the intricacies—and indeed the strange alchemy—of high performance fitness. And Dr Greg Hickey for allowing me to shadow him as he went about his work, patching up the playing group and keeping them healthy and well.

Thanks to Jenna Earle, Bronwyn Doig and Steve Wyatt, upon whom I could always rely to explain how a football club takes gifted young boys and turns them into organised, professional young men.

Thanks to Blair Hartley and Matthew Clarke from the recruiting team, along with Nick Austin, Luke Williams and Francis Jackson for their help understanding how a list is built.

Thanks to Emma Murray, Shane McCurry and Ben Crowe for giving me a privileged glimpse into how a club culture is born, and just how important it is to work on the mind as well as the body. The insights you all provided were—for me at least—among the most energising.

Thanks to Nicky Malady and Georgina Cahill and Josh Berriman for walking me through the media management process—and emotionally holding my hand down in the rooms in the last quarter of so many close wins and losses.

Thank you to all the volunteers who make the team function every week, from the doormen and water boys and game day assistants, to those who stud the boots and wash and fold the jumpers. And thanks to property manager Giuseppe Mamone, the busiest man at Tigerland (and the man who openly and often predicted a Crows-Tigers Grand Final, as early as round five).

Thank you to my friend and fellow Tiger tragic Dan Flitton (the prophet who predicted a Richmond premiership on the front page of The Age prior to round one!), along with Tony Greenberg, and my mother, for reading various versions of the text and catching errors of fact and grammar and punctuation. Your sub-editing was invaluable.

My most sincere thanks must go to the Tigers' head of coaching and football performance, Tim Livingstone, my point man at the club and who was unfailingly patient with everything from my "formal" requests (ie. constant text messages) for interviews and access, to my tendency to show up in his office unannounced. The book could not have been done without Tim's utter professionalism, and it would have been far less enjoyable to compile without his humour and grace.

But mostly, I want to thank Damien Hardwick. Quite simply, the book would never have been possible without his immediate blessing. Hardwick knew, going into this project, that he would be a central character, and that the way he operates would be shared with the world—that his temperament and philosophy and methodology would be exposed to the public. For all the changes that have taken place in the way football clubs operate, the coach remains the fulcrum around which all else swivels. Hardwick said yes quickly at the start of 2016, when he might have confidently expected Richmond to rise. But the decision to pursue the book again in 2017, coming off a 13th place finish, after every man, woman and child predicted his sacking, when they predicted this team to fail miserably, was truly courageous. But I want to thank him for more than mere permission.

I want to thank him for showing me just how much one professional can change the way they conduct themselves—how they can adapt to circumstance. And most importantly, I want to thank him for proving something I've long suspected. All my life, I've believed that footballers play their best when they feel loved by their coach. They like to be told what they do well more than what they've done poorly. I hope you'll permit me such a self-indulgent moment here.

I never played high level football. (Tall players who can't mark have little value.) But I did win a few plaudits by playing hard in the ruck, or spoiling meanly at centre half-back. I played in a high school team that won the state final, too. But I have a very clear memory of one of my happiest days in football, and it is unrelated to those achievements.

I was 14, and playing in a game at the old Melbourne High School oval in South Yarra. We were getting beaten, playing against Lalor Secondary College. A young forward named Lance Whitnall was tearing us apart.

But then at half-time our coach, Peter Wood, went around the room telling each one of us exactly why he thought we could win. And instead of screaming for effort or lamenting our lack of desire in those first two quarters, he told us to enjoy the game, and enjoy playing with one another. Then he pointed to each player, one by one, and told us what that person brought to the team. He loved the speed of that guy. The marking power of this one. He could not fault the desperation of another, or the foot skills of the boy next to him. He pumped up every one of us. He told me I would be playing on Whitnall, because he knew I was disciplined and had a thirst for tackling and bumping and knocking opponents over.

We all left the rooms on a high. Whitnall didn't get another kick or handball. We won comfortably, all of us playing to our strengths together. And that is what Hardwick drilled into his players all year. *Use your strengths. Play with connection. Celebrate together.* I firmly believe that the focus on these three pillars was one of the most crucial components—among many—that led to Richmond's rise this season.

I will miss my time inside the Richmond Football Club, profoundly. It was a dream excursion into a land unknown. Being inside a club, not just proximate to what Francis Bourke called "the tin gods", but to feel a trusted part of their collective endeavour is a high that will be hard to replicate. It is an addictive experience. I am suffering from withdrawal already.

That noted, I will also enjoy returning to the freedom of the grandstand. I watched most matches in my two years at Tigerland sitting in the media centre, behind glass, with other journalists and statisticians. In that hermetic environment, you don't cheer, you don't sit with a beer, you don't yell and don't despair—at least outwardly—and you also see no footy with your friends.

Back in the outer in 2018, I'll enjoy hearing the rumble of a stadium in full voice. I'll enjoy screaming with them once more. And I'll enjoy watching the play unfold, understanding much more clearly how each convoluted passage came to pass.

I heard recently that one of the assistant coaches who left Richmond in 2016 later ran into someone else from the club. This coach wasn't bitter, the person said, or even sad. He held no ill will toward anyone. He was magnanimous.

"I wouldn't change anything," he said. "I'll take every memory with me. I lived my dream."

And I lived mine.

—Konrad Marshall, October, 2017

→ **IN THE GEAR:** Pre-game on Preliminary Final, Konrad Marshall took the opportunity to be photographed with the Premiership Cup. He explains how he became part of the furniture: "Throughout it all I wore Richmond gear, to seem a (small) part of the team, and it did feel that way much of the time—never more so than at the MCG after a victory, when coaches, administrators and players would wander into the room, sing the song and walk with a happy spring in their step. They might tap a physio on the hand and say, "Good job, fella", or slap a player on the back and say, "Great game, mate", and then see me, pat my shoulder and say, "Well done, Konrad". I had done nothing, of course, but football clubs understand that theirs is a group endeavour. You wear the colours—you are part of the machine. For all this time, I felt like one tiny part of the engine driving Tigerland, albeit as an observer, a chronicler of a time that had its lows and highs."